ISBN: 9781313253123

Published by:
HardPress Publishing
8345 NW 66TH ST #2561
MIAMI FL 33166-2626

Email: info@hardpress.net
Web: http://www.hardpress.net

Croydon in the Past.

✠ ✠ ✠

Historical, Monumental, and Biographical.

ST. JOHN'S CHURCH, CROYDON.

In Memoriam Croydoniensium.

CROYDON IN THE PAST:

HISTORICAL, MONUMENTAL, AND BIOGRAPHICAL:

BEING A HISTORY OF THE TOWN AS DEPICTED ON THE

Tombs, Tablets, and Gravestones

IN THE

CHURCHES, CHURCHYARDS, AND CEMETERY

OF THE PARISH,

INCLUDING ALSO MEMORIALS OF THE NEIGHBOURING VILLAGES OF

BEDDINGTON, SHIRLEY, AND ADDINGTON;

PRECEDED BY ORIGINAL AND

INTERESTING HISTORICAL NOTES.

"De mortuis nil nisi bonum."

CROYDON:

PRINTED AND PUBLISHED BY JESSE W. WARD, "ADVERTISER" OFFICES,
14 & 15, KATHARINE STREET.

1883.

CROYDON :

PRINTED BY JESSE W. WARD, AT THE "CROYDON ADVERTISER"

STEAM PRINTING OFFICES, KATHARINE STREET.

PREFACE.

NEVER before, as far as we can learn, has an attempt been made to publish a work of this description, either in Croydon or elsewhere. Previous local historians have confined themselves to copying the laudatory inscriptions engraved on some of the brasses, tablets, and monumental marbles, erected in the chancels and aisles of the Churches, to keep in remembrance the names and deeds of the richer and more influential inhabitants who have passed away. The publisher of this work, not content with copying these obituary notices, has gone to the Graveyards and the Cemetery, and placed on permanent record the names, not only of the great ones, but also of those less favoured in this world, lying beneath the humble gravestone or monumental slab, on which their names and ages are recorded, with the date of their death, and on which, in many instances, their virtues are set forth in humble verse, or suitable Scripture text.

Many of these memorial stones will, by the operations of nature, in a few brief years crumble away, or be removed to make room for those of a later generation. Inscribed in the pages of this book, their names and deeds become permanently part of the past history of the town, and there are few residents who will not find in its pages, records of some dearly-loved ones whom they would gladly hold in their kind remembrance.

Interspersed with these lists of the departed are numerous short obituary notices, written in most instances by gentlemen who have known those of whom they write, while in the flesh, and who were pleased to have this opportunity of recording their testimony of departed worth.

Owing to the length to which these pages have run, in a few instances it has been deemed necessary to compress some of the inscriptions, especially where repetitions of Scripture texts occur, the publication of which would have extended these pages to an unwelcome extent without concurrent advantages.

In the introductory chapters will be found a brief but graphic History of the Town from the very earliest period, showing its gradual progress and subsequent rapid development, including many interesting matters and memorabilia, which have never before been published ; these have been collected by a diligent and unwearied search of every available source of information, and include an account of the now almost forgotten Canal, Tramway, and Atmospheric Railway. Many interesting documents from the State Paper Office, connecting this town with several important events in our national history, have been kindly placed at our disposal, and are now for the first time published, with explanatory notices.

Every endeavour has been used to make this work as complete as possible, so that all who feel an interest in the old town of Croydon may have within their reach a permanent and reliable record of Croydon in the Past.

Some idea of the work necessary to compile the book may be gathered from the fact that there are upwards of *four thousand five hundred separate names* given. The bare work of copying these would be in itself a task of considerable labour, but its magnitude is increased by the copious notes and brief biographies which are appended to the obituaries of the best-known residents.

We shall probably issue another edition when, in the course of time, the Cemetery contains a greater number of illustrious dead. In future editions we shall be happy to include further particulars of those, who, in the present edition, have not been in this way duly honoured. We have compiled from various sources of information all that we could gather, and have been cheerfully aided in the work by many old inhabitants, but we are conscious that there may be many omissions of records of departed worth which we would willingly rectify in future editions. We therefore cordially invite our friends to send to this office what notes they can, in the same spirit as we have written those already printed, and in accordance with the maxim we have taken for our motto, " *De mortuis nil nisi bonum.*"

CROYDON ADVERTISER OFFICES,
December, 1882.

INDEX TO HISTORICAL CHAPTERS.

HISTORICAL INDEX—*(Continued).*

INDEX TO CHURCHYARDS AND CEMETERY.

INDEX TO SURNAMES ON TOMBS, &c.

NOTE.

While this sheet (which, though first in the book, is the last printed) is passing through the press, a notable addition has been made to the dead lying in Addington Churchyard. Dr. Archibald Campbell Tait, Archbishop of Canterbury, has passed away, and, though offered a resting-place in the grand cloisters of Westminster Abbey, his remains are now side by side with his beloved wife, and in the same graveyard where so many of his predecessors are lying. He died on Advent Sunday, 1882, the fourth anniversary of his wife's decease, having nearly attained his 71st year.

The Early History of Croydon.

N commencing a brief epitome of the history of Croydon, we will endeavour in the first instance to give some idea of the configuration of the district in the pre-historic age. A dense forest filled up the whole of the country from the valley of the Thames to the South Wolds, the home of all kinds of wild animals, such as the wolf, the bear, the fox, the badger, and the wild cat. A great portion of this district was a swamp or morass, overgrown with rank verdure, impassable to all but the wild denizens of the woods. Just south of Croydon, the character of the country entirely changed; the valley in which the Old Town stands is the boundary line. This was caused by an alteration in the nature of the soil. The bed of London clay reaches to Thornton Heath, near the northern boundary of the parish. South of Croydon, the North Wolds commence; the hills are huge masses of chalk, raised by some great convulsion of nature from the bed of the sea; the bare soil thereon affords little nourishment for trees, and few, therefore, were to be found, except in the sheltered valleys.

In the forest range, the water from the hill sides gathered in the valley, forming swamps, eventually percolating into the soil, or finding an outlet by some small streamlet into the Thames valley. On the chalk hills, the water runs off very rapidly, making for itself channels, (though the nature of the soil prevented these channels becoming more than mere shallow brooklets, dry the better part of the year), to the lower levels; but there were some parts in the valleys where there were large stretches of level lands; here the water would naturally gather, forming bogs and swamps. The channels made by the passage of the water pouring down from the higher levels would, during the dry seasons, form a good level pathway, and we shall endeavour to trace the track of some of these brooklets, and show that most of our old roads are the dried beds of these hill streams.

The most northerly water-course affecting this town had its origin in the forest, where now the Crystal Palace stands, pouring down Collier's Water Lane to Thornton Heath, the pond there (now very considerably reduced) being the natural reservoir. A second stream came from the direction of New Thornton Heath, ran along the Whitehorse Road, and found its way by some circuitous route not clearly discernable, across North End, down Chapel Walk (where there was formerly a conduit), and Handcross Alley, joining the main stream near the Little Almshouses in Church Street. A third stream descended from the Park district and the higher ground beyond, passed down Mint Walk, crossed High Street at its junction with Surrey Street, thence down Scarbrook Hill, to a large pond situated in the triangle formed by Scarbrook Road, Church Road, and Church Street, and this pond, known in after years as Laud's pond, found an outlet partly across the Bogs, which we shall have to mention hereafter, and partly down the present Church Road, through the grounds of the Archbishop's Palace, where, in later years, it was artificially formed into fish ponds, round the churchyard, into Church Street, where it joined other streams. Laud's pond was also fed by springs, now utilised by the Water-works Company. Another stream came down the heights from Croham Hurst, pouring down Croham Lane, into the Southbridge Road, where it joined another stream, partially fed by springs rising in the grounds of Blunt House, and partially from a stream which came from Caterham and ran by the side of the Brighton Road, and the mysterious intermittent Bourne waters (of which we shall have to speak hereafter). This stream ran some little distance on the west side of the Old Town, but, being joined by a small brooklet from Duppas Hill and the Waldrons, it crossed the road near Chapel Passage, and shortly afterwards divided into two branches, one part running east and the other west of Union Street, thus form-ing an island, called to this day " Bog Island." The divided stream joined again just before reaching the church, and here, meeting with all the other streams we have mentioned, formed a tolerably strong current, sufficient to turn a mill. It now became the River Wandle, and made itself a course along the open ground at the back of St. John's Grove, crossed the course of the railway to Sutton, to Stubbs' Mead, where it formed a large marsh, yet known as Waddon Marsh, although the stream has long been confined to a channel, and the marsh converted into fertile pasture land. Almost all these water-courses were open until within the last 40 years. Since then, they have been covered in by the Board, and, in most instances, their old tracks have been converted into public roads. The running water is now confined to underground tunnels, and the bogs and swamps have been drained and converted into valuable building and garden land. Strangers, as they wander along the roadways of our old town, little think they are walking on the beds of ancient streamlets, and that in many cases, water, once such a source of trouble and annoyance to our forefathers, runs placidly under their feet in channels formed by the hands of man.

We have thus faintly endeavoured to show the track of the many water-courses to which we owe the foundation of the town. The earliest settlers in this island were undoubtedly the Celts, and naturally, in their settlements, they would seek to find combined wood and water—the two most necessary elements of their subsist-ence; these they would find conjoined in the district in which

Croydon now stands. The Druids, the priests of the tribes, required groves of oak for their religious worship, and these would readily be found on the borders of the forest ; and they had, combined with these, running streams, also sacred objects in their worship. They also required open spaces for their sacrificial rites. The bare chalk hills on the opposite side of the valley were available for this purpose. The names of the district point out the uses to which it was appropriated. Haling is simply a corruption of Halig, or Holy. The little island we have spoken of would form a safe retreat from the incursions of the wild denizens of the woods. Thus, every circumstance points to the feasibility of this district being considered, from the earliest time, holy or sacred ground.

When the Romans invaded this island, they doubtless found a small community gathered in this *Crag-dean*, or winding valley, and here they would be suffered to remain ; but the Romans, in accordance with their usual policy, united their principal stations by good roads, one of the principal of which, from Londinum to Regum (Chichester), passed through Croydon. The first station out of London was Noviomagus, the precise situation of which is disputed. Some archæologists place it at Holwood Park, where there is an ancient encampment still visible ; others at Woodcote, a retired little hamlet about two miles south of Croydon ; while a third party give Croydon the honour. We are inclined, however, to favour the idea that Woodcote is the more likely spot, partly on account of the numerous Roman remains found there, and partly on account of its splendid situation for defensive purposes, being situated at the mouth of a deep and natural gorge through the Wolds. There are also indications of a camp at Caterham Junction, on the opposite side of the valley, still called War Bank.

It is an undecided question which was the route of the Roman road through the town. It is scarcely probable that they would choose the lower road through the swampy ground of the Old Town, although some ancient maps of Surrey would seem to favour this supposition. The main thoroughfare through the town, along the High Street, in these old maps is only shown as a bridle-path. It is conjectured that at least two other Roman roads pierced through the parish, but all traces of them have been lost. We are, however, not without convincing proof of the presence of the Romans in the district. In 1871, the remains of a Roman villa were brought to light at Beddington while the workmen were employed in cutting the carriers on the Irrigation Farm, belonging to the Croydon Local Board. Various sepulchral urns, containing fragments of calcined bones, were dug up in the immediate vicinity, and numerous human skeletons have been laid bare, with iron spear-heads and bosses of shields, usually buried with their warriors. Many Roman coins have also been dug up in various parts of the town. At the foot of Duppas Hill is a farm called Coldharbour, signifying an outstation for Roman legionaries ; the name is common in the vicinity of Roman encampments. Beyond these simple facts, the 300 years' reign of the Romans in Britain is, so far as Croydon is concerned, a blank.

After the evacuation of this island by the Romans, the Saxons from Friedland and other parts of modern Germany, overran the country, introducing the worship of their mythic gods and heroes. They established the Heptarchy, dividing the island into seven different kingdoms. The smallest, although probably the most important, was Cent, embracing the counties of Kent and Surrey. Historians generally date the invasions by the Saxon tribes to the time of Hengist and Horsa, which the Venerable Bede says took place about 449 B.C.; but other chroniclers date the establishment of the Kentish Kingdom fully a century earlier. All these dates are, however, to a great extent, matters of supposition. There is no doubt that long before the retirement of the Romans, numbers of Saxons had settled along the southern and eastern coast of England, and they would naturally invite their brethren to join them when the withdrawal of the Roman legionaries had left the country defence-less. The Saxons introduced the worship of Woden, or Oden (from whom all their war-chiefs claim to be descended), and, wherever they settled, erected temples to his worship. We find his name very clearly traceable in the modern hamlet of Waddon, formerly spelt Waddens, and perhaps more doubtfully in the word Waldrons, formerly also spelt Waldons. The very name of Croydon is a cor-ruption of two Saxon words—*Crag-dean*, Saxon for winding valley, eminently descriptive of the locality. Some archæologists have favoured the idea that the name is derived from the Norman *Croi-dune*, chalk-hill, totally oblivious of the fact that the town was called *Croigdeane* at the time of the Norman conquest. Any persons ascending the hills at Caterham or Haling cannot fail to notice how the valley winds in a serpentine course from Croydon to Godstone, formerly a natural pass from the valley of the Thames, through the chalk-hills to the Wealds of Sussex. The Saxon "g" is pronounced soft, very similar to our modern "y"; thus it will be noticed that fully a century before the coming of the Normans, the pronunciation of the name of the town was nearly the same as at present.

The Rev. D. W. Garrow, in his work on the "History and Antiquities of Croydon," published early in the present century, sup-poses the word to have originated in two Saxon words, *crone*, sheep, and *dene*, valley, and this idea is supported to some extent by the spelling of the name in the Domesday Book, where the town is called *Croindene*. In contradiction to this, we have the word spelt just as pronounced at the present time by an old Saxon scribe in 962,—fully 50 years before the Domesday Book was taken. It must be remembered that the orthography of proper names was then, and for ages afterwards, in a very unsettled and uncertain state.

Whether Christianity was introduced into this country during the continuance of the Roman Government is not positively known; it is believed that some faint traces have been discovered during the later years of their rule. St. Augustine, to whom the honour of introducing Christianity is generally given, landed in Kent in 597, but as early as the latter half of the second century, Tertullian wrote that those parts of Britain which were inaccessible to the Romans had become subject to Christ. Three English Bishops attended the

Council of Arles, in 347, and at Rimini a few years afterwards. St. Augustine was the first who brought the English Church in connection with the Romish Church. The original Celtic race, driven to the inacessible regions of Wales and Scotland, were the first converts to Christianity. In the fifth century there was a famous Christian seminary at Bangor, in Wales, and another in the Isle of Iona, in Scotland. Probably, when Augustine landed, many of the Saxon race still worshipped Wodin. Slowly, but gradually, Christianity spread through the land, until, at the time of the invasion of Sweyen the Dane, the whole island was nominally Christian. The Danes were heathen, but soon after they settled here they also embraced the Christian doctrines. The missionaries of Christianity seemed to have adapted themselves to the people, and heathen festivals were made to coincide with Christian celebrations. For centuries the English Church celebrated Easter at a different date from the Romish Church ; this was caused by the fact that the day thus celebrated was really the festival of the Anglo-Saxon goddess *Eastre*, from whence the very name was derived. Christmas, too, was made to coincide with the celebration of the heathen god Yule, or Jule ; and we yet burn the Yule block at Christmas, little thinking we are celebrating an old heathen rite.

The missionaries, while thus making the old coincide with the new religion, also very judiciously erected their first places of worship near to or upon the site of the holy places of the heathens. We have shown that the valley in which old Croydon stood had for ages been esteemed, both by Celt and Saxon, a holy place. What more likely than that the first priest who brought the worship of Christ into this district should erect his little chapelry upon the very ground where our Pagan ancestors were wont to offer up prayers to their gods ? The first positive proof we have of a church in Croydon is found in an old Saxon will, dated in the year 960, of Beorhtric and Ælfswyth, which was witnessed by " Elfsies, preoster of Crogdæne."

When this country was divided into parishes we know not with certainty. Camden states that Honorius, Archbishop of Canterbury, about the year 636, first began to separate parishes in England, and Theodor, his successor, effected the complete organisation of ecclesiastical power in this island. He urged upon the rich landowners the necessity of building and endowing churches upon their lands, and, as an inducement, offered them the right of patronage. Some estates were large and some small, and this accounts for the great difference in the size of parishes. We should gather from this that there was a church in Croydon at this time, for the right of patronage never was vested in any private individual ; it always has been in the hands of the Archbishops of Canterbury. The immense size of Croydon parish arises from the fact that all the northern portions were wild forest land, and therefore, in those days, comparatively valueless.

THE DOMESDAY BOOK.

In 1080 William the Norman ordered a general survey to be made of the whole of England, which took six years in compilation, and the result of his labours we have in the world-famous Domesday Book, the most indisputable record of topography ever made. We naturally turn to that valuable book to ascertain what it says about Croydon, and we find this entry :—

> "THE LAND OF THE ARCHBISHOP OF CANTERBURY.
>
> "*In Waletone* Hundred.*
>
> "Archbishop Lanfranc holds in demesne, Croindeine. In the time of King Edward the Confessor it was assessed for eighty hides,† and now for sixteen hides and one virgate.‡ The land is for twenty ploughs. In demesne there of four ploughs and forty-eight villans,§ and twenty-five bordars,‖ with thirty-four ploughs. Here is a church and one mill of five shillings and eight acres of meadow. Wood for two hundred swine. Of the land of this manor, Restold holds seven hides of the Archbishop, and Ralph one hide, and from thence they have seven pounds¶ and eight shillings** for gable.†† In the time of King Edward and afterwards, the whole was worth twelve pounds, now twenty-seven pounds to the Archbishop, and to his men ten pounds ten shillings."

We gather from the Domesday Book that the extent of the manor or parish was 2,880 acres of arable land, eight acres of meadow, the remainder consisting of woods, heaths, and wastes. When a survey of the whole parish was made by the Danes, the extent was rated at 9,000 acres, which very closely approximates

---

* Literally Wall Town, now Wallington, a hamlet in the parish of Beddington.

† It is an unsettled question how much land was comprised in the Saxon hide. Some writers estimate it at 30 to 33 acres, while others gave the quantity as 120 acres. It really means the quantity of land sufficient for the support of one family, and therefore would be variable in quantity, according to the fertility of the soil.

‡ A virgate is generally understood to signify the fourth part of a hide.

§ Villans are persons who held land by certain tenures. They were of two descriptions. They were villans regardant, that is, annexed to the manor or land ; or else they were in gross, or at large, that is, annexed to the person of the lord of the manor, and transferable by deed from one owner to another ; in fact, they were nothing more than slaves, and could be punished for running away. They were generally granted some small plots of land, which they only held during their lord's pleasure. According to Blackstone, a villan could acquire no property, either in land or goods ; but if he purchased either, his lord might enter upon them, oust the villan, and seize them to his own use, unless he contrived to dispose of them again before the lord seized them, for the lord then had lost his opportunity.

‖ Bordars were those of a less servile condition. The word is supposed to be derived from the Saxon *bord*—a cottage. They held small houses on the manor, and paid with poultry, eggs, and other provisions for the lord's consumption, besides performing domestic services, such as grinding, threshing, drawing water, cutting wood, &c.

¶ The pound mentioned here is really a pound of silver, consisting of twelve ounces.

** The shilling consisted, as at the present time, of twelve pence, and was equal in weight to three of our shillings, thus the pound was worth 62s. of our money.

†† Gable, or gavel, is rent paid in money or kind, and sometimes by service to the king or any other lord—such, for instance, as performing military service, either in person or by deputy.

to the survey made in 1797, and still more recently, which fixes the total acreage at 9,872 acres.

In 1273, Archbishop Kilwarby obtained for the town the privilege of holding a market on Wednesdays ; and in 1276, the right of a nine days' fair, commencing on the vigil of St. Botolph, that is to say, on the 16th of May. In the year 1314, Archbishop Reynolds obtained the grant of a market on Thursdays, and a fair on the Vigil of St. Matthew. Archbishop Stratford, in 1343, obtained the grant of a third market to be held on Saturdays, and a fair on the Feast of St. John the Baptist. At the present time the Wednesday market has entirely disappeared. The corn and cattle market is still held on Thursdays, and a provision market on Saturdays. The fairs, too, are gradually disappearing, although a cattle fair is still in November, in a field near the southern boundary of the parish.

In the time of Queen Elizabeth the streets are described to have been deep, hollow ways, very dirty, the houses generally with wooden steps to them, and darkened with large trees growing before them (a peculiarity to the town retained almost to the present day), and the inhabitants generally were smiths or colliers.

DESCRIPTION AND PROGRESS OF THE TOWN.

WE have, in our previous pages, described the origin of the town, and shown how naturally the proximity of the great North Forest, and the ever-flowing streams of pure water in a pleasant winding valley, tempted the early settlers to choose this spot as a place of residence. The same temptations offered to colonists in Australia and New Zealand would induce them to settle in a similar manner. When Christianity was introduced, a church was built on the borders of the stream, and doubtless other buildings connected therewith followed ; though, singularly enough, we do not find the slightest trace of any monastic establishment in the parish, nor does it ever appear to have been the property of any feudal lord. From the very earliest period it has been an appanage of the Archbishopric of Canterbury, and thus we find Archbishop Lanfranc in quiet possession at the time the Domesday book was taken.

The town gradually spread, first along the margin of the streams, and then up the hill towards our present High Street. It is not known whether the Romans made the upper road through the town, or followed the lower road past the church, but along this upper road gradually congregated the principal places of business.

In that road we find the principal hotels, and when the only mode of travelling was on horseback or in litters, the posting houses would naturally be erected on the road generally traversed.

During the troubled times, when the rival houses of York and Lancaster struggled for supremacy, and trade was carried on under immense difficulties and amid great dangers, the shops were principally confined to the triangle formed by Surrey Street and High Street, having its apex at the back of the present Town Hall. Here were "the Rows;" so called from the fact that the tradesmen displayed their wares in rows, partially or wholly covered over, in the same manner as they do at the present time in the bazaars in Eastern lands and in some of our old fashioned fairs. At nights these rows were closed by gates, carefully guarded by watchmen. In all probability there would be one such gate near the "Old King's Head" inn, and another at the opposite extremity, where the "Robinson Crusoe" beer shop now stands. It is questionable whether there was any entrance from High Street beyond a narrow passage, which could be effectually closed by a door. There are two of these passages still in existence connecting with Surrey Street. Though this district is topographically divided into streets and lanes, yet it is still familiarly known by the inhabitants as "the Middle Row." With the advent of more settled times, tradesmen came more out into the front, and High Street became then, as now, the principal place of business in the town, narrow and inconvenient as it is for such a purpose. The narrowness of the street was not a matter of much consequence when only the noble and great rode in wheeled vehicles, and farmers brought the great bulk of their produce to market on horseback, and all merchandise which could not be conveyed by water, was carried from town to town on pack horses. For ages the roads were mere tracks through woods or across fields, choked with dust in summer, and almost impassable in winter. A bridge was a rarity. Where the stream was shallow, the traveller waded across ; where too deep, a rude ferry-boat was brought into requisition. In some few isolated instances, where the highways was a matter of national importance, such as the road between London and Dover, more care was taken. Around Croydon, excepting the main road to London, all the other roads were mere bridle tracks, such as many remain to this day.

Gradually wheeled vehicles became more and more common, and improvements in the roads grew absolutely necessary. McAdam introduced the art of road making, and soon excellent gravelled turnpike roads extended from town to town, and even by-roads shared in the general improvement. Stage-coaches commenced running from London to Croydon, and through to the south coast ; and every few hours the tradesmen were aroused by the sound of the guard's horn, as the Rocket or the Highflyer, or some other royal mail coach, dashed up to the "Greyhound" to change horses. In a few minutes the four reeking animals were removed, and four fresh ones took their places in the traces, and away the coach dashed down the Brighton road to the delight of all spectators. During the Regency, from 1810 to 1820, the semi-oriental pavilion at Brighton was erected by the Prince Regent, and the Prince with his boon companions frequently posted through the town on their journeys to and from Brighton.   Their example was followed by a host of imitators.   Part of the coaching business was transferred to a point near the " Red Deer " inn, on the Brighton road, where a row of stables were built, some of which, converted into dwelling houses, still remain, known as Crunden Place.

The proximity of the town to London naturally attracted the attention of gentlemen fond of sports, and Croydon became a great hunting centre.   Two packs of hounds (one fox and one stag), and a pack of harriers, were kept in the immediate vicinity.   For the accommodation of the hunting fraternity, hunting stables were established in various parts of the town, and it was no uncommon thing for Mr. Bignell, who was then the principal livery stable keeper, to turn out from forty to fifty hunters every morning during the season.

These, however, only enlivened the town at certain seasons. Croydon at other times was a dull sleepy place, and Thomas Frost, in his " Recollections," thus describes it as it was 50 years ago :—

" I see it now, in my mind's eye, as it were then, with Whitgift's hospital, dating from the reign of Elizabeth, and affectionately and reverently styled by my fellow-townsmen, ' the College,' forming its most conspicuous architectural feature at the point at which it was then entered by the high road from London ; and the bent old women and men sunning themselves in the trim little courtyard, a glimpse of which is obtained through the archway, by which it is entered from the street.   From that corner, the long narrow High street, stretching southwards, dull rather than quiet, with here a slow grey-tilted cart, and there a Brighton stage-coach, stopping to change horses, with the scarlet-coated guard on the back seat, equipped with post-horn and blunderbuss.   The grey tower of the old church—then the only one in the parish—was seen over the tops on the right, across a street, leading to the slums of the Old Town ; and looking after the coach, as it dashes off again to the sound of the horn, the royal arms over the entrance of a substantial edifice of very red brick, with a signboard swinging from a beam across the street, proclaimed the principal inn, from the windows of which the Tory candidates for the representation of the county were wont to address their supporters.   On the opposite side of the narrow street was the old butter market, to which farmers' wives brought butter, eggs, and poultry, in that golden age of Tory-Radical politicians of Cobbett's school, when farmers wore linen gabardines, as their forefathers had done since the days of Egbert, and their wives did not disdain to milk the cows, feed the poultry, and collect the eggs.   A little further on, with the best of the sleepy shops on the right and the left, was the local capitol, where farmers stood on market days, behind their samples of corn on the ground floor, while above them the justices sat to hear charges of poaching and other rural offences, and the Court of Requests to adjudicate upon claims for small debts."

Thus it will be seen that the town did not really commence on the London side till the old hospital was reached.   There may have been a few detached houses in North End, with pleasant gardens, fronted in the street with trees, but there was no continuous street. South of High Street, there were rows of houses down to the " Swan and Sugar-loaf Inn," beyond which was a toll-bar.   Middle Row and Surrey Street would be much the same as at present.

The north side of High Street was principally occupied by private houses, with gardens behind. The shops opposite Surrey Street, now occupied by Mrs. Smith, pawnbroker, and Mr. Plowman, butcher, formed an old manor house, the back garden running up to Keeley Road, and extending some distance lower down the street. The old Vine House, pulled down last year, was said to have been the old Dower House. On the opposite side was a row of mean shops, behind which stretched on a very large pond, fed by springs, the principal source of the river Wandle. This pond was called "Laud's Pond." It is now entirely filled up, and the springs diverted into the wells at the waterworks. A short distance lower down the street was the entrance to the Archbishop of Canterbury's Palace-ground, where the "Gun Inn" now stands. Across the road, at the corner of the Small Almshouses, ran a stream of water, which came down the hills in the direction of Addington, and joined the main stream just beyond the church. The Old Town must have been a dreadful place to live in ; the main street, during the winter months, or continuous wet weather, was rendered almost impassable. The running streams, which ought to have been kept pure, were made the receptacle of indescribable filth and refuse, which the inhabitants were too lazy or too negligent to carry elsewhere. At times, when the Bourne waters rose, there would be one to two feet of water running down the street, and the lower rooms of the houses on each side were, in consequence, flooded. No wonder that few but the very poorest occupied this part of the town, and that Frost described it as " the back slums." It is only right to say the district has considerably improved since the streams were covered in, and a thorough system of drainage was carried out.

An attempt was made early in the present century to establish the trades of calico printing and bleaching. A calico printing mill was erected near the edge of the large pond, at the back of Church Street, which we have previously described as " Laud's Pond," where the water was diverted to turn a wheel, but it does not appear to have been very successful, and soon was given up. The bleaching trade was carried on in a portion of the Old Palace, and for a time met with a better fate, but the bleaching factory has now been converted into a steam laundry, and the old bleaching-ground is used as a drying-ground for the laundry.

The present development of Croydon is really ascribable to the universal development of the railway system. When the means of communication were slow, merchants were obliged to reside near their places of business, but the general adoption of the iron roads and the steam horse introduced a new era. City men of all grades found how much more pleasant it was to live in open spaces, surrounded by trees and flowers, than in the dull, sombre, crowded streets, and soon discovered that, by the change, they benefited both in pocket and in person. The railway afforded them a prompt and ready mode of transit to and from business every morning and evening, and many of them were not slow in taking advantage of the new life thus opened out to them. On all the hills which overlook the older part of the town, pleasant residences sprang into existence, new roads were laid out, and farm after farm was swallowed up ; but, owing to the fact that the greater portion of the new dwellings, being either wholly or partially detached, Croydon has never lost its rural appearance, and no town in England of its size and population presents such a mass of green verdure and open spaces. A thorough system of drainage was adopted, and all polluting influences removed ; a plentiful supply of pure spring water supplied to every house ; until the old, dull, stagnant country town of Croydon has grown in a lifetime to be acknowledged as the healthiest and wealthiest suburb of the great metropolis.

The outlying portions of the parish, especially Norwood, received a great impulse when the Exhibition building was removed from Hyde Park to form the nucleus of the Crystal Palace on Sydenham Hill, within a few yards of the boundaries of the parish ; this undoubtedly has greatly aided the rapid progress of the town. Year by year the population rapidly increases, and when the town is incorporated, and is ruled by a municipal council, the inhabitants generally will take a more active interest in all that concerns its welfare, and many improvements, now deemed impossible, will be effected, the result being still more to aid its onward progress.

One other matter deserves notice. By the adoption of the new scheme for the management of the Whitgift Charity, Croydon now enjoys the benefits offered by one of the most important educational establishments in the kingdom, and it is confidently hoped that ere long the Whitgift School, though perhaps not rivalling Eton or Harrow, may fully equal Rugby, Winchester, and schools of that class. This is an advantage which many of our residential population will not fail to appreciate.

LOCAL NAMES AND THEIR ORIGIN.

 RETROSPECT of the names of the principal roads and places in the town and district may help to throw light on some part of the history of the town, which would otherwise remain uncertain and obscure. Successive races invariably leave their marks on the hills, valleys, and water courses. We shall endeavour to point out a few of these old literary landmarks.

In our previous chapters we have shown that the name of the town is derived from two Saxon words, *crag-dene*—crooked valley, and that in Haling, we have an old Saxon word signifying Holy ;

in Wadden. a reminiscence of the time when the mythical hero *Wodin* was the principal god of our forefathers ; and in Wallingham or Walleton, we find a trace of Roman rule.

Our principal water-course is the river Wandle, which rises in and about the town. *An* is Celtic, and *Avon* Cymric or ancient British, for a running stream. There are in England three or four rivers named Avon. Stratford-on-Avon will naturally rise to the mind of every lover of English literature, as the birth-place of Shakespeare. The addition *El* signifies little—thus Avondel, little river. Formerly the *v* was sounded soft like our modern *w*, hence it would be sounded Awondel or Wandle.

Coombe is a Celtic word, derived from *Cwn*, the letter *w* being sounded like double o. Cwn or Coom signifies a hollow by the side of a hill, generally an old water course—thus we have Coombe lane. Addiscombe is a corruption of Edgecoom, the edge of a valley.

Scarbrook is easily traceable to the ancient British word *Scar*, a steep hill, and *brook* or *broc*, running water. The word Scar frequently forms a portion of the names of towns ; thus we have Scarborough, the steep-hill town ; and any one acquainted with that delightful watering place, will at once acknowledge the propriety of the title. Scar or Scaur is in common use in Derbyshire and Westmoreland to denote the slope of a very steep hill.

Park or *Parc* is Celtic for an enclosure. Thus we have Park Hill, Park Lane, and so forth.

Norwood is simply an abbreviation of the words North Wood, to distinguish the district from the great South Wood. which formerly covered the Wealds of Kent and Surrey.

Bourne signifies a running stream, and is frequently found in combination with other words, to show the direction from which the stream runs, such as Westbourne, Eastbourne, Holborn or Hill Bourne.

Woodcote is from the Saxon *cote*, a small dwelling, from whence we derive our familiar word—cottage. The word, therefore, signifies the cottage by the wood.

Selhurst.—It is rather singular that in this word. apparently so different. we have nearly the same meaning. *Sel* in Saxon means a superior kind of dwelling, *hurst* is a wood. Hurst is a common terminal in this district, and is spelt in a great variety of ways, but they are all derived from the same root. The frequency of its use clearly proves the former woody nature of the country.

Croham-hurst is a wood where the crows have a ham or home. Birdhurst has, of course. a precisely similar meaning.

Shirley comes from *Shire*, a boundary. It is situated on the borders of Kent and Surrey.

Waldrons may be derived from either of two sources. The Saxon word *Weald* or wild, and *Dene* a valley. Though the Waldrons has no resemblance to a wild valley now. in days gone by. such might have been its characteristic. We are rather inclined to think it is derived from the same source as Waddon. as it was formerly spelt Walden. If so, this is another proof of the prevalency of the worship of the hero-god Wodin in this neighbourhood.

Ham.—In the ancient Cymric, this word means a narrow point, or enclosure of land where two rivers meet, and in that sense is still used in Wales and the bordering counties. The Saxons, however, used the word to represent any place which a man could call his own ; hence our word home. Wherever the Saxons settled this terminal is in constant use. Fully one half the towns and villages in Norfolk and Suffolk terminate in Ham. Wherever the Danes settled in numbers, as in North Lincolnshire, Yorkshire, Derbyshire, and Leicestershire—we find the towns ending in *by* or *thorpe*,— *By* being the Danish equivalent for the Saxon *Ham*.

Mint Walk is probably derived from the Saxon *Min*, a field ; the word would therefore mean the walk leading to the fields. On the opposite side of High Street is a narrow passage, called Meadow-stile,—the stile leading to the meadows. Some towns had a right of mintage, but though the Archbishops of Canterbury formerly possessed this right, we have no proof that they ever established a mint at Croydon.

Cold Harbour.—This word has long puzzled antiquaries. It is almost invariably found near a Roman military station, and is, therefore imagined to have been an out-station used by the Romans for their military purposes.

Pitlake is from the Saxon *leag*, feeding ground, signifying the feeding ground near or by the side of the pit.

Mear is a boundary line.

Norbury.—An abbreviation of Northborough. There were formerly several boroughs in the town. We have the same word in Norwoodbury. The word Borough has now come to signify an incorporated town ; originally it meant a certain manor or district, and was in general use before corporations were dreamt of.

Collier's Water is a place from whence the colliers or charcoal burners obtained a supply of water. Collier's Water Lane leads direct from the forest to Thornton Heath pond.

Whitehorse Road owes its name to Walter Whitehorse, who obtained the grant of a free warren in this district in the reign of Edward III.

Ing is a place where a family settled, such as Tooting, Worthing, Dorking, and so on. The addition of *ton, ham, bury, fold,* or *worth*, denotes a branch settlement. Thus Warlingham would mean the place where the children of the Warlings had settled. We find the word in Addington, Beddington, Kennington, Beckingham, Syding-ham, in the last two cases modified into Beckenham and Syden-ham. The same combination occurs all over the kingdom. Thus we have Birmingham, Nottingham, &c.

The Common is simply an unenclosed piece of free land, over which every cottager had a right of free soke, or grazing. Gradu-ally these places have been swallowed up by different Lords of the Manor, and sold in lots. In several old cities and towns the right of herbage on the common is restricted to the freemen of the place, who, in olden times, had the exclusive right of voting at elections of Members of Parliament.

Pump Pail.—In this peculiar title we distinguish the Norman word *Pale*, or district. This word is still frequently used in old law books. It would mean formerly the district entitled to the use of the pump which stood there.

Broad Green.—This was a wide open spot, with a green in the centre. Gradually, however, encroachments have been made, and the green has disappeared, though the title remains.

Caterham is an abbreviation of the Roman *Caster*, or Castle, and the Saxon *ham*. There are remains of an old Roman fort on Coppice Hill, in this parish.

Keston in the same way, was originally Cœster-ton, shortened down to Keston.

Beggar's Bush is evidently derived from the Saxon *Beeker*, or point. Any one standing on the south side of Croham Hurst will at once be struck by a similarity of this point to the Beeker or Prow of an old Saxon war ship. No doubt it was formerly called Beeker Bush, vulgarised into Beggar's Bush.

Wickham is derived from *Wic*, a street or way, with the terminal *Ham*.

Bottom is frequently used to signify low ground, hence Smitham Bottom, Chipstead Bottom, &c.

Penge is derived from the Saxon *Pen*, a hill, in Gaelic *Ben*. In Wales almost all the hills and mountains are called Pen, and in Scotland Ben.

Anerley, from *an* a stream, and *el*, small. The small stream running from Sydenham hill into the morass, which then occupied the ground on which Penge now stands.

Swan and Sugar Loaf.—This is the title of a well-known Inn at the junction of the Brighton and Selsdon roads. It was originally a farm house, and forms part of the property devoted by Archbishop Whitgift to his hospital. Formerly it was decorated rudely with the Archbishop's arms, a cone or sugar-loaf hat, and a bent crook, resembling the curve of a swan's neck; hence it obtained the name of the Swan and Sugar Loaf from the common people, who did not understand heraldic signs. When the house was licensed, it retained the name by which the farmstead was familiarly known.

RAILWAYS, TRAMWAYS, AND CANAL,

With some Account of the Trial of the Atmospheric System on the London and Croydon Railway.

TOWARDS the close of the last century, it became apparent to all men of business that some readier and cheaper mode of conveying goods from town to town must be devised. The old system of pack horses was already a thing of the past, and their places had been superseded by the so-called fly-vans,

which crawled along the roads at a maximum speed of two miles an
hour. The success of the Duke of Bridgewater's canal, connecting
Liverpool and Manchester, naturally drew attention to the compara-
tive ease and cheapness of water carriage, and in the year 1801, an
Act of Parliament was obtained for the making and maintaining
a navigable canal from the town of Croydon to join the Grand
Surrey Canal in the parish of St. Paul, Deptford : and also for the
purpose of supplying Croydon. Streatham, Dulwich, Norwood, and
Sydenham with water. The company formed by this Act was
empowered to raise by subscription £50,000 in shares of £100 each ;
and if that sum should be found insufficient, then £30,000 by
additional shares or by mortgage ; and in order to repay the sub-
scribers the Company was authorised to charge 3d per ton per mile
on timber, stone, coal, bricks, tiles, and other goods, and three half-
pence on dung, chalk, clay, lime, and such articles. The canal was
finished and opened on the 22nd of October, 1809, but the water-
works were never attempted.

The route followed by the canal was almost precisely the same
as the present London and Croydon Railway. When this line was
projected, an arrangement was made by which the canal became
the property of the railway company for the sum of £40,259,—a
very good bargain for the Canal Company, as it had never financially
speaking been a success, although it had during its existence been
extremely beneficial to the trading interests of the town. In the
construction of the railway the space occupied by the canal was
utilised wherever possible. It was finally closed in August, 1836,
having been in existence about 30 years. Some few traces of the
old canal are still visible at Anerley and Norwood. The terminus
basin was at West Croydon, on the spot where the West Croydon
Station now stands. The water was supplied by reservoirs at
Norwood and Forest Hill, and a pumping station at Croydon. There
were several locks on the route, two near Croydon, two at Forest
Hill, and several intervening.

About the year 1810 this canal was supplemented by a tramway,
which ran from the head of the canal to Merstham. This tram was
very different from our modern lines. Iron rails this shape—
L ⌐J—were laid on large blocks of stone by the side of the roads.
and the wheels of the tram carriages made to fit inside the upright
flanges, so as to run on the flat surfaces. Thus it will be seen that
the flanges instead of being on the carriage wheels, as in our present
tram cars, were on the metals. They thereby obtained this advantage, the cars could run on ordinary roads as easily as any other
wheeled vehicles. By means of this line great quantities of stone,
lime, fullers' earth, and bricks were brought from the pits and quarries
to the canal boats and shipped to London. In 1815, to save this
transhipment, the tramway was carried through to London, and the
terminus made at Wandsworth. A branch ran from Mitcham to
Shipley's Oil-cake Mills at Hackbridge.

The old line of trams ran alongside the Brighton Road on a
slight embankment between the highway and the stream of the
Bourne, a considerable portion of the route is now hidden by the

Haling Park palings, but some remains of the embankment are still visible near the Red Deer Inn.   It was brought round the corner of the Anchor Hotel, but instead of following the line of our present tramways, along South End and High Street, it made a detour to the left, turning round Southbridge Road, or it would be more correct to say, where Southbridge Road is now situate, all this part behind the houses in South End being then open fields.   From thence it passed along Church Road, originally called Tramway Road, crossing Church Street near to Elys Davy's Road, and thence up the Tamworth Road to West Croydon basin.   The London branch was carried alongside the Mitcham Road, and found its way *via* Mitcham and Merton to Wandsworth.   The present railway from Mitcham to London in many places follows the track of this old tramway.

These roads were very useful in saving an immense amount of labour, and shortly after the opening of the line between Wandsworth and Croydon, they were subjected to a practical test.   The draught of a horse on a good road is about twenty hundredweight, and strong horses, under ordinary circumstances, can draw about a ton and a half.   To show the superiority of the tramroads, twelve waggons were loaded with stones till each waggon weighed about three tons, and a horse being attached drew them with apparent ease a distance of six miles in an hour and three quarters, having been stopped four times, in order to show that it had the power of starting as well as drawing the load.   Additional carriages were added, but still the horse was able to draw them.   On weighing the load at the end of the journey it was found to amount to more than fifty-five tons.

The successful application of steam power on the Liverpool and Manchester Railway, in 1830, opened the eyes of thinking men to the fact that a new era had dawned upon the world.   The directors of this new line offered a prize of £500 for the best locomotive engine, and so moderate were they in their expectations, that they did not require the successful engine to accomplish more than ten miles per hour; but George Stephenson's engine, the *Rocket*, on its first trial, averaged fourteen miles, and in some places even reached what was then thought to be the enormous speed of 30 miles per hour.   It is most amusing to hear that this *excessive* rate of speed was denounced as dangerous to the health of the public.   In the prospectus of a railway proposed to be made to Woolwich, it was modestly suggested that twice the velocity of ordinary carriages might be attained, combined with greater safety.   An eminent writer, in the *Quarterly Review*, denounced these proposals as " visionary schemes unworthy of notice," and further on says " We should as soon expect the people of Woolwich to be fired off upon one of Congreve's *ricochet* rockets as trust themselves to the mercy of such a machine going at such a rate."

In 1830, it was proposed to construct a railway from London to Birmingham, but, owing to the opposition of certain lords, the act did not become law until 1832.   The bill excited immense attention throughout the kingdom, and very little notice was taken of a smaller bill which was passing through Parliament in 1834.   This was an act, authorising the construction of a line from London to Croydon, along the track of the old Canal ; and in May, 1839, this, the first railway line south of London, was successfully opened by the Lord Mayor.   For some time trains only ran once in two hours, from eight in the morning until ten in the evening, and the fare each way was 1s. 9d.   The third-class carriages were all open at the top, and remained so for many years.   In these days, 1s. 3d. is thought an excessive charge for riding both ways in a comfortable closed carriage.

The London and Brighton Railway was opened in 1841, and soon afterwards the two lines were amalgamated.   When the Croydon Railway was constructed, the art of railway engineering was in its infancy, and we should smile now at some of the appliances adopted.   The first sleepers on the Birmingham line were blocks of stone, but the directors of the Croydon line did not fall into this error.   From the first they employed wood, using what are technically termed hog-trough sleepers—shaped thus $\vee$, and these were for many years in use.   They, however, did not use the $\top$ rails.   In place thereof, narrow planks of wood were laid longitudinally along the sleepers, and firmly fastened thereto.   On these were affixed bars of iron, about half an inch in thickness and two inches broad, with screw holes bored at intervals, enabling these bars to be securely fastened to the wood.   These were found to answer tolerably well where the traffic was light and the speed moderate, but near the stations where the breaks are applied and the wheels bite, the iron was soon either worn out or loosened, requiring continual watching. Eventually it was found necessary to remove the rails and adopt the $\top$ rails, fitting into iron chairs, bolted to the sleepers, and fastened with wooden keys.   Many costly experiments, however, had to be tried before the present perfect system was finally adopted.

We have now to speak of the Atmospheric Railway.   Many of our readers are not aware that one of the most interesting experiments ever proposed for the improvement of our modern railway system was tried at Croydon.   In 1840, Messrs. Glegg and Samuda brought before the notice of the public their Atmospheric Railway project.   It was first tried on a portion of the then unfinished West London Railway, near Wormwood Scrubbs, and proved so successful, that the London and Croydon Company obtained parliamentary powers for laying down a line of atmospheric railway by the side of their other line from London to Croydon, and making an extension of the same from Croydon to Epsom—an arrangement by which there would have been eighteen miles of atmospheric line, half of which would run parallel with one worked by the locomotive engines. It having been found more convenient to lay the Atmospheric Railway along the eastern side of the tracks used by the locomotive trains, although the line leading to the Croydon Station, and thence on to the Croydon and Epsom Railway, branches off from that to Brighton on the west, this difficulty was overcome by the construction at the point of separation of the Brighton and Croydon lines, of a very curious viaduct, which crossed the locomotive lines at an ·extremely acute and oblique angle, over which the atmospheric line

A 2

was conducted ; the rise from, and the descent to, the ordinary level being provided for by slopes of one in fifty. This expedient, by which one railway was made as it were to take a flying leap over another, alongside of which it had been running for miles upon the same level, was then thought to be a marvellous achievement.

Upon the part that was completed in the summer of 1845, experimental trips were run, for the purpose of testing the machinery, and a speed of thirty miles an hour was obtained, with a train of sixteen carriages, and of seventy miles with six carriages. This was, however, frequently surpassed when the line got into full working order by the regular express trains of nine carriages filled with passengers. The distance between Forest Hill and Croydon is $5\frac{1}{4}$ miles, and this has been accomplished in the marvellously quick time of 2m. 47s., including the starting and pulling up. This showed an average speed of more than 100 miles an hour. Coming down the incline of the viaduct this speed was much exceeded. The sensation has been described to us, by a gentleman who was in the habit of travelling by this train, to have been very similar to that of falling from a height ; it fairly took the breath away. The motion was very regular and smooth, with not one half the rattle and jar there is on an ordinary train drawn by locomotives.

There were pumping engines at Croydon, Norwood, Forest Hill, and New Cross, though the last was never used, as the Atmospheric System was not worked beyond Forest Hill, the remaining portion of the journey being completed by the aid of ordinary locomotives. One great difficulty of the Atmospheric System was the starting of the train. To obviate this, the metals on the line coming into a station were raised, and those on leaving were made to decline slightly, thus the necessary impetus was more readily obtained. Another great difficulty was stopping the train at the precise point required. Occasionally in wet weather, when the metals were slippery, the breaks would not bite, and the train would run some considerable distance before it could be stopped. In a train drawn by an ordinary locomotive this is not a matter of much consequence, as the carriages can be backed to their proper place. but on the Atmospheric Railway there was no backing power, the passengers must alight wherever the train stopped. A third difficulty occurred at the flying bridge, previously mentioned, near the Norwood Station. Occasionally, when the train was very heavily laden, the motive power was insufficient to propel the train over the top of the bridge, and it would stop sometimes within a few yards of the summit. To obviate this a simple remedy was provided. The three or four foremost carriages were detached from the ordinary couplings and the power was usually found sufficient to carry them over the top to the commencement of the decline. They were then attached to the remainder of the carriages by a long rope, and the train again started. The extra momentum thus obtained on the decline was sufficient to pull the back carriages over the remainder of the ascent, and thus the whole train arrived in Croydon Station, one half towing the other half behind it.

It would be somewhat out of place in a work like this to enter into an explanation of the working of the atmospheric principle, and without diagrams it would be almost impossible to do so. It will be sufficient here to state that a tube 15 inches in diameter was laid on the sleepers in the centre between the metals, and securely fastened down. Every two or three miles, pumping stations were erected to exhaust the air therein. On the top of this tube was affixed a moveable valve, so constructed as to easily rise, and yet when in position to be hermetically sealed. A piston affixed to the foremost carriage was let into this tube, which was completely lined with a soft composition, filling up all the little irregularities, and the piston so fitted as to be quite air-tight, and yet to move with little friction. When the air was quite exhausted in the tube, it was kept closed until the train was ready, and then the piston, which we have stated was affixed to the foremost carriage, was placed in the tube and the end of the tube behind it was opened. The current of air rushing in behind the piston to fill up the vacuum, gave sufficient power to propel the train. The real weak point of the system was the difficulty of keeping the valve of the tube effectually air-tight. In ordinary weather there was no difficulty, but in very hot weather the composition by which the longitudinal valve was sealed became insufficient to retain the necessary solidity. This difficulty was thought to be overcome by the substitution of a new and harder composition; however, when the frosty weather set in this was found to be too hard. Eventually, after having been tried $2\frac{1}{2}$ years, and a very heavy expense had been incurred, it was found necessary to abandon the atmospheric and revert to the ordinary locomotives for traction power.

It is greatly to be regretted that a system apparently so full of promise should have been definitely abandoned for what appears to be so trivial a fault. It would have been thought that some other means might have been adopted for keeping the valve air-tight. Supposing this to have been the case, and the system had been extended, by the adoption of light atmospheric lines between the principal centres of population, what a revolution it would have made in our system of travelling. Imagine an atmospheric line at work the whole distance between London and Brighton, and trains propelled thereon at the same rate as the express travelled between Forest Hill and Croydon, we should see on our walls flaming placards announcing " Flying Atmospheric train from London to Brighton ; the whole journey in half an hour!" In the same way we might have trains from London to Croydon in five minutes, or to Margate in one hour, or Liverpool in two-and-a-half hours, and to Edinburgh in four-and-a-half hours, including time for refreshment at York. All these glowing anticipations doomed to disappointment, because a grease could not be found which would act properly in all states of the weather.

The Atmospheric Railway is, however, now a thing of the past, and it becomes our duty to speak of railways of the present. At the close of the Great Exhibition of 1851, it was decided to remove the Exhibition building to its present site on Sydenham Hill, where an army of workmen were employed in erecting the present Crystal

Palace, and laying out the beautiful surrounding grounds, under the superintendence of the late Sir Joseph Paxton. This naturally attracted attention to the beauty and salubrity of the surrounding neighbourhood. New houses sprang up in all directions, and from its contiguity to the palace and the many advantages it offered to residents, Croydon naturally shared in the general prosperity. Increased facilities for travelling became necessary, and new lines with additional stations were designed and rapidly completed, and, year by year, the population increased by "jumps and bounds."

Croydon is now connected with the London and North-Western Railway by several trains running daily to Willesden Junction ; with the Great Eastern Railway by trains to Liverpool Street *via* the East London Railway, which runs through the old Thames Tunnel ; with the London, Chatham, and Dover Railway by the branch line to Beckenham, *via* Norwood Junction ; and with the London and North-Western Railway by frequent trains both to Clapham and Wimbledon.

In 1879, it was determined by a number of gentleman, interested in the prosperity of the town, to bring the outlying portions into closer connection with the centre, and a system of street tramways was proposed. A company was quickly formed and the necessary capital subscribed. An act having been obtained, work was commenced forthwith, and in November 1880, the first portion, extending from North End to Thornton Heath Pond was opened. Other portions have since been gradually completed, and the whole of the original scheme carried out. Further extensions, however, are on the point of being made, extending the line to the Palace and Penge.

WHITGIFT'S HOSPITAL AND SCHOOL.

THE most prominent Institution in the town is the Hospital, College, or School, founded in the reign of Queen Elizabeth by Archbishop Whitgift. Standing in the very centre of the busiest part of the town, the quaint old hospital, or college as it is more familiarly called, attracts the notice of every visitor, while the spacious schools, lately erected in North End, out of the funds of the original bequest, are not only an ornament to the town, but promise to become, in a few years, one of the largest and most important educational institutions in the kingdom.

Archbishop Whitgift, the founder, presided over the diocese of Canterbury, during the latter years of the reign of " Good Queen Bess," and in the 38th year of that monarch's reign, he obtained letters patent for building a hospital at Croydon, with license of mortmain. The building was commenced on the 17th day of

January, 1596, and finished on the 29th September, 1599. The schoolmaster's house adjoining was not finished until the following year.

Stow, writing in 1600, says :—" This yeere, the most reverend father, John Whitgift, Archbishop of Canterbury, did finish that notable and memorable monument of our time, to wit, his Hospital of the Holy Trinitie in Croydon, in the county of Surrey, by him there founded, and builded of stone and brick, for the relief and sustentation of certain poor people. As also a fair school-house for the increase of literature, together with a large dwelling for the use of the schoolmaster, and these premises, he, through God's favourable assistance, performed and perfected for that (as I have heard him say) he would not be to his executors a cause of their damnation, remembering the good advice an antient father hath left written to all posteriteè. *Futior via est ut bonum quod quisquis post mortem, sperat agi per alios, agat dum vivit ipse per se.*" " It is much safer for a man to do good and charitable deeds by himself, whilst he liveth, than to hope that others will do the same for him after his death."

The execution of the work was entrusted to the Rev. Samuel Finch, Vicar of Croydon, who had to make the contracts and superintend the workmen. There is a book preserved in the manuscript library at Lambeth, entitled, " The particular accounts of the building of Trinitie Hospital in Croydon, and the statutes and ordinances belonging to the same," in which there is a very minute schedule of the expenses incurred in the building, the sum total of which amounted to £2,716 11s. 11d.

The good Vicar was accustomed to write a weekly letter to the Archbishop, detailing the progress of the work. Very fortunately some of these letters have been preserved, as they throw great light on the value of labour, and the manners and customs of the time. The workmen, while digging the foundations, discovered some skulls and other human remains, which seemed to have troubled the worthy Mr. Finch very considerably. He mentions the matter in two letters. In the first one he says, " There were three skulls dug out of the trench, next the highway leading to the park," [now George-street.] In the second, dated February 19th, 1596, he writes thus : " For the skulls there were four digged up indeede, and I presently upon finding the first did confer with Outred, and asked him if his conscience were cleare, and he said it was cleare ; I reasoned also with Morris, an old Welshman, that had dwelt there for a long time, and he knew nothing however; for the better satisfaction in the matter, I caused Hillarie to cast the measure of the ground this day, and we find the bodies did not lie within the compass of the house, for (to the end that the plot might be cast square) there was five foot taken in of the way against the ' George,' and four foot left out of the grounde (wherein the house stood) against the ' Crowne ' (as ' Mr. Dr.' Bancroft knoweth well), so that the skulls being in the trench next to the ' George,' Hillarie dare depose they were without the compass of the house ; besides there be many that can remember, when they digged in the midst of that street, to set a May-pole therein, they found the skulls and bones of a dead person ; so it is generally supposed that it has been some waste place wherein (in the time of some mortalitie) they did bury in, and more I cannot learn."*

In addition to the difficulty arising from the finding of the bodies, the reverend Clerk of the Works seems to have had considerable trouble with the workmen. In a letter to Mr. Wormall, the Archbishop's secretary, dated 8th Feb., 1596, he writes† :—

"Wolmer, the bricklayer, was here yesterday, to view the work. He says that he cannot come himself, but he will send some men from Westminster, but they will not come under one shilling and sixpence per day, and the labourers under one shilling. Hillarie says that he can get a man who can do the work creditably for sixteenpence per day, and labourers at the rate of £6 per year, thus saving 2d. a day wages. And besides the master workman must be here to confer with the carpenter. This much Hillarie told me, but he does not know that I have told your Grace. The yard is all fenced in strong and safe, and we have made an end of pulling down.‡ Now we have taken mortar making in hand, cleansing and levelling the ground, and on Monday next, Hillarie says we shall be ready for the foundation and the bricklayer. Weeks, the bricklayer, has been looking at your brick-clamps and says they are very good.|| We have had our sand from Dubber's Hill, for the Park faileth."

On the 18th February, he again writes, and says that Henry Blease and John Green, two of his parishioners, had undertaken the brickwork for 1s. 3d. per day. Blease had begun the foundations leading to London, and finding the ground made and false, he dug a trench in the ground 4ft. deep, and finding that he had come to solid ground, he filled up the trench with great flint and small stones and brickbats and rubbish, not confusedly but orderly laid on, and rammed strongly course upon course, strong and sure. In this work he used up the heap of stones, which his Grace had made the boys gather out of the churchyard, and also half-a-dozen loads of small stones fetched from Smithdome (Smitham) bottom. He found it necessary to make the foundations in the other parts of the building even stronger, and for this purpose provided carts to fetch great flint and chalk for the building, and small for filling. In this letter he asked his Grace to send him some more money, as he had been obliged to send William Tagburne to Smithfield to buy two horses ; for this purpose he had given him £5.

---

* In all probability, these were remains of the unfortunate men slain in the encounter between the Londoners and the troops from Tonbridge Castle, which took place near this spot after the battle of Lewes, that occurred in 1264.

† We have somewhat modernised both the spelling and the phraseology of the letters in order to make them more intelligible to our readers.

‡ An old inn, called the Chequer, formerly occupied the site of the present hospital. It was purchased by Archbishop Whitgift for the sum of £20. and a tenement adjoining cost him £30. Probably the pulling down, mentioned in this letter, referred to the old inn.

|| It would by this appear the Archbishop had been brickmaking, so as to have some ready for the work when he commenced building.

In his next letter, the Vicar acknowledges the receipt of £20, sent by William Tagburne, and then came the difficulty about finding the skulls and other remains which we have already mentioned. Had they been found inside the range of building, we do not know what would have been the consequences ; probably the Hospital would have been removed to some other spot. Towards the conclusion of this letter occurs a sentence which we give in its entirety, owing to its exceeding quaintness. "I thank God our grounde-work is greatlye commended by all that vewe the same. And I hope well that it will like his Grace at his comminge, for it is not slubbered up, but stronglye doone."

The next letter contains the copy of a contract with Nicholas and Christopher Richardson, citizens and freemasons of London, and Gabriel Anscombe, of Charlton, yeoman, who bind themselves under a penalty of £100 to bring to Croydon so much good and seasoned freestone, as shall be sufficient for the doors and windows of the Hospital, and shall work the same, and set them up in such necessary and ready manner, that the remainder of the work be not delayed, receiving or taking for the same 9d. the foot for windows, and 10d. the foot for door cases." Those interested in these matters can see the work performed under this contract, and will be able to compare the difference in prices between the Elizabethan age and the present.

The next letter is dated the 28th of February, in which the Vicar complains that the work has been delayed by this " goodlye seasonable weather, which would not serve for the laying of mortar," and therefore the work would not be ready for his Grace's inspection "untill Monday come seven-nighte."

In the next letter, dated March 3rd, the worthy Vicar is in great tribulation. Blease, one of the bricklayers, had made some complaint of the unskilfulness of the workmen. He seems to have been a grumbling fellow, never satisfied. He and Green, who are mentioned in a previous letter, were allowed 1d. per day more than the ordinary workmen to take charge of the bricklaying. Instead of laying his complaints before the Vicar, he reported the matter to Mr. Mills, a gentleman who had come on the part of the Archbishop to inspect the work. It would seem that Blease, who, it will be remembered, was recommended by Hillarie, soon began to complain of Hillarie, because he both set out the work and gave his advice to the workmen. "For," saith Blease, "if I be appointed one to take charge, 'tis reason I appoint the work and the workmen." The Vicar went to Blease to advise him to be content that Hillarie should exercise supervision, but Blease would not be content, and so the Vicar let the discontented bricklayer have " a bit of his mind." We quote his own words. " But, goodman Blease, I understand you shoot at another matter, which neither you, nor Hillarie himself, nor never a man here shall attain, if I know it, and that is, you would have the appointment of the workmen under you to make a gain of their wages ; as for example, here is Kilman, highly recommended to us, a good workman, who has 14d. a day, and you have made him promise you 2d. a day out of it, pretending that he is under you, and cometh in by you, when you give him neither meat, drink, nor lodging; and thus you would have us do with others; but you shall not have your will, and if Kilman thinks well to work for his Lordship for a shilling a day, he shall only receive that money, for there is no reason you should gain by his work to his Lordship's loss; for I have learnt this trick of you; when you gain by any of the men, you allow them to work as they please, but if they will not let you share their earnings, then you haste them on." Thus it will be seen that there were tricks in trade even in those days. The Vicar threatened Blease to take off his extra penny a day if he would not be quiet. Some short time afterwards, he was up to his old tricks again. He put on a labourer to work as a bricklayer, but Hillarie spied him before he had been at work an hour, and would only let him work as a labourer, and "then the fellow wrought 3 days and received 2s. 6d., a labourer's wages." He tried the same game on with two more men, but they were soon detected. "But," says the Vicar, "what are these matters to trouble my Lord with. We shall have enough hereof before the work is ended, and I told Mr. Mills 'tis no caveat to me, for I know in a multitude there will fail out such matters. If we cannot appease, we will thrust out such unruly persons."

The next trouble Mr. Fitch had to contend with was the bricks. Those which had been provided were insufficient, and he had to buy some. He went with the brickmaker to see the bricks before purchasing. We prefer to give the Vicar's own words. " Rednap came hither this day, and as soon as ever he came into the yard, and saw the bricks, his heart was dead ; he went to them and chose here one and there one, and knock on it, and said, ' he hoped there were better to be found in the Park.' To the Park we came, and there went from clampe to clampe, and we found one here and there good, but they did not equal his own expectation. Fain would he have excused himself, but his handie work spake against him, and we were so round with him, that he burst into tears, saying, ' he was never the like served in any work ; he was ashamed of it, he could not excuse it ; it was the wickedness and deceitfulness of the earth. And all be it, he could not thoroughly make amends, yet he could be content to do what lay in him, but not of that earth." Well, then, to the loom pits beyond Dubber's Hill we came, near Halinge gate, where bricks had been made in time past. There he found such mould as contented him, and with much parleying, was content to give my Lord the making of fifty thousand, and of ten thousand for waste (nothing in comparison, but as much as we could get him to yield to), and to make one hundred thousand more for the price he made for in the park, having all the necessaries found him as he had in the park. And there wood must be had from the farm, and water fetched in a cart from the other Halinge-gate. And these bricks will be ready for us before Whitsuntide. Only he requests His Grace to write to Sir John Box (in whose work he is) that he will be content to spare him till he has served our turn, which he knoweth he both may and will."

Unfortunately, at this point, these interesting letters cease, and we are left in doubt whether the Vicar or Blease conquered in the end, or whether Blease was turned out as an " unruly person."

The statutes of this Hospital inform us that it was founded for the benefit of at least thirty persons of both sexes, and so many more under the number of forty, as the revenues will permit, half the number must be inhabitants of Croydon, and half of Lambeth. One of them (who is also to teach in the school-house, built by the founder) is required to say public prayers mornings and evenings in the chapel on all working days, except Wednesdays and Fridays in the forenoon, and Saturdays in the afternoon, on which days, as also on Sundays and festival days, the poor people are to resort to the Parish Church of Croydon. All this has been altered ; there is a proper chaplain appointed, and he reads prayers three mornings in the week in the old chapel. The schoolmaster is now the head-master of the celebrated Whitgift Grammar School ; he, however, still resides in one of the houses adjoining the Hospital.

The Worshipful Company of Fishmongers provide a dinner for the poor people on the 23rd March in each year. The visitors of the company attend service in the Parish Church in the morning, and then return to the Hospital, and visit the kitchen to see that the dinner (for which they pay to the warden, £2 13s. 4d.) is cooking ; thus they take care the poor people are not defrauded of their repast, which takes place in the common hall. On leaving, the Fish-mongers place in the poor-box attached to the entrance gate, a half-sovereign, which, with any other monies which have been deposited therein, is taken out after dinner, and divided in equal proportions among the brothers and sisters. This old practice has never been once omitted for more than 250 years.

The Hospital, the building of which we have previously described, is in the form of a square, with a small court-yard and grass plat in the centre, very much after the fashion of the old colleges in Oxford and Cambridge.

Over the gateway, engraved on stone, are the arms of the See of Canterbury, with Archbishop Whitgift's, and the date 1597, in which year this part of the hospital was completed. Over the arms on a square stone are these words : Sanctæ Trinitati Sacri (sacred to the Holy Trinity). Over the gateway is this quotation from Prov. 28 c., " Qui dat pauperi, non indigebit " (he that giveth to the poor shall not lack.)

Entering the gateway, and crossing the grass plat, we come to the Common Hall, in which the business of the hospital was accus-tomed to be transacted. It is, however, now fitted up as a reading room and library, for the use of the brothers and sisters. Formerly an old picture of the " Dance of Death " hung over the chimney place ; this has, however, now been removed to the chapel. There were also kept in this room three antique wooden goblets, one of which held three pints, on which was inscribed—

What, sirrah, hold thy peace,
Thirste, satisfied, cease.

But these have all disappeared. There is an old water-colour painting in a frame, dated 1795, representing the front of the hospital, looking down North End, including a view of the old George Inn, with sign overhanging the street; over the fire-place is a framed Latin inscription, which formerly was annexed to the Whitgift monument in the Old Church, and was saved from the fire. The following is a copy of the inscription :—

> Gratia non miror, si fit divina Johanine
>   Qui jacit hic, solas credito gratus erat,
> Nec magis immerito Whitgiftus dicitur idem,
>   Candor in eloquio, pectore candor erat,
> Candida pauperibus posuit loca, candida musis,
>   E terris moriens candida dona tulit.

[TRANSLATION.]

> Some slight approach to evangelic fame,
> Lies buried here, which once was John by name :
> Of Whitgift's name, behold the dark abode,
> Fair was his speech, as from the heart it flowed,
> For want and learning a fair spot he gave,
> Then died, to meet a rich reward beyond the grave.

The business meetings of the Governors are now held in a room over the Common Hall, adjoining the Warden's apartments. This room presents no particular features; the arms of the Archbishop are carved on the wood panels over the fire-place. There is, however, kept in this room an old black letter Bible, strongly bound in wooden covers, mounted in brass; the New Testament is worn away. By an inscription inscribed therein, we find that it was presented to the hospital by Abraham Hartwell, " Reverendissimi Fundatoris Humillimus Serocitus " (the humble and most dutiful servant of the Reverend Founder) 1599, and was repaired at the expense of Thomas Lett, Esq , in 1813. It is a copy of a Bible, translated into English by order of Archbishop Cranmer, and there is a Prologue or Preface written by that dignitary. This is the first authorised English translation of the Scriptures, and varies considerably from the authorised version at present in use, which dates from James the First. The imprint runs as follows:—" Imprinted at London by the deputies of Christopher Barker, printer to the Queen's most excellent Majestie, 1595." Formerly this Bible was kept in the Common Hall, and previous to its removal there, was in use in the Hospital Church, where, as was customary, in former times, it was chained to the reading desk.

Over the outer gate in an upper room, called the Treasury, were deposited all the title deeds and other documents relating to the hospital. The most curious and valuable are Queen Elizabeth's original grant to the Founder, and the Archbishop's Deed of Gift of the several estates with which he endowed the hospital. They are both on vellum; the first neatly endorsed, and the margins beautifully ornamented with a drawing of the Queen in her robes, sitting in a chair of state, and the royal arms in different compartments. The other document is written in English ; the beginning is embellished with a drawing of the Archbishop in his robes, very artistically finished ; the margin contains his arms beautifully illuminated. A fire-proof room has lately been erected, in which these valuable documents are carefully preserved.

The right of presentation is vested in the Archbishop of Canterbury. The following is a copy of the form of presentation :— "(A. B.) by divine providence Archbishop of Canterbury, Primate and Metropolitan of all England, to our Beloved in Christ (C. B.) : Health in the Lord for ever. By these presents we grant unto thee, in consideration of thy bodily infirmity, of thy poverty, and age, the space and lodging of one of the poor brethren of the Hospital of the Holy Trinity in Croydon, of the foundation of John Whitgift, Archbishop of Canterbury, for the term of thy life, and for the sustenance of thy poverty, willing and strictly enjoining thee to keep and in all things observe the statutes and ordinances of the same Hospital. In testimony whereof, &c."

The Chapel is situated in one corner of the quadrangle. It is a very neat and unpretentious looking building. At the request of Whitgift, it was formally dedicated to the worship of God by the Bishops of London and Winchester, on the 10th of July, 1599, by the title of the Chapel or Oratory of the Hospital of the Holy Trinity at Croydon, of the foundation of John Whitgift, Archbishop of Canterbury. A fine portrait of the founder, painted on wood, formerly hung on the wall. It was taken down, under pretence of being cleaned, but has never been returned. It is now, we understand, hanging in some of the buildings of the Whitgift Schools, where it must be somewhat out of place, because underneath are the following lines :—

> Has Triadi Sanctæ Primi qui struxerat œdes,
> Illuis en veram Præsulis effigiem.

Which we read thus—

> A striking portrait of the Primate see,
> Who built this chapel to the Holy Three.

There are, however, a few objects of interest remaining on the walls, amongst which is a portrait of a lady, wearing a large ruff, with this inscription :—" A. D. 1616. Ætatis suœ, 38." This is said to be a portrait of a niece of the Archbishop, and it bears some resemblance to the portrait of Whitgift.

There is also a framed tablet affixed to the wall near the entrance door, which formerly hung over the mantel piece in the common hall. It is almost illegible, but on closer inspection it proves to be a full-length skeleton entering a kind of portal, around which are some indistinct Latin phrases.

Over the reading desk are two other tablets, with the following quaint inscriptions :—

" To the happy memory of the most Reverend Father in God, Doctor John Whitgift, late Archbishop of Canterbury, &c., his Grace's sometime faithful loving servant and unworthy Gentleman Usher, J. W., consecrateth this testimony of his ancient duty. Obiit 29th Feb., 1603."

> Pure saints by Heaven refined from earthly dross,
>   You duly can esteem your new increase,
> But our soul's eyes are dim to see the loss,
>   Great Prelate, we sustain by thy decease.

> We never could esteem thee as we ought.
>   Although the best men did thee best esteem ;
> For hardly can you square a mortal thought
>   That of so great worth worthily can deem.

The straight, sound cedar, new cut from the stem,
 As yet is scarcely missed in Libanus ;
This richer than the wise kings' richest gem,
 New lost, as yet is scarcely missed of us.

But years to come and our deserved society,
 I fear, will teach us more and more to prize
This matchless pearl—this fairest, fruitless plant,
 On whose top, Virtue sitting, touched the skies.

Presuming Horace, Ovid confident,
 Proudly foretold their books eternities :
But if my muse were like mine argument,
 The lines would outlive both their memories.

For their best masterpieces do contain
 But pictures of false Gods, and men's true faults,
Whereas in my verse ever should remain
 A true saint's praise, whose worth fills Heaven's great vaults.

Shine bright in the Triumphant Church, fair soul
 That in the Militant has shined so long ;
Let rarest arts thy great deserts enroll,
 I can but sing thee in a mournful song.
 And wish that with a sea of tears my verse
 Could make an island of thy honoured hearse.

L'ENVOY.

Cavendish in prose set Cardinal Wolsey forth,
 Who served him in that place, I served this Lord ;
He had his faults to write of, and his worth,
 Nothing in this man was to be abhorred.
 Therefore his theme much larger was than mine,
 But, Cavendish, my theme better is than thine.

 Let ivy-honor'd Bards adore,
 The muses and Perène's name ;
 I offer my unpractis'd tone,
 A rude probationer for fame.

On the south wall is a large frame, in the centre of which is the Archbishop's arms, surrounded by some Latin inscriptions in praise of charity. There is also another frame on the opposite wall containing a very lengthy poem, the greater portion of which is totally illegible.

The seats in the Church are plain oaken benches without backs, so that the poor people have no chance of resting themselves during the service, which simply consists in reading the prayers and lessons of the day. Occasionally there is a full service. Archbishop Tait once preached a sermon in this small chapel. The poor brethren are expected to attend service in the Parish Church on Sunday.

The site of the Hospital was formerly occupied by a public-house called the " Chequers." We find among the purchases made by the Archbishop for his Hospital these entries :—

The " Chequers " in Croydon cost £20.

A Tenement adjoining cost £30.

Another Tenement in Croydon, called Stay Cross, with one acre-and-a-half of land, cost £80.

Upon these I have builded my Hospital, school-house, and schoolmasters' houses.

The original yearly revenue of the institution, arising princi-

Whitgift's Hospital and School. **xxix.**

pally from the Archbishop's endowment, was only £185 4s. 2d., but it is now upwards of £2000.

Formerly the Warden and Brethren were a body corporate, with power to buy, purchase, and possess goods and chattels not exceeding £200 per year. Their common seal was a history of Dives and Lazarus, and the escutcheon bore the arms of the Archbishop. Now, however, all power is taken out of the hands of the Warden and Brethren, and is vested in Governors appointed under the new Scheme just sanctioned by the Charity Commissioners, and who have built and established the present noble Whitgift School out of the surplus funds of the original endowment.

STATE PAPERS CONNECTED WITH CROYDON.

MANY interesting matters throwing light on the history of Croydon in the Past, may be gathered from the Calendars of State Papers, and in the following pages we propose to give extracts from various State Papers and Letters, lodged in the State Paper Office in the British Museum, between the years 1588 and 1640, in which the town of Croydon is mentioned :—

Lease for 21 years of Waddon Manor and Snelsdon Meadow, Croydon parish, to William Whitgift, at an annual rent of £22 6s. 8d. Among the conditions are the following :—The tenant to inbarn half the corn in the manor, lay down half the compost, also to maintain the Archbishop's steward and officers, four days a year, when they come to keep courts and take the rents.

The extent of the Manor of Waddon is not know. It was given in the year 1127, by Henry I, to the Monks of Bermondsey, who in 1390 transferred it to Archbishop Courtney, and ever since that time it has been annexed to the See of Canterbury. A Court Baron is held annually in Easter week, and in former times a constable was appointed for the hamlet. There is a corn-mill in Waddon, which is mentioned in Domesday Book.

1590, 26th November.—Lease of 7 acres in Bushmead meadow, Croydon, called Southflake and Northflake fields, for 21 years at annual rental of 22s., to Edward Kidman.

1593, 30th October.—Lease for 21 years of 106 acres at Broadcombe, Croydon, to Edward Heath, at an annual rental of £2, with leave to dig trenches and lay down pipes for conveyance of water to the houses.

1597, 21st March.—Lease for 28 years of 8 acres of land at Broomy Lees, Croydon, timber excepted, at an annual rent of 8s., to Gabriel Salway.

1603, *Croydon, 24th Sept.*—Whitgift, Archbishop of Canterbury, and Bancroft, Bishop of London, to Cecil. This is a paper containing particulars of factious and ill-disposed clergymen who preferred petitions to the King against the government of the Church, and thanking the King for protecting the Church as reformed by the late Queen (Elizabeth).

This letter is addressed to Cecil, Earl of Salisbury, who was at that time President of the Council, an office equivalent to our Prime Minister—excepting that the President is appointed by the Monarch, while the Prime Minister is the choice of the House of Commons. At the time of the accession of King James, the hopes of the Presbyterian party were raised by the belief that he would make certain changes in the Episcopalian Church, established by his predecessor, as he had been brought up in the principles of the Kirk of Scotland. Various petitions were presented to the King, which however were coldly received, and doubtless this drew forth the letter of thanks mentioned above. As it was dated from Croydon, it is evident that the Bishop of London must at the time have been on a visit to Archbishop Whitgift at the Old Palace.

Further petitions followed, and, much to the alarm of the Bishops, the King ordered that a conference should be held at Westminster, in which the matter should be discussed. The assembly consisted of 20 Bishops and other dignitaries, while only four of their opponents were summoned. The Bishops, however, were dreadfully perturbed, and, being admitted to the royal presence before the Presbyterians were admitted, they threw themselves on their knees before him, and earnestly entreated him not to alter the constitution of the Church, nor to give the Puritans the triumph in the coming debate. The King condescended to lift the weight of fear from their hearts, for he told them he meant to give the Puritan party a sound flagellation. Of course, such being the royal determination, the result of the discussion was a foregone conclusion. James himself took a prominent part in the debate, and conducted it in that royal style which admits of no contradiction. He was in his true element. Theological discussion was his pride and glory, and he believed himself capable of silencing all Christendom. He held forth on all sorts of topics, and assured the anti-episcopal divines that, in his opinion, if there were no Bishops there would soon be no King, and that " a presbytery agreed with monarchy as well as God did with the Devil." The Reformers complained bitterly of the manner in which the discussion had been conducted, but James was inflated with the idea of his own unrivalled eloquence and ability. He boasted that he had " peppered the Dissenters soundly ; " " they fled me," he said, " from argument to argument like schoolboys."

Croydon, July 12st, 1602.—The Earl of Northumberland to Cecil.—This letter, in which is a letter enclosed to the King, says that he would have known more of certain matters, but Raleigh distrusted him.

The question naturally arises how this letter comes to be dated from Croydon, and it requires some insight into English history to understand its meaning or import. About this time Sir Walter Raleigh, who had married a sister of Sir Nicholas Carew, of Beddington, was suspected of being implicated in a plot to raise Arabella Stuart (cousin of the King) to the throne. Cecil, the Prime Minister, was jealous of the great ability of Raleigh, and wanted an excuse to

get rid of him.   The Earl of Northumberland was himself also suspected, but, to clear himself, had volunteered to visit Raleigh, then
on a visit to Beddington Hall, and endeavour to gain information.
It is evident Sir Walter distrusted him, and the Earl wrote the above
letter to Cecil while on his visit to Beddington.

Croydon, *July 9th*, 1603.—This is a letter written by Archbishop Whitgift to
King James, remonstrating against his letters to the Universities for restoration of
impropriate tithes.   He says he will attend His Majesty and personally make
known the inconvenience thereof, which will be the overthrow of the Universities
and learning.   Annexed to this letter is a statement by the Archbishop of the
inconvenience likely to result from the alteration of the University impropriations.

In this year King James was, as usual, short of money, and he
had laid his hands on certain tithes belonging to the Universities
spared by King Henry VIII, and this gave rise to a remonstrance
on the part of Whitgift, which, we believe, was successful, and the
property was restored.

1604.—On the 20th February we have notice of the presentation of Samuel
Finch to the vicarage of Croydon.

The presentation had lapsed into the hands of the King.   The
Rev. Samuel Finch was the son of the late Rev. Samuel Finch, who
superintended the erection of the Whitgift Hospital.   The first Mr.
Finch died shortly before Archbishop Whitgift, but it would seem,
at that prelate's death, he had not appointed another Vicar, and the
right of presentation lapsed into the hands of the King, who presented it to the gentleman above named.

1605.—*November 5th*, *Lambeth*.—On the above date (the celebrated gunpowder plot day), we find a letter from Archbishop Bancroft, who had succeeded
Whitgift in the Archiepiscopal See, saying that Thomas Percy had been seen
riding towards Croydon, and had reported " all London is up in arms."

Thomas Percy was one of the principal conspirators in the
gunpowder plot.   He engaged the house adjoining the Parliament
House, as it was the intention of the conspirators in the first instance
to break into the cellar underneath the building in which Parliament
sat.   He was a gentleman pensioner and therefore no suspicion was
excited when he took these premises.   It was afterwards found that
the cellars into which they wanted to penetrate were to let, and it
was Percy who took them, as he alleged, for the purpose of storing
wood for winter.   When the plot was discovered, the conspirators
fled in all directions, and it would seem that Percy in the first
instance turned his horse's head towards Croydon, but he and the
rest were eventually brought to bay at Holbeach House, on the
borders of Staffordshire, where he was shot in the struggle which
ensued.   In a very ancient history, we read " Thomas Percy and
Robert Catesby, Esquires, fighting back to back, were both of them
slain with one bullet."

The Percy above described was a relative of the Earl of
Northumberland, and suspicion fell on that nobleman ; and we find
a letter four days afterwards from the Earl to the King, which is
written from Croydon, although it is impossible to surmise what he
could have been doing at Croydon at the time.   He could not have
been a welcome guest at Beddington, where his treachery to Sir
Walter Raleigh must have been known.

The letter is dated Croydon, Saturday, November 9, 1609, and in it the Earl expresses his sorrow for having offended his Majesty, and fears that if the King expresses his displeasure, the world will cast imputations on his character, and he entreats his Majesty to save his loyalty from suspicion.

We might here remark that the Earl was apprehended and held in custody in the town for twelve years, at the same time as Sir Walter Raleigh. There are one or two other letters having reference to the Gunpowder Plot, or arising from the suspicions which gathered round that mysterious affair. About this time, Archbishop Bancroft died, and Archbishop Abbot was nominated in his place.

1612—*Croydon, July* 12.—Archbishop Abbot, in writing to the King, says that the lingering in England of the Spanish Ambassador, Don Pedro de Zuniga, is very suspicious. He had already secretly disbursed £12,000 to £13,000 in England, and tampers at night with the Lieger Ambassador from France. He was in England at the time of the Powder Treason, and God knows what share he had in that business.

Croydon, Aug. 3rd, 1612.—Archbishop Abbot to the King.—Zuniga has removed to the Lieger Ambassador, Alonzo de Velasquez, in the Barbican. Velasquez has been more free with his masses, having a bell rung, and holding several in the day. He sends scandalous reports of English affairs to Spain and Italy.

Croydon, Aug. 17th, 1612.—Archbishop Abbot to Rochester.*—Will, at the King's command, hold correspondence with the Venetian Ambassador.

At that time, the holding of masses in public was strictly prohibited, except at the official residences of the Ambassadors.

Westminster, Nov. 18, 1611.—Grant to the Earl of Nottingham of the manor of Haling and other lands, &c., in Croydon and Mitcham.

Charles, Earl of Nottingham, was the celebrated Lord Admiral, who commanded the British fleet which destroyed the Spanish Armada. He died at Haling House on December 14th, 1624. Previous to this grant, he must have had possession of the property, for it was granted to him on leave, under letters patent of the 34th of Elizabeth ; and his brother, Sir William Howard, died there in 1600. At his death this manor, by some means, was re-transferred to the Gage family, to whom it had been granted by Queen Mary. They, however, forfeited it during the reign of Queen Elizabeth for treasonable practices. Robert Gage took part in the conspiracy of of Babington and others against Queen Elizabeth, and he was beheaded in September, 1586. His brother, John Gage, incurred

---

* The Earl of Rochester, a handsome young Scotchman, who attracted the King's fancy ; after the death of Cecil, Earl of Salisbury, he became the reigning favourite, and was made Secretary of State. Rochester's connection with the Countess of Essex, her divorce, and re-marriage, in which the King took an active part, is one of the most disgraceful incidents in English history. The only redeeming feature in the affair is Archbishop Abbot's manly protest against granting the divorce. His brother Bishops who sat in conclave proved themselves ready tools for the accommodation of aristocratic licentiousness. After this marriage Rochester was created Duke of Somerset, but soon afterwards fell under the Royal displeasure from his connection with the Overbury murder. He and his wife were both arraigned and condemned to death. " But," says an old chronicler, " they had a lease of their lives granted them for ninety-nine years, yet so as never after to see the King's face again." The Earl of Essex, the jilted husband, lived to lead the Parliamentary armies in the great struggle which took place during the following reign.

imprisonment and forfeiture of his lands and tenements for har-
bouring George Besley, a proscribed Jesuit priest. On the death of
the Earl of Nottingham, they resumed possession, and sold it to
Christopher Gardener, Esq., in whose family it remained until 1707,
when it was purchased by Edward Stringer, Esq. He bequeathed
it to his widow, who married again to a gentleman named
Hamond, by whom she had issue. She left it to her grandson,
William Parker Hamond, who retained possession until quite
recently. The estate has lately been divided into lots, and resold to
various proprietors.

Croydon, Sept. 29th, 1612.—This is a note of the distribution of 42s. 6d. given
by the Duke of York, when he dined at Croydon, to the yeomen of Archbishop
Abbot's household.

The Duke of York was the eldest surviving son of James the
First ; he afterwards ascended the throne as Charles the First.

Croydon, Sept. 28th, 1614.—Archbishop Abbot to the Bishop of Peterborough.
In this letter, the Archbishop says the King wishes to know the truth of a report
that several silenced ministers, especially Mr. Dod and Mr. Cleaver, are suffered
to preach in his diocese ; and also that Mr. Catelyne, of Northampton, though
professing conformity when questioned, does not " use perpetuall conformity ;" the
refractory disposition of the people of that town cannot be borne with.

This was the commencement of the great struggle between
king and people, in which eventually the king lost both crown and
life. It is rather singular that even in the time of Charles the First,
the inhabitants of Northampton should have been celebrated for
their "advanced" views on religious matters, a characteristic which,
judging from recent events, they retain up to the present day.

London, July 31, 1619.—Chamberlain to Carleton.— The Lord Admiral went
to Chatham to see the ships in company with Sir Horace Vere and Lord Digby.*
He is very desirous to settle at Beddington, near Croydon, but Sir Nicholas Carew
will not give up his seat to him.

The Lord Admiral is the infamous Duke of Buckingham, who
had just superseded the Earl of Nottingham (Lord Charles Howard),
the grand old admiral, residing in retirement at Haling Park. It
would seem that he coveted the possession of Beddington House, but
Sir Nicholas Carew would not part with the family mansion. George
Villiers, Duke of Buckingham, succeeded the Earl of Rochester
in the favour of the King, and under his rule, this country was
disgraced both at home and abroad. Every office in the State was
given to his favourites, or sold to the highest bidder. His private
life was a long course of debauchery and wickedness. He accom-
panied Charles, Prince of Wales, in his mad-cap expedition to the
Court of Spain, and was responsible for many of the worst acts of
that foolish Prince. Eventually he perished by the hand of an
assassin at Southampton.

Croydon, Aug. 18, 1624.—Archbishop Abbot to Carleton.—Thanks for his favour
to Dr. Jermyn. Regrets his late nibs, but all suffer alike who do " not stoope sail
to that castle," though if they do, not certain of success. He (the duke) stands
higher than ever, cannot think what that presages.

This letter was evidently intended to be kept private ; the
language is enigmatical, and is difficult to understand. The Duke

---

* Afterwards Earl of Bristol.

hinted at, is the Duke of Buckingham, who was at that time in high favour with the king.

Croydon, Dec. 20, 1625.—Archbishop Abbot to Sec (Lord) Conway.—The Archbishop reports what took place at an interview between himself and certain messengers from the French Ambassador, who claimed as the Ambassador's chaplains, Pettinger, *alias* Wentworth, and Dupre, *alias* Forbes, two Roman Catholic priests in London.

This has reference to the persecution of the Catholics in England carried on with great severity during this reign. All Catholic priests were banished from the kingdom, excepting, of course, those belonging to the establishment of the Ambassadors, and the representatives of the kings of France and Spain were accustomed to claim as their servants, any priests who fell into the hands of the law. These disputes were continually recurring, and gave rise to much ill-feeling between the different monarchs.

Croydon, July 10th, 1627.—Archbishop Abbot of Canterbury to Sec. Conway. —The Archbishop says that he does not forget the message Lord Conway brought him on Thursday last, and because he has heard nothing from him since, sends to him to know what he is resolved touching the house or houses where he must remain. He enumerates the houses which belong to his see, and enquires whether the king will leave the choice to himself. or name one or two for him to reside in. He desires to know, because he has to make provision of wood, and coals, and hay, and when he has brewed, it is fit to know where he shall put it.

About this time the good old Archbishop incurred the Royal displeasure. It appears that one Robert Sibthorpe, Vicar of Brockley. in an assize sermon preached at Northampton, declared that even if the King commanded people to resist the law of God, they were to obey him, to show no resistance, no railing, no reviling —to be all passive obedience. To demonstrate the Scriptural soundness of his doctrine, he quoted the verse of the Book of Ecclesiastes, " Where the word of the King is, there is power ; and who may say unto him, What doest thou ? " Abbot, very properly, refused to licence the printing of this sermon. In vain the King (Charles I.) insisted. The Archbishop was suspended, and eventually ordered to reside at Canterbury. It is evident the above letter was written to Lord Conway while the matter was in abeyance. Bishop (afterwards Archbishop) Laud licensed the publication of the sermon. Sibthorpe was rewarded by being made Prebend of Peterborough, and Rector of Bishop Latimer. Some time afterwards Abbot was restored to the Archbishopric.

1633.—Nicholas to Capt. John Pennington.—The Archbishop of Canterbury is very sick and weak at Croydon, inasmuch as it is thought he will hardly escape or live long. P.S.—The Archbishop died on Sunday last.

1633, *Aug.* 29th.—Richard Kilvert to Sir John Lambe.—The funeral of the Archbishop will be celebrated at Croydon on Tuesday next, the funeral sermon to be preached by the Bishop of Rochester.

Archbishop Abbot was buried at Guildford, his native town, where he had founded a hospital and grammar school, which remain in existence to this date. As a reward for his servility, Laud was appointed to the vacant Archiepiscopal See, and King Charles the First was strengthened in his foolish ideas of the royal supremacy, in the enforcement of which both he and Laud perished on the scaffold. We have one or two letters from Laud, dated from Croydon, deserving of notice.

Croydon, Aug. 25th, 1634.—The Archbishop says that he has received Sir Thomas's letters, well fouled and worn. They bear date Aug. 4th, and came into his hands on the 23rd. He has had a little leisure (and but a little) for these three weeks, and now that his majesty is upon his return, he must return to grinding again.

Croydon, August, 1636.—In this we have an account of the journey of Archbishop Laud from Croydon to Oxford, in his coach and six, attended by fifty horsemen, all his own servants. He lodged the first night at Sir Thomas Roe's (Crauford).

This journey to Oxford was doubtless caused by the fact that Parliament had been called to meet in that city, on account of the great plague raging in London.

Croydon, Aug. 4th, 1636.—Archbishop Laud to Sir Thomas Roe, at his house at Crauford.— . . . If Sir Thomas comes to Croydon next week, he will be welcome, and will find it a pretty stiff journey as the ways are now.

Oatlands, Sept. 19th, 1636.—The Council to Archbishop Laud.—To take orders to remove inmates flying from London to Croydon in that time of infection.

It would seem the plague extended its ravages to Croydon, for the parish registers show that there died from the plague in this town —between the months of July, 1603, to April, 1604, 158; in the year 1625, 76; in 1626, 24; in 1631, 74; and between the 27th July, 1665, and the 22nd March, 1666, the number amounted to 141.

Under the date Sept. 11th and Oct. 6th, 1638, there are two letters from Archbishop Laud, written at Croydon, to the unfortunate Queen of Bohemia. This lady, the Princess Elizabeth, daughter of James I, married the Count Palatine, who was shortly afterwards nominated by the States of Bohemia, king of that nation, an office he foolishly accepted. This led to the terrible 30 years' war, which desolated the whole of Central Europe, and in which every European nation was more or less involved.

There are two or three matters of local interest in these records which we also publish :—

1634, *Croydon, May 20th.*—Returns made by the Justices of the Peace for the Hundred of Wallington and the Town of Croydon, which certify that they have suppressed 18 ale-houses and licensed 32.

1619, *Sept. 20th.*—Extract from the Churchwarden's Accounts of Croydon show that town, being opprest by the carriage of saltpetre to Kingston-on-Thames, has had the road measured, and found it 10 miles and 62 roods ; also that Richard Gilbert is threatened with ruin by the saltpetre men, who wish to dig for saltpetre in the shop which will stay his work.

1634.—Francis Vincent and Edward Batts to the Lords of the Admiralty. —These are two saltpetre men who set forth that they have made various applications to Sir John Tunstall, near Croydon, to inspect his pigeon house for saltpetre, which he refuses, saying that last time it was digged four feet deep, which he thought such a prejudice that he had it filled up with sand and gravel.

1636.—Petition of the Hundred of Kingston, Surrey, to the Council.—The petitioners complain that they are paid by the saltpetre men for carriage from Kingston to Croydon but for 7 miles, whereas it is 18 miles, and they are to have 6d. per mile for carriage, but the saltpetre men abate 18d. upon every load, and besides a truss of straw for every load, and make them wait with their teams many hours.

1637.—Petition of Francis Vincent, saltpetre man, to the Lords of the Admiralty.—Notwithstanding his Majesty's letters patent for making saltpetre, Sir John Tunstall, of Croydon, in no way obeying the commission, will not suffer petitioner to dig in his pigeon-house. He prays the Lords to take the case into consideration and order petitioner satisfaction.

Owing to the great scarcity of saltpetre, letters patent were issued in the reign of Charles the First, giving authority to the Lords of the Admiralty to employ men to dig for saltpetre wherever they thought possible to find it. This gave rise to innumerable complaints, as the men generally took a fancy to dig where they knew their digging would be a nuisance, and they had, in consequence, to be bought off. In one instance, it will be seen they took a fancy to dig under a tradesman's shop, and in another under Sir John Tunstall's pigeon-house, but Sir John refused them this privilege, and this led to complaints to the Lords of the Admiralty, as cited above. Whether Sir John eventually had to give way we do not know, as the letters on the subject unfortunately end here. Sir John Tunstall is frequently mentioned in the records of Croydon in the Past. It was in his name that Archbishop Laud purchased an estate in Albury, in the county of Warwick, afterwards exchanged for some lands at Horne, in Surrey, the rents and profits of which were to be yearly applied for the placing out of poor children of the said parish as apprentices ; and it was into the hands of Sir John Tunstall and other trustees, that Henry Smith, Esq., of London, in 1624, placed the sum of £1,000, with which an estate was purchased at Limpsfield, Surrey, the profits of which are to be devoted for ever to the relief of the poor of Croydon.*

1637, *Jan. 29th.*—Sir Thomas Walsingham having been sent for to the Board for having sold certain woods, called Westfield, in the parish of Croydon, to have them grubbed up, denied that he gave any warrant for it, and promised to give effectual orders to prevent the grubbing of any of his woods in that county without license from his Majesty or the Board. Thereupon he was discharged.

1637, *August.*—Petition of Nicholas Wood and John Wood to Archbishop Laud.—The petitioners say that in February last they bought of Olave Edlyn, of Ham Farm, in the parish of Croydon, lately deceased, tenant to Sir Thomas Walsingham, for £22, the wood in Westfield Coppice, containing 8 acres, and the same to grub up, if the statutes allow it, which it seems to do, if it be within two furlongs of the farmhouse, which it is. But since the sale, his Majesty has put forth a proclamation to restrain grubbing up of woods. The petitioners being fearful to offend, Sir Thomas Walsingham offered 40s. to secure them from damage, or else advises his tenant to tie them to his bargain, and get others to grub it. They pray the Archbishop to recommend their cause to the Council, that nobody be suffered to grub the said wood but petitioners.

It would seem that even so early as the reign of Charles I, the attention of the Lords of the Admiralty had been directed to the general grubbing up of the woods, from whence the supplies of oak timber necessary for the ships of war were obtained, and that a proclamation had been issued by the King to prohibit the practice.

Croydon, Sept. 7th, 1638.—Wiliam Dell to Sir John Lambe.—Think not I neglect you, though at every turn you abuse me. Your letters never come till

---

* Sir John Tunstall, who belonged to a Durham family, was a magistrate for the county of Surrey, and was Knighted at Theobalds, Surrey, on the 13th July, 1619. He is then described as of Carshalton, gentleman usher and esquire of the body of Queen Anne, consort of James I. In 1623, he lived at "Adgecombe," that is Addiscombe, in the house, in later years, occupied as a Military Seminary by the East India Company. He was buried at Croydon in February, 1651, and his wife, Lady Tunstall, in 1652 ; though there does not appear to have ever been a monument or tablet erected to their memory. It is rather curious that Sir John, who is named in so many wills, died intestate ; his next heirs were his grandsons, who were at time under age. They eventually succeeded to his property.

Thursday, which day your carrier goes out of town ; so that it is impossible to answer the same week. You need not doubt of my thinking of a new wife in haste. I rather think of my winding sheet this sickly time, or of joining myself to your friend Dr. Barkham, who, good man, *valedixit seculo*, and is lately turned hermit in Norwood, not far off.

Croydon, Aug. 5th, 1640.—William Dell to Sir John Lambe.—Archbishop Laud is content you should permanently settle the bearer (Mr. Pemberton) in the clerkship (St. Vedast), as he desires.

1639.—Information against John Lascoe for destroying the game about Croydon, and taking hares in Haling Wood.

1640, *Jan. 11th.*—Bond of John Lascoe and John Mantell, of Croydon, in the sum of £50 to the King, conditional that John Lascoe shall not take, kill, or destroy hares, partridges, or pheasants, then this present obligation to be void.

MEMORABILIA.

AT the present time, the Waldrons is the name of a district covered with stately mansions and villas. It may not be uninteresting to note a description of the district given by a writer early in the present century :—" Attached to the Haling estate is a piece of land called the Waldens, consisting of about 12 acres ; it is a high ridge of gravel soil, rising in a very steep ascent, forming a perfect shelter to the street, and descending in a declivity, as sudden, into a beautifully verdant valley, about five acres in extent. It was formerly enclosed by a park fence and stocked with conies. In the reign of Henry VIII it was occupied by Sir William Carew and used by him as a preserve for that species of game, to which purpose it was particularly adapted."

* * *

In Haling Park, there was formerly a fine grove of exotics and evergreens, which is referred to by the Poet Laureate, William Whitehead, in a poem entitled " Answer to an Epistle from a grove in Derbyshire to a grove in Surrey." William Whitehead died in 1785 ; he was the son of a baker at Cambridge, but evincing signs of genius, he was sent to Clare Hall, and eventually was made Poet Laureate.

* * *

Aubrey, in his celebrated work called the *Magna Britannia*, gives the following interesting account of the famous Vicar's Oak, which formerly stood on Norwood Hill :—" In the great wood, called Norwood, belonging to the Archbishop, was anciently a tree called the Vicar's Oak, where four parishes met, as it were, in a point. It bore mistletoe, which some were so hardy as to cut for the gain of selling it to the apothecaries of London, leaving a branch of it to sprout out. But they proved unfortunate after it, for one of them fell lame, and others lost an eye. At length, in the year 1678, a certain man, notwithstanding he was warned against it upon account of what the others had suffered, adventured to cut the tree down, and he soon broke his leg."

*   *   *

The parish register dates from 1538, and in it we find several remarkable instances of longevity in this parish, from which we extract the following :—Alice Miles, died on her 100th birthday, buried March 6th, 1634. Margaret Ford, aged 105, buried February 2nd, 1715. John Baydon, aged 101, buried December 12th, 1717. Elizabeth Giles, widow, aged 100, buried August 17th, 1729. And Elizabeth Wilson, from the " Black Horse," aged 101, buried March 17th, 1771.

*   *   *

Sir William Walworth, the famous Lord Mayor of London, who slew Wat Tyler upon his insulting Richard II, was keeper of the park which originally stood on Park Hill, and is said to have resided there. In the reign of Charles I, Francis Leigh, gentleman, of Addington, was keeper, and had a lodge in the park. He was *Reeve* of all the woods, had all the small spray, the doted and rotten trees, the bark of all trees felled, with grass for two cows in the park, and a fee of twopence a day. It was intended that a palace for the Archbishop of Canterbury should be erected in the park, but the purchase of Addington House rendered this proceeding unnecessary.

*   *   *

On the 25th day of July, 1505, word was brought to the town of Croydon that a man was lying dead in a close near Pollard Hill, which was putrified and stank in the most horrible manner. None of the officers could be induced to bring him in, whereupon he remained there until the Tuesday night following, being the 27th day, whereupon the Vicar (the Rev. Samuel Finch) hired a man named James Woodward, and they two went to him and found him lying on his back, with his legs pulled up to him, and his knees lying wide, his right hand lying on his right leg, and his left across his stomach, the skin of his face and the hair of his head beaten off by the weather, so that no portion of the lineaments of his face could be identified. He wore a rotten canvas doublet, and his hose ragged, a black felt hat, with a cypress band, and two laces tied at the end of the band. Woodward digged the grave hard by him, and the two pulled him in, each with a long pole.

*   *   *

Roger Pryce, leaning on a culver, charged with hail shot on his left side, his match in the same hand, the piece discharged suddenly and killed him presently, saving as much time as wherein he prayed the bystanders to pray to God for him, and so, falling down, desired God heartily to forgive him all his sins, and so he died the 25th July, 1585, and was buried on the 27th.

*   *   *

Elizabeth, daughter of John and Clemence King, wife of Samuel Flynche (primus), Vicar, in the space of *seven* years mother of *five* children at separate births, died the 17th November, 1589, aged *twenty-one years*.

In 1200, two women, who had stolen some clothes at Croydon, were pursued and captured at Southfleet, where they were imprisoned and tried by Lord Henry de Cobham and " many other discreet men of the county," who adjudicated them to undergo the fire ordeal. By this foolish and impious test, one of them was exculpated, and the other condemned and afterwards drowned in a pool called Bikepool. The two chief species of trial by ordeal were those of fire and water, the former being, in the opinion of some writers, confined to persons of high rank, and the latter only used for common people. But if the above case be correctly related, it is probable this distinction was not strictly observed.

In Church's History of England, he speaks of the Black Assizes at Oxford, in 1577, and of the assizes at Hereford in the reigns of King James and King Charles I, and says that a similar occurrence happened at Croydon. "The like chanced," says he, " some four years since at Croydon, in Surrey, where a great depopulation happened at the assizes; and the two judges, Baron Yates and Baron Rugby, getting their banes there, died a few days afterwards."

The following relic of Papacy is recorded in the parish register in the year 1596:—" Memoranda, that whereas Samuel Fynche, Vicar of Croydon, licensed Clemence King, wife of John King, brewer, to eat flesh in the time of Lent, by reason of her sickness, which license beareth date the 29th day of February ; and, further, that the said Clemence doth yet continue sick, and hath not yet recovered her health, know ye, therefore, that the said license continueth still in force, and, for the more efficacy thereof, is here registered according to the Statute in the presence of Thomas Mosar, churchwarden of the parish of Croydon, the 7th day of March, in the 38th year of the Queen's most gracious reign, and for the registering thereof is paid unto the curate 4d."

Among the many eminent men, who have at different periods filled the office of Vicar of Croydon, is one " black sheep." William Clewer, D.D., who was collated by Archbishop Juxon in 1660. This man seems to have been a thorough scamp. During the Commonwealth he made himself notorious as a prosecutor of Royalists. As soon as King Charles ascended the throne, he became an ardent Royalist, and managed to interest the Earl of Clarendon in his behalf, the result being that Archbishop Juxon presented him with the living of Croydon. He soon began a system of extortion and injustice, demanding very much more for tithes and fees than he was entitled to, which led to considerable litigation. Eventually, he was ejected from his benefice in 1684. After his deprivation, he was tried and convicted at the Old Bailey for stealing a silver cup, and ordered to be burnt in the hand. The following anecdote of him is recorded in Smith's " Lives of Highwaymen : "—O'Bryan, a well-known highwayman, who was afterwards hanged at Tyburn, meeting with Dr. Clewer, the parson of Croydon, coming along the road from Acton, demanded his money, but the reverend doctor had not a farthing with him. O'Brian was for taking his gown. At this, our divine was much dissatisfied, but perceiving the enemy would plunder him, quoth he, " Pray, sir, let me have a chance for my gown ; " so pulling a pack of cards out of his pocket, he further said, " We'll have, if you please, one game of all-fours for it, and if you win it, take and wear it." This challenge was readily accepted by the foot-pad, but being more cunning than his antagonist at slipping and palming the cards, he won the game, and the doctor went contentedly home without his canonicals.

* * *

During the Commonwealth, Sir William Brereton, a distinguished General serving on the Parliamentary side, was granted possession of the Archiepiscopal Palace at Croydon, and Mr. Jonathan Westwood was appointed Minister. In a book in the MS. Library at Lambeth, there is the following memorandum :— " In pursuance of the several orders of the Committee for the Reformation of the Universities, of the 15th January, 1650, and 28th January, 1851, it is ordered that Mr. Lawrens Steele, treasurer, doe from time to time continue and pay to Sir William Brereton the sum of £50 for the use of such ministers as have been, and shall be by him provided, to serve the cure of the Church of Croydon, in the County of Surrey, the same to be continued till further orders of the said trustees, and to be accounted from the last receipt, any order to the contrary notwithstanding." It was after the ejectment of Mr. Westwood that Dr. Clewer, the clergyman mentioned in the preceding paragraph, was appointed.

* * *

The frequency of highway robberies may be gathered from the fact that on March 31st, 1722, six men were hung at Thornton Heath, and in April, 1723, four other criminals were hung in the same place.

* * *

The last person condemned to the horrible punishment of hanging in chains was James Cooper, a highwayman, who was executed on a gibbet in Smitham Bottom, for murdering and robbing Robert Saxby, groom to John How, Esq., of Barrow Green, in the parish of Oxteed, in Surrey, on the 17th March, 1749, near Croham Hurst. The gibbet was erected a short distance below where the " Red Deer " now stands. At that time, it was an open space, and for years afterwards was known as Gallows Green.

* * *

The celebrated Jerry Abershaw, a noted highwayman, who for some years (from 1790 to 1795) kept the whole of Surrey in a state of alarm, was tried at Croydon Summer Assizes, in 1795, for the murder of David Rice, an officer, whom he had killed by a pistol-shot, at the same time wounding a second officer with another pistol. The evidence was very conclusive, but some clever barrister detected a flaw in the indictment, and he was acquitted. As he was leaving the dock, he was re-apprehended on a charge of shooting one Barbara Turner, for which he was tried, and this time, there being no flaw in the indictment, he was found guilty, and executed on Kennington Common, on the 3rd August, 1795.

We have the record of a terrible storm of hail, rain, with thunder and lightning, which occurred in and about Croydon on the 12th May, 1728, which exceeded everything ever before known. Several hailstones, being measured, were from eight to ten inches in circumference. Most of the glass windows which faced the storm were shattered, and beans, peas, &c., were quite cut off. Many beasts and sheep were driven into the ditches, and were there drowned. The vehemence of the tempest, it is said (although we should be inclined to doubt the fact), drove the hailstones several inches into the ground. In 1744, there was another violent storm, during which one Mark Welch was struck dead by lightning while riding in his cart in Smitham Bottom.

* * *

In the *Sporting Magazine* for November, 1792, we read that in the reign of James I, public horse races were established, and such horses as had given proofs of superior abilities became known and celebrated. Their breed was cultivated, their pedigrees, as well as those of their posterity (an imitation, perhaps, of the Arabian manner), were preserved and recorded with the utmost exactness. The usual places for exhibitions allotted for the fleetest racers were Gately, in Yorkshire ; Theobalds, on Enfield Chase, and Croydon. The race-course was on Parson's Mead, which was then an open space of ground, about fifty acres in extent.

* * *

It may interest some of the readers of these pages to know that before the present century, Parson's Mead extended from Mrs. Chatfield's residence at Broad Green to the old Manor House at North End, formerly occupied by the late Mr. Till, intersected only by the little footpath at the back of the Wesleyan Chapel. Alexander Caldcleugh, Esq. (a West Indian planter, it is believed), was the Lord of the Manor, and resided at Broad Green House about seventy years ago. At that time the inhabitants who resided in Barnaby Hotel, as it was called, possessed the valuable privilege of pasturing cattle in the Mead. Time changes all things, however, and a " change suddenly came over the spirit of their dream," for about the year 1830 an award of this important property was made, to the delight of some people and the disgust and discomfort of others. The Lord, of course, took the lion's share, and those freeholders who lived in Barnaby Hotel, and had, in legal phraseology, land where cattle could be *levant* and *couchant*, also had some dainty slices. As may be imagined, there was an awful outcry by those who were " left out in the cold," but as everything had been done according to law by Martin Knockholt, the surveyor, the disappointed soon settled down. The land was ultimately sold, and the present range of respectable houses are built on land where pony races were once run to the gratification of Her Majesty's lieges. Alexander Caldcleugh, the younger, left Croydon many years ago, and lived and died at Santiago, in South America.

* * * * *

BEDDINGTON.

Among the Rectors of Beddington, we find recorded the name

of John Leng, D.D., who, in 1723, was made Bishop of Norwich. Though appointed to the Bishopric, he continued to hold the Rectory of Beddington until his death, at the age of 62, occasioned by the small-pox, which he caught at the coronation of George II., in 1727. He was editor of two of the comedies of Aristophanes, and of the six Comedies of Terence. He was buried at St. Margaret's, Westminster.

* * *

The Rev. Charles Carew, another Rector, was beheaded in August, 1540, as an accomplice in the plot against King Henry VIII, for which his relation, Sir Nicholas Carew, also suffered. He was author of a " Treatise on the Mensuration of Land."

* * *

During a visit of Queen Elizabeth to Beddington Hall, Sir Francis Carew treated her Majesty to what was considered at the time to be " a rite merrie conceite." " He led her to a cherry tree, whose fruit he had on purpose kept back from ripening, at least one month after all cherries had taken their farewell of England. This secret he performed by so raising a tent or cover of canvas over the whole tree, and wetting the same now and then with a scoop or horn, as the heat of the weather required ; and so, by withholding the sunbeams from reflecting upon the berries, they grew both great and were a long time before they had gotten their proper cherry colour ; and when he was assured of her Majesty's coming, he removed the tent, and a few sunny days brought them to their full maturity."

* * * * *

ADDINGTON.

Addington was a much more important place in former times than it is at present. There were formerly two manors in the parish. In the year 1278, they belonged to Robert de Aguilon, who obtained the Royal licence to embattle his mansion at " Eddintone," the King (Henry III) granting him at the same time right of free warren in the manors. The old mansion, or castle, formerly stood on the hill overlooking the Church, and traces of this building have been turned up by the plough in very recent times. The hill is still called Castle Hill. About the year 1400, this house was pulled down, and a new mansion erected on the same spot, over the principal entrance of which was a stone bearing the following quaint inscription :—

> In fourteen hundred and none,
> There was neither stick nor stone ;
> In fourteen hundred and three,
> The goodly building which you see.

This house was pulled down in 1780, and the present mansion erected in another part of the park, which now forms the country seat of the Archbishops of Canterbury.

* * *

The manor in Addington was held by the King's cook, and furnishes an example of the tenure of estates by serjeanty. The holder of this manor is bound to attend the monarch's kitchen on coronation day, and to make a dish alled *Pastias*. He had the power to appoint a deputy, who had to make a dish called *Girunt*, or if *seym* (seam or lard) was added, it was called *Malpigernoun*. We believe the actual recipe for making this dish is not known. In a scarce work, published by the Society of Antiquaries in 1790, containing a collection of ancient cookery recipes of the 14th century, the following is given as the probable contents of the dish :—" It is made as a pottage, and consists of almond milk, brawn of capons, sugar and spices, chicken parboiled and chopped, &c." This service is still kept up, and at the coronation of Victoria this "dish of pottage" was presented. It was formerly the custom for the King, on receiving the dish, to confer the honour of knighthood on the lord of the manor. Now that the Archbishop of Canterbury is lord of the manor, we should suppose this old custom will be discontinued. The manor of Addington was held by the King's cook so early as the reign of Edward the Confessor.

THE OLD PALACE OF THE ARCHBISHOPS.

WE have no means of ascertaining, with any degree of certainty, when the Archbishops of Canterbury first resided in Croydon. In our previous pages we have shown that the Manor of Croydon has been from time immemorial annexed to the Metropolitan See. In former times the duties of the Archbishops were much more multifarious than at present, and their presence was frequently required at their different manors. This doubtless led them, in the first instance, to erect a dwelling, in which they could reside when they came to transact their business at Croydon. This building was first entirely composed of wood, but gradually this wooden erection was removed to make room for something more permanent and substantial. Legend says that so early as the days of Edward the Confessor, the Archbishop dwelt here occasionally, but all traces of this earlier building have long since disappeared, and the only reliable data remaining in support of this legend arises from the circumstance of the Confessor's arms being found in the great hall, impaled with those of England and France. We have positive proof that Archbishop Kilwardby lived here in the thirteenth century, as several of his official acts are dated from Croydon. From that time until the middle of the eighteenth century, there are few Archbishops who did not live more or less frequently in the Old Palace, where they had pleasant gardens, fish-ponds, vinery, bowling green, and other appurtenances of a nobleman's residence. Here they received Crowned heads, Princes, and Ambassadors, ordained Bishops, and transacted various affairs of State, some of which are recorded in our extracts from the State Calendar.

Among other monarchs who have visited the place, we may mention Mary I, Elizabeth, Charles I, and James II. The unfortunate James I of Scotland, who was taken prisoner by the English while on his passage to France, spent the greater part of his 18 years' captivity, in the Old Palace in the custody of Archbishop Arundel.

According to Ducarel, the Palace consisted of one large court, guard chamber, chapel, hall, buttery, kitchen, &c., besides other convenient and necessary apartments, amongst which a long gallery must not be omitted. Excepting the guard chamber, which is of stone, all the rest of the building is of brick. The greater part still remains standing, but the larger hall and guard chamber have been converted into a steam laundry, the chapel is used as a girls' schoolroom, the vinery changed into a private house, the fish ponds filled up, and the spacious gardens are now utilised as a drying ground in connection with the laundry.

The last Primate who resided here was Archbishop Hutton, who died in 1758; his two immediate successors, Archbishops Secker and Cornwallis, allowed the Old Palace to fall into decay, and in 1780 an Act of Parliament was obtained for selling the property, and on the 10th October in that year, Abraham Pitches, of Streatham, purchased it for £2,520. It was afterwards sold in lots, but the greater portion remains in the occupation of Mr. Oswald, who resides in a part of the house, while the other part is converted, as we have before stated, into a steam laundry. Such are the vicissitudes which this old building has undergone.

It was intended to have erected a country mansion for the Archbishops on Park Hill, where property had been leased for that purpose, but just at the time when the building was about to be commenced, the old Hall at Addington was offered for sale, and this, being deemed suitable, was purchased. By reference to our notice of Addington Church (see page 117), it will be seen that the Archbishops now make that their permanent dwelling-place, and in the village church and churchyard they find a last resting-place.

ARCHBISHOP TENISON'S SCHOOL.

IT is evident that there was formerly a Grammar School at Croydon, although we can give no account of it beyond the fact that in the register of Archbishop Courtney there is a memorandum of his having ordained one, John Makneyt, master of the Grammar School at Croydon, a deacon at Maidstone.

The only schools of remote date, beyond the Whitgift School already mentioned, is one founded by Archbishop Tenison in 1714. We learn that he purchased a farm and lands at Limsfield, in Surrey, of the then yearly value of £42. The school was originally established for ten poor boys and an equal number of girls, but an increase of revenue led to an increase in the number of pupils. The school was originally established in North End, and in 1791, was further benefited by a legacy of £500 from Mr. James Jenner, and £300 from Mr. William Heathfield, with other donations from charitable persons, and with this money a substantial brick building was erected, with commodious apartments for the master and mistress. In 1852, this school was taken down and removed to its present site, adjoining St. Peter's Church, in South End, where a handsome school-house has been erected in the Elizabethan style, after designs of Sir Gilbert Scott. It now forms, with the adjoining infant school, the parish school for St. Peter's district, and is under the supervision of the minister of St. Peter's Church.

ELYS DAVY'S ALMSHOUSES.

THE Founder of these almshouses was a citizen and mercer of London, born in Croydon, who, having obtained letters patent of King Henry VI, bearing date the 25th December, 1447, and also letters patent from Archbishop Stafford, together with letters from the Abbot and Convent of St. Saviour's, Bermondsey (who were thought to have an interest here), founded this almshouse on the 27th April, 1447, and called it Elys Davy's Almshouse. It was intended for the support of seven poor people (men and women), six of whom were to receive tenpence a week, and the seventh, to be called the tutor, one shilling. It was endowed with £18 a year, with some cottages situated near it, the rent of which cottages was to be applied to the expense of its repairs. The Vicar, Churchwardens, and four of the principal inhabitants of Croydon were appointed Governors; and the master and wardens of the Mercers' Company Overseers. The founder required that the clothes of the tutor and the poor of his almshouses should be " darke and browne of colour, and not staring, neither blazing, and of easy price cloth, according to their degree, that they should attend Divine service daily in the church of Croydon, and there ' pray upon their knees for the King in three paternosters, three aves, and a credo, with special and hartily recommendations ' of the founder to God and the Virgin Mary; that they should also say for ' the estate of all the souls abovesaid,' daily at their convenience, one ave, fifteen paternosters, and three credos; and that after the death of the founder, provided he should be buried at Croydon, they and their successors should appear daily before his tomb, and there say the Psalm *De Profundis*, or three paternosters, three aves, and a credo." After the Reformation, it became impossible to carry out these regulations, and in August, 1566, the original statutes were revised by Archbishop Parker, and the spirit, rather than the letter, of the benevolent donor's bequest is now adhered to.

The old almshouses bequeathed by the founder having become dilapidated, they were enlarged and improved in 1875, several smaller bequests having been made by different charitable individuals sufficient to justify an enlargement. The present buildings, situated near the tower end of the Church, now afford comfortable dwellings for 12 poor people, who each receive a monthly allowance of £1 17s., with a donation of 7s. 6d., eight sacks of coals, and a dole of bread at Christmas. The revenue may now be estimated at £200 per annum. Parties eligible to receive this charity must have been householders in Croydon for seven years, and the right of presentation is vested in the Vicar, Churchwardens, and other Governors.

THE LITTLE ALMSHOUSES.

THESE are situated at the angle of Church Street and Lower Church Street, and, when first erected, were doubtless intended for the parish poor. The date of their first erection is not known, but they must have been built previous to 1528, as in that year a rent-charge of twenty shillings was given them by Joan Price. In 1629, Arnold Goldwell gave £40 towards their erection; in 1722, they were described as "nine small, low, inconvenient houses;" and in 1775, they were enlarged by the addition of two new buildings for twelve poor residents, with funds supplied by the then Earl of Bristol, and a subscription raised amongst the inhabitants. The late John Blake, Esq., left the sum of £1,000 for the benefit of the poor of these almshouses, which was invested in consols. They now afford habitations for twenty-four poor persons, who, in addition to the free occupancy of the tenement, receive each a stipend of 29s. 4d. monthly, with an extra allowance of 10s. and 7s. 6d. on alternate years, an allowance of coals, and a dole of bread at Christmas, under the direction and management of the Churchwardens for the time being.

CROYDON IN 1851 AND 1882.

EW people can absolutely realise the great improvements which have been effected in the town during the lifetime of the present generation ; we therefore propose to lay before our readers a brief retrospect of some of the more important changes made in the residences of our inhabitants; together with notices of the additions and alterations made in our streets, roads, and public places, taking as our stand point the year 1851, the memorable year of the first Great Exhibition. It must be borne in mind in reading this chapter that all our remarks have '51 as their data, unless specially stated otherwise.

At that time the population of the whole parish of Croydon was 20,355, it is now over 80,000. There were then 81 streets, roads, and places, there are now nearly 400. The places of worship were in proportion—the Church of England had 4, namely, the old Parish Church of St. John the Baptist, St. James's Church, then called the district chapel of St. James, on Croydon Common ; the district church of All Saints at Norwood ; and a small Chapel of Ease at Shirley. The Nonconformists only mustered 6 chapels, namely, the Wesleyan in Church-path, North End ; the Congregational in George-street ; the old Baptist Meeting House in Pump-Pail ; Providence Chapel (Calvinistic) in West-street ; the Friends' Meeting House in Park-lane ; and a small Roman Catholic Chapel near Broad-green. There were in course of construction, St. Peter's Church, South End, and Christ Church, Sumner-road. There are now more than 50 buildings devoted to the worship of God. The Church of England have 18 ; the Congregationalists and Independents have 9 ; the Baptists (Calvinistic and General) have 8 ; the Wesleyan Methodists, 4 ; the Primitive Methodists, 3 ; the Free Methodists, 2 ; Friends, Free Christians, Christian Brethren, and Roman Catholics each 1, and four others not enumerated, besides about 30 Mission Houses, in which Divine Worship is regularly conducted every Sunday. Not only have they increased in number but also in size. In 1857, the Parish Church was really the only spacious place of worship in the town ; now there are at least a dozen others, which can accommodate equal, and in some instances, even larger congregations.

These pages are written in 1882. Year by year, doubtless, still further changes will occur which we may have to notice in future editions of this work. We commence first with

HIGH STREET.

No. 1, now tenanted by Mr. D. B. Miller, draper, was at the date we have mentioned, in the occupation of Mr. G. S. Stapleton, in the same line of business. There was an opening adjoining, leading to the George-yard, where Mr. G. Tice had some stables.

The Greyhound Hotel was tenanted by Mr. B. Bean, who was succeeded by Mr. Budden. The livery stable business in the yard was carried on by Mr. D. Freeman.

Nos. 10 and 11, now the extensive ironmongery establishment of Messrs. Hammond and Hussey, were then divided into two shops, Mr. Henry Hammond had one, and Mr. W. Mawle, grocer, the other. Shortly after this, Mr. Hammond entered into partnership with Mr. Purrott and took both shops, Mr. Mawle removing a few doors lower down the street. Messrs. Hammond and Purrott had for some years a branch shop in Surrey-street, at the corner of Scarbrook-hill.

Nos. 13 and 14 remain unchanged, Mr. J. Jordan, ironmonger residing in No. 13, and Mr. Page, fishmonger, in No. 14.

There was a saddler's shop at No. 15, and Mr. T. L. Robinson, father of Mr. W. Mosse Robinson, carried on the business of banker and wine and spirit merchant at No. 16, now the offices of the Union Bank. The wine and spirit trade was for some years carried on in the name of Messrs. Robinson and Son, and was removed to No. 15, the next door being entirely devoted to the banking business.

The King's Arms Hotel, now located in Katharine-street, faced High-street, partly on the site of Mr. Entwistle's wine and spirit stores. Mr. Stedall, upholsterer, had a shop adjoining, afterwards occupied by Messrs. Mawle and Sibery, grocers. The Board of Health had an engine station on part of the premises. In 1866 they were all pulled down to make an approach to the Central Railway Station, and Katharine-street was then built.

Mr. D. Davidson occupies the shop formerly tenanted by Messrs. Jarvis and Co. and Messrs. Lashmar and Co., drapers, at No. 18; and at No. 20, Mr. A. C. Ebbutt, upholsterer, has followed his father, Mr. John Ebbutt.

The house agency and auctioneering business now carried on by Messrs. Blake, Haddock, and Carpenter, was formerly carried on by Messrs. Blake on the same premises.

Mr. Baldiston, printer of the *Croydon Chronicle*, lived at No. 33. The old house, No. 40, remains in the possession of the same tenant, but several dilapidated tenements of the same class, nearly adjoining, have been removed and their places filled with handsome modern shops.

Friends'-road is quite a modern improvement. Formerly there was a narrow passage called Battersbee's yard on the site, in which stood three or four small cottages.

The surgery of Messrs. Carpenter, Whitling, and Lanchester, No. 53, was then the surgery of Messrs. Westall, Brown, and Ward. Dr. Westall lived in Dr. Whitling's house adjoining the surgery.

Messrs. Nalder and Collyer's brewery stood on the same ground, but it has swallowed up a private house adjoining.

Mr. Thomas Keen lived at the Elms, now the residence of Mr. T. R. Edridge.

Messrs. Crowley's brewery remains without change, excepting that their Mineral Water Works are carried on in what was formerly the private residence of Mr. Alfred Crowley.

Southborne (No. 65), the residence of Mr. R. Flint, was then in tenancy of Messrs. G. Bottomley and H. Thompson (now the celebrated Sir H. Thompson, of London), surgeons.

Crossing the road, we notice that Mr. Lambert's tobacco factory, removed to No. 101, formerly stood at the corner of West-street.

Messrs. Waghorne and Miles's coachbuilding establishment, No. 83, was then carried on in the name of Mr. S. Waghorne, coach and cart wheelwright.

Corney's yard was formerly called Corney's Rents.

The Bricklayer's Arms Inn was kept by Mr. J. Hamsher.

No. 93 still remains in the hands of Mr. R. Walton, grocer.

Laud-street, Whitgift-street, & Wandle-road, were not then built.

The ground where the County Court Office now stands was occupied by Mr. John Cox, corn and seed merchant.

Mr. John Goose, solicitor, lived next door at No. 105.

Mr. George Price, wine and spirit merchant (now Price and Son), still remains at No. 114. Mr. G. Bance, upholsterer, nearly adjoining, is another old resident.

The Green Dragon Inn was kept by Mr. Horatio Chesterman, who was succeeded by Mr. L. T. Hardy, Mr. W. Marten, Mr. H. Yates, and Mr. James Wood, the present tenant.

The London and County Banking Company was formerly located at No. 119, now the office of Mr. T. H. Ebbutt, furnishing undertaker. The premises at No. 120, where the bank is now carried on, have been erected by the company. It was formerly a pastry cook's shop.

Mr. W. T. Bance, grocer, tenanted No. 123, and Mr. J. Dubois, grocer, No. 124. The premises have been united by Mr. W. Stevenson, grocer.

The Town Hall remains externally the same, but great alterations have been made in the interior. The Literary Institution (now the Literary and Scientific Institution), at present located in the Public Hall, formerly occupied part of the premises. The lower room was the old Corn Market, where the farmers stood every Thursday showing their samples of corn. It has now been converted into a convenient justice room. Other changes have also been made. The Corn Market is now held in a large room attached to the King's Arms Hotel in Katharine Street.

The extensive premises occupied by Messrs. Pelton, grocers, were formerly divided into three shops.

No. 132 was a licensed house called the Masons' Arms.

A beer-house called the Horse Shoe, stood on part of the site of the American Stores Inn, kept by Mr. J. Bryant, popularly known as " Gaffer Bryant."

The *Croydon Chronicle* Office fills the place of the old Butter Market, where the farmers' wives stood with their butter, eggs, and poultry.

The present General Post Office, or the ground on which it stands, was occupied by Mr. J. Booker, corn and flour dealer, afterwards by Mr. Gough, grocer, and subsequently by Mr. Whittaker, provision dealer.

Messrs. Podmore and Martin's office at No. 145, was a tobacconist's shop.

4

Mr. Chas. Newton, postmaster, formerly carried on the postal business in the lower part of his stationery shop, the entrance being in Crown Hill. Before these premises were rebuilt, the post office was located in a little corner of the shop, but with a separate entrance.

NORTH END.

The Crown Hotel is one of the few houses which have not changed owners. It still remains in the hands of Mr. Thomas Green, though a portion of the premises have witnessed considerable changes. In 1865, a bank, called the English Joint Stock Bank, had an office in the shop adjoining the gateway. In 1869 this was used as a Fire Brigade Station.

The Police Station still remains at No. 6.

Just beyond the new premises lately erected by Messrs. Batchelar and Sons, upholsterers, was Archbishop Tenison's School, now removed to Selsdon Road. At that time Handcross Alley was continued from Church Street to North End, but the upper portion has been widened and is now called Keeley New Road.

The site on which the London and South-Western Bank is carried on was up to very recent times a private garden.

The old Wesleyan Chapel was in Church Path, at the back of the Railway Arms. It has now been converted into a schoolroom. A new and more spacious building was erected in 1857 in Tamworth Road.

The Croydon High School for Boys (principal, Mr. H. Turner) was an establishment for young ladies, kept by Mrs. Goring and Stafford. It was afterwards occupied by the Girls' Public Day School Company, until their removal to their new premises in Wellesley Road.

Crossing the road, the whole of Station Street and Station Terrace, now filled with handsome shops, was the site of a garden attached to North End House, which is hidden in the back ground. Poplar Walk was not laid out until 1852.

There was a small beer-shop, called The Telegraph, at No. 65, adjoining the small court known as Orange Court. Most of the houses up to Messrs. Drummonds' offices were private houses, several with rows of trees before them.

Messrs. Arnold and Coldwells' outfitting establishment was tenanted by Mr. Meredith, coal merchant, and Mr. Castledine, timber merchant.

The Whitgift Schools, now forming such a prominent feature in the street, were not erected until 1870. Previously to that time the site of the school and the playgrounds had been a market garden, tenanted by the late Mr. Alexander Henderson, the front to the street being filled with a row of mean shops, at the back of which was a yard, called Turner's yard, used partly for storing stone and partly as an iron foundry.

The handsome shops adjoining, occupied by Mrs. Halliwell and Messrs. Allsop and Wagner, tobacconists, were built in 1858 by the trustees of the Whitgift Charity, to whom the property belongs.

The extensive range of premises, extending from North Place

to the Swan Inn yard, forming the drapery establishment of Mr. Joshua Allder, was then occupied by about half-a-dozen different tenants.

Mrs. Harriet Scrivener was landlady of the Swan Hotel.

SOUTH END.

The entrance to Coombe Road has been improved by the removal of an old farrier's shop which formerly stood at the corner.

Mr. Philip Hubbert, surgeon, lived in Boswell House, now the residence of Mr. Barrow Rule, clerk to the School Board. Boswell Court was tenanted by Mrs. Colonel Kelly.

In No. 8 lived a Mr. Christopher Stone who announced himself as "Daily teacher of French, English, drawing, writing, arithmetic, and the flute," quite a combination of accomplishments.

Aberdeen Road is a new road. John Simm Smith, Esq., J.P., lived at Blunt House.

The old Swan and Sugar Loaf was tenanted by Mr. W. Meager.

There were only two houses in Selsdon Road between the Cattle Market and the Rail-view Beer-house, and four houses on the Brighton-road between Drovers' Road, the entrance to the Cattle Market, and the Red Deer Inn, the southern terminus of the Croydon tramways. All the streets and roads which cover the ground between Selsdon Road and Brighton Road were unbuilt, the space being clear pasture land. There was formerly a turnpike on the road, just below the Swan and Sugar Loaf.

CHURCH STREET.

No. 1, now the shop of Mr. G. C. Hyde, wholesale provision dealer, was formerly the back of Mr. Reading's tallow chandlery, and there was another tallow chandlery a few doors below Surrey Street. The inhabitants in those days did not object to a few foul smells. To show the primitive nature of the business carried on in this street at that time, we may notice that No. 10 was occupied by Hannah Howell, greengrocer and mangler, and at No. 19, the site of Messrs. Marshall and Son's outfitting shop, there lived a Mr. H. Battersbee, who also obtained his livelihood by keeping a mangle.

Mr. Wm. West carried on the butchering business on the same premises occupied by his son, Mr. S. West, the well-known meat contractor.

The old brewery down the yard, between Nos. 28 and 29, was tenanted by Mr. James Wood, who was followed by Mr. T. Williams.

The premises beyond were principally private houses ; Mr. J. G. West's grocery shop was tenanted by Mrs. Mary Ann Wilkinson, and Messrs. S. West and Co.'s by Dr. Wm. Chalmers.

In the old Palace Yard, Mr. Williamson, omnibus proprietor, occupied the site of Messrs. Russen and Son's premises.

Messrs. Starey and Oswald carried on the business of linen bleachers in part of the Old Palace, now known as the Palace Laundry.

The Gun Inn was occupied by Mr. W. Ewence, and Mr. T. L. Henley, surgeon, had a private house next door.

The old tan-yard, carried on by Mr. Edwards's father, was on its present site.

There was formerly a passage called Church Court, leading to the Girls' School of Industry, by the side of the church wall, now the site of the Gothic Cottage, occupied by Mr. W. D. Russell.

There were no houses opposite the Church ; the whole space covered now by St. John's Grove and St. John's Road was vacant ground. An uncovered stream, polluted with all kinds of filth, ran down the centre. It was not until 1851 that the old streams were turned into culverts by the Board of Health.

Most of the houses up to Elys Davy's Almhouses were private houses ; the " Rose and Crown " was kept by Mr. W. Russell.

The old Vine House, lately pulled down, was in the occupation of Mr. T. Martin, builder.

In the old shop at the corner of Ebbutt's Court, Mr. Jas. Clark, now residing at No. 29, carried on the business of a wood turner.

Messrs. J. and E. Grantham, London carriers, conducted their business in the yard occupied by Mr. A. Turner's veterinary forge.

Mr. T. G. Plowman, butcher, is one of the few who remain in the same shop.

A large building which covered the site of Mrs. Goddard's furniture warehouse and the Theatre Royal, was an Educational Institute, conducted by Mr. R. B. Paull, and there was attached to it a spacious hall, called the Croydon Lecture Hall. When the present premises were erected, Mrs. Goddard's shop was intended to be a provision market, but it was never fully occupied for that purpose and was soon closed.

SURREY STREET.

The " Three Tuns Inn " was kept by William Wateridge, veterinary surgeon. All the public-houses in this street seem to have been continually changing hands during the past thirty years. The " Three Tuns " has been successively tenanted by Mr. Wateridge, Mr. Wm. Richardson, Mr. C. S. Ward, Mr. S. Knight, Mr. J. Dossett, Mr. W. Smith, and the present landlord, Mr. G. Smith.

The lower part of the adjoining premises, now occupied by Mr. D. W. Smith, corn chandler, was originally the Old Gaol, where prisoners were confined before being taken before a magistrate, or while waiting their trial at the assizes. Mr. Thomas Pilbeam, the last parish beadle, then lived in the adjoining house. The lower part of the Town Hall has since been adapted for this purpose.

Nos. 5 and 6 are now occupied by Mr. G. Watson, greengrocer and fishmonger. Formerly they were divided, No. 5 forming the shop of Mr. Henry Plowman, furniture broker, and No. 6 was a beer-house and eating-house called the " Jenny Lind." In 1853 the " Jenny Lind " was closed, the two shops thrown into one, and occupied by Mr. Henley as a clothes and shoe warehouse. The " White Hart " beer-house at No. 9 was opened as the " New Jenny Lind," a title it did not long retain.

The first Gas Works, established by Mr. Overton, were situated in Overton's Yard. They were purchased by the Croydon Gas Company in 1846, and it was found necessary in 1869 to remove them to Waddon Marsh Lane, as more room was required than could be found on the old site.

The office of the *Croydon Times* is at the house formerly (previous to 1863) occupied by Mr. Loveday as an eating house ; and Parker's pie-shop (adjoining) still preserves its name and fame.

The " Dog and Bull Inn " was kept by Mr. Daniel Brown, who was followed in the tenancy by Mr. Wm. Goddard, Mr. Elijah King, Mrs. C. J. King, Mr. W. Wood, and Mr. W. G. Richards, the present tenant.

Crossing the road we find the " Britannia Inn," formerly kept by Mr. John Hunt, who was succeeded by Mr. Jas. Hathrill, Mr. Robert Cliff, and Mr. John Chappell, who has lived there since 1868.

In the butcher's shop (No 36) now occupied by Mr. Webb, the same trade has been carried on for many years. This row is popularly known as the Shambles, having in former years been entirely tenanted by butchers. Several yet remain.

The " Royal Oak Inn " is another proof of the quick change in tenancy. It was formerly kept by Mrs. Mary Ann Herring, then by Mr. A. A. Bignell, Mr. T. L. Ryott, Mr. G. Clifton, Mr. C. Maltby, Mr. C. H. Porter, Mr. W. E. Humberstone, and the present tenant, Mrs. E. M. Walter.

The " Old King's Head Inn," at the back of the Town Hall, is an exception to the rule of quick changes, Mr. Mark Griffin having lived there for twenty-five years. He was succeeded by Mr. Sadler, and afterwards by the present tenant, Mr. W. Jackman.

THE MIDDLE ROW.

King Street, Middle Street, and Market Street were formerly much more important places of business than they are at the present time, the removal of the butter market having materially affected the trade in this locality.

GEORGE STREET.

No. 1 has undergone several mutations. It was formerly occupied by Mr. Muigay, gentleman, then by Mr. C. Dowell, insurance agent, afterwards by Mr. C. Newton as a temporary post-office, while his own premises were rebuilding. When the Whitgift Schools were established, it was adapted for the residence of the Rev. E. H. Genge, assistant master.

No. 2 was the old school-room of the Whitgift Hospital, and was used for some time as the Lower School, which was afterwards removed to the new premises in Church Road. The Young Men's Christian Association then became tenants, and were followed by Mr. Webb, who used it as a musical instrument warehouse. It is now used as a class-room in connection with the Whitgift Grammar School.

No. 3, another portion of the Hospital buildings has been fitted up for the residence of Mr. R. Brodie, head master of the Whitgift

Schools ; for many years previously it had been tenanted by the Rev.
G. Coles, curate of St. James's Church, who was the chaplain to
the Whitgift College.

The remaining portion of this street, where there is now a row
of shops, was filled up with a number of detached private houses.
George Street proper then only extended as far as Park Lane. The
road, opposite thereto, now called Wellesley Road, was then called
New Lane, and contained only eight houses—some of them very
small. Mr. E. Russell lived near where the Public Hall stands.
The parish pound stood at the corner.

The old Congregational Chapel, which stood on the opposite
side of the road, was pulled down a few years since, and the present
spacious and handsome building erected in place thereof.

About this point the road took the name of Addiscombe Road,
and there were only a few straggling houses thereon. On the right-
hand side was Fairfield House with its grounds, occupied by Mr. A.
Twentyman as a school for young gentlemen. Beyond this was the
" George the Fourth Hotel,"—next a large piece of vacant ground
on which St. Matthew's Church and Lecture Hall have been erected.
This unoccupied ground extended up to the " Railway Hotel,"
occupied by Mr. W. Coulstock. Between this hotel and the bridge
was the residence of Mr. F. Slight, sec. to the London and Brighton
Railway.

Crossing over the bridge, there were a few houses on the high
ground on the right-hand side, beyond which was a farm called
Park Hill Farm, on which was the residence of John W. Flower,
Esq. This farm is now nearly wholly built on, and forms the site
of Park Hill Road, Park Hill Rise, Chichester Road, Fairfield
Road, and the other roads adjacent. On the left-hand side was
Cherry Orchard Road, then came Brickwood House and grounds,
and about half-a-dozen villas, principally inhabited by Professors of
the Military College. The whole of the remaining space from
Canning Road to the Ashburton Road, was taken up by the
Addiscombe Military Seminary and grounds, the property of the East
India Company.

Beyond the College grounds was Addiscombe Farm, occupied
by the Right Hon. Earl Ashburton. This terminated the town.
There were a few houses at Shirley and a Chapel of Ease.

The East Croydon station was then much smaller than at
present, althought it was on the main line of the South Eastern
Railway to Dover, Margate, Ramsgate, and Hastings. The New
Croydon portion had then not been added. There was no South
Croydon station.

PARK LANE.

On the left hand side of this lane, near its junction with George
Street, is a large gravel pit, the property of the London, Brighton,
and South Coast Railway. This was the old Fair Field, where the
annual pleasure fair was held for many years. The Cattle Fair is now
held in a field near the " Windsor Castle Inn," on the Brighton Road.
The lane (called Back Lane) formerly did not extend beyond Coombe

Road, but, by the opening of St. Peter's Road, there is a pleasant drive now open to St. Peter's Church and the Selsdon Road. All the land on each side is rapidly being built upon.

LONDON ROAD AND THORNTON HEATH.

The only houses on the right hand side of the London Road, beyond the West Croydon Station, were Oakfield House, Broad Green Place, and one other house near the entrance of St. James's Road. On the opposite side stood the " Fox and Hounds Hotel," (Mr. John Tebbutt, landlord), facing the station ; then came a long blank, until a few private houses were reached, which stretched up to Broad Green. It is rather singular that there was not a place of business on the London Road. We meet a few shops at Broad Green, and then fields up to Thornton Heath Pond, round which were congregated a few houses. Bensham Lane was entirely occupied by market gardens.

HANDCROFT ROAD AND THE DISTRICT ROUND.

This being a very old road (forming at one time the chief road through the " old town " of Croydon), has changed almost less than any other ; most of the small streets leading therefrom, including Adelaide Street, Albion Street, and Myrtle Street, were occupied, but Croydon Grove, Sumner Road, and Canterbury Road were only projected.

Mitcham Road consisted principally of a number of cottages congregated round the Barracks, called Barrack Town.

Derby Road was laid out, but not built on, and Parson's Mead, called New Road, was partially filled up on one side only.

ST. JAMES'S ROAD.

St. James's Road, commencing at Broad Green, was divided into three portions. In the first portion, extending from Broad Green to Windmill Road, there was scarcely a house beyond the few cottages at the commencement, and the mansion, standing near the corner of Windmill Road, called Croydon Lodge. All the dis-trict beyond, extending up to Gloucester Road, was known as Croydon Common, having originally formed portion of the common.

In the second portion, Messrs. Bulman and Co. had a steam saw mill, and then followed St. James's Episcopal Chapel, the Rev. G. Coles, curate. Beyond the church was Middle Heath Lane, occupied by gardeners, now called Sydenham Road. Opposite the church were some National Schools, which have been removed. The third portion of St. James's Road, extending from Windmill Bridge to Addiscombe College, now called Lower Addiscombe Road was entirely untenanted. On the left, some short distance from the road, were the newly erected Freemason's Almshouses. The grounds of the Military College occupied nearly the whole of the right-hand side of the road, beyond the junction with Cherry Orchard Road. The North Kent line was not constructed until 1870, at which time the Addiscombe Road station was erected.

CROYDON COMMON.

Until a few years previous to this time, the whole of Croydon Common was a vacant waste. Whitehorse Road led through it, on which there were a few houses. This road then extended through the district now known as New Thornton Heath, to the junction with Colliers' Water Lane. At the present time the far end is called Parchmore Road. The whole of this district was entirely covered with trees. Near the site of the Lambeth Waterworks reservoir were some public gardens, known as Beulah Spa Gardens. There was a branch of White Horse Road at the junction with Windmill Road, to the " White Horse Inn " on the Selhurst Road. The whole length of the road from this point to the " Jolly Sailors Inn," in South Norwood, was called Selhurst Road, on which there were a couple of farms, called respectively Selhurst Farm and New White Horse Farm. The greater portion of Norwood was a dense wood, inhabited by a few wandering gipsies.

WINDMILL ROAD.

This was originally called Selhurst Road, and in 1851 consisted of a few cottages gathered round the " Fisherman's Arms Inn." All the roads leading therefrom were open ground, the Cemetery was not laid out until 1861. The new Union Workhouse was erected in 1864 ; previously the old Infirmary on Duppas Hill Terrace had served for the Parish Workhouse.

RAILWAY ACCOMMODATION.

At that time the only railway stations in the parish were West Croydon, East Croydon, and South Norwood, then a small calling station on the edge of the bank at the Portland Road bridge. The only terminus in London was London Bridge station ; the line to Victoria was not constructed until some years afterwards. The number of trains daily to London from both stations combined was 34 up, and 35 down, now there are about two hundred each way. Croydon was then on the South Eastern Company's main line to Dover, Hastings, Portsmouth, Margate, Ramsgate, and Maidstone. Most of the trains had third class carriages attached, but these were quite open at the top, and passengers were thereby exposed to all the inclemency of the weather. Once a day, covered carriages were provided for third class passengers in the parliamentary train, in accordance with the provisions of the Act of Parliament. To seven of the up trains passengers were brought from Mitcham in omnibuses, free of any additional charge, and in like manner were conveyed thither from seven down trains.

Croydon in the Past.

THE PARISH CHURCHYARD.

THE PARISH CHURCH OF CROYDON, dedicated to St. John the Baptist, is situated at the junction of Church Street and the Old Town. The date of its dedication is unknown; in all probability it is one of the oldest Christian Churches in the kingdom, and is believed to have been erected on the site of a temple or place of heathen worship dedicated to Woden, the hero-god of our Saxon forefathers. Croydon has been from time immemorial an appanage of the See of Canterbury; and the Old Palace, portions of which still remain contiguous to the Churchyard, was up to the middle of the last century, one of the favourite residences of the Archbishops, several of whom were buried in the Church. The Old Church is supposed to have been almost entirely rebuilt by Archbishop Courtney, who occupied the Archiepiscopal see from 1381 to 1396. It was in the Early Perpendicular style, and consisted of a nave with aisles, porches on the north and south side, three chancels, a sacristy, and a massive tower at the west end. It was built exteriorly of flint with stone copings, and stone and flint within, filled up with chalk and rubble. In the interior were several ancient and beautiful monuments, notably among which was one to the memory of Archbishop Whitgift, and another to Archbishop Sheldon, and a third to Archbishop Grindall, the mutilated remains of which are yet to be seen. The most beautiful one, as a work of art, was carved by Flaxman in white marble, representing an angel carrying a female to heaven. This was erected to the memory of Mrs. Bowling, wife of Mr. James Bowling, of Southwark.

Unfortunately these are now things of the past, as the **Old** Church, so full of these interesting reminiscences, was totally destroyed by fire, caused by the over-heating of a flue, on the night

B

of the 5th of January, 1867 : a portion of the outer walls and the
tower alone remaining standing. The New Church, rebuilt on the
lines of the old one, with several improvements, from the designs
of Sir Gilbert Scott. was opened on the 5th of January, 1870. One
of the most attractive features of the present edifice is the magnificent oak roof of the nave and chancel. The pulpit, prayer desk,
and altar rails are most beautifully carved. They are the work
of the late Mr. Gaskin, of Croydon, by whom they were presented
to the Church. The font is a fine specimen of veined alabaster
artistically carved. The reredos, though a fine work of art, is too
small for so large a building. It is divided into three compartments—the Nativity. Crucifixion, and Resurrection. There are
several stained glass windows ; the principal one is the great east
window in the chancel ; the others have been presented at various
times. The following are the inscriptions on those erected to the
memory of the late J. W. Flower, of Park Hill :—

" In memory of J. W. F., who died April 11, 1873, aged 65."
" *Virtute vixit, memoria vi- it, gloria vivet.*"

Under the adjoining one—

" *In ornatum Domus Dei. Necnon ad cognatis dilectas commemorandus
hanc fenestram ponendam curavit.—J. W. F.*

Underneath the two windows in the opposite aisle—

" Erected to the memory of John Wickham Flower, born 11th August,
1807, died April 11, 1873, by his friend John Peter, 1874."

" *Omnes animæ evaderent ad terram. Utique homicida est homo hic. In
reliquo reposita est mihi corona justitiæ.*"

In the tower is a fine peal of bells cast by Taylor, of Lough-
borough, and a magnificent clock, with a set of chimes which play
every third hour, the machinery manufactured by Messrs. Gillett
and Bland, of Croydon.

The old churchyard was formerly much more limited in extent
than at present, and the number of burials in the old ground must
have been immense, the ground all round being raised several feet
above the level of the floor of the church. Up to the year 1830
it was the only place of sepulture in the town, excepting the small
burying ground attached to the old Baptist Chapel in Pump Pail.
It was, however, almost doubled in size in 1848, when the old
vicarage house was pulled down, and the site thereof, with the
garden adjoining, was added to the old ground. This, however, was
soon filled, and as the town had began to grow very rapidly, a new
and spacious Cemetery was opened in the Queen's Road, and the
old churchyard was finally closed by an Order of Council on the
1st of August, 1861. The whole extent of the ground is not much
more than two acres, and from this must be deducted the site of
the Church and several footpaths which cross it in various directions.

We might here remark that there are several ancient tombs which
we have been obliged to pass over, age having rendered the inscriptions totally undecipherable, and there are many others which we
have had great difficulty in reading, and doubtless in a few years

these epitaphs will also be quite obliterated. We have throughout
followed the ancient orthography, omitting only portions which
appeared to be superfluous in a work of this description.

In the Interior of the Old Church.

In the Old Church were several very interesting tablets and
monuments, and though they were all destroyed during the burning
of the Church, yet a work of this description would not be complete
without a brief description of the principal memorials.

In a recessed arch were the painted effigies of a man and
woman, kneeling before desks. Over the man was this
inscription—

Obiit 21 Jana., 1553, aet suae 69. Underneath in Roman capitals,
Heare lieth buried the corps of Maister Henrie Mill, Citezen and Grocer,
of London famous Cittie, Alderman and somtyme Shreve. A man
of prudent skill, charitable to the poore, and alwaies full of pitie.

> Whose soul wee hope dothe rest in blise,
> Wheare joy dothe still abounde.
> Thoughe bodie his full depe do lie,
> In earthe here under ground.

Over the woman—

Obiit 2 Aug., 1585, aet suae no age. Underneath—
Elizabeth Mill, his lovinge wyf lyeth also buried heare, whoe sixtene
children did him beare, the blessing of the Lorde, eight of them
sonnes and the other 8 weare daughters. This is cleare a witness
sure of mutuall love, a signe of greate accorde.

> Whose sole amonge the patryarks,
> In faithful Abram's brest,
> Thoughe bodie hirs be wrapt in clay,
> We hope in joye dothe rest.

On a black marble tablet was the following inscription—

Here lyes the body of John Pynsent Esq., one of the Prothonotories of
his Majestie's Court of Common-Pleas, who departed this life the
29th August, 1668.

> The meanest part of him is only told
> In this inscription, as this Tombe doth hold
> His worser part, and both these easily may
> In length of time consume, and weare away;
> His virtue doth more lasting honours give,
> Virtue, and virtuous souls for ever live;
> This doth embaulme our deade beyond the art
> Proud Ægypt used of old; his head and heart
> Prudence and pietie enricht, his hand
> Justice and charity did still command;
> Hee was the Churche's and the poore man's friend;
> Wealth got by law, the Gospell taught to spend.
> From hence hee learnt that wt is sent before
> Of our estates, doth make us rich far more
> Than what wee leave, and therefore did hee send
> Great portions weekly; thus did hee commend
> His faith by workes; in heaven did treasuer lay;
> Which to possess his soule is cald away.
> Here only is reserved his precious dust,
> Untill the resurrection of the just.

On a Sarcophagus, with an arched recess, was the effigy of a
Churchman in his scarlet robes, surmounted by the arms
of the Sees of Canterbury, York, and London. At the top
of the monument was the following :—

> Beati mortui qui in Dno moriuntur:—
> Requiescunt enim à laboribus suis.
> Et opera illorum sequuntur illos.
> Apoc. 14.

There was a Latin inscription above Archbishop Grindall's tomb.
We give the English translation for the benefit of our
readers who are not conversant with the Latin language—

Edmund Grindall, a native of Cumberland, Doctor in Divinity, celebrated for
his learning, prudence, and suavity of character; remarkable for constancy,
justice and piety; beloved alike by his fellow citizens and foreigners;
having returned from exile (to which for the sake of the Gospel he
submitted*), promoted to the summit of dignity by a gradation of
honours under the auspices of Queen Elizabeth, he governed successfully
the Churches of London, York, and Canterbury†, and when now no
loftier pre-eminence remained for him, released from the shackles of the
body, free and happy, he took his flight to Heaven on the 6th day of July
in the year of our Lord 1633, aged 63.

Besides the many offices of piety which he performed in his lifetime, when
near his death, he consecrated the greater part of his fortune to pious
purposes. In the parish which gave him birth he caused a handsome
Grammar School to be built which he richly endowed. To the foundation
of Magdalen College, where, when a boy, he drew his first nutriment from
the breast of Alma Mater, he added a scholar ; to Christ Church, where in
late years he studied, he left a grateful memorial; he increased the
treasury and library of Pembroke Hall, of which he was once a Fellow,
and afterwards Master, and assigned ample endowments to one fellow,
two scholars, and a lecturer in Greek ; he enriched Queen's College,
Oxford, with monies, books, and large revenues ; he gave £100 to the poor
of Canterbury; the residue of his property he dedicated to pious works ;
thus living and dying he was Benefactor to Learning, to the Church, and
to his Country.

Underneath the effigy were the following lines—

> Grindallus doctus, prudens, gravitate verandus
> Justus, munificus, sub cruce fortis erat.
> Post crucis ærumnas Christi gregis Anglia fecit
> Signiferum, Christus cœlica regua dedit.
> In memoria æterna erit justus.—Psal. cxii.

There were several other verses in Latin. He was successively
Bishop of London, Archbishop of York, and Archbishop of
Canterbury. He died the 6th July, 1583, aged 63. Some
time before his death he incurred the Queen's displeasure,
and was suspended from his office. In 1582 he was
restored to a great extent to his ecclesiastical jurisdiction,
but by that time he had the misfortune to become totally
blind ; he in consequence resigned his office, which was
accepted by Queen Elizabeth, but before the necessary for-
malities were completed, he died, and was succeeded by
Archbishop Whitgift.

---

* The Archbishop deemed it advisable to leave England upon the accession of
Queen Mary, and retired to Germany where he remained till her death.

† Grindall was in the year 1569 appointed Bishop of London ; in 1570 he was
translated to York, and in 1575 to Canterbury.

The oldest memorial in the Church was a brass near the entrance to the middle aisle. The inscription, it will be seen, bears the date 1390.

Hic jacet Egidius Seymor. qui obiit xxij. die Decembr, a dni mccclxxxx. cui 'aic ppiciet ds.

On a tomb on the north walk was the following inscription on a brass plate :—

Here lyes ye bodye of ye precious servant of God. Mr. Samuel Otes, Master of Arts and Minister of the Word in Croyden. whose Piety, Zeal, and Selfdenyal are the best monument of his Worth, Whose blessed memery lives, and needs not words to preserve it. He was placed there Ao. 1643, and deceased Ao. 1645, aged 30 years, having lived long, though he dyed young.

R (admire and learne) B.

There was also a monument to Archbishop Whitgift, the founder of the noble Charity in the North end. The figure was full size recumbent, with hands folded in the act of prayer. The arms on the tomb were those of the See of Canterbury, the See of Worcester, and the Deanery of Lincoln. The following was the inscription ;—

Post tenebras spero lucem.
Whitgifta Eborum Grimsbeia ad littora nomen
Whitgifta emisit. Felix hoc nomine Grimsbei
Hinc natus: non natus ad hanc mox mittitur hospes
Londinum: inde novam te Cantabrigia. matrem.
Insequitur, supraque, fidem suavi. ubere crescit ;
Petro fit socius: Pembro : Tradique magister :
Fitq. matri, Cathedræque Professor utrique
E. Cathedra Lincolna suum petit esse Decanum :
Mox Wigorn petit esse suum ; fit Episcopus illic :
Propæses Patrie, quo nunquam acceptior alter.
Post annos plus sex summum petit Anglia patrem.
Plus quam bis denos fuit Archiepiscopus annos.
Charior Elizæ dubium est, an Regi Jacobo ;
Consul utriq. fuit. Sis tu Croidonia testis
Pauperibus quam charus erat. queis nobile struxit
Hospitium, puerisq. scholam, dotemq. reliquit.
Cœlibis haec vitæ soboles quæ nata per annos
Septuaginta duos nullo enumerabitur ævo,
Invidia hæc cerneus moritur Patientia vincens
Ad summum evecto æternum dat lumen honori.

We append a translation of the above—

After darkness I hope for light.
Whitgift, of great, unspotted, holy name,
To Grimsby's regions wafted Yorkshire's fame ;
Not born to sojourn in a town like this,
He hastened to the great metropolis :
Thence, Granta, flew to thee : and as he grew,
The choicest food from thy sweet mixture drew ;
In Granta's bowers he rose to high degree,
Of Pembroke, Peter-house. and Trinity ;
Raised to th' exalted chair by Marg'ret* giv'n,
He spoke the faith and mysteries of Heav'n.
Lincoln, as Dean, proclaimed him all her own,
And Worcester hail'd him on her Bishop's throne.

---

* He was Margaret Professor of Divinity at Cambridge.

A Judge all mindful of his country's trust—
He prov'd that to be great is to be just,
For more than twice ten years, so rare a man,
Did England boast her Metropolitan ;
Subject to Sov'reigns of illustrious names,
The great Eliza, and the learned James,
To both a counsel and a friend he prov'd,
By both alike rever'd, alike belov'd.
How kind to want, the poor man's friend confest,
Let Croydon's town, let Croydon's poor attest ;
He rear'd, and by his bounty did supply,
A House for age, a School for infancy.
Such num'rous progeny we never knew
Of a long single life of seventy-two.
Envy beholds and sickens at the sight,
Victorious patience* crowns it with immortal light.

Then followed two verses in juxtaposition, and at the bottom
were the following lines---

Gratia non miror, si fit divina Johannes
Qui jacit hic, solus credito gratus erat.
Nec magis immerito Whitgiftus dicitur idem ;
Candor in eloquio, pectore candor erat.
Candida pauperibus posuit loca, candida Musis ;
E terris moriens candida dona tulit.

TRANSLATION.

Some slight approach to evangelic fame
Lies buried here, who once was John by name ;
Of Whitgift's name, behold the dark abode ;
Fair was his speech, as from the heart it flowed ;
For want and learning a fair spot he gave,
Then died to seek a bright reward beyond the grave.

Near this was a splendid monument to the memory of Archbishop Sheldon, representing the recumbent effigy of the
Prelate, in his archiepiscopal robes and mitre. His left
hand sustained his head, and in his right was a crosier.
Under the figure was a sarcophagus, on which was figured
a horrible mass of winged hour-glasses, skulls, bones,
worms, and dirt. The following inscription was on a
tablet above the statue—

Hic jacet Gilbertus Sheldon, Antiquâ Sheldoniorium familiâ, In agro
Staffordiensi natus, Oxonii bonis literis eruditus, S. Sⁿ. Theologiæ
Doctor insignis ; Coll. Omnium Animarum Custos prudens et fidelis,
Academiæ Cancellarius Munificentissimus, Regii Oratorii Clericus
Car. 1ᵐᵒ E. Martyri Charissimus, sub Serenissimo R Carolo II.
MDCLX, magno illo Instauratinis anno, Sacelli Palatini Decanus.
Londiniensis Episcopus ; MDCLXII, in secretoris concilii ordinem
cooptatus, MDCLXIII ad dignitatis Archiepiscopalis apicem evectus.
Vir—Omnibus Negotiis Par, omnibus Titulis Superior, in rebus adversis
magnus, in prosperis bonus, utruisque fortunæ Dominus ; pauperum
parens, literatorum patronus, Ecclesiæ stator. De tanto viro pauca
dicere non expedit, multa non opus est ; norunt præsentes, posteri
vix credent ; Octogenarius, animam piam et Cœlo Maturam Deo
rediddit v. Id. Novembris, MDCLXXVII.

TRANSLATION.

Here lieth at rest, Gilbert Sheldon, born in the county of Stafford of the
ancient family of Sheldons ; educated at Oxford ; a learned Doctor

---

* Evidently an allusion to the Archbishop's motto : Vincit quid patitur—
" He conquers who can endure."

of Divinity, a discreet and faithful Warden of All Souls' College, a most munificent Chancellor of the University, Clerk of the Royal Closet. held in the utmost esteem by the blessed Martyr, Charles I; in the year 1640, the great year of the restoration of King Charles II, appointed Dean of the Chapel Royal and Bishop of London ; in 1642, chosen a Member of the Privy Council ; in 1643, advanced to the summit of Archiepiscopal honour.

A man equal to every station, superior to every title, constant in adversity, virtuous in prosperity, superior to either event: father of the poor, patron of the learned, guardian of the Church, it is not right to say little of so great a man. to say much would be useless : his contemporaries knew his excellence, and posterity will believe it. At fourscore years he surrendered his pious spirit to God, mature for Heaven, on the 5th November, 1657.

A neat white marble tablet affixed to the wall, nearly opposite Sheldon's monument. bore the following inscription—

Beneath are deposited the remains of the most reverend John Potter, D.D., Archbishop of Canterbury, who died Oct. 10, 1747, in the 74th year of his age.

On the ground, adjoining the east-wall, on a black marble ledger—

Here lyeth the body of the most reverend Dr. Thomas Herring, Archbishop of Canterbury, who died March 13, 1757, aged 64.

Adjoining the above—

Depositum Gulielmi Wake, Archiepiscopi Cantuariensis, qui obiit 24 Januarii. 1736, Ætatis suæ 79, et Etheldra uxoris ejus, d 11 Aprilis, 1735. Ætatis suæ 62.

Here lieth the body of Sir Joseph Sheldon. Kt., some time Lord Mayor of London, the elde t son of Ralph Sheldon, Esq., who was the elder brother of Gilbert Sheldon, Lord Archbishop of Canterbury. He left issue two daughters Elizabeth and Ann, and died Augt. ye 16th, 1681, in the 51st year of his age.

Beneath this place were deposited the remains of Thomas Brigstock, Esq., he died of decline, 27th October, 1792, in the 17th year of his age. If a suavity of manners and goodness of mind could have preserved his life, he would not now been numbered among the dead.

Here under lieth Buried the bodie of Franc Tirrell, sometime Citizen and Grocer of London. He was a good benefactor to the poor of divers Hospitals. Prisons, and Pishes of London; and to the continuall relief of the poore fremen of the Grocers, he gave to this Pishe 200*l*, to build a new Market house. and 40*l*. to beautifie this Church, and to make a new Saintes Bell. He died in September 1600.

When the old Market House was pulled down in 1807, the following inscription was discovered " This Market House was built att the coste and charges of Francis Tirrell, citizen and grocer of London, who was born in this towne, and departed this worlde in Sept. 1600."

A column of marble supporting a funeral urn bore the following inscription—

Sacred to the memory of Mrs. Anne Bourdieu, wife of John Bourdieu, Esq., of Golden square, London. She departed this life the 23d March, 1798, aged 31.

> A virtuous daughter and a sister kind,
> A tender mother and a wife refin'd,

Who all the various duties of life sustain'd,
Inspir'd by wisdom, and by honour train'd,
Lies here entomb'd ; here virtue, beauty, grace,
Ready for heav'n, have run their earthly race ;
Yet to the shorten'd course of youth confin'd,
She shew'd but glimpses of her glorious mind ;
Where multitudes of virtues pass'd along,
Each moving onward in the lovely throng,
To kindle admiration, and make room
For greater multitudes that were to come ;
But her vast mind, rich with such gifts divine,
In heaven's eternal year alone could shine.

Here lieth interred the body of the truly pious and singularly accomplish'd Lady Dame Ruth Scudamore, daughter to Griffith Hamden, of Hamden, in the County of Bucks, Esq., first married to Edward Oglethorpe, Esq., sonn and heir to Owen Oglethorpe, in the County of Oxford, Knight, and by him had 2 daughters ; after to Sir Philip Scudamore, of Burnham, in the County of Bucks, Knight ; and lastly to Henry Leigh, Esq., sonn and heir to Sir Edward Leigh, of Rushall, in the County of Stafford, Knight, by him had one son named Samuel, now living. She dyed at Croydon March 28, 1649, being the 73d year of her age.

This lady was aunt to the illustrious patriot, Hampden, and to Edmund Waller, the poet. It is rather strange that she bears on her tombstone the name of her second husband, rather than that of her third.

Here lyeth the bodye of Nicholas Hatcher, of Croydon, gentleman, who was Captaine of a Troop of Horse, under his most sacred Majestie King Charles the First, and Yeoman-Usher in Ordinarie to His Majestie King Charles the Second, who departed this life the 29th of September, 1673, aged 69.

It is seldom we find puzzles or riddles on tombstones, but here is one which contains an anagram :—

Curteous Reader, know that here doth lye,
A rare example of true pietie,
Whose glorie 'twas to prove herselfe in life,
A vertuous wooman and a loyall wife,
Her name to you obscurely Ile impart,
In this her anagrame, " No arme but Hart ; "
And least you should joyne amis, and soe loose ye name,
Look underneath, and you shall find ye same.

Martha Burton, ye wife of Barnard Burton, Esq.,
deceased ye 20h day of November, and was buryed
ye 26h day. Anno D'ni 1668.

The following was the inscription on the tomb of a blind man :—

Memoriæ Sacrum. To the pious memorye of his religious Father Ralph Smith, who deceased the 26 of Sept. 1639, aged 83. Thomas Smith did lay this marble as a grateful testimonye of his filial duty.

So well thou lov'st God's house, tho' beinge blind,
Thou came oft hither, lighted by thy mind ;
Where thou did'st offer such a sacrifice,
As few do now present that have their eyes,
A bleeding harte of sinne in sorrow dround,
Sustained by Hope, and with Devotion crownd ;
Therefore thou dost deserve an abler pen,
Whose spritely lines mighte stir up zeale in men,

To write thine epitaph, I am sure of this
What thou dost want in words, thou hast in blisse.
[In early life Mr. Ralph Smith was yeoman of the guard.]

The last one which we insert from the interior of the Church was erected in the North Gallery :—

Sacred to the memory of John Parker, Esq., formerly of London, who died on the 6th March, 1706, aged 46 years, and is here interred. Also of Elizabeth, his relict, who died the 10th August, 1730, aged 70 years.

The pair, while they lived together, were a pattern of conjugal behaviour ; he a careful indulgent husband, she a tender engaging wife ; he active in business, punctual to his word, kind to his family, generous to his friend, but charitable to all ; possest of every social virtue. During her widowhood she carefully and virtuously educated five children, who survived her ; she was an excellent economist, modest without affectation, religious without superstition ; and in every action behaved with uncommon candour and steadiness.

In the Interior of the New Church.

There are very few memorial tablets in the present Parish Church. It contains the mutilated remains of the monuments of the Archbishops, and two small brass tablets saved from the fire. We publish the inscriptions *in extenso* :—

𝕺rate pro anima 𝕰lye 𝕯aby nuper 𝕮ibis et 𝕸erceri, 𝕷ondon, qui obiit iiij die mens' 𝕯ecembris, 𝕵nno 𝕯'mni 𝕸ill'imo cccclb. cujns anime propicietur 𝕯eus. 𝕵men.

TRANSLATION.

Pray for the soul of Elis Davy, late Citizen and Mercer of London, who died on the 4th December, 1455. God be merciful to his spirit. Amen.

Ely Davis founded an Almshouse in Croydon on the 27th April, 1447, for seven poor people, six of whom were to receive 10d. per week, and the seventh, who was called the tutor, 1s. This almshouse, somewhat enlarged, still remains in Church Street, near the tower end of the Church.

Here under are conteined the bodies of Thomas Parkinson, late Farmer of ye Parsonage of Croydon, and Elizabeth, his wife, which Thomas deceased the the 7 day of September, 1605, and Elizabeth the 30 Janvary, 1594.

The following marble tablet has also lately been erected—

John Singleton Copley, R.A., born 1737, died 1815. Inscribed by his grandchildren.

John Singleton Copley, father of the celebrated Lord Lyndhurst, was buried in the north chancel aisle of the Old Church. He was born in Boston, Mass., U.S., and came to this country in 1776. He painted portraits of several of the children of George the Third. His other productions are " The Death of Lord Chatham," " The Destruction of the Floating Batteries during the Siege of Gibraltar," " Brooke Watson saved from the Shark," all of which have been engraved.

*The following Tablets are affixed to the outer wall of the Archbishop's
Palace, near the Chancel End of the Church :—*

Martha Oswald, *d* July 2, 1848, *a* 51.
John Oswald, *d* Aug. 2, 1848, *a* 60.
Charlotte Oswald, *d* Dec. 2, 1856, *a* 27.
      Consecrated as a tribute of respect by his affectionate friends to the
                                memory of
Samuel Starey, *d* Oct. 28, 1809, *a* 52.
Elizabeth, his widow, *d* Aug. 17, 1833, *a* 76.

> The Stareys were the principal owners of the old Palace of
> Croydon. They were extensive bleachers, and their
> grounds reached from Pitlake on the East to the Gas
> Works on the West, and from Waddon Brook on the
> South to Barrack Field on the North. About sixty years
> ago pony races were occasionally ran in this field, which
> was partly surrounded by large elm trees ; and it is
> remembered that at the time of the rejoicings and
> illuminations that took place in 1816, after Waterloo,
> when " there was a sound of revelry by night," the boys
> were always to the front in those days as they are in the
> present, and were perched in the trees like so many crows, in
> order to witness the fireworks and the dancing on the
> officers' lawn in the Barracks.

------

*The following Inscriptions are taken from the Tombs and Tombstones
on the south side of the Church, South of the pathway ; including
the new ground added when the Vicarage House was removed :*

John Collier, whitesmith, *d* Feb. 12, 1834, *a* 65.
Jane Collier, his widow, *d* Jan. 10, 1837, *a* 68.

> Collier's Corner, at South End, near the Blue Anchor, then, as
> now a whitesmith's shop, was named after these worthy
> people.

Ann Bowling, wife of James Bowling, of the Borough of Southwark,
      d April 26, 1808, *a* 25.

> This is the lady in whose memory a magnificent marble
> monument, representing an angel bearing a female figure,
> the work of Flaxman, the eminent sculptor, was erected in
> the Parish Church. We regret to say this magnificent
> work of art was totally destroyed during the fire. Above
> the figures were these words—
>   " Then shall the good be received into life everlasting."

Under Sacred to the memory of Ann, the beloved wife of James Bowling,
of the Borough of Southwark (and daughter of the late Mr. James
Harris of this place) who after two days' illness only exchanged this
life for a better, on the 26th April, 1808, in the 25th year of her age.

        Bright excellence, with every virtue fraught,
        So may we be by thy example taught ;
        Pure in the eye of Heaven like thee appear,
        Should we this hour death's awful summons bear ;

> Like thee all other confidence disown,
> And, looking to the Cross of Christ alone,
> In meekness tread the paths thy steps have trod,
> And find with thee acceptance from our God.

Her husband, under the strongest bonds of affection, has caused this monument to be erected, in testimony of his everlasting regard, and gratitude to a most affectionate wife and kind friend.

Also Abraham Purshouse Driver, her son-in-law, *d* March 16, 1841, *a* 65.

Elizabeth, wife of Wm. John Blake, *d* Aug. 11, 1841, *a* 40.

Elizabeth, widow of the late Rev. Jas. Wykes, rector of Hazelbeach, in Northampton, *d* Jan. 16, 1844.
Also Ann Alicia Wykes, her daughter, *d* Dec. 1, 1848, *a* 45.
Also Geo. Penfold, solicitor, *d* Sept. 3, 1852, *a* 44.
Also in loving memory of Mary Caroline Haddon, daughter of Mrs. Wykes, *d* June 28, 1881, *a* 68.

> [Mr. G. Penfold held the office of Vestry Clerk of Croydon for many years having succeeded his father, Mr. Thos. Penfold. He was succeeded in office by Mr. John Drummond, solicitor, at whose death the office was given by the Vestry to Mr. Henry Seale, who still retains it.]

Ann Moore, *d* Sept. 27, 1787, *a* 35.

> Here lies, whose life is at end,
> A tender wife and earnest friend ;
> She resteth here with hope to be,
> Happy with her to all eternity.

Sarah Driver, wife of A. P. Driver, jun., of Walcot Place, Lambeth, *d* April 26, 1819, *a* 32.
Edward, her son, *d* May 20, 1821, *a* 8.
James, another son, *d* March, 1835, *a* 23.

> [The Drivers are descendants of Mr. A. Purshouse Driver, mentioned on Mrs. Bowling's tombstone. They seemed to have lived at Christchurch, in Lambeth, and afterwards moved to Mitcham, where the two sons were born.]

Mrs. Ann Norrish, *d* Jan. 15, 1834, *a* 56.
John Norrish, *d* June 10, 1846, *a* 83.

In memory of Elizabeth and Dinah Maynard, both wives of James Maynard.
Also James Maynard, *d* Jan. 14, 1756, *a* 75.

William Clifford, *d* Oct. 7, 1741.
Ann, his wife, *d* Oct. 9, 1749.

Elizabeth Theobald, of Woodside, *d* May 23, 1851, *a* 80.
William Theobald, *d* Feb. 15, 1856, *a* 88.

Alfred Bignell, *d* July 28, 1837, *a* 21.
Albert, son of Joshua and Ann Bignell, d Aug. 22, 1849, *a* 29.
Susan, wife of Albert Bignell, *d* Nov. 12, 1848, *a* 30.

Elizabeth Newport, *d* May 17, 1741, *a* 29.
Sarah, his wife, *d* Oct. 13, 1746, *a* 36.

William Whiteley, *d* Jan. 8, 1787, *a* 94.
Mary Whiteley, his wife, *d* June 4, 1773, *a* 74.

Edward Roberts, M.D., *d* Nov. 21, 1846, *a* 84.

John Smith, late of Southwark, son of Thomas Smith, Esq., of York, *d* Oct. 18, 1803, *a* 34.

In a vault, William, son of John and Jane Mann, *d* Jan. 2, 1841, *a* 50.
Also Sarah Mann, his sister, born Aug. 28, 1796, *d* Jan. 20, 1870.

John. son of John and Jane Mann, *d* Sept. 24, 1856, *a* 70.
Sophia Mann. his sister, *d* Feb. 7, 1865, *a* 61.
Also John Mann, *d* Feb. 16, 1818, *a* 63.
Mrs. Jane Mann. *d* June 19, 1835 *a* 76.

 Mr. Mann kept the butcher's shop in what was called " The Shambles,"
 Surrey Street, now occupied by Mr. Taylor.]

Thomas Mann, *d* May 24, 1840, *a* 57.
Louisa Taylor, *d* Sept. 24. 1841, *a* 16 months.
George. son of John and Ann Mann, *d* April 26. 1823, *a* 30.
Thomas, son of Richard and Mary Mann, and grandson of **John and Jane**
 Mann, *d* March 10, 1840, *a* 15.

Mrs. Elizabeth Rice. *d* Nov. 25, 1818, *a* 54.
Also. Eliza. wife of Joseph William Rice. *d* April 4, **1844, *a* 34.**
Joseph William Rice (formerly parish clerk). *d* Sept. 7, 1854, *a* 38.

John, the twin-born son of William and Anne Rice, died in his infancy
 March 11, 1752.
     Tho' twins by birth, to me the right
     Above my Brother given ;
     He to enjoy his friends on earth,
     But I the God of Heaven.

Also Mary Rice. daughter of the above-named **William and Anne Rice.**
 d Oct. 2, 1822. *a* 78.

William Rice, *d* May 2, 1793. *a* 82.
Ann. his wife, *d* Jan. 29, 1795. *a* 75.

Samuel Unstead, *d* July 22, 1851, *a* 65.
Sarah, his wife, *d* Jan. 23. 1853, *a* 62.
 Mr. Unstead carried on the business of cooper in the High Street.]

Mrs. Hannah Gravener, *d* March 14, 1744. *a* 42.
Mr. Henry Gravener, (formerly of South End), *d* Dec. 16, 1835, *a* 66.

Anna Main, *d* Aug. 18, 1831, *a* 78.
     Thy life is calmly closed at last,
     In tenderness and truth 'twas passed ;
     No more thy well-known form we see,
     But still we love to think on thee.

     He who thy fondness most did prize,
     Altho' not bound by kindred ties ;
     He who from childhood was thy care
     And like a son thy heart did share.

     To whom the name of Nurse will prove
     A spell to bring back all thy love.
     This tribute pays and trusts in that great day,
     The Lord of Life thy service will repay.

James Stapleton, *d* Nov. 14, 1750. *a* 75.
Also James Stapleton, *d* August 11, 1756, *a* 53.

James Giles. *d* August 24, 1848, *a* 50.
Lucy Elizabeth, his wife, *d* July 6, 12, *a* 54.
 [Mr. Giles was a predecessor of Mr. Stovell, poulterer, 112 (then of 108),
 High Street.]

Joseph Innes, youngest son of James and Sarah Innes, *d* Jan. 15, 1821, *a* 38.
Mrs. Sarah Innes, his sister, *d* Dec. 16, 1852, *a* 76.

On a tomb, Susannah, wife of John Phillipson, gent., *d* Feb. 23, 1796, *a* 33.
    Grieve not, dear friends, I was early called,
    Rather be prepared to obey the awful change.
Also the above John Phillipson, gent., *d* May 30, 1840, *a* 80.
 " Blessed is he whose unrighteousness is forgiven, and whose sin is covered."

On the sides of this tomb, Joseph, son of John Phillipson, gent., *d* June
  16, 1854, *a* 45.

> His pious memory here shall lay
> Till letters cut in stone decay.

Also Susannah, his daughter, *d* March 29. 1853, *a* 58.

> " Flee from evil and do the thing that is good and dwell for evermore.''

[Mr. Phillipson, was a corn merchant residing in George Street.]

Sarah, wife of James Innes, *d* July 22, 1823, *a* 72.
James Innes, *d* May 27, 1821, *a* 74.

Mrs. Patience Ridley, *d* April 9, 1794, *a* 72.
Also three of her daughter's children, who died in infancy.

> So sleep the saints, and cease to groan
> When sin and death have done their worst ;
> Christ hath a glory like his own,
> Which waits to cloathe their waking dust.

Mrs. Mary Gardner, *d* Jan. 1778, *a* 45.
Also Master Wm. Jas. Gardner, of Calcutta, in the East Indies, *d* May
  7, 1789, *a* 13.

> Endearing, lovely, virtuous, noble youth,
> Whose heart was goodness, whose affection truth ;
> Farewell, thy soul hath winged its joyful way
> To realms of bliss and never-ending day.
> Reader, stop, pause, think, thy frail state explore;
> Go home, be wise, thy just God adore.

Catherine, wife of Samuel Johnson, *d* Aug. 3, 1803, *a* 53.
Also Mr. Joseph Cooke, late of Northampton, surgeon, *d* Feb. 12, 1827,
  a 86.
Also Captain Samuel Johnson, late of Her Majesty's Royal Wagon Train,
  d July 10, 1828, *a* 44.

> The Royal Wagon Train was not a very distinguished
> Regiment, but it had its usefulness in picking up the sick
> and wounded on the field of battle, and no doubt it did
> good service both in the Peninsula and at Waterloo. In
> those far off days, when Croydon contained about eight
> or ten thousand inhabitants, the Barracks were full of
> soldiers, who gave a little life and animation to the other-
> wise deadly-lively town. The band numbered about 25 or
> 30, and no doubt discoursed most eloquent music every
> afternoon, opposite the officers' quarters, and as that was
> almost the only enjoyment the townspeople had, the
> Barrack yard was the shady promenade, especially on
> Sundays. That music is now a thing of the past, and
> almost all who heard it have joined the majority.

Richard Messenger, *d* Dec. 31, 1818, *a* 69.
James Messenger, his son, *d* Aug. 29, 1858, *a* 76.
Mary Ann, his wife, *d* Oct. 9, 1863, *a* 74.

[Mr. Richard Messenger was originally a pawnbroker, residing in the opening
  adjoining the Old Butter Market, which occupied the site of the
  Croydon Chronicle office.]

Mary, wife of Richard Messenger, *d* Nov. 15, 1797, *a* 45.
Mary, only daughter, *d* April 30, 1828, *a* 46.
James Andrews, her husband, *d* Dec. 14, 1849, *a* 59.

Mary Messenger, *d* Oct. 22, 1781, *a* 74.
Mary, daughter of John and Mary Messenger, *d* Feb. 3, 1792, *a* 3.

Mary, wife of Richard Messenger, d Jan. 21, 1844, a 65.
Also Richard Messenger, her husband, d Feb. 7, 1853, a 74.

John Messenger, d Jan. 11, 1811, a 73.
Mary Messenger, his wife, d Jan. 26, 1821, a 77.
Also Richard Messenger, their son, d Oct. 22, 1877, a 10 months.

Emma Willis Bance, daughter of George and Mary Bance, d Jan. 24, 1838,
    a 3 years 10 months.
Mary Ann Bance, d July 16, 1838, a 7 years 7 months.
Eliza Brett Bance, d May 28, 1851, a 14.

William Hideman, d June 11, 1781, a 42.
Elizabeth Hideman, d Jan. 11, 1807, a 72.

Michael McCarty, d Dec. 19, 1822, a 49.
    Beloved and respected through life, lamented in death
    by all who knew him.
    [Mr. McCarty kept a livery stable in George Street, where Mr. Waters' coach
    building establishment now stands. He was the father of the late
    beadle.]

Sarah, his wife, d April 23, 1823, a 50.
Maria McCarty, d April 15, 1809, a 15 months.
    Our Great Jehovah from above,
    An Angel he did send,
    To fetch his little harmless dove
    To a place that has no end.

Elizabeth, wife of Robert Streeter, d July 11, 1857, a 78.

Elizabeth, wife of Thos. Eagles, d July 4, 1798, a 65.
Thomas Eagles, d Oct. 13, 1798, a 61.
    [Mr. Eagles left a sum of money to the churchwardens to keep this tomb in
    repair, the remainder to be distributed in bread to the poor.]

Richard Clements, d March 27th, 1823, a 19.
Mary Clements, his mother, d May 17, 1825, a 51.
Mary Barker Clements, her daughter, d Feb. 29, 1828, a 25.
John Clements, the father, d July 17, 1840, a 81.

On a tomb, Hic Jacet Joannes Bouchier, obiit 17 Mai, 1774, ætat 74.

John Oxden, d Oct. 10, 1780, a 55.
Also Elizabeth Oxden, d Oct. 14, 1796, a 67.

Elizabeth Morris, late of Lewes, Sussex, obiit March 10, 1785, ætat 59.

Mrs. Mary Adcock, d Oct. 31, 1808, a 70.
Also Mary, wife of William Meguinness, d July 29, 1820, a 73.

George Wildgoose, surveyor, d Feb. 26, 1806, a 61.
Ann, his wife, d July 9, 1824, a 84.

Richard Whiffin, d April 11, 1809, a 40.
Lucy Whiffin, his widow, d Dec. 7, 1820, a 48.

Mary Ann, wife of Thos. Cooper, d Jan. 15, 1835, a 70.

James Bull, of Pangdean, Sussex, d Sept. 4, 1828, a 25.
    The character of the deceased was marked by an undeviating regard to the best
and most lasting interests of friendship. As a son, brother, and friend, in each
relation he stood without blemish. This stone is erected by a few friends to
commemorate his virtues while living, and to show their regard for his memory
now that he is departed.

Thomas, son of Robert and Fanny Bennett, d May 9th, 1824.
    Deeply lamented by his surviving relatives and friends.
Also Mrs. Margaret Todd, d April 18, 1810, a 74.

Joseph Killmaster, *d* April 19, 1834, *a* 62.
Leah, his wife, *d* April 27, 1834, *a* 60.
Louisa Bullen, granddaughter, *d* Dec. 16, 1854, *a* 3.
[Mr. Killmaster was a carpenter, residing in the Old Town.]

Richard Gould, *d* April 30, 1804, *a* 32.
John Gould, his brother, *d* Feb. 10, 1834, *a* 67.

Mrs. Mary Freebody, *d* Nov. 17, 1786, *a* 51.

Thomas Walton, *d* Sept. 25, 1783, *a* 46.
Jane, his wife, *d* Nov. 7, 1806, *a* 67.

Sarah Whittaker, daughter of Daniel and Patience Stagg, *d* suddenly Aug.
2, 1842, *a* 54.
Henry Whittaker, her husband, *d* March 5, 1869: interred in St. Peter's
Churchyard.

Mary, wife of Michael Copp Horton, Esq., *d* Jan. 8, 1784, *a* 51.
Also Michael Copp Horton, Esq., *d* March 3, 1808, *a* 88.
An uncommon energy and correctness of mind, a mild and placid disposition,
a heart warmed to the prick of sorrow and of Christian charity rendered his
length of days a blessing to himself, his relations and friends, and his last
hours resigned, composed, and happy.

Sarah, wife of Peter Green, *d* March 28, 1789, *a* 70.
Peter Green, her husband, *d* May 22, 1793, *a* 73.
John Green, *d* Dec. 22, 1802, *a* 39.
Also Sarah Poole Purnell, wife of the above, *d* Feb. 80, 1838, *a* 68.
" Great are the troubles of the righteous, but the Lord delivereth them
out of all."
[This lady was married twice, but chose to have her name on the tombstone
of her first husband.]

Wm. Skey Purnell, *d* May 15, 1820, *a* 40.
Mrs. Sarah Glover, *d* Sept. 18, 1820, *a* 31.

Ann, wife of Mr. W. F. Rivers, *d* April 26, 1852, *a* 42.
Also W. F. Rivers, *d* June 8, 1854, *a* 43.

Mr. James Sant, *d* Jan. 18, 1837, *a* 86.
[Grandfather of the present celebrated artist.]
" When the Eye saw him then it blessed him."
Martha Sant, his daughter, *d* Dec. 8, 1863, *a* 88.
James Trusler, died Jan. 9, 1853, *a* 47.
Dorothy, wife of Henry G. Ward, *d* July 23, 1807, *a* 42.
Also Henry G. Ward, their son, *d* May 31, 1814, *a* 18.
Also Henry G. Ward, his father, *d* May 10, 1834, *a* 68.
Mary, wife of Henry G. Ward, *d* June 11, 1846, *a* 85.
[Evidently a second wife.]

Vault. Here lieth the body of William Unwin, second son of the late Rev.
Wm. Cawthorne Unwin, rector of Stock-cum-Ramsden, Essex, and
great nephew of John Unwin, Esq., whose remains are interred near
here, who departed this life May 8, 1806, *a* 19.
Also on the left-hand side of this stone lie the bodies of Mary Ann Unwin,
his only sister, who died Sept. 24th, 1799, *a* 29; and of Elizabeth
Shuttleworth, his aunt, who died Jan. 29, 1795, *a* 40; also his
mother, Anne Unwin, who died May 10, 1825, *a* 75.
John Unwin, Esq., *d* Sept. 21, 1789, *a* 76.

A small gravestone bears this remarkable inscription—

R + E, son of Robert and Ann, *d* Nov. 30, 1792.

Robert Smith, only child of Robert and Elizabeth Smith, d Dec. 11, 1788, a 17.
Also Robert Smith, Esq., his father, d Feb. 20, 1815, a 68.
Also Elizabeth Smith, his mother, d Feb. 22, 1830, a 80.

Sarah, wife of John Cockrell, d Sept. 27, 1823, a 65.

> Resigned to him who gave thee breath
> And calm'd thy soul in hour of death,
> Tho' pain and sorrow long endured,
> By Christian faith and hope secured.
> Beyond the grave all sorrows cease,
> And rest in perfect bliss and peace,
> If we in life but copy thee
> Our future state will happy be.

Also John Cockrell, d Jan. 10, 1837, a 78.

George Olive, d March 9, 1792, a 39, and four of his children.

Mr. Richard Swift, d June 26, 1789, a 76.
Philadelphia, his wife, d Feb. 1, 1794, a 76.

In memory of John Viney, inventor of the Patent Wheel, obiit July 27,
    1742, ætat 63.

Rebecca, wife of John Viney, d August 14, 1791, a 58.

Patience, wife of Daniel Stagg, d Jan. 9, 1832, a 67.
Daniel Stagg, her husband, d Oct. 30, 1844, a 79.
Thomas Stagg, grandson, d July 23, 1848, a 23,

> My time on earth so soon did pass away;
> Because God called I could no longer stay,
> A rapid consumption brought me to the grave,
> I trust in Christ my precious soul to save.

Elizabeth daughter of Francis and Jane Jones, d March 9, 1797, a 25.

> Fragrant the rose, but it fades in time,
> The violet lives, but quickly past its prime,
> While lilies hang their heads and soon decay,
> And whiter snow in minutes melt away,
> Such and so withering are our early joys
> Which time or sickness speedily destroys,

Also, Ann Jones, her sister, d Sept, 15, 1833, a 58.
At the back of this stone we read—
Mary Jones, d Feb. 28, 1791, a 29.
Francis Jones, her father, d April 30, 1804, a 63.
Jane Jones, her mother, d Sept. 14, 1817, a 83.

Mary, wife of George Agate, d March 19, 1791, a 62.
George Agate, died August 4, 1799, a 62.
    [Formerly a nurseryman in Southbridge Road.]

Mr. James Martin, bricklayer, d Jan. 19, 1808, a 61.
Arenia Martin, his wife, d Sept. 18, 1816, a 64.
Also Harriot Martin, his daughter, d Jan. 31, 1851, a 64.

Harriot Martin, wife of Thomas Martin, d Dec. 4, 1819, in the 20th year
    of her age and the second of her marriage, leaving an infant daughter.
Also, Arenia, her daughter, d Jan. 2, 1820, a two months.

> A lovely infant and a model wife
> All to this vault must sadly be consigned
> Thus, all we hold most dear to us in life
> With grief and sorrow are to death resigned.

Also, Thomas Martin, builder, d Jan. 30, 1866, a 68.
Also, Rebecca Collins Martin, second wife, d Nov. 14, 1876, a 73.
    [Mr. Martin carried on his business at the back of the Old Vine House,
    Church Street, lately pulled down, and the site covered with shops.]

Richard Gould, *d* April 30. 1804. *a* 32.

> Weep not, dear friends, altho' on earth
> My time with you is past,
> With Christ above I hope to meet.
> Where happiness will last.

Also, John Gould, his brother. *d* Feb. 16. 1834. *a* 67.

Mrs. Mary Thornhill. *d* Oct. 9. 1830. *a* 39.

William, infant son of Edward and Sally Percival. *d* March 6. 1847. *a* one year and five months.

Edward Percival. *d* Nov. 3. 1847. *a* 30.
Sally Percival. *d* April 26. 1861. *a* 46.

James Halfhide. *d* July 23. 1807. *a* 72.
Mary Halfhide, his wife. *d* Jan. 20. 1830. *a* 90.

William Cock. *d* March 3. 1787. *d* 33.
James Tweedalle Adair Richardson. *d* May 18. 1812. *a* 2.

Margaret Cock. *d* Sept. 29. 1817. *a* 62.
Bridget, wife of George Richardson and daughter of the above. *d* Dec. 12. 1830. *a* 48.
Mr. George Richardson. her husband. *d* July 4, 1861. *a* 79.

Elizabeth Rutter. *d* Dec. 14. 1786. *a* 70.
Also, Daniel, her husband. *d* Jan. 30, 1790. *a* 80.

James Johns, *d* Oct. 19. 1830. *a* 57.
Sarah Johns, his wife. *d* June 4, 1858. *a* 75.

Susan Stevens. *d* April 19. 1831. *a* 44.
Geo. Thos. Smith, her nephew. *d* April 10. 1823. *a* 4.

> 'Tis Jesus from his mercy seat
> Invites me to his rest,
> He calls poor sinners to his feet
> And makes them truly blest.

Vault.—Alice Brigstock, wife of Richd. Brigstock. *d* March 18. 1750. *a* 59.
Also, Richard Brigstock, her husband. *d* Nov. 14. 1779, *a* 89.
[The Brigstocks were originally brewers in South End.]

On one side, Elizabeth Farley. *d* May 18, 1823, *a* 80.
On the other, Frances, wife of John Farley, *d* Jan. 30, *a* 49.
John Farley, *d* 10 April, 1824, *a* 69.
Jane Farley, his sister. *d* Oct. 17, 1838. *a* 89.

Henry Stanford Purser. *d* Aug. 4. 1830, *a* 48.
Harriet, his wife. *d* March 9. 1829. *a* 45.
Also four children who died in infancy.

Jane Farley. wife of Thos. Farley, *d* Oct. 23. 1783, *a* 73.
Thomas Farley, *d* Sept. 4, 1808, *a* 95.
Thomas Farley, his son, *d* June 22, 1835, *a* 83.
Catharine, his wife, *d* Dec. 11, 1858, *a* 85.

Vault.—Mary Breary. *d* April 28. 1785. *a* 28.
James Meagher, *d* July 10. 1795. *a* 67.
Robert Meagher, *d* Sept. 6. 1807, *a* 36.
Francis Meagher, *d* Oct. 10. 1826. *a* 73.
Harriott Meagher, *d* May 17. 1827, *a* 16.

Martha, wife of James Scott. *d* Dec. 24, 1827, *a* 51.
James Scott. *d* Aug. 9, 1853, *a* 74.

Sarah, wife of Charles Collier, *d* Aug. 29, 1809, *a* 68.
William, her son, *d* Oct. 4, 1802, *a* 22.
Charles Collier, whitesmith. *d* Sept. 23, 1820, *a* 81.

c

Jane Frances. daughter of Wm. Bryant, *d* April 5, 1860, *a* 22 months.

Ann, wife of Jonas Sturt, *d* Nov. 18, 1792, *a* 37.

> Long as the good congenial worth revere,
> As worth departed prompts the gushing tear.
> So long to virtue just and urged by woe,
> For three, the heart shall grieve, the eye shall flow,
> And whilst by friendship led or grief opprest,
> We tread these limits where thy reliques rest,
> With thy loved image shall thy virtues rise,
> Sooth the keen pang, and train us for the skies.

Jonas Sturt, blacksmith, *d* Oct. 26, 1829, *a* 68.

Mrs. Mary Roffey. *d* Feb. 9, 1787, *a* 36.
Mrs. Mary Wasdall, *d* March 1, 1825, *a* 81.

James Trusler, *d* Jan. 9, 1853, *a* 47.

Sarah Partridge, singlewoman. for 55 years an inhabitant of this parish, *d* Nov. 2, 1790, *a* 74.
John Partridge, Esq., *d* Feb. 27, 1809, *a* 90.

Eleanor Elizabeth Bennett, daughter of John and Eleanor Bennett, *d* March 2, 1858, *a* 5.
> " Though lost to sight to memory dear."

William Eades. *d* Sept. 8, 1818, *a* 9.
Frances Charlotte Eades. *d* March 14, 1826, *a* 75.
James Bryant Eades, *d* July 8, 1826, *a* 78.
Anna Maria Rich, their daughter, *d* May 10, 1825, *a* 33.
   [Mr. Eades was an undertaker.]

William Eades, *d* Oct. 31, 1831, *a* 45.
Mary Elizabeth, his wife, *d* Sept. 26, 1851, *a* 66.
William Eades, their son, *d* Feb. 27, 1847, *a* 37.

Martha, wife of James Scott, *d* Dec. 24, 1827, *a* 51.
James Scott, *d* Aug. 9, 1853, *a* 74.

Sarah, wife of James Booth, *d* April 13, 1792, *a* 36.
> Weep not for me my children dear,
> Although you're left behind,
> Prepare yourselves to follow me,
> And bear me in your mind.

Also Mr. Robert Rogers, *d* Jan. 24, 1836, *a* 85.
Mrs. Hannah Rogers, *d* Sept. 11, 1836, *a* 85.

Thomas Rice, *d* June 12, 1797, *a* 18.
John Rice, *d* Oct. 5, 1806, *a* 28.
Also William Rice. *d* Nov. 15, 1814, *a* 62.
> The man who meant well and acted boldly.

Elizabeth, wife of Henry Stent, *d* July 13, 1806, *a* 31.

Robert, only child of Robert and Elizabeth Smith, *d* Dec. 11, 1788, *a* 7.
Robert Smith, Esq., his father, *d* Feb. 20, 1815, *a* 68.
Elizabeth Smith, his mother, *d* Feb. 22, 1830, *a* 80.

Elizabeth Sarah Brooke, *d* July 11, 1844, *a* 65.
Daniel Thompson Brooke, *d* Feb. 5, 1837, *a* 68.
   [Mr. Brooke left a sum of money to the churchwardens of the parish, the interest of which is spent on bread for the poor.]
   [Some other names not decipherable.]

Margaret Charlotte Watts, eldest daughter of Lieut.-Col. Watts, *d* May 13, 1825, *a* 28.

Mary West. d Sept. 15, 1827, a 74.
Edward West, d Aug. 23. 1830, a 76.

John Harris. surgeon. d Sept. 22. 1823, a 79.
Ann. his wife, d Sept. 7, 1809. a 69.
Joseph Bottomley, grandson. d Nov. 12, 1799. a 21.
Harriott Bottomley. his mother. d Oct. 12, 1826, a 32.
Catharine Harris Bottomley. d Oct. 16, a 6.

Elizabeth. wife of Edward Hughes, d Dec. 6, 1822, a 68.

Martha. relict of Roger Griffin, Esq., of Clerkenwell, d June 30, 1822, a 90.

Robert Harris, Esq., magistrate of the County of Surrey, d Sept. 24, 1907, a 70.
Mary, his widow, d Nov. 13. 1828
Mary, his daughter. d Nov. 2. 1843.
Susanna, his daughter, d Feb. 18, 1871.

By reference to the *Gentleman's Magazine* we find that Mr. Harris. who died in the Commission of the Peace for the county. was originally a druggist in St. Paul's Churchyard. He had a son named Francis, who was brought up to the medical profession, and practised in Croydon, He died on the 5th May. 1849. and was buried at Mitcham, where there is a monument erected to his memory. He married Harriet St. Clair Kelly. daughter of Lieut.-Colonel Kelly, of the 1st regiment of Life Guards. who died in India. Colonel Kelly's wife was buried in St. Peter's Churchyard, where her name is recorded on a tomb, together with her husband's, which will be found noticed under the proper heading.

Mrs. Jane Nockalls, d Jan. 15. 1813. a 98.

Mrs. Lucy Wilson, d May 23. 1832, a 83.

Mrs. Hester Russell. d March 10. 1817, a 82.

Elizabeth Harris, May 12. 1823, a 18.
Mrs. Ann Harris. d Nov. 26, 1826. a 56.
Thomas Mackinder. who died suddenly the same day, a 55.
Elizabeth Mackinder, his relict, d June 1, 1833, a 69.
Mary Harris d March 27, 1840. a 29.

George Leonhard Steinman, Esq., d Jan. 4, 1830, a 72.
Susanna. his relict. d Oct. 14. 1842, a 80.
Louisa Bastin. their youngest daughter, d July 13. 1823, a 34.
[Mr. Steinman's son published a History of Croydon.]

Charles Church. d June 10, 1827, a 37.
> Weep not dear Friends, although on Earth,
> My time with you is past,
> With Christ above we hope to meet,
> Where happiness will last.

John Duncan. d April 20. 1825, a 65.
Sarah, his relict, d May 28, 1825, a 60.
> Dear friends, forbear to mourn and weep,
> While in the dust we sweetly sleep,
> This frailsome world we've left behind,
> A crown of glory now to find.

George Drake, Esq., d April 21, 1800, a 60.

Mrs. Mary Herbert, d April 7, 1805, a 75.

Mrs. Elizabeth Horn, d Feb. 11, 1809, a 77.

Mrs. Phœbe Lovejoy, *d* Aug. 3, 1802, *a* 30.

Jane George, wife of Richd. George, *d* Dec. 31, 1820, *a* 71.
Sarah, second wife of Richd. George, *d* Feb. 22, 1828, *a* 47.
Richard George, *d* Aug. 30, 1849, *a* 88.

Rebecca Sutton, *d* March 20, 1810, *a* 34.
John Sutton, her husband, *d* Dec. 7, 1816, *a* 39.

Mary Brunsden, spinster, *d* June 2, 1819, *a* 61.
Miss Elizabeth Wright, *d* July 5, 1849, *a* 78.

Mrs. Hester Lloyd, relict of the late Rev. Thomas Lloyd, of Hereford
Cathedral, *d* June 30, 1840, *a* 73.

Thomas Dax, Esq., *d* March 28, 1834, *a* 80.
Ann, his widow, *d* Feb. 27, 1844, *a* 82.

Thomas Dax, Esq., senior master of the Court of Exchequer [no age nor
date].
Anne Elizabeth Dax, his relict, *d* April 19, 1861, *a* 62.
                    Grata et Œterna Memoria.

George Bell, gent., *d* April 19, 1849, *a* 42.
            Relying only on the merits of his Saviour.
Jenet Bell, his widow, *d* April 16, 1855 [no age].

William Higgs, of Church Street, Croydon, *d* Jan. 20, 1856, *a* 58.

Isaac Hadfield, who died in Demerara, Feb., 1847.
Mary, his wife, *d* Feb. 23, 1850, *a* 50.
        This Stone is erected by their affectionate children.

Mr. Thomas Hall, *d* Oct. 18, 1859, *a* 70.

Mr. Thomas Small, *d* Jan. 30, 1851, *a* 44.

Emma Sophia Knight, *d* April 30, 1851, *a* 48.

Berthia, wife of Wm. Tidy, *d* Jan. 27, 1837, *a* 46.
William Tidy, the respected sexton of this parish for 34 years, *d* March
11, 1866, *a* 76.
    Keep innocency, and take heed unto the thing that is right, for that shall give
    a man peace at last.

William Hillier, *d* Sept. 17, 1853, *a* 18.
Thomas Green, *d* June 27, 1855, *a* 61.

David Tidy, *d* March 8, 1826, *a* 62.
Thomas Albert Lockwood, *d* March 1, 1826, *a* 2½.
Richard Tidy, *d* May 24, 1838, *a* 57.
Lucy, his wife, *d* Dec. 16, 1839, *a* 53.

John Allen, news agent, 31, Surrey Street, *d* March 21, 1854, *a* 32.

Hannah, wife of John Gibson, *d* Sept. 14, 1853, *a* 56.

Andrew Stranger, *d* March 17, 1854, *a* 3 months.
Charlotte Stranger, *d* April 25, 1858, *a* 24.

George Samuel Goddard, *d* June 14, 1854, *a* 74.
        " He died trusting in the merits of Christ, an heir of that righteousness
                    which is by faith."
                Here shall we rest until that great judgment morning,
                When the last trump shall sound its awful warning;
                When the Archangel's voice, midst peals of thunder,
                Shall break the iron bands of death asunder,
                Tear up the graves, the elements confounding,
                And thro' the caverns of the deep resounding;
                Proclaiming through each lone sequestered lodgment,
                Awake, ye sleeping dead, and come to judgment.

Ellen, wife of John German, *d* April 27, 1859, *a* 27.
> We laid her in the hallowed grave
> In hope of Him who died to save.

Michael Newman, *d* Dec. 29, 1854, *a* 66.

Mary Winter, *d* Oct. 18, 1856, *a* 86.

John Geal, *d* Oct. 31, 1859, *a* 82.
Mary Geal, his wife, *d* Jan., 1861, *a* 73.

Edward Albrey Russell, son of Edward Russell, *d* March 30, 1861, *a* 26.

Ann Waters, relict of the late Mr. Joseph Waters, *d* Feb. 17, 1860, *a* 79.
> Lived beloved and died lamented.

Emily Boyce, wife of Robert Boyce, *d* March 9, 1859, *a* 59.

A tomb, now standing in the centre of the Churchyard, formerly stood outside the wall of the Old Church, enclosed with iron rails, backing up to the tomb of Archbishop Sheldon. When the church was rebuilt, this tomb (with the coffins) was removed to its present site. The following are the inscriptions thereon:

Beneath this tomb repose the remains of the Right Hon. Lady Catharine Sheldon, late Phipps, who died in January, 1738.

John Sheldon, Esq., of Mitcham, who died in March, 1752.

The Right Hon. Constantine Phipps, Baron Mulgrave, who died in September, 1775.

The Right Hon. Lady Lepel Phipps, Baroness Mulgrave, who died in March, 1780.

Richard Sheldon, Esq., of Lincoln's-inn-fields, who died the 15th February, 1795, aged 72 years.

William Sheldon, Esq., nephew of Richard Sheldon, Esq., also interred here, who died December 23, 1811, aged 38.

Thomas Henry Sheldon, Esq., brother of the above, who died Feb. 5, 1817, in his 70th year.

> [These two gentlemen were sons of William Sheldon, brother of Richard Sheldon, mentioned above.]

It is rather curious that John Sheldon, whose relatives had his tomb backed up to that of Archbishop Sheldon, does not appear to have been any relation of that dignitary. This John Sheldon was second son of William Sheldon, of Mitcham, gent., and grandson of William Sheldon, who in his will, dated 9th September, 1699, describes himself " of London, Draper, and now inhabitant of Clapham, in the county of Surrey." John Sheldon was the second husband of Lady Catherine Annesley, only daughter and heiress of James, third Earl of Anglesey, by Lady Catherine Darnley, natural daughter of James II. She was relict of William Phipps, Esq., only surviving son of Sir Constantine Phipps, Lord High Chancellor of Ireland, and by him had, with other issue, a son, Constantine Phipps, created (for some reason which we have not been able to ascertain) Baron Mulgrave of New Ross, in the Peerage of Ireland, 3rd September, 1767, and he was buried in the same tomb as his mother, as the inscription thereon testifies. The burial of John Sheldon and some of his relatives at Croydon was probably in consequence of having, by accident, resided in this parish at the time of his wife's death, she desiring in her will to be buried " in the parish churchyard where I dye." She was consequently buried at Croydon, and he was, at his desire, buried with her. The Phipps and Sheldon tomb is composed of stone, with white marble panels. During the removal of the coffins from the side of the Church wall to their present resting-place, it was seen that the coffin containing the remains of Lord Mulgrave had been filled up with wax, evidently with the intention of preserving the body. The will of Lady Catherine Sheldon is worthy of notice. After devising her property, she leaves the care of her children " to my much-loved and honoured mother, Catherine, Duchess of Buckingham," but if she refused the guardianship, she then commits them to the care of " my aforesaid husband, he having always been to me a most indulgent, tender, and affectionate husband, and to my dear children has always been a most kind and loving Father. . . . And I order and direct my Executor to dispose my funeral in the following manner, that is to say I will be buryed in the Parish Churchyard, where I dye, and to be carried in a Hearse, with only one pair of horses, without escocheons, plumes, or any other ornaments. I will have no coach nor attendance to follow me. I will have no pall bearers, chief mourner, nor mourners, but I will have six of my nearest poor neighbours to carry my body from the hearse to the grave ; to each of them I will give ten shillings and sixpence. I will have no torches for I direct that I shall be carried out of my house in the morning at the break of day. I will that there be no rings given in remembrance of me, and tis my desire that all herein mentioned concerning my funerall be as punctually performed as any other part of my Will, and lastly, I do hereby appoint my loving husband, John Sheldon, Esq., Sole Executor." In the will of John Sheldon, he is described as " John Sheldon, of Mitcham, in the county of Surrey, Esquire." He directs, " And I will that I be buried with the Right Honourable Lady Catherine, my late dear deceased wife, who lyes in Croydon Church Yard. The Funeral and expence of repairing the vault and laying a marble slab with an inscription, not exceeding one hundred pounds." After reciting a variety of legacies, comes this peculiar item, " to John Johnson, an infant about ten years old, the son of Ann Osborn, the now wife of John Bishop, £500." He left the residue of his estate to his nephew, Richard Sheldon. There is not a word in any of these documents relating to Archbishop Sheldon. In some histories it is stated that John Sheldon was the son of the Archbishop, but it is impossible this can be true, as that dignitary never was married.

Henry Hatten, d Oct. 30, 1839, a 68.

John Recks, d Jan. 4, 1861, a 47.

James Window, Esq., of Craig's Court, London, and Addiscombe Road, d Feb. 26, 1859, a 68.

The following lines were formerly on a rail—

> Thou shalt do no murder, nor shalt thou steal,
> Are the commands Jehovah did reveal ;
> But thou, O wretch, who without fear or dread
> Of thy tremendous Maker, shot me dead
> Amidst my strength and sin, but, Lord forgive,
> As I through boundless mercies hope to live !

Caroline, wife of George Matthew, d July 20, 1858, a 70.

George Washford Matthew, d April 18, 1860, a 75.

[Mr. Matthew was a stage-coach proprietor, and ran a coach to London before the railway was opened.]

> Long before the screech of the locomotive was heard, and when many of the tradesmen of the town occasionally walked to and from London, Mr. Matthew (" Georgy," as he was commonly called), a kind-hearted unsophisticated man, was for many years proprietor and driver of one of the old Croydon coaches. It was rather a slow coach, it is true, but it was always considered very safe, and there was an old joke, often repeated over the morning glass, that upon one occasion, when Mr. Matthew held up his whip, and hailed a Croydon tradesman who was walking to town, the pedestrian, looking round with a twinkle in his eye, said, " Can't ride this morning, Mr. Matthew. I'm in a hurry, and want to get to town early." But there were coaches in those days, and the mail, that went the pace, viz., " The Times," " The Age," and other Brighton coaches, well horsed and often driven by noblemen and gentlemen, which rattled through the town at ten miles an hour.

> " Alas ! alas ! where are they gone,
> The coach, the bays, and greys ?
> Alas ! alas ! where are they gone,
> The light of other days ? "

> " Though the coachmen of old are dead,
> Though the guards are turned to clay,
> You will still remember the " yard of tin,"
> And the mail of the olden day."

Elizabeth Elgie, d Aug. 12, 1860, a 64.

Ann Phillips, d March 10, 1861, a 71.

Elizabeth Janet Watson, d Jan. 18, 1859, a 86.

Mary Polhill, born Jan. 24, 1767, died May 25, 1858.

William Steward Owen, Esq., of Duppas Hill Place, d Nov. 26, 1855, a 64.

[One of the first members of the Croydon Local Board of Health.]

James Waters, d April 3, 1853, a 31.
Elizabeth Waters, his mother, d Oct. 15, 1857, a 61.
J. V. Routledge, his son-in-law, d Jan. 17, 1859, a 31.
John Waters Routledge, his son, who died at sea, Aug. 7, 1874, a 17.

Charlotte, wife of Wm. Agate, d Aug. 4, 1850, a 72.

George Agate, d March 19, 1850, a 80.
May, his wife, d April 4, 1850, a 78.

Ann, daughter of Edward and Ann Bond, d July 24, 1850, a 23.
Edward Bond, d Jan. 8, 1856, a 60.

Ann, wife of Thomas Pretty, d May 7, 1848, a 76.

Edward Dickenson, gent., *d* Nov. 8. 1827, *a* 71,
Mary Magdalene Dickenson, died at Vauxhall, Lambeth, June 7, 1841, *a* 76.

Mary Brumsden, *d* June 22, 1811, *a* 61.

Elizabeth, wife of Patrick Drummond, solicitor, *d* Aug. 29, 1845, *a* 73.
Patrick Drummond, her husband, *d* Nov. 5, 1845, *a* 79.
Also, Mary Drummond, their daughter, *d* Nov. 17, 1871, *a* 67.
    " All that are in the graves shall hear his voice, and shall come forth."
                                JOHN v. 28.
    [These were the father, mother, and sister of the late John and the present William Drummond, of North End.]

Thomas Miller, *b* Nov. 3, 1767, *d* Dec. 14, 1855.
         " My flesh also shall rest in hope."
The deceased was a gentleman of considerable musical abilities, and was the first person to officiate at the organ erected in 1794, and destroyed in the fire. Mr. Miller filled the post of organist for some years without fee or reward.

Wm. Curtis, *d* Oct. 4, 1853, *a* 53.

Mary, wife of Richard Mann, *d* June 17, 1850, *a* 58.
Richard Mann, her husband, *d* Sept. 17, 1856, *a* 68.
    [Mr. Richard Mann was a tallow chandler and plumber.]

Knivett Leppingwell, *d* Sept. 21, 1849, *a* 72.

Charles James Messenger, *d* Sept. 19, 1851, *a* 32.

Margaret, wife of Robert Corney, *b* Feb. 17, 1785, *d* Feb. 17, 1850.
Mr. Robert Corney, her husband, *b* May 25, 1787, *d* Jan. 28, 1868.
Maria, their daughter, *b* Feb. 27, 1812, *d* Nov. 26, 1851.
    [Ancestors of Mr. Corney, pipe-maker, of High Street.]

Harry, son of John and Ann Grantham, *d* Nov. 2, 1853, *a* 46.
          His frame no more shall pain or sickness know,
          For gentle death has closed the scene of woe.
Also Mr. John Grantham, his father, *d* April 16, 1856, *a* 81.
Sarah, his wife, *d* April 30, 1856, *a* 67.

Gabriel Shaw, Esq., only son of Charles Shaw, Esq., of Lawton in Cheshire, and of Elizabeth Ludlow, his wife, *d* Feb. 11, 1851, *a* 75.
    Beloved and lamented by all who knew him.

Ann wife of Mr. David Grantham, *d* July 21, 1852, *a* 46.

John Cream, *d* June 1, 1851, *a* 53.

Joseph Noble, of Wood Street, Cheapside, *d* Nov. 27, 1857, *a* 39.

Plumer Eyles, formerly of Lewes, Sussex, *d* June 3, 1851, *a* 85.

John Blake, *d* Feb. 23, 1852, *a* 72.
    John Blake was for many years the principal auctioneer in in Croydon. He was wealthy, and a gentleman of unblemished character, and was highly valued by all who knew him, not only for his wonderful business habits and integrity, but for his benevolence, his hospitality, and his *bonhomie*. His whole life had been spent in the parish, and had been one of almost incessant activity in the path of usefulness.

Edward Grantham, Esq., *d* June 13, 1852, *a* 71.
Elizabeth Jane, his sister, *d* Jan. 14, 1865, *a* 80.
    [Mr. Grantham was a surveyor of considerable eminence.]

In this vault are deposited the remains of Robert Wells Eyles. Esq.. late of Brickwood House, a magistrate for the County of Surrey. *d* Oct. 15. 1853. *a* 70.

Sarah Susannah. his wife. *d* June 20. 1830. *a* 56.

Mary Ann. their youngest daughter. *d* Sept. 23, 1828, *a* 14.

> Their remains are deposited in a vault in the church of St. Martin, Ludgate. London.

On the side panels, John Brown Eyles, of St. Andrews Court. Holborn, *d* Nov. 26, 1863, *a* 69.

Robert Meyrick, youngest child of Edward and Sarah Eyles. *d* July 4, 1855, *a* 6 years 5 months.

In the cemetery are interred the remains of Mary Anne, sister of R. W. and J. B. Eyles. *d* April 28, 1868.

Also their sister. Ann Elizabeth Eyies, *d* May 19, 1870, *a* 73.

James Robinson Esq., of Croydon and Queen Street Place, London, *d* Aug. 4. 1853. *a* 63.

Maria. wife of Wm. Inkpen, *d* Aug. 8, 1855. *a* 56.

> Each moment since her dying hour,
> My loss I keenly feel.
> But trust I feel the Saviour's power,
> To sanctify and heal.

Also Wm. Inkpen, *d* Oct. 28, 1873, *a* 85.

> [The deceased left the sum of £600 to the inhabitants of the Little Alms-houses.]

> Mr. Inkpen was the principal coach proprietor in Croydon, and like his old friend and competitor Mr. Matthews, he almost always drove one of his own teams. His coaches were always well horsed, and all the appointments were good ; and, if he did not go the pace that kills, he generally accomplished the journey to or from London in a little over an hour. Mr. Inkpen was highly respected by his fellow-townsmen, and always won golden opinions from his numerous passengers. He was, perhaps, a little narrow-minded and prejudiced, and had such a horror of and dislike to railways that he was never known to enter one of their carriages. He was a man of property, chairman of the Board of Guardians, and died at a ripe old age.

> > " The sun is set that once shone out,
> > So bright upon these teams ;
> > The night has come, and all that's past,
> > Seem but as fleeting dreams."

Elizabeth King, *d* Dec. 19, 1857, *a* 82.

Henry Clark, late of Rudgwick, Sussex, *d* July 3, 1858, *a* 33.

Benjamin Bailey, for many years sergeant in the Fusilier Guards, *d* Feb. 1, 1858, *a* 76.

Elizabeth, his widow, and formerly wife of Charles Strudwicke, *d* Nov. 30, 1858, *a* 77.

Eleanor Kirkham, *d* March 17, 1860, *a* 45.

James Latter, *d* March 15, 1857, *a* 59.

Benjamin Weller, *d* Oct. 25, 1856, *a* 52.

Mrs. Unity Elizabeth Weller, *d* Jan. 29, 1857, *a* 51.

Ellen, beloved child of Henry and Elizabeth Mary Richards, *d* March 12, 1855, *a* 11.

Richard Priddy, *d* Feb 5, 1851, *a* 71.
Mary Priddy, his widow, *d* Jan. 28, 1856, *a* 72.
    [Mr. Priddy was a maltster, living on Crown Hill.]

Robert Wm. Bond, *d* April 23, 1855, *a* 22.
Emma Hannah Bond, *d* May 17, 1859, *a* 30.

Elizabeth, wife of Henry Downing, died Jan. 7, 1855, *a* 71.
Henry Downing, *d* at Thelnetham, Suffolk, Jan. 5, 1859, *a* 79.

Archibald Henry Greeves, *d* May 28, 1854, *a* 45.

William Wickens, *d* April 15, 1854, *a* 45.
Julia, the truly and dearly beloved wife of William Hallett, corn merchant, of High street, and widow of the above William Wickens, *d* Aug. 6, 1860.

> How then ought I to live,
> While God withholds the kind reprieve,
> To live well die never,
> To die well and live for ever.
> To bear from the world of grief and sin,
> Eternally with God shut in.

Rev. Brice Fletcher, *d* Sept. 11, 1854, *a* 83.

> Looking unto Jesus.

Mary, wife of the late Samuel Taylor of the Borough, *d* Jan. 19, 1854, *a* 83.
Emily Frances Adams, her grandchild, *d* March 27, 1841, *a* 16.

John, son of the late Rev. Jno. Geo. Hodgson, M.A., vicar of this parish, *d* Dec. 23, 1853, *a* 9.
    " He shall gather the lambs in his arms and carry them in his bosom."

Wm. Wright, *d* Dec. 3, 1868, *a* 42.

Sarah, wife of Mr. A. R. Sewell, *d* Sept. 12, 1853, *a* 50.
    What is your life? It is even a vapour that appeareth for a little time and then vanisheth away.

Charles Henry Large, youngest son of the late Robert Large, Esq., of Great Clacton, Essex, *d* Aug. 29, 1853, *a* 56.

Benjamin Day, nephew of George Day, of the Railway Bell Inn, Croydon, *d* Jan. 10, 1860, *a* 18.

William Johnson, saddler, *d* April 6, 1853, *a* 52.

Rebecca Chesterman, *d* Aug. 27, 1852, *a* 35.
Horatio Chesterman, *d* Jan. 8, 1853, *a* 40.

Theodore H. A. Fielding, *d* July 11, 1851, *a* 70.
    And merciful men are taken away; none considering the righteous is taken away from the evil to come.

Mrs. Martha Stead, of the Gun Inn, *d* Dec. 9, 1862, *a* 64.
William Stead, her son, *d* March 2, 1853, *a* 29.
Susanna, Wm. Stead's wife, *d* July 20, 1851, *a* 28.
William Stead, of the Gun Inn, *d* Aug. 5, 1855, *a* 56.
    Husband and father of the above, who, after a succession of domestic troubles during his stay in Croydon, departed this life in the full conviction of inheriting a better one; beloved and respected by all who knew him.

William Cheetham Hales, *d* Jan. 3, 1859, *a* 41.

Edward Booth, *d* Sept. 13, 1859, *a* 53.

> O reader, observe this stone erected here,
> Contains a loving Father, tender parent dear,
> Who sought no honours, betrayed no trust,
> But strove in all his dealings to be just,
> This truth he braved in every path he trod,
> An honest man is the noblest work of God.

Hannah, wife of Mr. John Battersbee, *d* Dec. 28, 1853, *a* 75.

Sarah Morley, wife of Mr. John Morley, *d* Sept. 4, 1852, *a* 63.

Here lieth the remains of Charles Yewens, " who when living was a man, now of his kindred dust," born Aug. 23, 1798, died Sept. 3, 1860.

Susy Margaret, his infant daughter, *d* Aug. 28. 1855, *a* 3.

Joshua Bignell, late livery stable keeper, *d* May 8, 1850. *a* 67.

    Mr. Bignell kept for a number of years the celebrated hunting stables near the Derby Arms Inn. He was a kind-hearted, humane, and upright man, though occasionally a little *brusque* in his manners, and hot-tempered. " Old Josh " was not only well known at Melton and Rugby by all the sporting men who rode with the Quorn and the Pytchley, but also by all the swells who sported scarlet in the Midlands. He was a hater of humbug, and a lover of horses, and the man would have had a hot time of it who failed in carefully nursing a hunter after a hard day's run with the " Old Surrey " or the Stag Hounds. Poor " Old Josh ! " What would be your feelings now if you could see the dilapidated state of the old stables which were formerly kept so neat and trim, both by yourself and subsequently by your son Atwood, who was veritably a " chip of the old block."

Ann, his wife, *d* April 27, 1867, on her 84th birthday.

James Bennett, late of the Derby Arms, *d* March 19, 1849, *a* 60.

Sarah Bennett, his wife, *d* Jan. 20, 1875, *a* 85.

Elizabeth, her daughter, who died on her passage to Port Phillip, South Australia, Dec. 20, 1848, *a* 27.

Sarah, wife of Attwood Bignell, daughter of James Bennett, of the Derby Arms, *d* Aug. 5. 1849, *a* 30.

James Bennett, her brother, *d* May 6, 1860, *a* 43.

Major-General Sir Ephraim G. Stannus. C.B., for many years Lieut.-Governor of the Honourable East India Company's Military College at Addiscombe, *d* Oct. 21, 1860, *a* 66.

    There is a marble tablet erected to the memory of this gentleman in St. James's Church by his brother officers. Before his appointment to Addiscombe College he served with considerable distinction in various campaigns in India, Arabia, and Persia. Some years before Sir Ephraim Stannus was governor, the discipline at the College was not perhaps quite so strict as it might have been, and there were sometimes quarrels and fights between the cadets and the roughs of the town. The cadets were nicknamed *puppies* because (it was said) they hunted and tortured cats, and whenever the offensive word was applied to these spirited lads, a row was sure to ensue, and many a fight took place in the town and at Addiscombe, resulting in broken heads and damaged noses.

Jane, wife of Wm. P. Robinson, *d* Nov. 9, 1833, *a* 38.

Christopher John Robinson, her son, *d* Nov. 9, 1833, *a* 11 days.

    " Man cometh up and is mowed down as a flower, he fleeth as it were a shadow, and never maketh a stay."

Charlotte Davidson, youngest daughter of the late James Davidson, M.D., Professor in Imnechel College, Aberdeen, *d* March 16, 1848.

Catharine Rachel, daughter of Dr. Wm. Chalmers, *d* Jan. 26, 1831, *a* 13.
Elizabeth Margaret, his wife, *d* May 28, 1846, *a* 52.
Wm. Chalmers, M.D., *d* Oct. 13, 1862, *a* 76.

Eliza, wife of James Constable, *d* Dec. 8th, 1849, *a* 29.
Ellen, wife of Charles Arnold, *d* Sept. 1, 1872, *a* 30.
George, husband of Maria Constable, *d* Jan. 4, 1881, *a* 39.

Emily Kerrell, *d* June 27, 1853, *a* 20.

William Wood, *d* Aug. 3, 1854, *a* 66.
Rhoda Shepherd, *d* Nov. 15, 1858, *a* 43.
Jabez Towell, *d* Oct. 6, 1855, *a* 3 years.

> Jesus, lover of my soul,
> Let me to thy bosom flee,
> While the raging billows roll,
> While the tempest still is high.
> Hide me, oh, my Saviour hide,
> Till the storm of life is past,
> Safe into the haven guide,
> Oh, receive my soul at last.

Amelia Mary, daughter of Robert and Lucy Titman, Drill-Sergeant Grenadier Guards, *d* Feb. 7, 1858, *a* 4.
Lucy Jane, her sister, *d* April 10, 1854, *a* 9 months.

> See from earth, the fading lily rise,
> It springs, it grows, it flourishes and dies,
> So these fair flowers, scarce blossomed for a day.
> Short was the blossom, early the decay.

Wm. Bowman, son of John and Mary Bowman, of Leatherhead, *d* Aug. 22, 1851, *a* 70.

Salome, wife of Mr. John Eames, *d* April 3, 1856, *a* 26.

> Led by simplicity divine.
> She pleased and never tried to shine.

Mrs. Rebecca Peters, wife of Thomas Peters, *d* June 21, 1852, *a* 23.
Eliza Mary, her daughter, *d* Feb. 6, 1853, *a* 1 year 5 months.

Edward James Croft, *d* Nov. 10, 1855, *a* 46.
Edward Charles Croft, his son, *d* Oct. 8, 1860, *a* 23.
Chas. Sidney Smith, *d* June 3, 1859, *a* 59.

G. J., *d* June 16, 1860.

> I shall go to him, but he shall not come to me.

Kate Sarah Ebbutt, *d* April 17, 1857, *a* 7 months.

Elizabeth, wife of Wm. Lamb Bennett, *d* March 23, 1860, *a* 36.

> A good wife and tender mother.

Major Berners, late of the Royal Artillery, *d* May 80, 1853, *a* 57.

Elizabeth, daughter of Morris and Elizabeth Hughes, *d* March 18, 1854, *a* 20.

> Then farewell, dear child, farewell,
> Though severed still, our hearts are one,
> In distant spheres, awhile farewell,
> We part to meet again anon.

Mrs. Catharine Spencer, *d* June 29, 1855, *a* 71.
John Spencer, her husband, *d* Sept 10, 1832, *a* 47.
Thomas Spencer, her son, *d* June 5, 1877, *a* 40.

The following tombs are in the narrow strip of land at the tower end of the Church between the footpath and the road.

George Hicks, butcher, died May 3, 1845, *a* 29.

Joseph Coomber. *d* Oct. 4. 1831, *a* 21.
Martha Coomber, his mother. *d* Nov. 28. 1831, *a* 39.
James Coomber, his father. *d* Dec. 1850. *a* 84.

Sarah Markham. *d* Aug. 2, 1827, *a* 39.
Charles Strudwicke. *d* Feb. 3. 1853. *a* 65.

Eliza Holliday, *d* Nov. 24. 1835, *a* 72.
Argent Holliday. *d* Dec. 8. 1835, *a* 30.
Richard Holliday. *d* Dec. 28. 1835, *a* 74.
　　　[The Hollidays were a well known Waddon family.]

Elizabeth, wife of John Young. *d* Jan. 24. 1822. *a* 38.
Also 9 of her children, who died in their infancy.

　　　　　　Ah, solemn death, that by commission comes,
　　　　　　To call a loving wife and tender mother home,
　　　　　　No longer to assist her partner in his cares,
　　　　　　No more advise her offspring in their tender years.

George Weller, *d* Jan. 10, 1802, *a* 28.

Alexander Cummings. *d* Aug. 3, 1841. *a* 53.

Ann Woodward, *d* Jan. 7, 1858.

　　　　　　Farewell, vain world, we've had enough of thee,
　　　　　　And value not what thou canst say of me,
　　　　　　Thy smiles I court not, nor thy frowns I fear,
　　　　　　All's one to me, my head lies quiet here.

James Woodward, her father. *d* Jan. 20, 1846. *a* 74.
Jane, his wife, *d* May 27, 1846.
　　　　　　In death we were not parted.

Here lies the remains of an Honest Man—John Kennedy, late Quarter-
　　　Master of his Majesty's Royal Wagon Train, *d* Jan. 28, 1804, *a* 49.
Christiana Kennedy, his wife, *d* Aug. 10, 1818, *a* 63.

John Stagg, *d* Aug. 1. 1833. *a* 79.
Hannah Stagg, his wife, *d* Dec. 21, 1835, *a* 70.
Mary Ann Stagg, *d* March 22, 1845. *a* 45.

Sarah, wife of Thos. Skinner, *d* Aug. 24, 1849, *a* 70.

John Williamson, *d* March 21. 1822, *a* 83.
Sarah, his wife, *d* May 17, 1827, *a* 70.
John Williamson, his son, *d* March 12, 1833, in the prime of life.

Walter Wilson, *d* Sept. 1, 1831, *a* 58.
Sarah, his wife, *d* April 15, 1834, *a* 57.

---

*The following Tombs lie in the space between the South side of the
Church and the Footpath.*

There are a few ancient stones laid near the Church walls, which came out
　　of the old Church. We give the inscriptions in full :—

Here lyeth interred ye body of Svsana Legatt, ye wife of Mr. George
　　Legatt, citizen and Dry Fishmonger of London, ye only davghter of
　　Mr. Richard Shalleros, of ye Parish of Croydon, yeoman, aged 24
　　years, leveing one son. Shee departed this life ye 9th day of Sept.
　　in ye yeare of our Lord God, 1679.

Sara, the wife of Jonathan Andrews, of London, marchant, dyed the 1 of
　　October, 1645.
　　　　[This is the oldest tombstone in the Churchyard].

In memory of Mr. George Lowen, late of London, butcher. He married Mary, the only daughter of Mr. Joshua Pennyall, of Croydon, butcher, by whom he had issue one daughter, who died in her infancy, and all three hereunder be interr'd. He died Oct. 26, 1741, aged 43 years. His said wife died before him, that is to say, the 26th day of February, 1727, in the 22d year of her age.

Joshua Pennyall, *d* May 13, 1758, *a* 84.

Mrs. Ann Callant, widow (eldest daughter of Thomas Morton, Esq., of Whitehorse), *d* Feb. 11, 1733, *a* 72.
Jane Callant, wife of Robert Callant, *d* Feb. 19, 1736, *a* 52.

Martha, second wife of Robert Callant, *d* Sept. 16, 1754, *a* 45.
Robert Callant, *d* Feb. 7, 1764, *a* 72.

Mrs. Elizabeth Brown, *d* April 23, 1833, *a* 60.

William Hills Tanner, *d* Nov. 12, 1720, *a* 74.
Walter Hills Tanner, his brother, *d* Sept 26, 1717, *a* 79.
Elizabeth Hill, wife of Richard Hill, *d* Feb. 10, 1720, *a* 25.
Richard and William Hill, infant sons.
    [This family were Tanners by name and Tanners by trade.]

Thomas Farnes, *d* Nov. 31, 1779, *a* 44.
John Farnes, his son, *d* March 17, 1796, *a* 53.
Sarah Farnes, his wife, *d* April 28, 1805, *a* 85.
Also John and Mary Davey, of this parish.
    [Mr. Farnes was in his day the principal builder in the town, and to his hands
    was entrusted the reconstruction of the roof of the Old Church in 1760.]

Mary, widow of Robert Mackett, *d* Aug. 22, 1786, *a* 83.

Alexander Caldcleugh, Esq., of Broad Green, *d* Jan. 18, 1809, *a* 55.
Elizabeth, his daughter, wife of William Plaskett, Esq., of Old Burlington
    Street, *d* Nov. 24, 1832, *a* 41.
Elizabeth, widow of Alexander Caldcleugh, Esq., *d* Feb. 8, 1835, *a* 67.
    [Mr. Caldcleugh was the last owner of the chancel. He sold it to the parish
    shortly before his death.]

Joseph Williams, citizen and grocer of London, *d* June 5, 1759, *a* 57.

John Harley, gentleman, *d* Jan. 15, 1705, *a* 62.
Mary Harley, his wife, *d* March 7, 1715, *a* 74.

Charles Smith, *d* Nov. 11, 1845, *a* 40.

Charlotte Mary Oswald, 1856.

Elizabeth, relict of James Moulton, gent., *d* Feb. 10, 1772, *a* 67.

Daniel Richard, Esq., of Waddon, *d* Dec., 1743, *a* 82.

Mr. Robert Sulley, *d* March 17, 1835, *a* 56.
Jane, relict of above, *d* April 3, 1843, *a* 66.
Also Alfred Richard and Elizabeth Marshall, *d* Nov., 1832.

Ann Peach, daughter of Hugh and Mary Peach, *d* Oct. 20, 1716, *a* 32.

Thomas Merredew, *d* July 17, 1847, *a* 75.
Elizabeth, his wife, *d* July 7, 1853, *a* 74.

Charlotte Merredew, daughter of John and Sarah Merredew, *d* Feb. 17, 1860 [no age].
John Merredew, *d* Sept 2, 1806, *a* 36.
Eliza, his daughter, *d* Sept. 3, 1823, *a* 21.
Sarah, his wife, *d* Jan. 16, 1826, *a* 63.
Edmund, his son, *d* Sept. 18, 1848, *a* 50.

Christopher Margett. d Oct. 12. 1808, a 68.
Robert Margett, her nephew. d Nov. 13. 1856, a 82.
Sarah, his wife, d May 10. 1856, a 84.
> [Mr. Margett was a greengrocer. and for a number of years occupied the shop
> now belonging to Mr. Browning in Church Street. "Margett's Yard"
> takes its name from him.]

Ann, wife of Thomas Part, d June 24. 1792. a 39.
> Long as the good congenial worth revere,
> As worth departed prompts the gushing tear,
> So long to virtue just and urged by woe,
> For thee, the heart shall grieve, the eye shall flow,
> And whilst by friendship led or grief opprest,
> We tread these limits where thy reliques rest,
> With thy loved image shall thy virtues rise.
> Sooth the keen pang and train us for the skies.

Benjamin Hayward, d Aug. 19. 1816, a 46.
> An affectionate husband.
The eye of him that hath seen me shall see me no more. Thine eyes are
upon me, and I am not.

Also Benjamin. son of the above. A most lovely infant and an only child.
He was taken from his distress'd parents Aug. 24, 1815, a 2 years and
2 months.
> Of such is the Kingdom of Heaven.

Elizabeth, wife of Joshua Hayward. d June 18. 1799, a 37.
Joshua Hayward, her husband, d Dec. 31, 1850. a 93.
> [Grandfather to Mr. Hayward of the Windsor Castle Inn, on the Brighton
> Road.]

Walter Lewen, d Aug. 14, 1781, a 81.
Elizabeth, his wife, d March 9. 1788, a 74.

Ann, daughter of John and Mary Fulker, d April 11. 1826, a 2 years and 8
months.
Mary Fulker, her mother. d April 8, 1847, a 43.
John Fulker, her father. d Nov. 19, 1860. a 65.

Robert Smith, of Streatham. d Feb. 21, 1825, a 63.
Mary Smith, his wife. d Dec. 29. 1853, a 77.
John Smith, d April 26. 1838. a 35.
Robert Smith, d March 16, 1859, a 64.

John Walder, d Feb. 24. 1766, a 34.
Jane, his wife, d Nov. 7, 1817, a 83.
Ann, his daughter, d June 9. 1831.

In memory of Mr. John Harris, an honest man and skilful florist, d Jan. 4,
1811, a 59.
> Fond to admire creation's various powers
> In all the fragrance and the hue of flowers
> He marked their rising from the earthly tomb
> Swell into verdure,—redden into bloom ;
> Die to revive through Nature's wond'rous maze,
> Emblem of man ! the source of holy praise ;
> And now his body in the earth is lain,
> Like them, tho' dead, to rise and bloom again.

Mrs. Ann Brown, d Feb. 19, 1831. a 72.
Mr. Thomas Brown, her husband, d May 24, 1831, a 62.
Elizabeth Ann Brown, d March 28, 1833, a 64.
Mr. Henry Brown, her husband, d May 21, 1843, a 66.

Sarah Chapman, d May 8, 1844, a 51.
James Chapman (her husband), d March 24, 1852, a 80.

Here lies the body of Anna, the loving and beloved wife of Roger Anderson, of London, youngest of the seven sons of William and Bridget Anderson, of this parish. She was daughter of the Rev. Dr. Casson, Rector of Sutton in Herefordshire, and one of the Prebends of Hereford Minster, a great sufferer during the time of Cromwell's usurpation, for his firm adherence to the Church of England, and his loyalty to the royal martyr. She died 19th Jan., 1723, in the 74th year of her age. Finis coronat opus.

Mortis trophæum de corpore Henrici Hoar, medico-chirurgi, qui prisci candoris et humanitatis se exemplum præbuit et plane bonus fuit licet optimis comparetur. xi Februarii obiit, anno salutis MDCCIX, ætatis LXXII. Annis ille senex fuit et candore; sed illum dixerunt omnes non satis esse senem.

[He was married at Gatton, in this county, on the 21st June, 1677, to Jane, eldest daughter of John Hedge, of that place, by whom he had issue two daughters.]

Susan Anderson, d Feb. 19, 1776, a 80.
William Johnson, d Oct. 26, 1776, a 42.
Mary, his wife, d March 13, 1788, a 52.
George Fullick, d May 3, 1808, a 45.
Eliza Fullick, d Sept. 4, 1819, a 92.

William Haydon, d Oct. 8, 1824, a 74.
Amey Haydon, d July 19, 1820, a 64.
Ann, wife of James Haydon, d Feb. 4, 1829, a 45.
James Haydon (her husband), d Jan. 15, 1858, a 76.

Rachel Levens, d Dec. 20, 1744, a 65.
Richard Levens, d Sept. 16, 1748, a 77.

James Chapman, d Feb. 3, 1841, a 47.

In memory of Ursula Swinbourne, who, after fulfilling her duty in that station of life her Creator had allotted her, and by her faithful and affectionate conduct, in a series of 35 years, rendered herself respected and beloved while living, and her loss sincerely regretted by the family she lived with, departed this life the 5th January, 1781, aged 55. Reader, let not a fancied inferiority from her station in life prevent thy regarding her example : but remember according to the number of talents given shall the increase be expected.

Edward Daniel, d May 5, 1782, a 54.
Edward Daniel, d July 22, 1827, a 75.
Elizabeth Daniel, d Oct. 5, 1834, a 71.

John Gray, d Dec. 5, 1841, a 27.

Ann Buckland, wife of Samuel Buckland, d Oct. 31, 1826, a 68.
Samuel Buckland, d Aug. 28, 1805, a 55.

Anthony Matthew, d Nov. 2, 1835, a 63.

Wm. Hancock, d Oct. 3, 1870, a 76.
Mary Hancock, his wife [rest illegible].

John Knight, d June 12, 1766, a 66.

> Afflictions sore long time I bore,
> Physicians was* in vain,
> Till death did seize, and God did please,
> To ease me of my pain.

[This verse is repeated *four* times in the Churchyard and *seven* times in the Cemetery].

---

* This word has been variously mis-spelt ; in some cases the word " where " being used.

Sacred to the memory of Henry Haldane, Esq., Student of Physic, who
departed this life the 28 January, 1810, in the 23 year of his age.

> With manners gentle, and with zealous mind,
> Both formed complete, to benefit mankind ;
> The healing art he sought with keen desire,
> Thro' fume pestiferous, and contagion dire.
> Careless of self, intent on other's case.
> This mortal frame severe disorder seize ;
> Him, fierce cathartic and horrid coughs assail,
> O'er which no skill or science could prevail ;
> Tyrannic Death, who viewed him as a foe.
> Stretch'd forth his dart, and struck the deadly blow :
> Down sank the youth : his earthly part soon lies,
> But to its God, the dismal spirit flies ;
> There placed with Seraphs in the realms above,
> In joy, in peace, in happiness and love ;
> They to his soul all joyous comfort bring,
> While to their God they hallelujah's sing.
> Avaunt ! thou tyrant, where is then thy sting ?

Wm. Brown, gentleman. *d* Nov. 25, 1807, *a* 57.
Mrs. Mary Brown, his mother, *d* Jan. 8, 1816, *a* 94.

Jane, wife of Thomas Weaver, of Park Hill Farm. *d* Jan. 3, 1849, *a* 42.
> The memory of the just is blessed.

Richard Codnor Henley, of Abbotts Kerswell, Devonshire. *d* Sept. 21, 1848,
a 25.

William Hollands, *d* April 10, 1826, *a* 76.
> Forbear, my friends, to weep,
> Since death has lost its sting :
> Those Christians that in Jesus sleep
> Our God will with Him bring.

Francis Merritt, *d* April 11, 1733, *a* 60.
> In this dark bed doth lie,
> A husband dear and so must I.

Mary Ward, *d* Jan. 21, 1823, *a* 73.
Thomas Ward, *d* June, 1789, *a* 71.

George Godsalve, *d* April 1, 1763, *a* 50.
Sarah, his wife, *d* June 21, 1790, *a* 80.
Richard, Sarah, John, and Martha, who died in their minority.
Also, Mrs. Sarah Read, mother of the above, *d* June 28, 1822, *a* 75.
Thomas Read, *d* Sept. 18, 1823, *a* 83.
Sarah Godsalve, widow of Wm. Coward, Esq., of Brixton, *d* June 22, 1849,
a 70.
> [There is a small stone tablet in St. Clement's Church, Hastings, erected to
> the memory of Mr. Coward, who died Sept. 27th, 1823, aged 70.]

Elizabeth Coombes, *d* July 28, 1771, *a* 69.
Thomas Coombes, her son, *d* Oct. 9, 1761, *a* 39.
Elizabeth Coombes, her daughter, *d* Nov. 14, 1775, *a* 48.
William Coombes, another son, *d* Oct. 15, 1794.

John Puzey, *d* June 26, 1833, *a* 40.
> For here we have no continuing city, for we seek one to come.

Thomas, son of Thomas and Mary Mayhew, *d* Jan. 5, 1800, *a* 9.
Mary, his mother, *d* May 10, 1826, *a* 67.

Henry Skinner, *d* Dec. 19, 1842, *a* 75,
Mary Skinner, *d* Oct. 6, 1844, *a* 72.

Hannah, wife of Wm. Thornton, of Waddon, *d* May 24, 1844, *a* 56.
Wm. Thornton, her husband, *d* Nov. 29, 1858, *a* 72.

D

John Henry Cazenove. Esq., of Waddon, *d* Jan. 24, 1817, *a* 80. Universally benevolent, generous, and social, his virtues will live in the remembrance of his grateful relatives who have erected this monument.

George Brooks. *d* June 27, 1852, *a* 31.
Hannah Mary Brooks, his daughter, *d* Sept. 19, 1863, *a* 6.

Mary, beloved wife of Richd. Sanderson, of Norbury House, *d* Sept. 24, 1826, *a* 68.

Richard Sanderson, merchant and citizen of London, *b* at Wigton, in Cumberland, *d* Aug. 20, 1837, *a* 75.

Martha, daughter-in-law of William Higgins, Esq., and sister-in-law of Richd. Sanderson, Esq., *d* Feb. 6, 1820, *a* 58.

West of the Footpath leading to the South Porch.

Mary Anne Bone, *d* May 13, 1826, *a* 38.
Thomas Bone, *d* Nov. 19, 1828, *a* 48.

David Hoar, *d* May 14, 1804, *a* 75.

William John Bodkin, *d* Jan. 28, 1812, *a* 46.
Thomas Bodkin, his son, *d* Jan. 23, 1873, *a* 62.

William Bodkin, *d* May 30, 1798, *a* 65.
Mary, his wife, *d* March 5, 1821, *a* 77.
Mary Elizabeth, wife of Percival Barker, daughter of William Bodkin, *d* July 2, 1816, *a* 47.
   Like her father, she died lamented, and her memory will ever be respected by all who knew her.
Thomas Barker, her son, *d* Oct. 15, 1826, *a* 26.

John Haythorne, *d* Nov. 19, 1760, *a* 48.
Mrs. Hannah Right, *d* Sept. 2, 1778, *a* 64.
Thomas Farnes (late of Waddon), *d* Dec. 12, 1818, *a* 71.
Hannah Farnes, his wife, *d* Jan. 6, 1835, *a* 82.

Sophia, wife of C. W. Farnes, of Waddon, *d* Sept. 4, 1831, *a* 34.
Also Charles Wright Farnes, *d* Nov. 29, 1863, *a* 68.
                    Buried at Forest Hill.

William Budgen, *d* Sept. 21, 1816, *a* 81.
William, his son, died Oct. 31, 1788, *a* 2 years and 4 months.
Mary, his daughter, *d* May 15, 1803, *a* 19.
Thomas, his son, *d* March 1, 1805, *a* 23.
Ann Budgen, his wife [remainder obliterated].

Ann Moore, daughter of Wm. and Ann Budgen, *d* June 6, 1820, *a* 40.
John Moore, her son, *d* Aug. 7, 1820, *a* 11.

Josiah Holdship, *d* Dec. 24, 1833, *a* 37.

Clarissa Cotman, *d* Jan. 26, 1838, *a* 26.
Edward Cotman, her father, *d* Aug. 30, 1840, *a* 68.
   [This gentleman lived opposite the Duke's Head Inn, South End, and died through eating poisonous mushrooms.]

Thomas Berrington, *d* Aug. 8, 1840, *a* 51.
Mary, wife of Francis Berrington, *d* July 19, 1868, *a* 71.
Francis Berrington, *d* Nov. 22, 1857, *a* 71.
William Berrington, *d* Dec. 28, 1864, *a* 73.
Susan, his wife, *d* Dec. 7, 1866, *a* 72.
   [Mr. Thomas Berrington was a butcher residing near the top of Crown Hill.]
The Manns, the Berringtons, and the Streeters, were for many years the principal butchers in the town.

Robert Thornton, of Waddon, *d* May 22, 1837, *a* 78.
Eliza Thornton, *d* March 18, 1850, *a* 88.

Anne, wife of James Slarke, clerk, *d* July 13, 1826, *a* 54.
> The subscribers to the National Girl's School established in this place, of which she was the exemplary and useful mistress for upwards of 20 years, have erected this stone as a mark of their approbation, and a public testimony of her worth.

James Slarke, her husband, *d* Oct. 16, 1843, *a* 73.

William Tegg, *d* Aug. 14, 1792, *a* 43.

Isaac Wheeler, *d* June 26, 1789, *a* 33.
Mary Costin, his wife, *d* Nov. 29, 1821, *a* 73.

1272537

William White, late of Duppas Hill, bricklayer, *d* Aug 23, 1837, *a* 90.
> Earth walks upon Earth like glittering gold,
> Earth says to Earth we are but mould,
> Earth builds upon Earth, castles and towers,
> Earth says to Earth, all is ours.

Sarah, wife of James White, bricklayer, *d* Jan. 17, 1854, *a* 60.
> Lament we may for those that were dear to us, but not as without hope, even Jesus wept at the death of Lazarus.

Over a vault.—James Overton, *d* May 15, 1831, *a* 66.
Ann Overton, his wife, *d* June 14, 1835, *a* 74.
William Overton, grandson, *d* Sept. 27, 1835, *a* 2 years 6 weeks.
Henry James Overton, grandson, *a* 22.
Mary, wife of Henry Overton, *d* March 5, 1844, *a* 47.
George Thomas, her son, *d* April 12, 1860, *a* 28.
Henry Overton, *d* Jan. 11, 1864, *a* 74.

> Mr. Henry Overton, a self-made man, was an old inhabitant, who was well known and highly respected. He was a thorough John Bull—warm-hearted, rich, and generous— and he possessed considerable skill as an engineer and a mechanic. He not only built his own brewery, but also built up a good connection with it. He was a very enterprising and public spirited man. In proof of this it may be mentioned that he purchased the original gas works from the proprietors, and conducted them profitably for some years. In 1847, however, the works becoming too extensive for the grasp of one individual, the present company was formed, and in 1859, the works were removed from Overton's Yard to their present site, at Waddon Marsh.

William Creswick, *d* March 10, 1857, *a* 85.
Mary, his wife, *d* Sept. 21, 1827, *a* 54.
Gideon, their son, *d* Nov. 4, 1801, *a* 26.
John, another son, *d* Oct. 2, 1809, *a* 27.
> [Mr. Wm. Creswick was an old ringer, and when he died a dumb peal was rang.]

Charles Girling, licensed victualler (Dog and Bull Inn), *d* Aug. 8, 1833, *a* 47.
Charles, his son, *d* Dec. 24th, 1827, *a* 6 years.
Henry Pembridge, another son, *d* Dec. 24, 1827, *a* 5 years.

William Wood, *d* Feb. 19, 1792, *a* 36.
John Clarke, *d* March 3, 1819.

Thomas Burgess, *d* July 18, 1837, *a* 54.
> This stone was erected by his master in grateful recollection of twenty years faithful service.

Thomas Burgess, his son, *d* Dec. 29, 1858, *a* 30.

Mary Anna, wife of Thomas Overton, *d* Nov. 15, 1826, *a* 37.
Thomas Overton, *d* Oct. 22, 1846, *a* 55.
Jane, their daughter, *d* April 26, 1829, *a* 2 months.

Isaac Pratt, *d* Sept. 29, 1839, *a* 29.

Joanna, wife of Joseph Cook, *d* April 15, 1832, *a* 77.
Joseph Cook, *d* Jan. 18, 1834, *a* 77.
William Cook, their son, *d* Dec. 24, 1825, *a* 41.

James, son of James and Mary Mayhew, *d* Sept. 1, 1847, *a* 19.
James Mayhew, *d* Aug. 15, 1853, *a* 70.
> [Formerly landlord of the Royal Oak Inn.]

Hannah, widow of the Rev. John Smith, rector of Carlton, in Norfolk, *d* April 6, 1794, *a* 90.
Paulina Smith, her daughter, *d* Jan. 15, 1813, *a* 78.

Rebecca Simmons, wife of Francis Simmons, *d* Nov. 12, 1818, *a* 40.
Francis Simmons, her son, *d* in infancy.
Ann, her daughter, wife of Jas. Hendred, *d* Nov. 29, 1826, *a* 26.
Jas. Francis Hendred, *d* in infancy.
Francis Simmons, *d* Aug. 11, 1833, *a* 58.

John Norman, sexton of this parish upwards of 36 years, *d* March 27, 1803. *a* 72.
Mary Ann Norman, his wife, *d* Aug. 9, 1832, *a* 92.

Mr. John Burchett, *d* Jan. 7, 1826, *a* 89.

Harriet Fanny, daughter of Fredk and Mary Wagner, *d* May 9, 1810, *a* 3½ years.
> We trust thou'rt gone before
> To bloom, and praise, and to adore
> Thy God, our Saviour and our Friend,
> Who will protect such to the end.

Sarah, wife of William Wickens, *d* June 6, 1814, *a* 56.
Elizabeth Wickens, his second wife, *d* May 12, 1824, *a* 57,

Mrs. Ann Parish, *d* Jan. 3, 1823, *a* 58.
George Wenham, *d* Sept. 2, 1839, *a* 12.
> Grace 'tis a charming sound,
> Harmonious to the ear,
> Heaven with the echo shall resound,
> And all the earth shall hear.

Elizabeth, wife of Henry Mascall, *d* Oct. 21, 1828, *a* 75.
Fanny, his second wife, *d* Jan. 6, 1832, *a* 51.
Henry Mascall, *d* Oct. 22, 1835, *a* 72.

Sophia, wife of James Tidy, *d* July 17, 1820, *a* 36.
Sophia, her daughter, *d* Dec. 26, 1824, *a* 5.
James Tidy, her husband, *d* Sept. 12, 1832, *a* 45.

Mrs. Mary Keates, *d* Oct. 19, 1830, *a* 29.
Mary, infant daughter, *d* Oct. 23, 1830.

Thomas Turner, *d* July 6, 1811, *a* 44.
Sarah, her daughter, *d* April 20, 1830, *a* 36.
Sarah, his wife, *d* June 3, 1828, *a* 63.
> Here cloathed in peace, may her dear ashes rest,
> Who suffered sore with heavy pains opprest,
> Who always was a true and faithful friend,
> Remaining good and perfect to the end.

Mary Ann Churcher, of Thornton Heath, *d* March 13, 1837, *a* 64.
John Churcher, her husband, *d* May 15, 1838, *a* 65.
Both deeply regretted.

George Couchman, *d* December. 30, 1832, *a* 71.
Elizabeth Couchman, *d* Jan. 12, 1838, *a* 77.

Sarah Couchman, *d* Nov. 28, 1841, *a* 41.
Thomas B. Thirkel, her grandson, *d* Aug. 5, 1846, *a* 2.

James Thomas Page, eldest son of Jasper and Martha Page, *d* May 11, 1820, *a* 22.

> A youth is laid beneath this stone,
> Death nipped the bud, the blossom's gone,
> Be still each parent's sighing heart,
> Time is but short that we shall part,
> When we again in glory meet,
> 'Twill turn past bitters all to sweet.

Edward Jasper Page, *d* Dec. 29, 1851, *a* 17.
Martha Deborah, eldest child of Henry Tyson and Martha Dale, *d* March, 26, 1861, *a* 3.

Jasper Page, *d* Aug 29, 1814, *a* 41.

> Alas, a husband, father, brother, friend,
> Ah, one who all these names so well deserved,
> Lies here entombed, his pains are at end,
> Then why lament, since Heaven hath him preferred.

Martha Page, widow, *d* Oct. 10, 1855, *a* 80.
Also 4 of her children.

Benjamin Ives, *d* May 18, 1811, *a* 27.

> Death little warning to me gave,
> And quickly brought me to my grave,
> I from my friends did quickly part
> And lost my life by horse and cart.

John Fisher, *d* Dec. 27, 1838, *d* 66.
Sarah Fisher, *d* June 10, 1843, *a* 74.

Sarah, wife of James Paine, *d* May 4, 1748, *a* 31.
James Paine, *d* June 13, 1757, *a* 77.

Mary, wife of Wm. Page, of Purley Cottage, *d* Dec, 21, 1847, *a* 78.'

Jane, wife of Joseph Lynn, of Chelsea Hospital, *d* Oct, 17, 1820, *a* 45.
She was a truly pious and charitable woman.

Robert Rice Lynn, her son, *d* March 12, 1838, *a* 42.
Elizabeth, sister to Joseph Lynn, *d* Oct. 24, 1844.

Wm. Lynn, *d* March, 1770, *a* 61.
Jane, his wife, *d* May, 1801, *a* 84.
Father and mother of Mrs. Williams and Mrs. Coates.

James Dabner, *d* Aug. 29, 1834, *a* 77.

Elizabeth Elliott, *d* Jan. 17, 1833, *a* 41.

William Filby, *d* May 23, 1810, *a* 81.
Ann Filby, his wife, *d* Dec. 17, 1815, *a* 80.

Thomas Morris, late of St. Andrew's Undershaft, London, *d* Jan, 23, 1837, *a* 46.

Thomas Creasey, *d* July 23, 1844, *a* 28.

George Soan, *d* Feb. 8, 1820, *a* 83.
Elizabeth Soan, his wife, *d* Aug. 11, 1829, *a* 86.
John Soan, *d* Jan. 14, 1833, *a* 64.
Elizabeth, his wife, *d* Sept. 20, 1826, *a* 62.

Joseph Porter, *d* July 16, 1834, *a* 69.
> A lingering sickness did me seize.
> No physician could me ease,
> I sought for means but all in vain,
> Till God did ease me of my pain.

Ann Porter, his wife, *d* Dec. 24, 1850, *a* 70.

James Cross, *d* Dec. 17, 1845, *a* 36.
Matilda, his daughter, *d* Dec. 31, 1845, *a* 19 days.
Charles James, his son, *d* April 15, 1858, *a* 14.

Jane Hiscock, wife of John Hiscock, *d* May 2, 1824, *a* 73.
John Hiscock, her husband, *d* April 11, 1823, *a* 64.
> Know, O Reader, his departure was sudden, therefore be ye ready, for in such
> an hour as ye think not, the final summons cometh.

> [Mr. Hiscock was one of the last of the private brewers. He kept the Globe,
> in the Old Town.]

Richard Smith, *d* Aug. 23, 1832, *a* 38.
Mary Ann, his daughter, *d* July 24, 1827, *a* 3.
Ann, his daughter, *d* Oct. 8, 1833, *a* 16.
Richard, his son, *d* June 4, 1847.

Ann, wife of George Clifford, *d* June 18, 1809, *a* 32.
George Clifford, *d* Dec. 7, 1810, *a* 67.
Ann, wife of George Clifford, *d* Jan. 16, 1838.

The following are the inscriptions on the East (chancel) end of the Churchyard.

John Ebbutt, *d* Feb. 3, 1813, *a* 66.
Ann, his wife, *d* Sept. 18, 1814, *a* 58.
Thomas Ebbutt, his son, *d* Sept. 1, 1832, *a* 41.
Abi, his wife, *d* July 22, 1851, *a* 60.
> [John Ebbutt was grandfather of Mr. A. C. Ebbutt, upholsterer, of 20 and 24,
> High Street.   Thomas Ebbutt was his uncle.]

Mrs. Susanna Blake, Sept. 3, 1811, *a* 21.
William Blake, her husband, *d* April 15, 1842, *a* 64.
Hester, second wife of Wm. Blake, *d* March 5, 1852.
> [Mr. Blake caused a stained glass window to be erected in the Old Church, to
> the memory of his uncle.]

Thomas Blake, builder, *d* Aug. 10, 1830, *a* 88.
Mrs. Elizabeth Alcorn, his sister, *d* May 2, 1823, *a* 81.

Robert Henry, son of Nicholas and Mary Jayne, of the Crown Inn, *d* Feb.
   24, 1832, *a* 10.
Richard Henry Williams, their nephew, *d* Sept. 20, 1832, *a* 21.
Nicholas Jayne, *d* Nov. 15, 1847, *a* 65.
> [Ancestor of Messrs. J. B. and F. N. Jayne.]

Richard James Jones, *d* July 27, 1837, *a* 71.

Hiram Matthews, *d* May 16, 1834, *a* 40.

Elizabeth Molineux, *d* March 7, 1842, *a* 59.
Thomas Molineux, *d* April 19, 1845, *a* 55.
> [Formerly an architect residing in High Street.]

John Morrison, late of the Isle of Madeira, merchant, *d* April 17, 1824,
   a 55,

William Woolnough. *d* June 21, 1832. *a* 50.
Charlotte. his wife. *d* May 21. 1828.
Augusta Mary, second daughter. *d* Oct. 24. 1856. *a* 40.

This gentleman was agent or clerk to the Croydon Canal Company, who were the principal carriers in Croydon, and conveyed nearly all the heavy goods in barges to the Thames, consisting of stone. lime. Fuller's earth, and timber. bringing back as a return freight. coals and other heavy goods for the town and neighbourhood. The canal was about ten miles in length. with numerous locks and two reservoirs. one at Forest Hill (now utilised for other purposes). and the other at Norwood. which may still be seen on the left hand side of the Crystal Palace Railway. The canal was an immense source of amusement to the inhabitants, for in summer there was the pleasure of boating. fishing. and bathing, and in winter the delightful exercise of skating.

George Champniss, *d* Feb. 21. 1825, *a* 53.
A good husband. a fond father. and an honest man.
[For many years landlord of the Swan and Sugar Loaf. South End.]

Mrs. Mary Champniss. *d* July 25. 1826. *a* 52.

James Moody. *d* March 23. 1826. *a* 40.
Sarah. his wife, *d* July 6. 1832. *a* 50.

Sarah Kirton. *d* Aug.. 2. 1834. *a* 19.
Jane Charlotte Maria, daughter of Wm. and Sarah Taylor. *d* Aug. 21, 1845, *a* 18.
William Taylor, *d* May 18. 1849. *a* 74.

Mrs. Comfort Shaw. *d* March 8. 1836. *a* 26.

William Wildgoose. *d* June 22. 1818. *a* 72.

Sarah Long. wife of Giles Long. *d* Jan. 26. 1833. *a* 76.
Giles Long. *d* Dec. 26. 1831. *a* 81.
Elizabeth. their grand child. *d* Dec. 2. 1844. *a* 21.
Giles. son of Giles and Frances Long. *d* May 8. 1848. *a* 18.
Sarah Long. his sister. *d* Oct. 1, 1851, *a* 19.
Ann Long. his sister. *d* June 8. 1852. *a* 24.
Emily Charlotte, daughter of William and Mary Long. *d* Dec. 6. 1852, *a* 19.
Mary. wife of William Long. *d* Oct. 22. 1854. *a* 59.
John Frederick, her son. *d* April 11. 1857. *a* 20.
Frances Long. wife of Giles Long. *d* March 6. 1871. *a* 71.
Giles Long. her husband, *d* June 18. 1881. *a* 81.
[Late coal merchant. of East Croydon Station.]

Susan Cazalet. daughter of Wm. and Mary Cazalet. of Austin Friars, *d* May 14. 1825. *a* 51.
Maria, her sister. *d* March 4, 1827. *a* 44.
Sarah. her sister. *d* Sept. 16. 1836. *a* 60.
Mary Cazalet, *d* Sept. 15, 1840. *a* 68.

Sophia, eldest daughter of the Rev. J. L. Chirol, *b* 1806, *d* 1825.
This damsel is not dead but sleepeth.

Rev. J. L. Chirol, one of Her Majesty's Chaplains. *b* 1765, *d* 1837,

Elizabeth, wife of Wm. West, *d* Oct. 22. 1846. *a* 42.
Emily. her daughter, *d* Aug. 6. 1838. *a* 1 year 8 months.

Reuben, fifth son of Robert and Mary Godfrey, d June 29, 1826, a 19.
Jane, his sister, d April 11, 1839, a 32.
Catharine Taylor Godfrey, d Oct. 10, 1851, a 37.

Thomas Stunnell, d Jan. 23, 1840, a 55.
Robert Godfrey, d July 18, 1850, a 89.
Mary, his wife, d Jan. 31, 1859, a 84.
[Formerly master of the Workhouse.]

Mrs. Elizabeth Bance, d April 5, 1819, a 80.
Judith, wife of Wm. Bance, d April 23, 1817, a 61.

Samuel Davis, Esq., d June 16, 1819, a 59.
Frances, his fifth daughter, d Feb. 5, 1853, a 80.
Frances, daughter of Samuel and Henrietta Davis, d May 10, 1828, a 18.
Anne, sister of Samuel Davis, Esq., d Feb. 18, 1833, a 75.
   [In the Old Church there was a stained glass window erected to this gentleman's
      memory.   He resided at Birdhurst.]

Mrs. Tryphina Smith, wife of Robert Smith, d Sept. 19, 1818, a 24.
Mrs. Sarah Jeffries, his mother, d May 19, 1828, a 72.
Mrs. Jane Smith, his second wife, d Oct. 9, 1853, a 34.
Elizabeth, her daughter, d May 4, 1837, a 11.
Sarah Ann, daughter of George and Martha Smith, d Feb. 22, 1851, a 10.
Martha, wife of Geo. Wm. Smith, d April 11, 1858, a 42.
         A kind affectionate wife and tender mother.

Eleanor Streeter, d Feb. 28, 1816, a 14 years.
John Shove, d Dec. 20, 1818, a 2 years.
William Streeter, his brother, d Oct. 18, 1826, a 35.
John Streeter, d Sept. 17, 1837, a 75.
Elizabeth Streeter, d June 22, 1838, a 73.
Henry, their son, d Jan. 1, 1841, a 46.

Mrs. Mary Haines, wife of John Haines, d Aug. 18, 1815, a 62.
John Haines, d Sept. 10, 1830, a 76.
Elizabeth Haines, d Dec. 19, 1853, a 61.

Henry Bance, d Jan. 25, 1821, a 53.
Mary, his wife, d Nov. 15, 1826, a 58.
         A kind affectionate wife and tender mother.
   [Mr. Bance was a builder, residing in High Street, nearly opposite to the
      Town Hall.]

William Chatfield, Esq., d May 30, 1821, a 65.
Mary Chatfield, his wife, d July 19, 1821, a 65.
Charles Chatfield, Esq., their youngest son, d Nov. 23, 1876, a 77.
James Chatfield, Esq., of the Hon. E. I. Co.'s Civil Service, Madras, d
      March 5, 1813, a 29.
   [Mr. Charles Chatfield was formerly a wine merchant, in High Street (now
      G. Price & Son), and resided for many years at Broad Green House,
      London Road.]

William Chatfield, jun., Captain 1st. Regt. Madras Cavalry, died in India,
      Aug. 10, 1820, a 37.
George Chatfield, Esq., d Jan. 16, 1819, a 29.
Mary, his sister, d Oct. 23, 1844, a 58.

Frances, wife of John Chaloner, d Jan. 14, 1844, a 34.
            Tho' lost to sight to cherished memory dear,
            A beloved Wife and Mother sleepeth here ;
            For fifteen years the sad affliction bore,
            Her hopes in Heaven, a rich reward in store.
   [Mr. Chaloner was for many years coachman to the late Thomas Keen, Esq.,
      father to Baroness Heath.]

George Butt, *d* April 18, 1831, *a* 64.
Ann Fenner, his wife, *d* Aug. 16, 1853, *a* 72.
  [Mr. Butt was a dairyman living in Duppas Hill Lane; after his death his
    widow married again to a person named Fenner.]

Richard Siggars, *d* May 2, 1835, *a* 15.
Martha Haines, *d* Nov. 11, 1858, *a* 56.

Timothy Harding, *d* Jan. 13, 1825, *a* 76.
Ann Harding, his wife, *d* Jan. 3, 1840, *a* 76.
  Timothy Harding was the earliest printer in Croydon. He was
    also a bookseller and stationer, and kept a circulating
    library filled with the trashiest novels and romances of the
    day, and we are informed that his office was one of the
    smallest, his types the most old-fashioned, and his little
    press the most primitive. He kept one journeyman, on
    engaging whom, it was always made a *sine qua non*
    that he should fill up his spare time by working in the
    garden. In those days, as may be imagined, there were few
    inhabitants, and but little printing was required, and Mr.
    Harding's business consisted chiefly in printing the play-
    bills for old Beverley, manager of the Theatre, the
    summonses and other forms for the Court of Requests,
    and, on rare occasions, a little bill and lesser catalogue for
    an auctioneer. On one occasion the old gentleman indulged
    his fancy by writing, printing, and illustrating a little
    brochure, entitled the " Beauties of Sanderstead," which
    had a frontispiece (executed on wood) representing a lady,
    in deep distress, reclining by a weeping willow over a tomb
    in a churchyard. It will thus be seen that Mr. Harding
    was not only an author and printer, but illustrator of his
    own little work, and it is doubtful whether any of his
    successors possess such a combination of talents. Old
    Mr. Harding was quite a character. He was very taciturn,
    took snuff, and was somewhat Pickwickian in appearance.
    His dress always consisted of nankeen breeches and white
    stockings, low shoes, light vest, and dark coat, and he
    might be seen at any time of the day standing on the
    upper step of his front door,* looking at passers-by either
    under or through his spectacles.

Mary, wife of H. W. Looker, Esq., *d* Sept. 17, 1819, *a* 45.
  Let me live the life and die the death of the righteous,
  O let my latter end and future state be like hers.

William, son of Wm. and Elizabeth Smith, *d* Jan. 8, 1845, *a* 29.
Sarah Sylvia, wife of George Kemp, baker, *d* Aug. 28, 1850, 23.

Susanna, wife Mr. Richd. Scott, *d* March 10, 1849, *a* 59.

Thomas Page, *d* March 2, 1849, *a* 64.
  Also three children died in their infancy.
  Why should we lament that our little ones are crowned with victory.

Edith Harriet Page, *d* June 12, 1871, *a* 79.

Mrs. Jane Gruaz, *d* June 18, 1844, *a* 87.
Comfort Master Page, *d* June 23, 1868, *a* 57.

---

*Now Mrs. Dempster's, 110, High Street.

Benjamin Chrees, d Aug. 7, 1818, a 56.
Mary, his widow, d Sept. 4, 1841, a 80.
John Chrees, his son, d April 18, 1866, a 64.

John Chrees ("Johnny" he was called) was the son of a well-to-do glover in London, but we are not aware whether he succeeded to his father's business. If he did, it must have been for a short time, for he was continually in Croydon. He was very gentlemanly in his manner, and was always well dressed, and no doubt the cut of his clothes and the canary-coloured gloves which he sported, were the envy of the young gentlemen of the period. Like his namesake, Johnny Gilpin, he was a "citizen of famous London town." He was also a *bon vivant*, and was in the habit of telling amusing stories to his friends about the Corporation Luncheons and Dinners, and of the fun and pleasure he had when he went swan-hopping with a merry party up the Thames. We believe that he was a mason, but we know that he was a back-bone Conservative, and at election times when the committees met at the Greyhound,—

> "In and out through the motley rout
> The little man kept hopping about."

now running to the printer with copy, and anon hunting up a voter; at these stirring times he occasionally wrote and said some smart things. But, alas! for our old friend, "a change somehow came o'er the spirit of his dream." Fortune seemed suddenly to forsake him, but his friends— his first cousins were Messrs. John and Wm. Drummond— never did, and in his old age he always received the same amount of respect that he was accustomed to in his palmy days.

Charles Thompson, d March 6, 1818, a 71.
Mary, his wife, d July 13, 1834, a 83.
Mary Ann Thomson, her daughter, d Oct. 8, 1853, a 76.
Charles Pratt Thomson, her son, d Oct. 21, 1857, a 75.

Mary, wife of Cooke Webster, d April 9, 1818, a 25.
Elizabeth, his second wife, d April 17, 1832, a 27.
Cooke Webster, d Dec. 15, 1839, a 51.

Nicholas Dundas Anderson, d Aug. 29, 1818, a 16.
[This young man was drowned while bathing in the pond or canal made on the grounds of Addiscombe Military Seminary, and used by the cadets in the preparation of their military works. The canal has long been filled in.]

Janet, wife of Joshua Ryle, Esq., d Feb. 23, 1828, a 35.
Joshua Ryle, d May 14, 1828, a 42.

George Smith, d May 12, 1820, a 65.
Mary, his wife, d Jan. 25, 1837, a 73.
George, his son, d Feb. 10, 1831, a 41.
Thomas Smith, d Sept. 10, 1831, a 43.
Robert Smith, d. Dec. 26, 1819, a 22.
Matilda Ann Bain, d Feb. 27, 1837, a 24.
Mary Ann Inkpen, d March 31, 1832, a 13.

Emma, wife of James King, d Nov. 11, 1865, a 54.

David Thomas, *d* April 20, 1817, *a* 30.

Sarah, wife of T. H. Thomas, son of the above, died at Antigua, West
Indies, Aug. 30, 1840, *a* 29.

Ann Elizabeth Ida, her daughter, *d* Nov. 8, 1838, *a* 1 yr. 9 mths.

Edward Champniss, son of George and Mary Champniss, *d* Jan. 27, 1821,
a 11.

> When the fatal trump shall sound,
> When the immortals pour around,
> Heaven shall thy return attest,
> Hail'd by myriads of the blest.

Mary Champniss, his sister, *d* Nov. 1822, after an illness of two days, *a* 15.

Joyse Field, *d* Jan. 6, 1829, *a* 76.

John Field, *d* March 22, 1830, *a* 85.

Hannah Field, *d* Nov. 3, 1848, *a* 64.

Thomas Field, her husband, *d* Jan. 8, 1858, *a* 78.

> [Mr. Thomas Field left £50 to the poor of the parish of Croydon, which was
> distributed by the Churchwardens shortly after his death.]

Thomas Elias, son of Thomas and Mary Corker, *d* April 14, 1819, *a* 1 year
5 months.

Amelia Elizabeth, his sister, *d* May 1, 1831, *a* 10.

Mary, his sister, *d* Oct. 7, 1841, *a* 16.

> God will redeem my soul from the power of the grave, for he will receive me.

Mary Ann Paine, *d* Sept. 22, 1846, *a* 39.

Mary Ann, wife of Thomas Paine, *d* Jan. 3, 1849, *a* 70.

Harriot, daughter of Abraham Burnett, *d* May 21, 1819, *a* 17.

Mary, her sister, *d* April 23, 1821, *a* 9.

Abraham Burnett, *d* Nov. 21, 1844, *a* 71.

William Burnett, *d* March 15, 1836, *a* 30.

Wm. Brown, *d* Oct. 24, 1825, *a* 59.

Margaret, his wife, *d* Feb. 12, 1829, *a* 74.

> [Abraham Burnett was a farmer, and tenanted a farm called Fox Farm in
> Selsdon Lane. He formerly lived in an old house which occupied the
> site of the present theatre, to which access was obtained by going
> down three or four steps.]

Rebecca King, *d* April 27, 1832, *a* 31.

Elizabeth Hardy, her sister, *d* Dec. 12, 1860, *a* 52.

John Cope, *d* June 26, 1825, *a* 77.

Elizabeth, his wife, *d* Jan. 16, 1828, *a* 79.

Thomas Turner, *d* Feb. 12, 1829, *a* 58.

Mrs. Christian Turner, his wife *d* June 30, 1849, *a* 82.

James Turner, her son, *d* April 3, 1860, *a* 67.

William Turner, veterinary student, *d* Jan. 21, 1828, *a* 23.

> After lingering a year and nine months from dissecting a diseased animal,
> beloved and lamented by all who knew him.

Robert Marshall, *d* July 25, 1839, *a* 46.

Mary Marshall, his wife, *d* April 14, 1860, *a* 65.

> [Mr. Marshall was landlord of the Blue Anchor, South End. The house was
> managed by his widow for many years after his death.]

Elizabeth Simmons, *d* Dec. 28, 1836, *a* 61.

Richard, her husband, *d* Nov. 8, 1851, *a* 72.

Sarah, his daughter, *d* Sept. 29, 1819, *a* 21.

Eliza, another daughter, *d* Aug. 21, 1835, *a* 23.

Mrs. Mary Hall, *d* Feb. 12, 1820, *a* 82.

Mrs. Jane Hall, *d* Nov. 1, 1822, *a* 62.

Mrs. Anne Hall, *d* March 1, 1845, *a* 95.

Rebecca Knapp, *d* July 2, 1819, *a* 42.
Wm. Jerome Knapp, her nephew, *d* Oct. 23, 1821, *a* 12.
Sarah Anne Knapp, *d* Oct. 13, 1818, *a* 54.

Daniel William, son of Wm. and S. Johnson, *d* June 12, 1817, *a* 7½ years.
Sarah, his mother, *d* Nov. 26, 1847, *a* 68.

Richard Ray, *d* May 29, 1818, *a* 36.
Edward Ray, *d* Dec. 19, 1841, *a* 33.
Mary Amoore, his grandmother, *d* Sept. 25, 1850, *a* 88.
Mary, widow of Richard Ray, *d* April 17, 1850, *a* 68.

    [The Rays were plumbers and glaziers. They had shops in High Street and
      South End.]

Edward Ray, *d* Jan. 24, 1817, *a* 59.
Susanna Stevens Fidler, his daughter, *d* Nov. 14, 1818, *a* 33.
Susanna Ray, his widow, *d* Nov. 11, 1822, *a* 67.
Mary Ann Ray, her daughter, *d* Sept. 13, 1852.

Wm. Trask, *d* April 10, 1846, *a* 63.

Mrs. Mary Hullett, *d* Nov. 16, 1848, *a* 67, widow of William Hullett,
    Minister of the Philadelphian Chapel, Plymouth, who *d* Feb. 8, 1818,
    a 57.

Mary, wife of Henry Stagg, grocer, *d* April 25, 1841, *a* 39.
Mary Churchill, her mother, *d* July 21, 1844, *a* 83.

Jane Dodd, *d* May 2, 1861, *a* 69.
> Let this vain world engage no more,
>   Behold the gaping tomb,
> It bids us seize the present hour,
>   To-morrow death may come.
> The voice of this alarming scene,
>   May every heart obey,
> Nor be the heavenly warning vain,
>   Which calls to watch and pray.

George Dodd, her husband, *d* March 1, 1864, *a* 71.
    [The deceased was a bricklayer in Handcroft Road.]

John Dennis, *d* Oct. 13, 1818, *a* 55.
Mary Dennis, his wife, *d* Feb. 12, 1855, *a* 85.

George Skinner, *d* May 2, 1822, *a* 21.
William Skinner, *d* June 10, 1835, *a* 38.
John Skinner, *d* Oct. 31, 1843, *a* 45.
Jeremiah Skinner, *d* Nov. 24, 1845, *a* 42.

    [John Skinner met with his death in a somewhat singular manner. He was at
      work on a haystack on Haling Park Farm, and fell therefrom; the
      prong of a fork ran into his thigh, from the effects of which wound he
      died.]

John Skinner, *d* July 10, 1817, *a* 54.
Ruth Skinner, his wife, *d* Aug. 24, 1852, *a* 82.

Mary Ann Buzin, *d* Nov. 10, 1817, *a* 48.

Henry Hibbitt, *d* March 23, 1810, *a* 54.
Ann, his daughter, *d* July 23, 1819, *a* 30.

Sarah Unstead, *d* June 25, 1835, *a* 75.
Wm. Unstead, her husband, *d* Oct. 30, 1838, *a* 77.

Thomas Herring, *d* Feb. 28, 1845, *a* 40.
    [Thomas Herring kept the Royal Oak Inn, Surrey Street; his widow succeeded
      him.]

David Skene, Esq., formerly a merchant in London, *d* March 9, 1817, *a* 58.
> This stone is erected by his brother George Skene, Esq., of Skene, in Aberdeenshire, and the family, as a small tribute of respect and acknowledgment of his scientific abilities.

Joel Turner, mason, *d* Aug. 23, 1819, *a* 55.
Ruth, his wife, *d* Jan. 15, 1824, *a* 58.
George, his son, *d* July 7, 1840, *a* 50.
Edward Markby, *d* Feb. 16, 1814, *a* 29.
William Markby, *d* Dec. 23, 1823.
Elizabeth Markby, their mother, *d* Nov. 7, 1835, *a* 76.
Mary Ann Markby, *d* Nov. 3, 1849, *a* 56.
Mrs. Mary Markby, *d* March 22, 1813, *a* 72.
James Markby, *d* Nov. 30, 1822, *a* 69.
Frederick Markby, *d* May 21, 1833.
> [The Markbys were stationers and had a shop at the entrance of Park Street High Street.]

William, son of Francis Potter, *d* May 12, 1843, *a* 31.
Francis, his brother, *d* Sept. 16, 1849, *a* 27.
Sarah, wife of John Potter, *d* March 15, 1843, *a* 27.
Alfred Charles, son of Charles Potter, *d* April 1856, *a* 2.
> [The Potters were fellmongers in Surrey Street, down what is now called Fellmonger's Lane.]

John Grantham, Esq., *d* Jan. 9, 1814, *a* 66.
Elizabeth, his widow, *d* Aug. 5, 1137, *a* 87.
> [This gentleman was a surveyor and land agent.]

William Musgrove, *d* June 24, 1813, *a* 53.
Elizabeth Smith, *d* Jan. 4, 1822, *a* 51.
Edward, her husband, *d* May 17, 1830, *a* 68.

Samuel Hemmans, late of Chatham Dockyard, *d* June 14, 1819, *a* 74.
Ann, his widow, *d* Oct. 22, 1833, *a* 81.
Susannah Hinton, her sister, *d* Dec. 18, 1845, *a* 85.
Samuel Hood Hemmans, Lieut. R.N., *d* at Ceylon, May 2, 1854, *a* 62.
Mary Eliza Hemmans, *d* Feb. 15, 1872, *a* 81.
Thos. Hinton Hemmans, Lieut.-Colonel, *d* Nov. 17, 1873, *a* 79.
Ann Hemmans, *d* April 1, 1875, *a* 75.
> The Hemmans family originally came from Mitcham; they had a brewery, now pulled down, at Lower Mitcham. In 1820, Wm. Hood Hemman was Churchwarden of that parish, and his name is cast on one of the bells. The tombstones, from which these inscriptions are taken, have lately been replaced by new stones, probably by some members of the family.

Lieut.-General Francis Grose, *d* May 8, 1814, *a* 56.
Rev. Francis Devis Grose, his son, *d* Dec. 2, 1817, *a* 28.
Mrs. Fanny Grose, wife of Lieut.-General Grose, who having suffered with great patience and resignation a most painful illness for 18 months, *d* Jan. 12, 1813, *a* 46.
> Behold the bricks and mortar cover,
> The best of wives, the kindest mother.

> [General Grose occupied a mansion, called Limes House, on the Whitehorse Road. The house has been pulled down, and the grounds attached thereto are now built upon.]

Thomas Head, *d* Dec. 17, 1840, *a* 58.
Mary, his wife, *d* May 8, 1848, *a* 65, and 7 children.

Elizabeth Rood, widow, after an illness of 5 years, *d* June 1, 1839, *a* 70.

Richard Turner, d Nov. 26, 1828, a 56.
William Mitchell Wood, d Oct. 19, 1845, a 45.

Maria, wife of James Clark, d Jan. 13, 1839, a 54.
> It is not well or wise,
> To mourn for thee with endless pain,
> There is a better world above the skies,
> Where we hope to meet again.

Henry Graham, d July 25, 1826, a 22.
George Graham, his father, d Nov. 7, 1826, a 54.
Eleanor Butcher, his daughter, d Oct. 14, 1841.

Richard Virgoe, d June 24, 1844, a 73.
Elizabeth, his wife, d July 27, 1848, a 76.
> To God I cried, who to my help
> Did graciously repair,
> In trouble's dismal day I sought,
> My God with humble prayer.

Elizabeth Hotchkiss, d Dec. 31, 1850, a 84.
James, her husband, d Jan. 2, 1851, a 79.

Edward Lulham, Esq., d Nov. 22, 1840, a 60.

William Basingwhite, d May 21, 1857, a 74.
Mary Ann, his wife, d June 24, 1874, a 84.
Mary Ann, his daughter, d Oct. 13, 1834, a 20.

Richard Allingham, d March 27, 1818, a 10.
> Oh, when fair youth that every promise gave,
> Sheds its sweet blossom in the lasting grave,
> Our eyes o'erflow with many a streaming tear,
> And each sad bosom heaves a sigh sincere.

Elizabeth, his sister, d April 10, 1826, a 11.
Anne, his sister, d Feb. 5, 1831, a 17.
William, his brother, d May 21, 1838, a 17.
Richard Allingham, his father, d Sept. 29, 1841, a 66.
Eliza, his mother, d Jan. 30, 1849, a 68.

Samuel Berry, d May 18, 1817, a 53.
Elizabeth, his wife, d March 15, 1841, a 85.

Mary Ann, wife of Robert Bance, d July 31, 1841, a 37.
Robert Bance, her husband, d Jan. 31, 1847, a 47.
Eliza Bance, her daughter, d Nov. 11, 1850, a 16.
George Bance, her son, died at Melbourne, Australia, Jan. 10, 1853, a 17.

Emily Gooch, wife of Robt. Gooch, M.D., d Jan. 21, 1811, a 25, and third
   of her marriage.
Sarah, second wife of Robt. Gooch, d March 28, 1833, a 45.
Robert Gooch, M.D., d Feb. 16, 1833, a 45.
> [Ancestors of Sir Daniel Gooch, M.P.]

William Elliott, Esq., of Woodside, d Nov. 10, 1809, a 65.

Hannah, wife of James Down, d Jan. 23, 1813, a 63.

George Allworthy, d Aug. 28, 1823, a 74.
Mary, his wife, d Nov. 9, 1824, a 69.

James Spence, d May 18, 1814, a 75.

Robert Rosier Ray, d May 20, 1838, a 65.
Elizabeth, his first wife, d Sept. 17, 1814, a 38.

James Mann, d April 3, 1837, a 63.
Catharine, his daughter, d Aug. 6, 1849, a 40.

Sarah, wife of Henry Simmonds, *d* Sept. 26, 1846, *a* 26.
Elizabeth Baker, *d* Aug. 18, 1826, *a* 75.

Edward Henry Francis, *d* May 5, 1842, *t* 57.
Theodore O. Francis, his son, *d* June 20, 1842, *a* 19.
John Robt. Francis, *d* Feb. 14, 1846, *a* 34.
Alfred Edward Francis, *d* April 20, 1846, *a* 28.
> [Mr. Francis kept a boarding-school, and lived nearly opposite the New Inn, in South End.]

Mary King, *d* May 19, 1832, *a* 60.
James King, her husband, *a* April 3, 1841, *a* 71.

William Wilmshurst, *d* Jan. 25, 1837, *a* 30.
Fanny, his mother, *d* May 12, 1838, *a* 55.
William, his father, *d* Dec. 7, 1853, *a* 77.
Esther Wilmshurst, *d* June 26, 1854, *a* 38.
> [For many years the Wilmshurst family carried on the business of carpenters and builders, at 85, North End. The premises were removed to form the entrance to the Whitgift School.]

Henry William, son of Wm. Barnes, Esq., *d* March 14, 1846, *a* 1 year 6 months.
Elizabeth, wife of George Tant, *d* May 13, 1848, *a* 84.

William Vickery, *d* Dec. 19, 1839, *a* 47.
Elizabeth Vickery, *d* Feb. 3, 1855, *a* 63.

Abraham Wall, *d* Sept., 22, 1826, *a* 43.
Salome, his wife, *d* Jan. 12, 1840, *a* 67.

James Hopwood, *d* Feb. 13, 1822, *a* 79.
Mary, his wife, *d* Jan. 13, 1826, *a* 82.

Edith, wife of Thos. Penfold, solicitor, after a long and painful illness, which she bore with Christian fortitude, *d* Dec. 18, 1827, *a* 54.
Henry, her son, *d* April 23, 1822, *a* 25
James Moore Penfold, his brother, *d* Oct. 22, 1831, *a* 25.
Mary Jane Penfold, his sister, *d* Feb. 6, 1830, *a* 11.
Clarissa, his sister, *d* April 4, 1830, *a* 36.

Mary, wife of Edward Oldaker, *d* Sept. 26, 1838, *a* 53.
Edward Oldaker, *d* Sept. 27, 1840, *a* 76.
David Freeman, his son-in-law, *d* Sept. 7, 1858, *a* 40.
> [Mr. Oldaker formerly kept a confectioner's and baker's shop on the site of the premises now occupied by the London and County Bank.]

John Roff, *d* April 13, 1846, *a* 32.
> Weep not for me, my wife and children dear,
> I am not dead but sleeping here,
> Just like a blossom plucked from a tree,
> So death has parted you and me.

John Bradford, licensed victualler, *d* May 9, 1838, *a* 61.
> Oh, magnify the Lord with me,
> With me exalt His name,
> When in distress to Him I called,
> He to my rescue came.

Mrs. Ann Bradford, his wife, *d* Dec. 22, 1843, *a* 58.
Charles Bradford, his son, *d* March 15, 1845, *a* 25.
> [Mr. Bradford, described above as a licensed victualler, kept the Hare and Hounds at Waddon.]

Elizabeth, wife of Charles Gates, *d* Feb. 22, 1833, *a* 26
Wm. Richard Gates, her son, *d* Feb. 15, 1852, *a* 27.
Emily, her daughter, *d* Jan. 30, 1850, *a* 13.

Mary, daughter of John and Mary Peters, *d* Sept. 19, 1812, *a* 30.
> Death with his dart has pierced my heart,
> When I was in my prime,
> Mourn not for me my parents dear,
> It was God's appointed time.

Mary Peters, her mother, *d* Nov. 4, 1819, *a* 69.

George Stanford, *d* Aug. 8, 1839, *a* 63.
Mary, his wife, *d* March 16, 1852, *a* 66.
> [Mr. Stanford was landlord of the Swan Inn, North End.]

William Black, *d* Jan. 24, 1847, *a* 70.

Nathaniel Neale, *d* Jan. 4, 1846, *a* 55.

Mary Ann Meredith, *d* Sept. 3, 1845, *a* 70.
John Treadaway, bricklayer, *d* Feb. 1 1853, *a* 73.
Elizabeth, his wife, *d* Nov. 18, 1856, *a* 80.
Charles Crame, *d* June 14, 1833, *a* 47.
James Crame, *d* Feb. 9, 1837, *a* 54.
> [The Crames kept the Gun Inn, Church Street.]

John Adams, *d* Oct. 11, 1826, *a* 66.
> Weep not for me, my children dear,
> I am not dead but sleeping here ;
> I am thus as you must be,
> Prepare yourselves to follow me.

Eliza, wife of Joseph Haynes, *d* Jan. 10, 1845, *a* 45.

Mr. Richard Rowland, *d* May 17, 1831, *a* 69.
Susanna, his wife, *d* Jan. 13, 1848, *a* 82.

Nicholas Smith, *d* Nov. 9, 1825, *a* 50.
Robert Smith, *d* April 27, 1810, *a* 42.
Jeremiah Selmes, *d* May 30, 1853, *a* 50.
Hannah, wife of Nicholas Smith, *d* July 4, 1854, *a* 82.
> [Jeremiah Selmes was a butcher in Surrey Street, on premises now occupied by
> Mr. Cottle, draper.]

John Rogers, *d* Oct. 4, 1819, *a* 67.
Hannah, his wife, *d* April 15, 1837, *a* 77.

Elizabeth Atkins, *d* May 23, 1819, *a* 65.
Joseph Atkins, sen., *d* Oct. 26, 1821, *a* 77.
Joseph, son of James Atkins, *d* March 2, 1851, *a* 22.

Richard Brown, *d* Sept. 8, 1830, *a* 62.

Thomas Goodwin, *d* June 17, 1825, *a* 32.
> [Mr. Goodwin was a butcher, residing on premises adjoining the King's Head,
> Surrey Street, and while he was lying in his coffin, the King's Head took
> fire, and they were obliged to get the coffin and the body out of the
> window. It would seem that the lead coffin burst with the heat, and
> had afterwards to be soldered up again.]

Sarah, wife of Wm. Selmes, *d* Nov. 19, 1852, *a* 52.
Wm. Richardson Selmes, *d* July 21, 1873, *a* 66.
> [Mr. W. R. Selmes kept a butcher's shop in High Street, near the Town Hall,
> in one of the shops now occupied by Pelton Bros., grocers.]

Nicholas Payne, *d* March 28, 1843, *a* 46.
Sarah, his wife, *d* Nov. 27, 1855, *a* 52.
David, his son, *d* Feb. 20, 1851, *a* 22.

Thomas Thorne, *d* Jan. 15, 1828, *a* 55,
Mrs. Mary Boyd, widow, *d* Feb. 14, 1861, *a* 88.

Elizabeth, wife of John Brooker, *d* Nov. 11, 1856, *a* 71,
John Brooker, *d* Oct. 1, 1869, *a* 76.

Mary Brown, wife of Richard Brown. *d* Aug. 17, 1817, *a* 52, (with a cancer
in her breast). Memento mori.

> Let the Lord be ev'r in your mind,
> Before your body's here consigned.
> That your Redeemer may always see,
> Your soul's prepared for eternity.

> My God, He thought it just and right,
> In haste to put my soul to flight,
> And with His hand upon my breath,
> Consigned my breath to eternal death.

Miss Christiana Roy, *d* Sept. 19, 1824, *a* 15.
Mrs. Ann Taylor, *d* Oct. 1, 1831, *a* 84.
Mrs. Mary Roy, *d* Feb. 19, 1835, *a* 53.
Miss Harriet Roy, *d* July 27, 1839, *a* 30.

John Hughes, *d* Sept. 3, 1873.
Mary Ann, his wife, *d* Dec. 24, 1847.
Maria Hawkins, their eldest daughter, *d* April 30, 1872.

Elizabeth, widow of Capt. Mayne, Dublin, *d* July 27, 1825, *a* 66.

Ann Day, *d* Jan. 31, 1820, *a* 79.
William Day, her grandson, *d* Sept. 27, 1830, *a* 25.

George Butt, *d* Jan 23, 1834, *a* 29.
James Butt, his father, *d* March 29, 1839, *a* 66.

William Ward, *d* April 5, 1812, *a* 33.

William Hills Rice, *d* May 10, 1811, *a* 36.
Elizabeth, his wife, *d* March 18, 1804, *a* 29.

Enoch Redman, *d* Jan. 16, 1790, *a* 51.
Ann, his wife, *d* Oct. 4, 1793, *a* 47.

The truely deserving and justly lamented Mr. William Hills, late of Southwark, butcher, *d* Sept. 24, 1779, *a* 77.

> He was a sincere and honest man, an unparallel'd friend to friendless orphans,
> one of whom lives through his paternal care humbly to dedicate this stone
> to his memory. Now he rests from his labour, and his works do follow him.

Mrs. Bridget Rice, *d* March 13, 1811, *a* 62.
Thomas Rice, *d* July 18, 1818, *a* 79.
Christopher Hughes Rice, their son, *d* Aug. 23, 1835, *a* 35.
The infant son of Thomas and Bridget Rice, *d* April 12, 1776.

> How suddenly alas from me,
> You're snatched my infant boy,
> Tho' parted here, in bliss I hope,
> To meet in lasting joy.

Mrs. Catherine Yeatman, *d* July 18, 1825, *a* 79.

John Cheel, *d* June 6, 1821, *a* 27.

> Youth is laid beneath this stone,
> Death nipped the bud, the blossoms gone,
> Be still each parent's sighing heart,
> Time is but short that we shall part,
> When we again in glory meet,
> 'Twill turn past bitters all to sweet.

Mrs. Elizabeth Osman, *d* April 23, 1843, *a* 83.
Ann Martha Griffin, her granddaughter, *d* Oct. 2, 1857, *a* 14.

> Weep not for me, it is in vain,
> Your loss, dear parents, is my eternal gain.

E

Joseph Matthews, *d* June 23, 1826, *a* 77.
Sarah, wife of Wm. Laing, *d* Oct. 29, 1829, *a* 31.
William, her son, *d* Sept. 24, 1844, *a* 21.

Mrs. Amy Batten, *d* Nov. 15, 1844, *a* 89.
Amy Batten, her daughter, *d* Nov. 2, 1842, *a* 62.
Susanna, wife of Thomas Batten, *d* Oct. 23, 1821, *a* 29.

[Mrs. Amy Batten and her daughter kept a dame's school in North End, on part of the premises now occupied by Mr. Allder's shop.]

Abraham Metcalf, *d* Dec. 20, 1843, *a* 79.
Ann, his wife, *d* Nov. 29, 1843, *a* 69.

[Abraham Metcalf was the last warden of Whitgift Hospital, while it remained a corporate body. He steadily refused any alterations and innovations, and nothing could be done until after his death.]

Fanny, wife of Richard Older, *d* Nov. 19, 1810, *a* 44.
Rebecca Older, her daughter, *d* May 3, 1826, *a* 54.

[Mr. Richard Older was a bricklayer and builder.]

Champion Bennett, *d* Dec. 9, 1787, *a* 50.
Elizabeth Bennett, *d* Jan. 28, 1814, *a* 74.
Mary, her daughter, *d* Oct. 20, 1838, *a* 69.

William Ashby, *d* June 20, 1828, *a* 56.
Elizabeth, his wife, *d* April 15, 1835, *a* 61.

Winifred, wife of John Stedman, *d* Oct. 23, 1835, *a* 58.
John Stedman, *d* March 16, 1837, *a* 62.

[The deceased was a baker, residing at 16, Surrey Street (now the Royal Oak Brewery Office), in which business he was succeeded by his son. Another son was a violet grower on Thornton Heath.]

Richard Pampillon, *d* Oct. 12, 1788, *a* 45.
Sarah, his widow, *d* March 1, 1833, *a* 80.

On a vault near the North Entrance :—

Mrs. Sarah Burnett was born in this parish Jan 1, 1673. She died in London, Feb. 17, 1742, and was buried here.

> Boast not, vain man, whoe'er thou art,
> Of high birth, riches, strength, or power,
> For they no comfort can impart,
> When thou art at thy dying hour,
> Be meek and humble while on earth,
> Delight in being good and just,
> Nor riches, strength, nor power, nor birth
> Will be distinguished in the dust.

Mr. William Burnett, *b* Jan. 29, 1685, *d* Oct. 29, 1760.

> What is man ?
> To-day he's drest in gold and silver bright,
> Wrapt in a shroud before to-morrow night ;
> To-day, he's feasting on delicious food,
> To-morrow, nothing eats can do him good ;
> To-day he's nice, and scorns to feed on crumbs,
> In a few days, himself a dish for worms ;
> To-day, he's honoured and in great esteem,
> To-morrow, not a beggar values him ;
> To-day he rises from a velvet bed,
> To-morrow, lies in one that's made of lead ;
> To-day, his house tho' large he thinks too small,
> To-morrow, can command no house at all ;
> To-day, has twenty servants at his gates,
> To-morrow, scarcely one will deign to wait ;

To-day, perfumed and sweet as is the rose,
To-morrow, stinks in everybody's nose ;
To-day, he's grand, majestic, all delight,
Ghastly and pale before to-morrow night.
Now, when you've wrote and said whate'er you can,
This is the best that you can say of man !

North side of the Church, between the Church and the Footpath.

Joseph Shonfield, *d* Aug. 19, 1847, *a* 63.
Hannah Maria, his wife, *d* March 16, 1861, *a* 86.

William Day, *d* Feb. 26, 1832, *a* 42.
Joseph, his eldest son, *d* July 7, 1865, *a* 42.
Mary, his wife, *d* Dec. 12, 1868, *a* 78.
Mark Cooper, youngest son, *d* March 8, 1874, *a* 43.
William, his brother, *d* June 18, 1877, *a* 48.

Ann Woolford, *d* Jan. 13, 1827, *a* 39.
Thomas, her husband, *d* Aug. 30, 1836, *a* 63.

John Woolford, *d* Oct. 17, 1833, *a* 64.
Anne, his wife, *d* Dec. 6, 1827, *a* 59.

[Thomas and John Woolford were the last tenants of Blunt Farm, which extended beyond St. Peter's Church. It is now almost entirely built on. The old farm house remains standing in South End, and has been converted into four shops. The farm buildings extended behind the house, stretching across what is now called the Southbridge Road.]

Mrs. Martha Page, *d* Oct. 11, 1829, *a* 56.
Maurice Page, her husband, *d* June 14, 1838, *a* 68.

[Mr. Maurice Page was the ancestor of Mr. W. Page, the well-known fishmonger in High Street. He established the business in 1785.]

Joseph Dean, *d* March 26, 1777, *a* 43.

> Oh wife, most dear, my time is past,
> My love remain'd while life did last,
> And now for me no sorrow take,
> But love my children for my sake,
> My body now is turned to dust,
> My soul to Christ in whom I trust.

Thomas Meager, *d* March 10, 1733, *a* 58.
Martha, his wife, *d* June 3, 1755, *a* 76.
Thomas Meager, of Coombe, *d* April 27, 1804, *a* 77.
Martha, his wife, *d* March 10, 1802, *a* 64.
Thomas Meager, Esq., *d* Sept. 20, 1833, *a* 59.

Thomas Meager, of Whitehouse, yeoman, *d* Feb. 24, 1742, *a* 55.
Elizabeth Meager, his wife, *d* Oct. 23, 1747, *a* 56.
George Meager, yeoman, *d* April 18, 1830, *a* 77.
William Meager, yeoman, *d* Dec. 12, 1830, *a* 82.
Mary Meager, *d* April 10, 1847, *a* 77.

[The Meagers were for more than a century tenants of the Whitehouse Farm, Selhurst.]

John Meager, brewer, *d* Dec. 3, 1804, *a* 48.

Benevolent to all, strictly just in his worldly concerns, he industriously accumulated for others that he was not permitted to enjoy, but is now gone to meet his just reward.

John Thomas Haydon, *d* May 14, 1829, *a* 13.
Wm. James Haydon, *d* April 17, 1842, *a* 24.
Thomas H. Haydon, their father, *d* April 10, 1845, *a* 51.

Edward Nangreave, *d* Nov. 20, 1831, *a* 52.
Alice, his widow, *d* Jan. 6, 1832, *a* 49.

Ann, wife of Wm. Boulton, *d* March 25, 1824, *a* 75.
> Stop here awhile and shed a tear
> Upon the dust that sleepeth here
> As you are now, so was I,
> A rainbow floating in the sky.

Mary Wooderson, *d* June 4, 1824, a 49.
Martha Elizabeth Wooderson, her granddaughter *d* April 9, 1839, *a* 10.
Elizabeth, wife of Joseph Neville, surgeon, *d* Dec. 3, 1839, *a* 31.

Joseph Bell, late of Duppas Hill, *d* May 24, 1821, *a* 61.
Amey Bell, *d* Feb. 24, 1856, *a* 83.
Lucy Bell, *d* Feb. 6, 1809, *a* 78.
> [The Bells were originally saddlers in the High Street.]

William Newton, *d* Jan. 15, 1831, *a* 68.
Wm. Shirley Newton, his son, *d* Dec. 5, 1860, *a* 69.
Charles Newton, *d* April 22, 1842, *a* 45.
Elizabeth Mary, his wife, *d* Aug. 18, 1836, *a* 31.
> [Ancestors of the present Postmaster of the town.]

William Hodgkins, *d* Sept. 12, 1794, *a* 41.
Mary Hodgkins, his wife, *d* Feb. 4, 1815, *a* 62.
> [The family of Hodgkins were for many years carpenters in the Old Town.]

North side of the Tower :—

John Roberts, *d* Nov. 22, 1829, *a* 58.
Mary, his wife, *d* Oct. 16, 1830, *a* 58.
> Lovely and pleasant in their lives they were,
> Not long divided they together are ;
> Their bodies to this tomb, their souls on high
> Waiting the coming day of victory.

Richard Pettifer, *d* March 17, 1820, *a* 43.
Walter Godfrey Pettifer, *d* Jan. 20, 1840, *a* 30.

Wm. Attridge, *d* Dec. 12, 1832, *a* 74.
> This ritual stone thy son doth lay
> O'er thy respected dust,
> Only proclaims the mournful day,
> When we a parent lost.

Abigail Attridge, his wife, *d* Feb. 24, 1856, *a* 73.

Jane Weller, *d* Feb. 27, 1833, *a* 22.
Edmund Weller, *d* Dec. 6, 1834, *a* 34.

Martha Castledine, *d* April 22, 1830, *a* 25.
Sarah Castledine, her daughter, *d* Aug. 13, 1832, *a* 37.
William Castledine, *d* Feb. 17, 1870, *a* 77.
> [Mr. Castledine was a timber merchant and one of the earliest members of the
> Local Board ; but having some interest in the property purchased by
> the Board for the Cemetery, he was obliged to resign his office.]

Elizabeth, wife of Samuel Marston, of Selhurst Farm, *d* Feb. 16, 1825, *a* 36.
> Oh, solemn death, who by commission comes,
> To call a loving wife and tender mother home,
> No longer to assist her partner in his cares,
> No more to advise her offsprings' tender years.

Mary, wife of Henry Ray, sen., *d* Oct. 9, 1772, *a* 73.
Henry Ray, *d* Nov. 22, 1776, *a* 70.
Edward Ray, *d* Aug. 31, 1800, *a* 72.
Elizabeth Ray, his wife, *d* Aug. 20, 1819, *a* 79.
William Ray, *d* Jan. 30, 1845, *a* 70.
John Ray, *d* March 2, 1837, *a* 31.

Theodosia Maria Keallee, *d* April 4, 1796, *a* 75.

Robert Henbrey, *d* May 28, 1845, *a* 63.
Jas. Edward Henbrey, *d* Jan. 2, 1819, *a* 3.
Mrs. Jane Henbrey, *d* April 2, 1855, *a* 73.
 [Mr. Henbrey was a corn dealer, carrying on business at 62, South End, now
  occupied by Mr. H. Yates.]

John Pidgeon, trunkmaker, *d* Sept. 11, 1790, *a* 32.
Ann Pidgeon, *d* July 21, 1823, *a* 84.
Peter Pidgeon, farrier, *d* March 13, 1829, *a* 88.

Ralph Thrale, *d* Oct. 11, 1842, *a* 29.
Ralph Thrale, his father, *d* June 21, 1843, *a* 62.
Susannah Thrale, *d* Feb. 12, 1854, *a* 71.
 [Mr. Pidgeon lived on what is now called Scarbrook Hill, where he carried on
  business as a trunk maker. He was succeeded by Mr. Thrale, whose
  name occurs above. This gentleman added the ironmongery to the
  above business, and eventually disposed of it to Messrs. Hammond and
  Purrott (now Hammond & Hussey, of High Street). Some of the old
  inhabitants even now call Scarbrook Hill, " Pidgeon's Hill."]

John Pidgeon, *d* Nov. 13, 1795, *a* 61.
 Here in the grave I lay,
 And wait his will to prove,
 For he that turned me into clay,
 Will raise me in his love.

Mary Piggott, *d* Aug. 27, 1822, *a* 84.
George, her husband, *d* Jan. 28, 1824, *a* 89.

Steward Farley, baker, died in the Great Almshouses, April 13, 1796, *a* 71.

Martha Weller, *d* Nov. 18, 1825, *a* 60.
Richard Weller, *d* Nov. 20, 1833, *a* 71.
John Drewett, his son-in-law, *d* April 30, 1846, *a* 59.
Mary Ann, his wife, *d* Dec. 24, 1848, *a* 59.

George Tilbury, *d* March 5, 1787, *a* 40.
Elizabeth, his wife, *d* Feb. 8, 1830, *a* 77.
George, his son, *d* Dec. 12, 1830, *a* 48.

Sarah Blumsum, of Thornton Heath, *d* March 9, 1828, *a* 63.
Richard, her husband, *d* Oct. 26, 1830, *a* 70.
 [Mr. Blumsum was a gentleman, residing at Thornton Heath.]

Martin Maslin, *d* April 17, 1851.
Eliza, his wife, only daughter of Wm. Turner, of Epsom, *d* April 23, 1837

Priscilla Bennett, *d* Sept. 1, 1798, *a* 45.
 With great affliction I was sore opprest,
 By Night, nor yet by Day, I had no rest,
 Till my sweet Saviour heard the voice of me,
 And by his Mercy from my pain set free.

North side of the Path leading from Church Road to
Church Street.

Sarah Ann Kemp, *d* March 27, 1832.

Sarah Ann Lloyd, *d* Dec. 14, 1844, *a* 49.
John Smith Lloyd, *d* March 5, 1846, *a* 80.
Anne, wife of Alfred Lloyd, *d* Jan. 8, 1856, *a* 25.

John Brown, *d* Nov. 23, 1850, *a* 47.

James Bain, *d* April 6, 1853, *a* 84.
Mary Ann, his wife, *d* June 28, 1864, *a* 77.
Caroline, his daughter, *d* Oct. 23, 1843, *a* 23.
Emma Bain, his daughter, *d* June 5, 1855, *a* 38.

Mary Eliza Vigars Broughton, *d* June 18, 1839, *a* 24.

Richard Dean, *d* April 22, 1853, *a* 72.
Elizabeth, his wife, *d* Feb. 7, 1837, *a* 62.

Lucy Rogers, *d* April 21, 1832, *a* 55.
James, her husband, *d* Aug. 16, 1840, *a* 80.

John Bates, *d* Nov. 23, 1824, *a* 40.
> A lingering sickness did me seize,
> No physician could me ease,
> I fought for means, but all in vain,
> Till God did ease me of my pain.

Hannah Bates, his wife, *d* Feb. 26, 1855, *a* 73.
Henry Bates, his brother, *d* Oct. 12, 1832, *a* 39.

Elizabeth, wife of John Bell, *d* June 9, 1825, *a* 57.
John, her husband, *d* Oct. 12, 1840, *a* 65.
John William, their son, *d* July 13, 1828, *a* 22.
George Henry, another son, *d* Dec. 24, 1842, *a* 36.

John Maknis, *d* Feb. 19, 1823, *a* 63.
Ann, his wife, *d* Jan. 7, 1830, *a* 66.
John Simonds, *d* Jan. 8, 1832, *a* 39.

Thomas Edwards, *d* May 4, 1824, *a* 32, and two children.

Ann, wife of Charles Bray, *d* Dec. 29, 1840, *a* 34.
Charles, her husband, *d* June 17, 1845, *a* 32.
Sarah, wife of Chalkley Bray, *d* Aug. 2, 1849, *a* 76.
   [Mr. Chas. Bray kept the Canteen at the Barracks.]

Ann Abercrombie, *d* Oct. 12, 1843, *a* 58.
James, her brother, *d* March 11, 1844, *a* 61.

Elizabeth Dixon, *d* June 8, 1841, *a* 61.
Sarah Cliff, *d* July 3, 1842, *a* 73.

Mrs. Charlotte Cooper, *d* July 10, 1829, *a* 86.
Mrs. Salome Wiltshire, *d* Dec. 8, 1822, *a* 58.
> Earthly cover, to thy care
> We commit our parent's dust ;
> Safe and calmly keep them sleeping
> Till the Lord demands the trust.

Mary Ann Wiltshire, her daughter, *d* Aug. 17, 1853, *a* 64.
John Wiltshire, *d* Oct. 7, 1813, *a* 57.
James Wiltshire, his son, *d* Feb. 21, 1822, *a* 35.

James Robinson, *d* June 14, 1812, *a* 46.
Mary, his wife, *d* Dec. 15, 1845, *a* 66.

George Bell, wine merchant, Seething Lane, London, *d* Dec. 8, 1822, *a* 38.

James Friday, *d* July 3, 1821, *a* 83.
Lydia, wife of William Fox, *d* Jan. 26, 1826, *a* 34.
William Fox, her husband, *d* Oct. 2, 1857.

Mary, wife of Henry Linfield, *d* Feb 10, 1826, *a* 37.

> Oh ! husband dear, my time is past,
> My love remained while life did last,
> But now for me no sorrow take
> But love my children for my sake.

Robert Vigar, *d* Dec. 11. 1826, *a* 65.
Sophia Eliza Vigar [rest illegible].

Deborah Pullen, wife of Joseph Gillingham. *d* April 28, 1822, *a* 35.
Mary Ann, second wife. *d* Sept. 14. 1847, *a* 46.
Joseph Gillingham, *d* May 24. 1850, *a* 63.
  [Mr. Gillingham was a veterinary surgeon; his descendants (son and grandson) still carry on the business in Church Street.]

Annabella Marsh, wife of Samuel Marsh, *d* Nov. 6, 1772, *a* 29.
William Marsh, *d* July 22. 1778, *a* 76.
Anne Marsh, his widow, *d* Dec. 8. 1782, *a* 73.
Samuel Marsh, Esq., *d* March 12. 1795, *a* 58.
Capt. John Marsh, 62nd Regt., *d* Feb. 27, 1798, *a* 21.
Frances Elizabeth, widow of Samuel Marsh, Esq., *d* Oct. 27, 1861.

Robert Nicholson, *d* March 13. 1832, *a* 43.
Sarah, his wife, *d* May 12. 1860, *a* 72.

Mary, wife of William Gardener, miller, *d* Dec. 9, 1810, *a* 64.

James Allen, whitesmith, *d* Dec. 23, 1858, *a* 51.

John, son of Major D'Arley, *d* Nov. 23, 1828, *a* 17.

Charles Massie, *d* Oct. 22, 1807, *a* 75.
Sarah, his wife, *d* Oct. 3. 1815, *a* 82.

Henry O'Neil, *d* June 21, 1833, *a* 38.

John Adams, *d* March 2, 1827, *a* 66.

Mary Wood, of Duppas Hill. *d* May 21, 1828, *a* 62.
Mary, her daughter, *d* Feb. 23. 1831, *a* 23.
William Wood, *d* May 24, 1841, *a* 15.

Christiana Mennie, *d* May 21. 1828, *a* 64.
Robert, her husband, *d* June 5. 1833, *a* 63.

Michael Weller, *d* Jan. 8, 1826.
Sarah, his wife, *d* Sept. 29, 1836.

Mrs. Edith Pitman, *d* March 6, 1833, *a* 81.
Edward Pitman, *d* Dec. 5, 1837, *a* 96.

William Bourton, *d* April 10, 1824, *a* 67.
Margaret Bourton, *d* Oct. 2, 1837, *a* 84.

Mary, daughter of Thomas Pascall, *d* Oct. 28, 1824, *a* 15.

> Let this vain world engage no more,
> Behold the gaping tomb,
> It bids us seize the present hour,
> To-morrow death may come.

Esther, daughter of Henry and Martha Pascall, who sweetly fell asleep in Jesus, Jan. 25, 1810, *a* 24.

> Sleep sweetly, thou lump of lifeless clay,
> For soon the trumpet shall proclaim the day,
> When Christ, thy Lord, will with a shout descend,
> At which the mansions of the tomb shall rend,
> And those that sleep in Him again shall rise,
> And with shouts triumphant mount the skies.

  [The Pascalls were potters and brickmakers at Norwood, and the business is still carried on by their descendants.]

John Arnard Fichal, Esq., *d* June 20, 1823, *a* 49.

Ann Wright, *d* Nov. 20, 1834, *a* 85.
James Wright, *d* Sept. 30, 1841, *a* 91.

Robert, youngest son of John and Mary Moore, died in Australia, 1854, *a* 34.
George, eldest son, died in New Zealand, Oct. 6, 1877, *a* 72.
John Moore, *d* Nov. 12, 1842, *a* 63.
Mary, his wife, *d* May 5, 1843, *a* 61.

Elizabeth, wife of John Batchelor, *d* Dec. 20, 1833, *a* 61.
John Batchelor, *d* Jan. 20, 1837, *a* 59.
Martha Batchelor, *d* Oct. 16, 1849, *a* 12.

Richard Puplett, *d* July 22, 1855, *a* 57.
　　[Mr. Puplett drove one of the oldest coaches from London to Croydon.]

By the side of the Church.

A. Vander Kiste, *d* Jan. 9, 1810, *a* 68.
　　　　Thou must die, go reader and repent.
　　[Mr. Vander Kiste was a surgeon, having an extensive practice in the town. The Watsons were his descendants—Mrs. Watson was his daughter.]
Also Frances Ann Watson, *d* April 18, 1826, *a* 57.
Benjamin Watson, *d* April 30, 1833, *a* 59.

END OF PARISH CHURCHYARD.

ST. JAMES'S CHURCH.

THIS Church is situated at the intersection of St. James's Road and Sydenham Road. It was built in 1828, and consecrated by Archbishop Howley on January 31st, 1829. When first erected it was called the District Chapel of St. James. It was the first Episcopalian place of worship erected in the parish after the Mother Church, and at the time of its erection was in a very isolated part of Croydon Common, though now surrounded on all sides by well-kept roads and handsome villa residences. The present church is a brick building in the Pointed Style of architecture, with square tower at the west end. A new chancel has lately been added, and it is intended at some future day to take down the present church and rebuild it of stone on a larger scale and more elaborate character. At the east end, over the communion table, is a handsome stained glass window representing several of the miracles of Jesus Christ. It bears the following inscription :—" To the glory of God and in loving memory of Henry Campbell Watson, M.A., for 13 years Incumbent of this Parish ; born 29th of April, 1828, died 8th of January, 1879. This window has been erected by his relatives, friends, and parishioners, as a tribute of their love and esteem." There are two smaller windows in the new chancel. On one is depicted St. John the Baptist, and is inscribed as follows :—" In loving memory of Alice Emily Goldsmith, this window is erected by her sorrowing relatives. March 10th, 1882." The adjoining window, containing a representation of St. Barnabas, is also erected to the memory of the same lady " by her lovers and friends." When the East India Company's Military Seminary was in existence at Addiscombe, the cadets attended St. James's Church, and in the interior are several tablets erected to the memory of officers educated at Addiscombe, and in the churchyard the officials were wont to be buried. We commence with a description of the tablets in the interior :—

In memory of Major-General Sir Ephraim Stannus, Knight, K.C.B., and Colonel of the 3rd European Light Infantry on the Bombay Establishment, who after a long career of distinguished services in India, Arabia, and Persia, was selected by the Hon. E.I.C. for the arduous and responsible position of Lieut.-Governor of the Military Seminary at Addiscombe, where in the exemplary discharge of his duty, he died suddenly on the 21st Oct., 1850. Erected by a few of his oldest friends in token of the high estimation in which he was universally held,

[This gentleman was buried in the Parish Churchyard.]

To the memory of Frederick Charles Grindall, 2nd Lieutenant in the Corps of Bengal Engineers, who was drowned while bathing in the River Indus, at Attok, in the East Indies, on the 18th July, 1849, in the 24th year of his age and 5th of his services. This tablet is erected by those of his brother officers to whom he was known, in friendship and in regret—a tribute to his amiable disposition and his distinguished gallantry.

In memory of Eneas R. R. Macdonell, *a* 22 ; Norton Edward Eden, *a* 20; George Battine, *a* 21 ; officers of the Hon. E. I. Co.'s Engineers; and of James Battine, *a* 18 years, Bengal Light Cavalry, who were drowned in the River Medway, Dec. 15th, 1855. Erected by their brother officers as a mark of sorrow for their loss.

Aaron Penley, Esq., late of the H. E. I. C. College, Addiscombe, *d* Jan. 15, 1870, *a* 64.

George Collingwood, Esq., for many years a resident of St. Saviour's, Southwark, *d* Oct. 23, 1878, sincerely respected by all who knew him.

Sacred to the memory of Margaret Mary Rogers, wife of Robert Rogers, of Croydon, *d* Oct. 31, 1851, *a* 50.

West End and South Side of the Churchyard.

Thomas Heydon, *d* Jan. 25, 1852, *a* 20.
Catherine Heydon, his sister, *d* Jan. 6, 1853, *a* 18.
Hannah Heydon, his mother, *d* Jan. 14, 1878, *a* 66.

John Mott, *d* Aug. 11, 1839.
Julia, only daughter of [Here the inscription suddenly terminates].

Charles, second son of John Charles Bristowe, *d* Oct. 10, 1840, *a* 20.

Elizabeth Shaw, widow, *d* June 2, 1859, *a* 83.

Lucy, wife of Daniel Beck, *d* March 14, 1847, *a* 58.
Eliza, her granddaughter, *d* Oct. 1, 1843, *a* 1 year and 10 months
Daniel Beck, *d* Oct. 1, 1857, *a* 68.
Chas. John Beck, his grandson, *d* Dec, 13, 1878, *a* 25.
    [Mr. Daniel Beck was for some years master of Archbishop Tenison's school while it was located in North End. He was afterwards actuary of the Savings Bank.]

John Swindale, Esq., resident of the Island of St. Christopher, West Indies, *d* Dec. 14, 1833, *a* 82.

Sarah Lunn, *d* Nov. 1, 1845, *a* 58.
William Lunn, *d* July 29, 1869, *a* 82.
Ellen Maria Moore, their granddaughter, *d* Oct. 9, 1869, *a* 12.
       Departed this life an angel dear,
       In all her ways an angel she appeared,

Henry Bailes, *d* Nov. 13, 1831, *a* 66.
       Reader, the time is short!
Maria Firby, *d* Nov. 14, 1841, *a* 89.
Hannah Pickering Firby, *d* March 13. 1857, *a* 63.
    I heard a voice from Heaven saying unto me " Blessed are the dead which die in the Lord."

Caroline, wife of P. H. Byrne, *d* Nov. 12, 1860, *a* 57.
Philip Henry Byrne, *d* Nov. 7, 1864, *a* 70.

Louisa Augusta Thomson, *d* Feb. 12, 1843, *a* 27.
Jane, wife of Charles Pratt Thomson, *d* Jan. 21, 1853, *a* 61.

Diana, wife of William Fairman, *d* Oct. 23, 1849, *a* 49.
>She was an affectionate wife and a tender mother, and sincerely respected by all who knew her.

William Fairman, her husband, *d* July 13, 1868, *a* 68.

James Fairman, her son, *d* Aug. 3, 1874, *a* 56.
>[The Fairmans (father and son) were bricklayers, residing in Cherry Orchard Road.]

Sarah Oliphant, *d* Dec. 16, 1840, *a* 47.

Thomas Holliday, her brother-in-law, *d* April 22, 1840, *a* 38.
>[Mrs. Oliphant kept a ladies' school in South End. It was for many years the leading educational establishment for young ladies in the town.]

John Parsons, Esq., *d* Oct. 8, 1837, *a* 61.
>He was an affectionate husband, a kind and sincere friend, and his memory will ever be cherished by his widow.

Frances, his widow, *d* March 24, 1848, *a* 65.

Henry, son of Harriet and Robt. Loveland, *d* June 17, 1834, *a* 2¼.

Mrs. Harriet Loveland, her mother, *d* Sep. 13, 1855, *a* 52.
>Beloved, if God so loved us, we ought to love one another.

Charlotte Kettle, *d* Aug. 26, 1854, *a* 34.
>This stone is erected by her brothers who best knew her value and most deeply lament her loss.

John Kettle, her father, *d* Dec. 1, 1858, *a* 75.

Mary, wife of John Kettle, *d* May 9, 1833, *a* 73.

Sarah, wife of John Kettle, *d* July 9, 1851, *a* 66.
>Mr. John Kettle was a livery stable keeper and horse dealer, residing in Addiscombe Road, nearly opposite Ashburton Road. When the Military College was in existence, most of the pupils hired their horses from Mr. Kettle ; and the professors and others who could afford to keep a horse of their own generally dealt with Mr. Kettle. Many a general officer in the Indian Army will have a lively recollection of this old gentleman's horses, some of which he kept to let out to the cadets, and were more celebrated for bone and spirit than for flesh.

William Smith, of Addiscombe, *d* March 16, 1835, *a* 68.

Robt. Smith, his grandson, *d* Sep. 16, 1849, *a* 10 months.

John Little, *d* Oct. 3, 1832, *a* 68.

Andrew Little, his son, *d* June 22, 1837, *a* 18.

Elizabeth Little, his wife, *d* April 26, 1855, *a* 70.

John Foster, *d* June 12, 1833, *a* 63.

Elizabeth Foster, his daughter, *d* Jan. 7, 1837, *a* 13.

John Foster, his son, *a* July 5, 1839, *a* 19.

Sarah Foster, his widow, *d* Nov. 21, 1861, *a* 82.
>" The orphan's friend."

Sarah Ann, daughter of John and Sarah Piper, of Peckham, *d* Oct. 12, 1843, *a* 4¼

John Piper, her father, *d* June 20, 1850, *a* 40.
>Oh, Thou that hearest prayer, unto Thee shall all flesh come.

Sarah, wife of William Aldridge, *d* Jan. 13, 1842, *a* 47.

Mrs. Harriet Aldridge, *d* June 20, 1882, *a* 68.

John Richardson, *d* Jan. 7, 1836, *a* 83.

Rebecca Richardson, his widow, *d* Feb. 20, 1841, *a* 70.

William Furance, *d* March 31, 1831, *a* 59.
Lucy Furance, his daughter, *d* May 27, 1833, *a* 22.
Hannah Furance, his wife, *d* Jan. 27, 1841, *a* 51.

William, son of Thomas and Mary Pascal, *d* Nov. 28, 1841, *a* 7.

James Sturt, *d* Feb. 22, 1842, *d* 79.
> Free from all care and pain, asleep my body lies,
> Until the trumpet calls the dead in Christ to rise.
> Why mourn we for departed friends
> Since death all sin and sorrow ends ?
> A life well spent no doubt brings peace
> And joys that never more shall cease.

Lucy Sturt, his wife, *d* Nov. 15, 1852, *a* 96.

Joseph Eldershaw, *d* March 26, 1837, *a* 27.
Amelia Eldershaw, his mother, *d* Dec. 25, 1859, *a* 74.

Charles Elton Prescott, *d* May 25, 1832, *a* 58.

Ann, wife of William Bailey, *d* July 17, 1816, *a* 42.
Mary, his second wife, *d* Dec. 17, 1833, *a* 48.

Anne Cornfield, *d* Oct. 18, 1839, *a* 48.
John Cornfield, her husband, *d* March 26, 1857, *a* 69.
> [The Cornfields were for several generations bakers on the Common.]

Sarah, wife of Paul Rogers, *d* Nov. 12, 1843, *a* 79.
Paul Rogers, *d* Feb. 11, 1845, *a* 82.

William John Weller, *d* Aug. 20, 1864, *a* 25.

Ambrose Verral, *d* July 3, 1832, *a* 66.

Miss Sarah Loch, *d* Feb. 16, 1833, *a* 62.

Sarah Salmon, *d* Oct. 13, 1831, *a* 58.
John Salmon, her husband, *d* Jan. 27, 1837, *a* 76.
Sarah Salmon, his sister, *d* Dec. 5, 1858, *a* 84.

Anne Isabel, daughter of J. C. Dempster, *d* June 13, 1867, *a* 6 weeks.
> Fold her, O Father, in thine arms
> And let her henceforth be
> A messenger of love between
> Our human heart and thee.

Norah Emma, her twin sister, *d* March 1, 1868, *a* 10 months.

William Cowling, *d* Sept. 4, 1834, *a* 72.

Mrs. Ann Sully, *d* June 18, 1841, *a* 87.
Julia Maria Metcalf, granddaughter, *d* Feb. 24, 1837, *a* 17.
Ellen E. Metcalf, *d* March 10, 1849, *a* 51.
Edward Barnard Metcalf, *d* April 4, 1850, *a* 62.

John, son of George Baillie, late of the Medical Establishment at Addiscombe, *d* April 3, 1845, *a* 18.
> This young man, at the time of his untimely death, was one of the most promising pupils in the Addiscombe Military College. One day, while larking with a number of other cadets in the college grounds, they took into their heads to commence pulling a large garden roller along one of the walks. Unfortunately young Baillie's foot slipped, and he fell immediately in front of the roller, which passed over his body before it could be stopped. From the effects of this accident he died a few hours afterwards.

Wm. Paterson, son of Capt. W. Paterson, R.N. *d* May 31, 1831, *a* 17.

James, eldest son of the Hon. and Rev. James St. Leger, *d* Oct. 17, 1829, *a* 17.

Lydia, widow of the late John Mathison. *d* 1853.

James Smith, *d* Feb. 8, 1830. *a* 44.
> An honest man is the noblest work of God.

John Macrone, *d* Sept. 9, 1837, *a* 28.

John Bordwine, twenty-five years Professor of Fortification at the neighbouring Military Seminary. *d* Feb. 21, 1835, *a* 57.
Elizabeth, his wife, *d* April 17, 1850, 78.

> Erected by the Cadets of the Hon. E. I. Co.'s Military Seminary.

Sergt. Robt. Dodd, of the Royal Regiment of Artillery, after a service of 21 years at Addiscombe, where he died universally respected and regretted, May 12, 1838, *a* 52.
Elizabeth Dodd, his relict. *d* May 16, 1859. *a* 78.

David Bruce, *d* August 12. 1859, *a* 60. Deceased was formerly of the Royal Artillery, and was for 22 years Sergeant and Sergeant-major at the Military College, Addiscombe, and by strict integrity and affability, he was highly esteemed by all who knew him.
Adelaide Vincent, *d* Sept. 26, 1860, *a* 22.

Esther Jayne, wife of Jas. B. Jayne, *d* Dec. 23, 1860, *a* 26.

Alfred Sheppard, *d* April 19, 1863, *a* 42.
> When round my grave ye come and weep,
> Think that ye hear me say to all,
> Upon the tomb no tear must fall,
> God giveth his beloved sleep.

Mrs. Sarah Lewes, his mother, *d* Aug. 29, 1866, *a* 78.

Thomas Daniels, *d* Aug. 19, 1865, *a* 63.

Frances White, *d* Jan. 24, 1865, *a* 92.

William Henry Witt, *d* Jan. 25, 1865, *a* 32.
> Each moment since his dying hour
> Our loss we keenly feel,
> But trust we feel a Saviour's power
> To sanctify and heal.

Catherina Elizabeth Stanford. *d* Dec. 18, 1869, *a* 25.
> Tender in age, but strong in faith,
> She looked above and feared not death.

William Ford, *d* Oct. 1. 1846, *a* 41.
Anastasia Ford, his daughter, *d* Oct. 10, 1854, *a* 16.
Cecilia Ford, his widow, *d* May 3, 1860, *a* 53.

Elizabeth, the faithful and affectionate wife of William Mawle, *d* Aug. 12, 1860, *a* 38; also two infant children.
> Oh! where are the lost, whom we loved on this earth,
> With whose memory our bosoms yet glow,
> Their relics we gave to the place of the dead
> But their glorified spirits before us have fled
> To the land which no mortal may know.

[Mr. Mawle was a member of the firm of Mawle and Sibery, grocers. Their shop was pulled down to make the entrance into Katharine Street.]

Susannah Still, *d* Nov. 3, 1863, *a* 79.

Mrs. Mary Reynolds, *d* Sept. 19, 1856, *a* 54.

Elizabeth, widow of Edward Burbidge, of Aldersgate-street, London, *d* May 20, 1840, *a* 44.

Miss Sally Brown, *d* Nov. 10, 1861, *a* 83.

John, son of S. & E. Cousins, *d* Aug. 17, 1848, *a* 1¼.
Samuel, his brother, *d* June 20, 1862, *a* 5¼.

> Dear to their parents, to their God more dear,
> Two little brothers sweetly slumber here,
> Blest is their state, from sin and sorrow free,
> To us they died! they live, O Lord, to thee.

William Cousins, of Dagnall Park, *d* Jan. 30, 1875, *a* 33.

James Broughton, *d* Nov. 25, 1861, *a* 39.

Charles Baker, *d* May 12, 1861, *a* 22.

Ludee Elizabeth, wife of William Barclay Chadwick, Esq., Capt. 2nd
Surrey Militia, *d* April 27, 1846, *a* 52.

Kate, daughter of George Masters, *d* March 1, 1860, *a* 4.
George Masters, her father, *d* Dec. 6, 1866, *a* 46.

Master John Leonard Roth, *d* Sept. 4, 1848, *a* 4 months.
Sarah Roth, his mother, *d* March 8, 1848, *a* 21.

> Vain world, with all thy busy cares
> And glittering joys, depart ;
> A nobler guest demands my time.
> 'Tis Jesus claims my heart.

Chas. Edwd. Collins, *d* Aug. 26, 1845, *a* 5 months.
Emily Collins, his mother, *d* Jan. 23, 1846, *a* 20.
Richard Collins, *d* July 22, 1848, *a* 31.

> Blessed state beyond conception,
> Who its vast delights can tell ?
> May it be my blissful portion
> With my Saviour there to dwell.

William Davies, *d* Sept. 17, 1857, *a* 57.
Maria Davies, his wife, *d* Dec. 18, 1867, *a* 68.

Eliza Gilding, *d* Feb. 24, 1842, *a* 38.
Mary Elizabeth Shepherd, *d* Feb. 18, 1843, *a* 5.
[The Gildings kept a school in George Street.]

Benjamin Cooper, *d* June 9, 1859, *a* 68.

> Submissive to thy will, my God,
> To thee, my partner I resign,
> And humbly bow before thy rod,
> I mourn, but dare not to repine.

Richard Bagot, Esq., *d* Jan. 7, 1840, *a* 19.

Mary Ann, wife of W. W. Lambert, *d* May 30, 1860, *a* 57.
John Wm. Lambert, *d* March 22, 1864, *a* 73.
Henry Stone Lambert, M.D., their eldest son, who died at sea, July 5,
1871, *a* 39, and was buried off Brindisi.

Wm. Dyer Thomas, M.D., Deputy-Inspector General of Hospitals, *d*
March 24, 1837, *a* 60.
Rosa Thomas, his wife, *d* March 9, 1861, *a* 80.

William Johnson, of Church-street, *d* Nov. 22, 1868, *a* 85.

Bevan Powle, *d* Oct. 4, 1861, *a* 47.

Walter Edwd., son of John Tidey, farmer, of Woodside, *d* Sept. 26, 1856,
a 2¼.
Annie Patience, his sister, *d* April 28, 1867, *a* 17.

Mary Anna Field, *d* March 17, 1854, *a* 67.
Honoria Field, her sister, *d* Jan. 5, 1875, *a* 75.

Caroline Frances, wife of Wm. Day, Esq., *d* July 9, 1849, *a* 75.
William Day, *d* Feb. 1, 1853, *a* 81.
> [Mr. Day lived at Ringstead House in the Whitehorse Road, near the West Croydon Baptist Chapel.]

Elizabeth, wife of Rev. Geo. Coles, incumbent of this district, *d* Feb. 19, 1862, *a* 56.
George Godiom, her son, died at Melbourne, Australia, Sep. 14, 1854, *a* 23.
Rev. George Coles, *d* Jan. 22, 1865, *a* 65.
Thomas Fenning Coles, his son, *d* Dec. 12, 1879, *a* 38.

> The Rev. George Coles was son of Mr. Thomas Coles, of St. Mary Abchurch, London, who married on the 30th Nov., 1799, Miss Elizabeth Fenning, sister of William Fenning, Esq., of Ravensbury, in the parish of Mitcham, and afterwards of Christchurch, Surrey, an eminent calico printer. He was the first incumbent of St. James's Church, and held the office from 1829 to 1865. He was also Chaplain to the Whitgift Hospital. He had a brother named Thomas Coles, who also married a Miss Fenning, in all probability a sister of his wife. It will be seen that the rev. gentleman had a son called Thomas Fenning Coles, whose death is recorded above.

Isabella, second daughter of James and Mary Skinner, of Bedford Park, *d* Dec. 24, 1865, *a* 12.
> And all wept and bewailed her, but Jesus said " Weep not, she is not
> dead, but sleepeth."

John Smith, *d* April 15, 1861, *a* 68.
Martha Smith, his relict, *d* March 20, 1871, *a* 75.
Mrs. Elizabeth Ann Brook, her sister, *d* Jan. 10, 1856, *a* 69.

Miss Caroline Goddard, *d* Dec. 11, 1853, *a* 30.

Elizabeth Lamb, *d* July 7, 1861, *a* 83.
James Burton Hayward, drowned at Gallipoli, June 5, 1859, *a* 18.
Caroline Louisa Hayward, *d* May 25, 1866, *a* 14.

Mrs. Priscilla Strike, *d* April 4, 1863, *a* 73.
Robert Strike, her husband, *d* Nov. 22, 1880, *a* 93, for 36 years baker and servant to the Hon E. I. Company.

John Hayr, *d* Aug. 1. 1865, *a* 51.
> This languishing head is at rest,
>   Its thinking and aching are o'er,
> This quiet immoveable breast
>   Is heaved by affliction no more.

George Gates, *d* Feb. 6, 1869, *a* 54.

Clara Ellen Freeth, *d* March 3, 1861, *a* 3.

Wm. Homfray Foulkes, *d* Jan. 9, 1857, *a* 1.
> This lovely bud, so young and fair,
>   Called hence by early doom,
> Just came to show how sweet a flower
>   In Paradise could bloom.

Griffith Cadwallader Foulkes, *d* Aug. 19, 1857, *a* 5.

Mary, wife of Cornelias Amos, *d* Feb. 12, 1859, *a* 85.

Margaret Elizabeth Case, *d* March 5, 1858, *a* 68.
Priscilla Case, *d* July 30, 1871, *a* 77.

Caroline Grace Cooke, *d.* Jan. 9, 1859, *a* 59.

George Spiers, of High-street, *d* Oct. 1, 1859, *a* 28.

[George Spiers was nephew to the late Mr. W. H. Campart, hatter, High
Street.   He had accepted an appointment as correspondent or reporter
to a Lewes paper, but his career as a journalist was cut short by his
decease in the prime of life.   He was a genial young man, and a
vivacious companion.   He had no family, and his widow afterwards
married the late Mr. Bowden, ironmonger].

Joseph Cross, *d* Dec. 31, 1858. *a* 31.

> Though lost to sight, to mem'ry dear,
> A beloved husband lies sleeping here.

Susan Matheson, *d* Sept. 17, 1860, *a* 7½.

William George Matheson, *d* Oct. 28, 1878, *a* 23.

Mrs. Phillis Oliviere, *d* Sep. 29, 1859, *a* 58.

George Ward, *d* Dec. 17, 1859, *a* 78.

Charlotte Wells, his daughter, *d* Nov. 28, 1865, *a* 55.

Mr. William Grace, *d* Jan. 20, 1859, *a* 53.

William Collard, *d* Dec. 7, 1860, *a* 82.

Mary, his wife, *d* July 9, 1862, *a* 77.

Thomas, son of W. S. & J. Walker, *d* Dec. 28, 1865, *a* 6.

> The short-lived beauties die away,
> So bloom the human face divine ;
> When youth its pride of beauty shows ;
> In their spring the colours shine,
> And sweeter than the virgin rose.

Caroline Edith Mary Case, *d* Feb. 5, 1858, *a* 7.

Fredk. Jas. Case, *d* Feb. 9, 1858, *a* 6.

> They were lovely in their lives, and in death were not divided.

Frances, their grandmother, *d* June 2, 1861, *a* 70.

Charlotte, wife of Wm. Crawley, *d* Nov. 25, 1855, *a* 32.

> Though lost to sight to mem'ry dear,
> A beloved wife lies sleeping here,
> Her loss I very much deplore,
> But hope to meet and part no more,
> Where grief and pain for ever cease,
> And all is calm and joy and peace.

Elizabeth, wife of J. M. Hoffmeister, Esq., Paymaster R.N., *d* May 21,
1858, *a* 53.

Thomas Cummins, *d* Feb. 12, 1855, *a* 56.

Ann Cheesman, his sister, *d* Dec. 20. 1861, *a* 68.

Maria Lyke, *d* May 31, 1855, *a* 64.

Charles James Whitaker, *d* Oct. 13, 1855, *a* 69.

Martha Whitaker, his wife, *d* Nov. 28, 1859, *a* 73.

John Morgan, *d* Jan. 31, 1858, *a* 56.

Mary Morgan, his wife, *d* Feb. 6, 1880, *a* 83.

William Maughan, *d* Jan. 23, 1860, *a* 55.

James Stock, Master Mariner of Hull, *d* May 1, 1863, *a* 76.

> I left my home in perfect health,
> We little thought of death so nigh,
> But God saw good to take me hence,
> And with His will we must comply.

Eleanor, wife of Joseph Gower, July 15, 1866, *a* 49.

Thomas Sibery, *d* May 20, 1866, *a* 44.

James Winburn, *d* Dec. 27, 1866, *a* 53.

Henry Cornelius Thomas, surgeon, *d* Nov. 5, 1858, *a* 57.

Lucy Jane Frost, *d* Jan. 20, 1851, *a* 29.
Mary Frost, her daughter, *d* June 8, 1851, *a* 3.

John Wenman, *d* Aug. 22, 1856, *a* 30.
Only trust me.

William Cochrane, Corporal in the Grenadier Guards, *d* March 30, 1860, *a* 25.

Edward, son of George Cooper, surgeon, *d* Aug. 2, 1868, *a* 13.

William Edwards, who was killed by the falling of the Railway Bridge, Gloucester-road, March 20, 1865, *a* 36.

Elizabeth Graves, *d* May 10, 1865, *a* 26.
Thomas Graves, *d* July 23, 1863, *a* 63.
Elizabeth Graves, his wife, *d* Dec. 25, 1871, *a* 73.
William Graves, *d* May 28, 1872, *a* 31.
Norman Alfred Graves, *d* July 22, 1872, *a* 5.   Also four more children.
Louisa Elizabeth Graves, their mother, *d* Dec. 5, 1880, *a* 41.
    [Members of the Graves' family, livery stable keepers and cab proprietors.]

Edward Daniel, *d* March 27, 1864, *a* 31.
So fall asleep in slumber deep,
Slumber that knows no ending.
    [Mr. Daniel was a coach painter, and lived in Mead Grove.   He was greatly respected, and died after a few days' illness, leaving a widow and two children.]

Eliza Asman, wife of Mark Griffin, *d* May 23, 1873, *a* 68.

George Scambler, *d* Oct. 4, 1865, *a* 54.
James Dawson, *d* Dec. 29, 1853, *a* 71.

Eliza Cooper, *d* Aug. 14, 1866, *a* 47.

John Parry, Esq., late of St. Helen's Place, London, *d* June 6, 1867, *a* 91.
Jane Peck, his niece, *d* Dec. 31, 1870, *a* 63.

John Bateman, Esq., *d* Oct. 1, 1853, *a* 70.

Charlotte, wife of Edwd. George Gilbert, *d* Aug. 7, 1858, *a* 41.

James and Mary Penfold rest in Christ.

Robt. Martin Leeds, Esq., many years in the Hon. E. I. C.'s Service at Addiscombe, *d* Aug. 21, 1853, *a* 80.
    [This gentleman was purveyor to the Addiscombe College, and had the superintendence of all the provisions sent in by the tradesmen. He was succeeded in the office by his son, Robert Johnson Leeds, who is also buried in another part of this churchyard.]

Ann Feldwick, *d* March 8, 1858, *a* 79.
Charlotte, her sister, relict of J. W. Francis, of North End, *d* April 2, 1872, *a* 79.

Needham Kilmorey Cooke, son of Lieut. Cooke, R.N., after a protracted illness, entered into the joy of his Lord, Aug. 14, 1844, *a* 21.
    By his desire this tablet proclaims that the sole foundation of his bright assurance of acceptance with God, which enabled him to approach death with unclouded composure, was the finished work of Jesus Christ.
He hath clothed me with the garments of salvation; he hath covered me with the robe of righteousness.

Elvira, wife of Lieut. Cooke, *d* July 8, 1847.
    [Lieut. Cook was professor of Naval Architecture in Addiscombe College.]

F

Rev. James Penfold, M.A., *d* June 14, 1858, *a* 55.
Mary, his wife, *d* May 5. 1882, *a* 76,
Emily Grace, his second daughter, who after a short illness, entered into
  her heavenly rest on the night of her earthly Sabbath, July 10,
  1853, *a* 14.

South Side of the Church.

Lieut.-Co George Fredk. Penley, late of the Bombay Army, *d* May 14,
  1869, *a* 74.
  [Col. Penley was a well-known figure on the platforms of all Church Missions.
    During the decade 1860-1870, he was an active worker in all the religious
    and benevolent movements in Croydon ; and he died, as he had lived,
    with the respect of all who were privileged to know him].

Eiizabeth Soan, wife of Josiah Matthew, *d* June 12, 1847.

John Lock, *d* Sept. 30, 1832, *a* 24.
  Dearest wife and mother dear,
  Think of one a sleeping here,
  And passing stop and drop a tear,
  And pray be kind to my children dear.

Henney Longhurst, *d* April 22, 1861, *a* 68.

Thomas Chlist, late of the Volunteer Inn, *d* July 16, 1858, *a* 58.

Harriett, daughter of Wm. and Harriett Batchelar, *d* Sept. 15, 1852, *a* 11
  months.
  Beneath this rail, so feebly raised,
    Harriett gently sleeps.
  Here shall the sighs of grief be heard
    For here her parents weep.
  Here rest, Harriett, free from pain,
    And free from mortal care,
  Parent and child will meet again
    And wiped be every tear.

Clarissa Palmer, *d* Feb. 27, 1855, *a* 33.
Sabina Elliott Palmer, *d* Sept. 4, 1844, *a* 17.
  Where Jesus is I fain would be,
  I faint my much-loved Lord to see,
  Earth twine no more about my heart,
  It is far better to depart.

Richd. Palmer, *d* Feb. 2, 1836, *a* 74.
  Glory to Thee, who so oft has kept,
  And hast refreshed me whilst I slept,
  Grant, Lord, when I from death shall wake
  I may of endless life partake.

Anne Heather, *d* May 9, 1865, *a* 34. and infant daughter.

Rev. Richard Crampton Fell, died at Windermere, after a short illness, to
  the inexpressible grief of his wife, Aug. 8, 1866, *a* 61.
  [The Rev. R. C. Fell lived in George Street. at the house which was then
    No. 12, now No. 81. He was a great scholar, and (in conjunction with
    the Rev. E. F. Beynon, Rector of Chelsham) wrote a work on the Life
    of Alderman Kelly, the well-known publisher, who originated the plan
    of publishing works in weekly parts. Mr. and Mrs. Fell were known
    and respected for their simple Christianity and unostentatious bene-
    volence to the poor. One of the new roads on the Friends' School
    estate is named after them].

Eleanor, his widow, *d* April 18, 1882, *a* 82.

William Ralph, met his death on the London and Brighton Railway, March 18, 1869, *a* 30.
Alice Ralph, his wife, *d* July 1, 1876, *a* 33.

Sarah, wife of Henry Cooper, *d* Dec. 19, 1864, *a* 59.
Henry Cooper, *d* Sep. 4, 1882, *a* 83.
Edward Cooper, his son, *d* June 28, 1855, *a* 27.

Thomas Elison Deaton Howard, *d* July 18, 1863, *a* 57.

Elizabeth, wife of Nathaniel Barton Cooke, *d* June 9, 1869, *a* 44,   A'so two children.

John Sedgwick, *d* Jan 15. 1847. *a* 67.
Thomas Sedgwick, his son, *d* May 17, 1853, *a* 6.

Beneath this stone are deposited, till the morning of the Resurrection the remains of Jane, the most dear wife of Lieut.-Col. Jacob. To her it was eminently given to " adorn the doctrine of God our Saviour in all things," by " her work of faith and labour of love," and especially " by the ornament of a meek and quiet spirit." After a few hours of most patient suffering, she fell asleep in Christ on the 11th of March, 1853. *a* 35.
After a brief interval of 15 months from the departure of his dear wife, were deposited by side of her, the remains of her beloved husband, Lieut.-Colonel William Jacob (late of the Bombay Army).
What he was in His sight, the death of Whose saints is precious, that day will declare. What he was in his own eyes is recorded in the following words in his last will—" A Sinner saved by grace." He entered into rest 16th June, 1854, *a* 54.

Elizabeth, daughter of the Rev. Richd. Clark. M.A., *d* Dec. 18, 1847, *a* 75.
Sarah Ann, relict of Robt. Naylor, Esq.. formerly relict of Edwin Le Grand, Esq., surgeon of Canterbury, sister-in-law of the above, *d* Dec. 31, 1847, *a* 75.

Louisa, wife of the Rev. C. Arnold, M.A., *d* Oct. 25. 1854, *a* 73.
Harriett Louisa, her daughter, *d* Aug. 20, 1878, *a* 59.

Ellen Jane Leeds, *d* Nov. 10, 1855, *a* 16.

> Oh! not in cruelty, not in wrath,
> The reaper came that day,
> 'Twas an angel visited the green earth
> And took the flower away.

Caroline Ann Leeds, her sister, *d* May 20, 1856, *a* 12.

> To thee, O Lord, we her resign,
> Our loss is her great gain.
> The lovely gift was wholly thine,
> Why then should we complain ?

Robt. Johnson Leeds, House Steward, at Addiscombe College, *d* May 11, 1867, *a* 63.

Caroline Ann Girling, *d* Sep. 29, 1852, *a* 27.

Thomas Hayward, *d* May 26, 1855. *a* 38.
Esther Wilhelma Hayward, his mother, *d* April 11, 1875.
Richd. William Hayward, his father, *d* April 29, 1824, *a* 43.
Richd. Hayward, eldest son of the above, *d* July 2, 1847, *a* 33.
Francis, second son, *d* June 9, 1851, *a* 25.

James Parker, *d* March 28, 1860, *a* 47.
George Parker, his father, *d* Dec. 15, 1861, *a* 75.
Martha Parker, his mother, *d* Dec. 15, 1862, *a* 74.
Agnes Esther Smith, niece, *d* May 5, 1866, *a* 16.

John Russell. *d* Jan. 22, 1855, *a* 75.
Eleanor Russell, his widow, *d* Feb. 26, 1880, *a* 89.

Joseph Neville, surgeon, *d* Sept. 12, 1850, *a* 48.
> If the soul can cast itself upon God, and place an entire confidence in Him, death is no more than a sigh, or a short passage from one life to another.

Frank Hay Neville, *d* Aug. 11, 1861, *a* 26.

John Pollard, *d* Aug. 1, 1860, *a* 45.
> A father of the fatherless and a judge of the widow is God in His holy habitation.

Elizabeth Gardner, *d* July 23, 1856, *a* 32.
James Gardner, *d* March 27, 1861, *a* 76.

Charles Farebrother, *d* July 25, 1852, *a* 41.
Anne, his wife, *d* April 24, 1867, *a* 55.

Sarah Jepson, *d* Oct. 15, 1851, *a* 47.

Mary, wife of Joseph Smith, *d* March 1, 1858, *a* 62.
Joseph Smith, *d* Nov. 25, 1862, *a* 64.

John Rose, *d* Aug. 6, 1864, *a* 59,

Herbert, son of Solomon Child, *d* April 2, 1863, *a* 16.

Mary Ann Lewis, *d* May 2, 1859, *a* 6.
> A lovely girl lies sleeping here,
>   Short was on earth her stay,
> For at the age of six years old
>   Alas ! 'twas took away.

Mrs. Sarah Dean, *d* Jan. 19, 1862, *a* 69.
Mary Hannah Dean, *d* Dec. 5, 1850, *a* 10 months.
Florence Edith Dean, *d* July 7, 1867, *a* 2.
George Dean, *d* Nov. 15, 1878, *a* 87.
> [Mr. George Dean was a well-known nurseryman. The West Croydon Baptist Chapel, Thornhill Road, and roads adjacent, now cover the site of his gardens and grounds.]

George Keys, *d* March 22, 1865, *a* 75.
Jane Keys, his wife, *d* Jan. 30, 1876, *a* 79.

Phœbe Downing, 37 years pew opener at St. James's Church, *d* Nov. 22, 1865, *a* 75.
> This stone was erected by the congregation of St. James's Church as a tribute of sincere respect for her long and faithful service.

Sophia Morris, 37 years pew opener at the same church, *d* Jan. 24, 1866, *a* 85.
William, son of George and Phœbe Downing, died in the Crimea, Jan. 24, 1855, *a* 29.
George Downing, his father, after a lingering illness of 32 years, *d* Feb. 4, 1861, *a* 79.

William Dyer, *d* Oct. 31, 1854, *a* 33.
> My time on earth so soon did pass away
> Because God called I could no longer stay,
> A rapid consumption brought me to my grave
> I trust in Christ my precious soul to save.

James Steer, *d* Dec. 5, 1858, *a* 64.
Matilda, his wife, *d* June 12, 1860, *a* 58.
Letitia Steer, their daughter, *d* Nov. 28, 1857, *a* 14.
George, their son, *d* July 9, 1842, *a* 16.

Joseph Dyer, *d* April 24, 1840, *a* 8.

> Weep not, dear friends, altho' on earth
> My time with you is past,
> With Christ in heaven we hope to meet
> Where happiness will last.

William Russell, *d* May 31, 1854, *a* 25.
Sarah Russell, his wife, *d* Jan. 6, 1860, *a* 34.

James Cox, Esq., of Broad Green Place, *d* Jan. 7, 1862, *a* 83.
Mary Cox, his widow, *d* May 15, 1867, *a* 92.
Ann Cox, their youngest daughter, *d* March, 1847, *a* 15.
John Brookes Cox, *d* Sept. 4, 1851, *a* 22.
Mary Cox, daughter, *d* Sept. 1, 1877, *a* 50.
Alexander Thomas Cox, *d* Aug. 25, 1850, *a* 84.
John, eldest son of James Cox, whom he survived six months, *d* July 21, 1862, *a* 59, leaving a widow and daughter, who inscribe this tablet to his fondly cherished memory.
Ann Cox, his wife, *d* April 22, 1875, *a* 77.

Catherine Brooks, *d* Feb 9, 1853, *a* 44.

Mary, wife of Wm. Russell, sen., *d* July 27, 1853, *a* 64.
William Russell, her husband, *d* Oct. 13, 1855, *a* 55.

George Freeman, *d* March 28, 1853, *a* 17.

Thomas Everest, *d* Aug. 28, 1848, *a* 46.

Francis Williams, *d* May 10, 1861, *a* 76.

To the memory of my brother, William Loft, Esq., *d* Sept. 13, 1842.

George Forshaw, *d* June 23, 1841, *a* 27.

Michael Brennan, *d* Jan. 11, 1848, *a* 30.

George Stevens, *d* Oct. 4, 1863, *a* 68.
Elizabeth, his wife, *d* Dec. 20, 1841, *a* 47.

William Sharp, *d* April 18, 1865, *a* 79.

James Ford, bricklayer, *d* July 3, 1839, *a* 49,
Mary Ford, his wife, *d* April, 7, 1873, *a* 83.

Robert Cates, *d* June 27, 1845, *a* 59.
Thomas Cates, his son, *d* March 20, 1849, *a* 25.
Elizabeth Cates, his wife, *d* March 14, 1856, *a* 70.
Robert Cates, another son, *d* March 7, 1859, *a* 36.
Harriet Cates, *d* March 24, 1839, *a* 23.
Mrs. Sarah Storey, her sister, *d* Sept. 27, 1841, *a* 27.

Thomas Stagg, *d* July 6, 1846, *a* 62.
Mrs. Ann Stagg, *d* Dec. 11, 1846, *a* 65.
Mrs. Jane Stagg, *d* Aug. 20, 1848, *a* 61.
> [Mr. Stagg was for many years landlord of the Windmill Inn, St. James's road.]

Francis Marshall, *d* Dec. 24, 1836, *a* 71.
Elizabeth Marshall, his wife, *d* April 30, 1851, *a* 80.

Ann, wife of Geo. Nevill, Thornton Heath, *d* Sept. 28, 1839, *a* 40.

Mary, wife of John Gabitass, *d* Jan. 6, 1839, *a* 90.
John Gabitass, *d* Feb. 6, 1841, *a* 82.
> Also three great grand children.

Mary, wife of John Meager, of Walter Green Farm, *d* March 15, 1848, *a* 39.

Elizabeth, wife of Fredk. Snee, *d* March 5, 1870, *a* 71.
Frederick Snee, *d* July 2, 1877, *a* 80.

Elizabeth, wife of William Dyer, *d* Jan. 21, 1867, *a* 70.
William Dyer, *d* Feb. 4, 1871, *a* 76.
[Mr. Dyer was a road contractor, and lived in Parson's Mead.]

Mary, wife of Walford Appleby, *d* Feb. 15, 1857, *a* 67.
Walford Appleby, *d* Nov. 19, 1867, *a* 81.
[Mr. Appleby lived for many years at what is now No. 45, North End.]

Harriett Andrew, wife of Henry Appleby, *d* Easter Day, 1865, *a* 39.
Alfred William, her son, *d* Nov. 25, 1868, *a* 8.

Anthony Mean, *d* June 1, 1858, *a* 54.

Robert Hall, *d* Aug. 28, 1851, *a* 71.
Richard Hall, his son, *d* July 21, 1867, *a* 51.

Thomas Willoughby Holledge, *d* March 28, 1850, *a* 56.
Sarah, his widow, *d* Nov. 12, 1874, *a* 79.

William Elliffe, *d* Sept. 30, 1847, *a* 42.
> Prepare, my friends, do not delay,
> All in my prime was called away.

Alice Hempstead, *d* Sept. 30, 1860, *a* 83.
Alice Goulding, her daughter, *d* Sept. 13, 1858, *a* 58.

John Chatfield, *d* Nov. 28, 1854, *a* 57.
Sophia Chatfield, *d* Oct. 22, 1849, *a* 24.
Caroline Chatfield, *d* June 6, 1857, *a* 19.

Elizabeth Horner, *d* Sept. 10, 1841, *a* 52.

John Holloway, *d* Aug. 11, 1843, *a* 65.
Chas. Lonsdale, Esq., late Capt. 21st Fusiliers, *d* Feb. 26, 1846, *a* 60.

William Crosby, *d* June 2, 1849, *a* 54.
Isabella Wrigley, *d* Nov. 10, 1854, *a* 77.

William Etherington, *d* Aug. 23, 1862, *a* 58.
[Formerly landlord of the Star Inn, Broad Green.]

Henry Gill Harding, *d* Aug. 24, 1851, *a* 21.
Mary Ann Harding, *d* Oct. 18, 1853, *a* 28.
James Smithson Harding, *d* May 1, 1868, *a* 72.
Ann Harding, *d* Aug. 16, 1877, *a* 88.

Mary, wife of James Collis, of Bensome Lane, *d* April 2, 1847, *a* 44.
Mrs. Amelia Zuber, her sister, *d* Jan. 26, 1870, *a* 73.

Samuel Selmes, *d* Nov. 27, 1852, *a* 80.
Ann Maria Jane Selmes, *d* July 11, 1856, *a* 80.

James Hayward Evans, *d* Nov. 19, 1848, *a* 20.

Louisa Claudina Arnold, *d* Feb. 24, 1862, *a* 31.

John Harris Archer, *d* May 9, 1844, *a* 10.

Frank Wells, *d* Nov. 30, 1858, *a* 10.

Elizabeth Hall, *d* Sept. 17, 1845, *a* 81.
Jane Hall, her daughter, *d* March 9, 1848, *a* 46.

Thomas Watson, draper, *d* March 12, 1857, *a* 30.

Joseph Bebb, *d* May 30, 1849, *a* 86.

Thomas Dale, *d* Dec. 23, 1847, *a* 82.
Sarah Dale, his wife, *d* Feb. 26, 1848, *a* 80.

Elizabeth Mary Roberts, *d* Dec. 8, 1846, *a* 33.
Mrs. Mary Roberts, her mother, *d* Aug. 27, 1849, *a* 64.

Jane Lucy Parker, *d* March 31, 1848, *a* 4.
> O flower of bloom, too brief for human love,
> To Heaven's ark too soon, returning dove,
> One solace leaves us not with thee, sweet child,
> To God in beauty pure and undefiled.

Jane Dartnell, *d* Sept. 5, 1862, *a* 57.
John, her husband, *d* Nov. 23, 1861, *a* 63.
> [Member of the well-known firm of Close and Dartnell, plumbers, glaziers, and painters, of North End.]

Diana Dawes, *d* Jan. 21, 1847, *a* 82.
Daniel Dawes, *d* Dec. 10, 1849. *a* 67.

Elizabeth Meager Bunyer, wife of Andrew Gale, *d* July 29, 1848, *a* 41.
> Forsake me not, O Lord my God,
> Not far from me depart,
> Make haste to my relief, O Thou
> Who my salvation art.

Andrew Gale, her husband, *d* Aug. 10, 1882, *a* 75.
> [A road contractor, late of the Whitehorse Road.]

Daniel Howell, *d* April 24, 1845, *a* 34.
> Death little warning to me gave,
> And quickly brought me to my grave;
> I from my friends did quickly part
> And lost my life by horse and cart.

William Hoyle, who met his death with an accident on the Dover Railroad, May 24, 1846, *a* 22.
> Mourn not for me, my life is past,
> I loved you while life did last,
> Mercy show and pity take,
> And love my infant for my sake.

William Torrington, *d* March 9, 1862, *a* 62.

Sarah Davies, *d* Sept. 17, 1865, *a* 70.
Mary Ann Davies, *d* Nov. 12, 1862, *a* 51.

Ann, wife of Wm. Castledine, *d* Jan. 10, 1865, *a* 78.

William Pugh, *d* March 31, 1865, *a* 61.

Florence, daughter of George Stamper, *d* April 12, 1865, *a* 20.

Louisa Mary Ann Roper, *d* June 7, 1869, *a* 34.
Robert Roper, her father, *d* Nov. 16, 1881, *a* 70.

Margaret Mary, wife of Robt. Rogers, *d* Oct. 31, 1856, *a* 51.
Emma, his second wife, *d* Feb. 9, 1860, *a* 38.

Charlotte de Merveilleux, *d* May 14, 1864.
Matilda de Merveilleux, *d* Aug. 23, 1867, *a* 35.

Philip, eldest son of George and Augusta Chasemore, of Waddon, *d* Sept. 4, 1848, *a* 22.
George, his brother, *d* Feb. 22, 1853, *a* 24.
Augusta, their mother, *d* Aug. 21, 1855.

Mary Ann, daughter of John Wood, *d* Feb. 14, 1864, *a* 6.
Harriet, her sister, *d* March 5, 1864, *a* 1 year and 7 months.
> Dear to their parents, to their God more dear,
> Two little sisters sweetly slumber here;
> Blest is their state, from sin and danger free.
> To us they died; they live, O Lord, to Thee.

Thomas Ward, *d* June 12, 1855, *a* 77.
Caroline Jane, wife of Robt. J. Ward, *d* March 16, 1873, *a* 44.

Louie, daughter of the late Wm. Godson, *d* Aug 7, 1875, *a* 21.
Mary Ann Kettle. *d* July 6, 1861, *a* 60.
To the memory of Darling Addie, born May 27, 1863, slept Feb. 22, 1867,
For of such is the kingdom of heaven.

END OF ST. JAMES'S CHURCHYARD.

ST. PETER'S CHURCH.

THE district Church of St. Peter's is very pleasantly situated on the brow of a hill, near the South end of the town. The land on which it stands, and the graveyard adjoining, was given by Mr. John Russell, of Dunlewey House, Bedford Park, who died July 9th, 1864, and lies buried near the northern side of the tower. The Church itself is a very handsome structure, and was built in 1850-1, from designs by Sir G. Scott. A finely-proportioned spire was placed on the tower in 1864, but was burnt down while being finished; it was rebuilt and completed in 1865. The churchyard is full of graves, and it is expected that it will be closed almost immediately by an Order in Council. There are no tablets in the interior, but several memorial windows. The most prominent is one over the Communion table, the central portions of which represent the five most prominent Evangelists—St. Peter in the centre; on the left hand, SS. Matthew and Mark; on the right, SS. Luke and John. In the north aisle is a window erected by the relatives of a lady named Rhodes, representing the Christian graces—"I was hungry and ye gave me meat; I was thirsty and ye gave me drink; I was naked and ye clothed me; I was a wanderer and ye took me in; I was sick and ye visited me; I was in prison and ye came unto me." Miss Rhodes was a blind lady, and lived at South End. She was very charitable, and contributed largely towards the building of this Church. In order to increase the funds she had a little work published, called *The Anglo-Indian Family*, written by a lady who now resides in the neighbourhood of Reigate. There are three other windows adjoining, which bear the following inscriptions :—" In memory of Edward Peplar Smith, and Henrietta Frances, daughter of Charles Bailey, 1852;" "In memoriam Georgii Smith, vicino agro Selsdonensi et Francesca Maria, ejus uxoris Poni curavit Johannes Henricus corum filius, 1852;" "In memoriam Thoma James et Rebecca ejus filii iii., filia iiij., hanc fenestram tirri ferrerum." Another window has lately been added by Mr. J. S. Wright, in memory of his wife. Underneath is this inscription :—" To the memory of Eliza, the beloved wife of James Spurrier Wright, of Duppas Hill Terrace; at rest, June 15, 1880." In the trefoils at the top are angels bearing banners, on which is inscribed "Alleluia." The centre window represents St. Ann teaching the Virgin Mary from the Book of Holy Writ. On the open page are inscribed in Latin the prophetic words that a virgin should bear a child who should be called Emmanuel. On the right hand side is depicted Mary of Bethany at the feet of Jesus, with Martha in the background. Underneath, Ruth brought before Boaz with the gleaned wheat in her arms. At the bottom, the Syro-Phœnician woman touching the hem of Jesus' garment. On the right hand we see Esther pleading for her people before the king ; underneath is the Annunciation—" Blessed art thou among women ; " and at the bottom, the infant Moses in his cradle is brought before Pharaoh's daughter." There is another memorial window adjoining the one above described, placed there by the late Dr. Westall (who practised for many years in Croydon) to the memory of his only son.

The South East Side of the Churchyard.

Charles Miller, *d* Sept. 15, 1878.

> Mr. Charles Miller formerly lived in the Waldrons, and was the son of the late Thomas Miller, Esq. (gentleman and a scholar), who resided in Church Street for a number of years. He was also brother of George Miller, Esq., the well-known barrister, who still resides in Church Street. We believe that Mr. Charles Miller had an appointment in the Treasury, which he held for many years.

Lydia, wife of Thos. Farley, of Clapham, *d* Jan. 24, 1880, *a* 86.

> My presence shall go with thee, and I will give thee rest.

Henry Constable Roberts, *d* July 29, 1881, *a* 29.

> This gentleman, who had only recently been married, was cut off in the prime of life, not only to the intense grief of his sorrowing family, but to the sincere regret of his numerous friends, to whom he had endeared himself by his kindness, his amiability, and his *bon homie*.

Mark Cooper Day, *d* March 8, 1874, *a* 43.

> [Mr. Day was a carpenter and joiner, and had his workshops in Park Street.]

Juliet Nunes, fell asleep Jan. 9, 1872.

Mary, wife of Christopher Bartlett, *d* Oct. 11, 1871, *a* 60.
Christopher Bartlett, her husband, *d* Dec. 2, 1878, *a* 61.

> Mr. Bartlett was a self-made man, and was much respected by all who knew him. He was an old inhabitant of the town, and like thousands of other frugal, industrious, and fortunate men, he raised himself by perseverance and integrity from an humble position to one of comparative affluence. It is often said that Fortune wearies of carrying the same man ; but Mr. Bartlett must have been one of Fortune's favourites, for she never seemed to tire of carrying him, although he was not a feather weight. His first important work was laying out the street, now called West Street. He then purchased a large plot of land, beyond the Swan and Sugar Loaf, where he erected a number of houses. Bartlett Street commemorates this gentleman's enterprise. Mr. Chas. Davis continues the timber business established by the deceased.

Edith Jane, second daughter of Howard and Julia Nalder, *d* March 25, 1867.
This memorial is erected by her brothers and sisters.

Catherine, wife of C. R. Gilson, *d* Jan. 29, 1872, *a* 34.

Robert Russell, youngest son of James and Mary Russell, *d* Dec. 26, 1870, *a* 68.
Sui appetens nunquam.

Ann Russell, *d* March 2, 1877, *a* 61.
Having survived her beloved husband six years.

George Harker, *d* Aug. 1. 1869, *a* 35.
Harriett Harker, his wife, *d* Dec. 15, 1867, *a* 32.
The best of wives and mothers.

Maria, wife of John Simm Smith, *d* Feb. 18, 1867, *a* 71.
John Simm Smith, of Blunt House, Croydon, *d* Oct. 7, 1877, *a* 85.
Mr. John Simm Smith was a retired physician, and resided with his family at Blunt House for many years. His son is now one of the respected churchwardens of St. Peter's.

Arthur Charlesworth, an infant, *d* Nov. 12, 1871.

Emily, youngest daughter of Henry Langford, *d* Nov. 1, 1865, *a* 22.

Joseph Silver, M.A., of Trinity College, Cambridge, *d* Feb. 1, 1855. *a* 59.
William Silver, M.A., of Trinity College, Cambridge, his brother, *d* Dec. 26, 1867, *a* 63.
[These two gentlemen were well-known in the literary circles in the town and neighbourhood. They resided in the house now occupied by Dr. Lanchester, Park Lane.]

In loving memory of our little darling Edith Mary, *d* Oct. 8, 1873; and Alfred Edwin Graves, *d* Aug. 6, 1879.

Mary Anne Mackenzie, *d* July 20, 1874. *a* 82.
I look for the resurrection of the dead, and the life of the world to come.

Rebecca, widow of Thos. Miller, Esq.. *d* Dec. 23, 1860, *a* 85.
[Mrs. Miller was the widow of Mr. Miller, whom we have before mentioned as the first organist of St. John's Church, see page 24.]

Mrs. Mary Ann Dudman, *d* Jan 13, 1875, *a* 86.
She is not tasting death, but taking rest,
On the same holy couch where Jesus lay,
Soon to awake all glorified and blest,
When the day breaks and the shadows flee away.

Henry Roffey, *d* Nov. 10, 1881, *a* 31.
" We trust that those we call the dead are breathers of an ampler day for ever nobler ends."
[Mr. Roffey was a young man of great promise. He had only (on his marriage with Miss Entwistle) taken the business of Mr. Francis Warren, bookseller, about twelve months before his lamented death.]

Frederick Puzey, *d* Jan. 5, 1873, *a* 35.
[Mr. Puzey carried on the wine and spirit trade at the corner of Katharine Street, now conducted by Mr. Entwistle.]

In grateful recollection of his zeal on behalf of their spiritual welfare, and of his many estimable qualities, this stone is erected by members of the Congregation of Christ Church, Nassau, Bahamas, to the memory of the Rev. William Strachan, who died the 10th of August, 1866, in the 74th year of his age, after spending 53 years of his life as a Clergyman of the Church of the Bahamas, during 30 of which, and until his resignation through loss of sight, he was Rector of the parish of Christ Church.

Ann Hodgson, *d* Feb. 2, 1875, *a* 91.

Ann, wife of Fredk. Bean, *d* Nov. 17. 1863, *a* 47.
Frederick Bean. her husband, *d* Feb. 28, 1870, *a* 57.

Thomas Brooks, late H.E.I.C.S., *d* Feb. 19, 1864, *a* 67.

Walter Heygate Lambert, *d* Ash-Wednesday, 1866, *a* 13 months.

Augustus le Forestier, died at Samarang, Java, March 17, 1852.
Elizabeth, his wife, *d* Feb. 22, 1867, *a* 63.
Thomas Wallis, her brother, *d* Feb. 8, 1868, *a* 51.

Albert, son of George and Mary Ann Bance, *d* Sept. 20, 1867, *a* 27.
George Bance, *d* June 15. 1873. *a* 75.
Mary Ann Bance, *d* Feb. 24, 1880, *a* 76.

> [Mr. George Bance was an undertaker, and founded the business still carried on by his son.]

Ann, wife of Commander Leven Charles Fredk. Walker, R.N., *d* Dec. 27, 1867, *a* 68.
Commander Walker, *d* Sept. 7, 1876, *a* 74.

Mary Ann, wife of James Skinner, *d* Aug. 21, 1868, *a* 41.

> Her children arise up and call her blessed ; her husband also,
> and he praiseth her.

Samuel Hopkins, of South End, *d* June 29. 1870. *a* 63.

> [Formerly a grocer and cheesemonger, 23, South End.]

Ada Emma, daughter of D. W. C. and E. Ardley, *d* Nov. 15, 1870, *a* 3 years and 7 months.

William Allen Willmot, *d* Nov. 2, 1872, *a* 1¼.

> "And Jesus called a little child unto him."

John Allen Davis, of South End, *d* Aug. 11, 1868, *a* 26.
John Davis, his father, *d* May 20, 1873, *a* 68.

> [For many years landlord of the Swan and Sugar Loaf Inn.]

Martha Embly, *d* Nov. 2, 1873, *a* 45.

Mary Ann, wife of Chas. Samuel Coppin, *d* Jan. 9, 1875. *a* 26.
Elizabeth, wife of Chas. James Coppin, *d* Jan. 14, 1877, *a* 62.

Mary Ann, daughter of Curtis and Hannah Crippen, *d* June 25, 1867.
James Wells, youngest son of the above, *d* Sept. 11, 1871, *a* 72.

Ann Bickley, *d* Nov. 29, *a* 69.

Gertrude Elizabeth, child of Owen and Sarah King, *d* Nov. 15, 1870, *a* 1 year and 5 months.
Ethel Marion, her sister, *d* Jan. 2, 1874, *a* 3.

Mary Ann, wife of Wm. Harris Rule, D.D., Wesleyan Minister, *d* Feb. 26, 1873, *a* 69.
James Ulric, son of Barrow Rule, grandson of the above, *d* Oct. 10, 1873, *a* 10 months.

> [The Rev. W. H. Rule is still a prominent minister in the Wesleyan Church, and the author of several religious works. His son, Mr. Barrow Rule, is now clerk to the School Board.]

George Baker, *d* Dec. 26, 1870, *a* 67.

Emma, the fond and cherished wife of H. J. Hammon, Esq., of the Limes, Croydon, *d* June 29, 1851, *a* 44.
Charles Henry, her eldest son, *d* May 12, 1861, *a* 18.

Jane. wife of George Luckins, *d* Feb. 1, 1866, *a* 49.
Susan, wife of George Luckins, *d* Oct. 28, 1881, *a* 64.

Louise Stubbington, *d* Oct. 16, 1881, *a* 79.

George Hatch, *d* Sept. 7, 1866, *a* 44.
Charlotte, his wife, *d* April 30, 1879, *a* 56.

Francis Joseph Page, *d* June 4, 1867, *a* 9 months.

William Herring, *d* Feb. 5, 1858, *a* 57.
[A well-known eccentric barber in the Middle Row.]

Anne, wife of H. J. Whitling, *d* Nov. 28, 1862.

Sarah Hilling, *d* May 6, 1863, *a* 49.
John Hilling, her husband, *d* Oct. 14, 1864, *a* 50.

Chas. Wm. Wilbraham, *d* Oct. 26, 1868, *a* 64.

Annie Elizabeth Cooper, *d* May 27, 1872, *a* 9.
Kate Hillier Cooper, *d* June 17, 1872, *a* 16 months.

William Davey, *d* May 30th, 1879, *a* 84.

Francis Edward, son of F. and J. Wood, *d* May 5, 1873, *a* 5.
Blanche Wood, *d* Jan. 29, 1875, *a* 1.

Arthur Searle, *d* April 12, 1869, *a* 7 months.

Mary Ann Groom, *d* Sept. 26, 1870, *a* 3½
He shall gather the lambs with His arm, and carry them in His bosom.

James Duncan Kennedy, *d* Feb. 10, 1869, *a* 47.
Erected by a friend from his boyhood in affectionate remembrance.
"I sought the Lord, and he heard me, and delivered me from all my fears."

James Mardell, *d* Nov. 3, 1867, *a* 74.

Miriam Roffey, *d* April 10, 1862, *a* 49.
James Roffey, *d* April 14, 1877, *a* 64.
[Mr. Roffey in his younger days was huntsman to the stag hounds kept in
this neighbourhood, and was well-known and highly respected by the
gentlemen attending the hunt.   He afterwards successfully carried on
the well-known inn near the Cattle Market, called the Stag and
Hounds.]

George Duckett, *d* March 2, 1864, *a* 42.
We cannot Lord, Thy purpose see,
But all is well that's done by Thee.

Walter Talbot, *d* March 2, 1858, *a* 62.
Sarah Talbot, his widow, *d* Aug. 10, 1867, *a* 72.

Robt. Ray, *d* Sept. 2, 1856, *a* 59.
All gracious God, Thy will be done,
'Twas Thou that didst the blessing lend
And though withdrawn, I'm not alone,
Thou art the widow's faithful friend.
[Robt. Ray was a market gardener, and lived at Ivy Cottage, in the Selsdon
Road, near the railway viaduct.]

Lucy Maria Beck, *d* July 2, 1850, *a* 27.
Sarah Elizabeth Wilbraham, her sister, *d* Jan. 31, 1865, *a* 45.

William Lewis Janson, *d* April 18, 1872, *a* 41.

Sophia Matilda, daughter of Lewis and Sophia Burnand, *d* May 20, 1859,
a 17.
Chas. Robt. Burnand, *d* Dec. 1, 1879, *a* 29.

Jane, wife of James Davies, Esq., *d* May 24, 1868, *a* 58.

Eliza, eldest daughter of Edward Jones, Esq., *d* May 30, 1857, *a* 24.
Edward Jones, her father, *d* Sept. 3, 1865, *a* 87.

Maria Jones, her mother, *d* Feb. 8, 1877, *a* 88.

Ellen Bailey, *d* July 11, 1874, *a* 21.

John Collier, *d* Dec. 23, 1857, *a* 64.
Alfred Waller, his grand nephew, *d* March 3, 1874, *a* 8 months.
Elizabeth Collier, his widow. *d* Dec. 16, 1881, *a* 80.

Charles Collier, *d* Oct. 3, 1863, *a* 73.
Elizabeth, his wife, *d* June 28, 1878, *a* 77.

Joseph Bud, *d* Oct. 19, 1865, *a* 73.
Harriet Hadwen Bud, *d* Nov. 11, 1881, *a* 81.

Joseph Turner, of South End, *d* Oct. 26, 1865, *a* 62.

Richard Chas. Scott, *d* July 19, 1865, *a* 67.

He is gone, but gone to his rest,
No more on this earth to complain
Of sin, that his soul oft oppressed,
But with Jesus for ever to reign.

Colonel Edward Kelly, late 1st Regiment of Life Guards, died at Tirhoot, in India, Aug. 6, 1828; also in memory of Maria Louisa Kelly, his wife, died Dec. 22, 1860.

" God forbid that I should glory save in the Cross of our Lord Jesus Christ."
This frail memorial is erected by their affectionate daughters.

Ann Louisa Kelly, their eldest daughter, *d* Dec. 23, 1880.
Emma, her sister, wife of G. F. R. Sutton, *d* Jan. 26, 1866.
Anna Maria Kelly, sixth daughter, *d* Nov. 4, 1868.

Colonel Kelly was in his younger days one of the finest men in the British Army, and was esteemed one of the best swordsmen. He took an active part in the Battle of Waterloo, and was greatly praised for his gallantry by the Duke of Wellington in his dispatches. He afterwards served in India, where he died, and was buried. The place mentioned on the stone is " Tirhoot," but we have reason to believe it should be " Ticoot." He married a lady from Mitcham, by whom he had issue six daughters, three of whom lie with their mother in this churchyard. A fourth married Mr. Francis Harris (son of Mr. Robt. Harris, for several years an active magistrate for this county) who practised in the medical profession in Croydon, but afterwards removed to Mitcham, where he died in 1849. Mrs. Kelly, it will be seen, survived her husband thirty-two years, and lived during the whole of that time at Boswell Court, South End, Croydon.

Charlotte Battersbee, *d* March 31, 1875, *a* 74.

Susan Baldwin, *d* Dec. 14, 1866, *a* 69.
Emma, her husband, *d* May 23, 1868, *a* 76.

George Albert Privett, *d* Sept. 14, 1860, *a* 2.

Thomas Penson, of North End, *d* Jan. 21, 1859, *a* 58.

Fanny, daughter of Martin and Harriet Holliday, *d* Sept. 11, 1859, *a* 22.

Wm. Dean, *d* July 2, 1869, *a* 79.
Sarah, his wife, *d* Dec. 28, 1873, *a* 82.

George Hall, *d* Dec. 3, 1867, *a* 54.
Ann Hall, his mother, *d* June 4, 1871, *a* 89.

Thomas Jacob, *d* Oct. 22, 1858, *a* 39.

John Andrews, *d* Nov. 2, 1865, *a* 47.
Not lost but gone before.

Charlotte, wife of Geo. May, of London, *d* June 6, 1856, *a* 43.

Rebecca Rowlandson, her mother, widow of the Rev. M. Rowlandson,
D.D., vicar of Warminister, Wilts, *d* Dec, 16, 1867, *a* 91.
> " It is well, for God has ordered it." This was her motto through life; it kept
> her happy, and resting in Jesus only as her rock and stay, her end
> was peace.

George May, Esq., of Pittarrow, Croydon, *d* Oct. 6, 1876, *a* 66.
> The memory of the just is blessed.

Ann Gordon, daughter of Chas. Engström, *d* Aug. 9, 1876, *a* 7 weeks.

Emily Jane, daughter of Lieut.-Col. M. L. Rowlandson, *d* March 10, 1858,
a 22.
> The word of Christ dwelt in her richly, it was her delight, and in it she
> meditated day and night. Amongst her last words were " I am not in
> the least afraid." O Death, where then was thy sting: O Grave,
> where thy victory. Thanks be unto the Lord, who giveth us the victory
> through our Lord Jesus Christ, we have redemption through His blood.
> All my springs are in Thee.

Also Sarah Louisa Mary Rowlandson, *d* July 16, 1858, *a* 24.
> Soon called to follow her sister she so tenderly had loved, with her she now
> rests in peace.
> " The blood of Jesus Christ, His Son, cleanseth us from all sin. Jesus
> Christ, the same yesterday, to-day, and for ever." Here, she said, is
> the pillow upon which I rest my soul. " And they sung, as it were, a
> new song before the Throne," and God shall wipe away all tears from
> their eyes.

Major-General George Rowlandson, Royal Madras Artillery, *d* March 31,
1875, *a* 56.
> A faithful and consistent servant of Christ and his country He is entered
> into his rest.

Maud Mary Elizabeth Simkins, *d* May 1, 1867.
> I was dumb, I opened not my mouth, because thou didst it.

Hannah Crippen, *d* May 5, 1877, *a* 83.
Elizabeth, her sister, *d* March 7, 1878, *a* 76.

Sarah Thorp, *d* Nov. 20, 1859, *a* 64.
James Thorp, her husband, *d* Aug. 16, 1864, *a* 71.

Mark Bartlett, *d* March 6, 1862, *a* 76.
Emma, wife of Wm. Bartlett, *d* Nov. 2, 1868, *a* 45.

Ellen Wilton, *d* Aug. 21, 1861, *a* 1 month.
> Oh, not in cruelty, not in wrath,
> The reaper came that day.
> 'Twas an angel visited the green earth,
> And took the babe away.

Henry Herbert, infant son of Henry Long, *d* July 16, 1864.
Martha Jones, niece of Henry Long, *d* March 19, 1869, *a* 5.

Ann, wife of Commander Jas. Grant Raymond, R.N., *d* Aug, 25, 1859, *a* 62.
J. Grant Raymond, R.N., *d* May 27, 1863, *a* 67.

Chas. Benjamin Gurrey, *d* Jan. 15, 1861, *a* 38.

Walter Ricardo, Esq., of Haling Grove, *d* April 14, 1859, *a* 37.

Thomas Chas. Willoughby, *d* June 14, 1872, *d* 30.
Thomas Benjamin Willoughby, *d* June 16, 1875, *a* 68.

Jane, wife of Jeremiah Gilbert, *d* Jan. 22, 1859, *a* 36.
Edith Millicent Gilbert, infant daughter.
Jeremiah Gilbert, *d* Feb. 10, 1869, *a* 1 month.

Mary Ann, wife of Cuthbert W. Johnson, Esq., *d* Oct. 5, 1861, *a* 57.
Cuthbert W. Johnson, barrister-at-law, *d* March 8, 1878, *a* 79.

Mr. Cuthbert Wm. Johnson resided at Waldronhyrst, in The Waldrons, Croydon. He was one of the earliest members of the Local Board of Health, and for many years was the highly-esteemed chairman, and ruled that body to the satisfaction of all. He was a gentleman of considerable ability, and was bred up to the law, but devoted himself more particularly to agricultural pursuits, and was connected with several influential agricultural journals, to which he frequently contributed. It is pleasing to bring to memory the recollection of Mr. Johnson, who was a stately gentleman, combining in himself the best points of the old school. Seated in his canopied chair, with his velvet cap, in sober evening dress, he looked as if he had stepped out of an ancient frame hanging on the walls of some family mansion. He was always faultlessly clean, and close shaven. His entire appearance and manner conveyed a sense of dignity, self-possession, and somewhat stiff politeness. He listened with patience to the long debates in which the members of the Board were accustomed to indulge, and occasionally enlivened the proceedings with a little mild pleasantry. Nothing seemed to ruffle him or disturb the placidity of his temper—a most necessary qualification in any gentleman called to preside over meetings where persons of opposite opinions meet to discuss public matters. His death was a great loss to the town.

James Gooderson. *d* July 3, 1881, *a* 62.
Florence, child of James and Harriet Gooderson, *d* March 2, 1874, *a* 16 months.

Richard Barrow, *d* Nov. 15, 1859, *a* 62.

John Sawyer, died suddenly, Nov. 11, 1871, *a* 62.
> Farewell, farewell, yet not a long adieu,
> For I, if faithful, soon may be with you,
> In blissful regions, where no sin, no pain,
> Nor parting pangs shall sunder us again.

Ann Sawyer, his wife, *d* Sept. 25, 1879, *a* 72.
> Tender parents and friends sincere—
> Loved and lamented much—lie buried here.

Jane Mary Baylis, *d* Oct. 16, 1860, *a* 34.

Elizabeth, wife of James Pilbeam, *d* March 17, 1866, *a* 68.

James Woodroffe, *d* Sept. 2, 1844, *a* 52.
Sarah, his wife, *d* Jan. 26, 1864, *a* 69.
Eleanor, his daughter, *d* Aug. 26, 1881.

Morris Hughes, *d* Jan. 23, 1863, *a* 63.
Elizabeth, his wife, *d* May 17, 1879, *a* 68.

Samuel, son of John and Rebecca World, *d* May 13, 1870.
> There is a happy land, far, far away,
> Where saints in glory stand, bright, bright as day.

Edward Gower, *d* July 21, 1859, *a* 68.
> [Mr. Gower kept the New Inn, South End.]

Harriet Rebecca, daughter of William and Harriet Claxton, *d* Sept. 4, 1869, *a* 1.

Martha Gray, *d* Dec. 30, 1860, *a* 32.

> Brought up in tender care,
> Her parents and her brothers loved her dear.

Elizabeth, wife of George Gray, *d* July 20, 1859, *a* 34.

Henry Gower, *d* Jan. 29, 1877, *a* 57.

Alphonso Francis Matthey, Esq., late of Messina, *d* Oct. 13, 1854, *a* 56.

Ann, daughter of John Grantham, Esq., *d* July 5, 1859.

John Burt, *d* Oct. 12, 1875, *a* 66.

Marion Walker, *d* Feb. 24, 1877.
Marmaduke Tyson Walker, *d* March 29, 1877.

Thomas James Roff, son of Thomas Roff, *d* Oct. 11, 1875, *a* 17.

Sophia, wife of Thomas Stevens, *d* March 17, 1856, *a* 57.
Thomas, her husband, *d* April 11, 1873, *a* 76.

> [Formerly landlord of the Surrey Drovers, Selsdon Road.]

James Wm. Hoare, of South End, *d* Nov. 3, 1854, *a* 19½.

> A youth is laid beneath this stone :
> Death nipped the bud, the blossom's gone.
> Be still each parent's sighing heart,
> Time is but short that we shall part ;
> When we again in glory meet,
> 'Twill turn past bitters into sweet.

Rebecca Hoare, his mother, *d* Oct. 19, 1865, *a* 64.

Mary Snelling, *d* May 24, 1855, *a* 58.

Robert Roff, *d* April 5, 1875, *a* 48.

George Munton Bryant, *d* Jan. 21, 1853, *a* 48.

Hannah Bush, after a long and painful illness, *d* Feb. 11, 1872, *a* 53.

George Joseph Hope, *d* March 13, 1866, *a* 60.

Alice Liston Harris, daughter of George Harris, of Bedford Park, *d* July 21, 1860, *a* 12.
Louisa, widow of George Harris, Esq., and grandmother of the above, *d* Aug. 28, 1867, *a* 80.

Mary Ann Bance, *d* July 19, 1862, *a* 64.

> A dutiful wife and affectionate mother : much regretted.

Wm. Thomas Bance, her husband, *d* March 28, 1873, *a* 80.

> [Mr. Bance carried on the business of grocer and cheesemonger at 123, High Street, part of the premises now occupied by Mr. Stevenson.]

John Galloway, *d* Nov. 8, 1853, *a* 67.
Frances Galloway, *d* June 14, 1867, *a* 92.

> This is not our home. May we all more earnestly seek a heavenly one.

Jonathan Peed, of Brighton Road, *d* July 28, 1854.
Sophia, his wife, *d* Aug. 17, 1878, *a* 88.

> [Mr. Peed was for many years shepherd on the Haling Park Farm. He is father to Mr. Peed, the celebrated horticulturist, of South Norwood.]

Emily Morton Tippett, *d* Feb. 2, 1854, *a* 4 years and 9 months.
Mary Ann, her sister, *d* Feb. 12, 1854, *a* 2 years and 3 months.

> Sweet little flowers, your blooms are fled,
> Your tender leaves are pale and dead,
> And scattered—once so rosy red—
> In the cold tomb.

G

Wm. Hodgkins, *d* Dec. 27. 1854, *a* 78.
Catherine, his wife, *d* July 31. 1865.
Fanny Hodgkins, *d* Jan. 12. 1853, *a* 18.
    [Mr. Hodgkins was landlord of the Running Horse, in the Old Town.]

William Phipps, *d* July 29, 1862, *d* 60.
Martha Phipps, *d* May 7, 1868, *a* 70.
                    Hail, sovereign love, that first began,
                    The scheme to rescue fallen man ;
                    Hail, matchless free eternal grace,
                    That gave their souls a hiding place.
    [Mr. Phipps was formerly a well-known tradesman in High Street.]

Patience Pearce, *d* March 17, 1857, *a* 61.

Jane, wife of Abraham Brown, *d* June 5, 1853, *a* 60.

Mary, wife of George Cooper, *d* Jan 9, 1863, *a* 81.
George, her husband, *d* Oct. 24, 1866, *a* 79.

Frances Sarah Gedge, *d* Jan. 11, 1863, *a* 71.

George Tate, of Brockham, *d* Oct. 21, 1853, *a* 72.
Ann Tate, his daughter, *d* Aug. 5, 1841, *a* 15.
        Both buried at Pump Pail.
Catherine Tate, his wife, *d* Sept. 20, 1850, a 80.

William May, *d* Dec. 12. 1858, *a* 34.
Emily Jane May, his daughter, *d* Feb. 8, 1869, *a* 34.

George Batchelar, *d* Jan. 25, 1853, *a* 83.

Francis Charles Saker, *d* July 17, 1865, *a* 5 months.
Eva Ellen Saker, *d* Aug. 28, 1865, *a* 2.

John Wood, *d* Feb. 20, 1854, *a* 68.

Sarah Chapman, *d* Jan. 26, 1855, *a* 79.
Rev. Edward Chapman, her husband, *d* Dec. 7, 1858, *a* 86.

Rev. Thomas Dove, Wesleyan Minister, 14 years Missionary in Western
    Africa, *d* Dec. 1, 1859, *a* 59.

Josiah Dulake, *d* July 11, 1861, *a* 59.
Jane Dulake, his wife, *d* Oct. 2, 1863, *a* 60.
    [Mr. Dulake kept the Star beerhouse in Southbridge Road. He died from the
    effects of a fall. Coming down stairs one day rather hurriedly, his foot
    slipped, and he fell from the top to the bottom, breaking his neck.]

Samuel Waghorne, *d* Oct. 2, 1858, *a* 69.
Harriett, his widow, suddenly called to her rest May 13, 1867, *a* 78.
Thomas Waghorne, her only son, *d* Aug. 28, 1868, *a* 46.
    [Formerly a coachbuilder in High Street, now Waghorne and Miles.]

Mary, wife of Joseph Jordan, *d* Dec. 6, 1855, *a* 36.
Mary, her daughter, *d* Jan. 11, 1855, *a* 4.
Ann, her daughter, *d* April 7, 1850, *a* 1¾.
William, her son, *d* Oct. 29, 1863, *a* 17.

Elizabeth, daughter of George and Elizabeth Price, *d* April 25, 1853, *a* 9.
Elizabeth, her mother, *d* Jan. 19. 1867, *a* 63.
Edward, her son, *d* Jan. 29, 1875, *a* 35.

Elizabeth May, wife of William Green, of Granville Square, London, *d*
    March 31, 1863, *a* 47.
Emily Jane Suckling, her niece, *d* March 12, 1858, *a* 7.
                    Another lamb now safe from heat and cold,
                    Is gently gathered to the heavenly fold.

Phillip Babbidge, son of John Petter, *d* Oct. 3, 1853, *a* 2; also 3 children.

Mary, wife of Peter Paul Grellier, of Wormwood Street, London, *d* Feb. 8, 1855, *a* 80.

Mary Ann, wife of Napoleon Belcher, *d* May 3, 1859, *a* 80.
> Universally beloved and much regretted by all who knew her.

Elizabeth, wife of Edwin Winscom, *d* Jan. 21, 1853.

Edwin, her son, *d* Jan. 8, 1853, *a* 2.
> [Mr. Winscom was the first accountant to the Local Board of Health.]

James Street, *d* March 31, 1873, *a* 68.

William Barnes, born May 13, 1811, *a* 17.
> My days are like a shadow that declineth, and I am withered like grass.

Sophia Barnes, born July 28, 1841, *a* 17.
> I cried unto him with my mouth, and he was extolled with my tongue.

Frances, wife of Wm. Barnes, *d* June 11, 1862, *a* 51.

> The mother's voice we used to hear,
> Alas, too often heard in vain,
> Her anxious words of hope and fear,
> Will never reach our ears again.
>
> Oh, may we weigh with solemn thought,
> The holy counsel which she gave,
> Now to the heart more dearly brought,
> As here we sorrow o'er her grave.

Wm. Chuter, *d* March 21, 1861, *a* 43.
> [Landlord of the Cricketers' Arms, West Street.]

Mary Mullett, *d* May 16, 1861, *a* 43.
> After many years great suffering, borne with Christian fortitude.

George Graves, *d* March 31, 1860, *a* 58.

> Free now from every care and pain,
> Asleep my body lies,
> Until the trumpet calls
> The dead in Christ to rise.

Lucy Sophia Cooper, *d* Jan. 20, 1854, *a* 23.

Robert Lashmar, youngest son of John Lashmar, *d* May 22, 1853, *a* 49.
> [The Lashmars kept for many years one of the principal drapery establishments in High Street, afterwards Jarvis, now D. Davidson.]

Bertha Emberson, *d* April 16, 1853, *a* 5.

Ernest John Emberson, *d* April 27, 1853, *a* 9.
> [The father of these children carried on the school in High Street now under the management of the Rev. Dr. Roberts.]

John Battersbee, *d* Nov. 23, 1863, *a* 74.
> [Old John Battersbee was a collar maker in High Street. There was a court called Battersbee's Court on the site of the Friends' Road.]

Harry John, son of George and John Stapleton, *d* March 27, 1854, *a* 9 months.

Frank Thomas, his brother, *d* Jan. 17, 1856, *a* 8 months.

Walter James, brother, *d* April 26, 1858, *a* 1 month.

George Stapleton, *d* Aug. 17, 1869, *a* 48.

John Eldridge, *d* Oct. 12, 1854, *a* 64.

Ann Eldridge, his wife, *d* March 26, 1864, *a* 73.
> [Mr. Eldridge was one of the Inspectors of Weights and Measures for the County of Surrey.]

Edward Price, *d* Dec. 31, 1860, *a* 70.

Elizabeth, his wife, *d* May 11, 1873, *a* 71.

Sarah. wife of John Budgen, of Addiscombe Road, *d* June 18, 1869, *a* 95.
John Budgen, her husband, *d* July 5, 1869. *a* 81.

    John Budgen was the principal watchmaker in the town. His
old-fashioned shop was at the south corner of Mint Walk—
now an oil and colourman's. He was well-known in his
day as a most upright, honourable, and skilful man at business. He had filled all the usual parish offices with credit
to himself and benefit to the town, and in the waning of
life he retired to George Street, in order to live near his
old friend, Mr. Wm. Inkpen. Here he enjoyed his *otium
cum dignitate* for a few years, when, to use a figure of
speech, the clock of life, with all its delicate and compli-
cated machinery, was abruptly stopped by the hand of
Time. He left handsome legacies both to the hospital and
the little almshouses. On reference to the parish register
we find that in 1780, Mr. Budgen's father, who like himself, was a clever watchmaker, was appointed to erect the
chimes in the old church tower, where they remained in
operation until the sacred edifice was consumed by flames.

Marion Henrietta Boobier, *d* Jan. 9, 1855, *a* 31.

Robert Wood, *d* March 14, 1857, *a* 9.
Robert Wood, his father, *d* Sept. 21, 1870, *a* 52.
    [Mr. Wood was a milkman, and also verger at St. Peter's Church.]

Sophia Jane Richards, *d* Aug. 22, 1854, *a* 14 months.
Arthur James Richards, *d* Aug. 31, 1858, *a* 17 months.

> Farewell, dear infants, you are gone
> To Heavenly rest and love,
> Thus early called to Christ away,
> To dwell with Him above.

Elizabeth Harvey, *d* Nov. 16, 1874, *a* 73, forty-six of which were passed in
faithful service and friendship with the family, who erect this stone
to her memory.

John Gunn, *d* Nov. 9, 1865, *a* 59.
Ann Gunn, his wife, *d* Aug. 15, 1869, *a* 60.

> Dear honoured parents, we must trust
> Your precious bodies to the tomb,
> Here in the Churchyard's hallowed dust,
> Sleep calmly through night's transient gloom.

Elizabeth Finnis, relict of Gilbert Finnis, of Dover, *d* March 22, 1862, *a* 90.
    The stone was erected by her daughter, S. Cook.
    [The husband of the deceased was a brother of Colonel Finnis, the first
victim in the Indian Mutiny, and a relative of Sir John Finnis, who
once filled the office of Lord Mayor of London. Mr. Gilbert Finnis
several times filled the office of Mayor of the Borough of Dover.]

William Sibley, *d* July 14, 1865, *a* 49.

Lucy, wife of Thomas Swaine, of Thornton Heath, *d* May 14, 1855, *a* 73.
Thomas Swaine, her husband, *d* March 12. 1862, *a* 81.

Mrs. Sarah Cotman, of South End, where she resided more than half a
century, *d* Jan. 4th, 1855, *a* 81.
        Hodie mihi cras tibi.

Also Mr. John Cotman, her son, *d* Jan. 6, 1868, *a* 56.
    [Mrs. Sarah Cotman's husband died from the effects of eating poisonous
mushrooms.]

Frederick John Steer, *d* Feb. 7, 1865, *a* 5.

Mary Ann Lurway, *d* June 23, 1874, *a* 78.

Joseph Ford, Esq., late of the War Office, Pall Mall, died suddenly at Beaford, North Devon, Sept. 13, 1866, *a* 68.

Maria, his relict, died at Alton, Hants, April 22, 1881, *a* 85.

Samuel Slarke, *d* Aug. 15, 1864, *a* 60.

> " And what doth the Lord require of thee, but to do justly and to love mercy, and to walk humbly with thy God."

Ann Slarke, *d* April 6, 1866, *a* 57.

> [Mr. Slarke was a plumber, and sexton to St. James's Church. His father was clerk at the Parish Church.]

George Thomas White, chorister, *d* May 13, 1875, *a* 9.

George Lawrence, *d* Feb. 5, 1877, *a* 49.

Rose Alice, his daughter, *d* Sept. 26, 1866, *a* 6 months.

Amy Maude, his daughter, *d* Jan. 1, 1873, *a* 5.

Thomas William Lawrence, *d* Aug. 22, 1863, *a* 10 months.

Caroline Georgina, his mother, *d* Jan. 5, 1864, *a* 38.

> " Labour not for the meat which perisheth, but for the meat which endureth unto everlasting life, which the Son of Man shall give unto you, for them hath God the Father sealed."

> [Members of the family of Lawrence and Son, clothiers, Surrey Street.]

Susannah Giles, wife of James Giles, *d* June 15, 1864, *a* 49.

Eliza, wife of Thomas Weaver, of Park Hill Farm, *d* Dec. 6, 1862, *a* 54.

Thomas Weaver, her husband, *d* Aug. 28, 1872, *a* 63.

> [Mrs. Eliza Weaver was the second wife of Mr. Thomas Weaver. She was unfortunately killed by being thrown out of a chaise.]

Frederick Wagner, *d* Feb. 8, 1863, *a* 64.

Joseph Mitchell, *d* Feb. 8, 1879, *a* 87.

Mary Ann, his wife, *d* Feb. 9, 1879, *a* 78.

George Richard, son of George and Sophia Matthews, *d* Sept. 24, 1863, *a* 6.

Charles Ernest, an infant, *d* Feb. 25, 1874.

James Alphonsus King, *d* March 31, 1863, *a* 53.

James King, sen., his father, *d* March 27, 1865, *a* 83.

Elizabeth May, wife of John Hinchcliff Williams, *d* Oct. 31, 1864, *a* 54.

John Hinchcliffe Williams, her husband, *d* Feb. 8, 1869, *a* 59.

Jane, wife of George Smithers, *d* Sept. 25, 1864, *a* 37.

George Smithers, *d* Oct. 22, 1881, *a* 62.

> [Mr. Smithers resided at Duppas Hill, but in business he was the well-known fishmonger at the foot of London Bridge.]

Francis Oswald, *d* Nov. 20, 1877, *a* 42.

> Thine eyes shall see the King in his beauty.

William George Stephens, *d* Sept. 3, 1863, *a* 18.

Ellen Victoria Stephens, his youngest sister, *d* Jan. 8, 1874, *a* 6.

Anna Stephens, *d* March 11, 1881, *a* 22.

Matthew Pratt, of Brigstock House, Thornton Heath, *d* Dec. 18, 1879, *a* 61

Abi Susannah, his wife, *d* Jan. 18, 1866, *a* 35.

> This monument is erected by her affectionate husband as a tribute of love to her whose loss he must for ever mourn.

> [There was a tablet placed in the old Parish Church to the memory of this lady, a very few days before the destruction of the church. It was totally destroyed in the fire.]

John William Ebbutt, *d* July 26, 1875, *a* 58.

Clement Theodore Long, taken to rest Jan. 14, 1778, *a* 6 months.

Herbert John, son of John William and Elizabeth Lulham Jarvis, *d* Feb. 4, 1864, *a* 2.

Kate Mary Ann, her daughter, *d* June 8, 1870, *a* 10 and 7 months.

Elizabeth Johnson Jarvis, her grandmother, *d* Oct. 19, 1877, *a* 85.

Anne, wife of Mr. James Brown, *d* Aug. 5, 1871, *a* 18.

Annie Roberts, called to her rest Nov. 15, 1873.
   Her infant children, Maude and George Herbert, are sleeping with her.
         Where your treasure is, there will your heart be also.

Francis Dally Fisher, *d* June 29, 1873, *a* 51.

Patience Hobbs, *d* Dec. 3, 1863, *a* 67.

Charles Alborough Garard, *d* Feb. 4, 1877, *a* 48.

North side of the Churchyard.

Amy, wife of Thomas Holliday, *d* Feb. 4, 1866, *a* 77.

Thomas Holliday, *d* Oct. 16, 1870, *a* 80.
   [For many years a night watchman in High Street.]

Mr. Cornell, *d* Feb. 8, 1865, *a* 68.

Mrs. Ann Peters, *d* Oct. 13, 1863, *a* 61.

Edward Peters, her husband, *d* Dec. 1, 1865, *a* 79.

Mary Sophia, daughter of John and Mary Eldridge, *d* Dec. 29, 1881, *a* 5 months.

Richard Avery Sawyer, of North End, *d* July 21, 1864, *a* 60.

Sarah Sawyer, his wife, *d* Feb. 13, 1875, *a* 74.
   [Mr. Sawyer was a boot and shoemaker in North End.]

Mary Ann Jackson, *d* May 4, 1866, *a* 40.
             In faith she lived, in love she died,
             Her life was asked, but was denied.
   This tablet is erected by her affectionate brother, Wm. Dulake, 2nd Battalion,
   24th Regiment, Rangoon.

John Edward, only son of John Fuller, Esq., late Lieut. H.M's. 71st Regiment, *d* Oct. 6, 1861, *a* 27.

Martha Hayward, *d* Feb. 12, 1871, *a* 62.

Ebenezer Hayward, her husband, *d* Feb. 11, 1872, *a* 63.

Sarah Wood, her daughter, *d* Oct. 3, 1879, *a* 30.

Alice Jane Russell, wife of Wm. Russell, of South End, *d* Nov. 12, 1863, *a* 43.
             Forget thee? Never! To the latest breath
             We shall remember thy calm bed of death.
             What humble trust! what holy hope! what joy,
             'Mid dying pangs, could every thought employ!
             Yes! in that moment thou didst seem to be
             At peace with God, and God at peace with thee.

Mary Vickers, *d* Jan. 14, 1862, *a* 24.

Mary Elizabeth Hayward, *d* Dec. 25, 1874, *a* 25.
             In life much beloved, in death much lamented.

Emma Ann Taylor, *d* Dec. 13, 1868, *a* 25.
             When musing, sorrow weeps the past,
                And mourns the present pain,
             How sweet to think of peace at last,
                And feel that death is gain.

Fredk. J. Muskett, *d* March 31, 1871, *a* 8 months.
Fredk. Rigden, his brother, *d* Dec. 22, 1872, *a* 8 months.

Elizabeth Bowring, *d* Feb. 6, 1873, *a* 27.

Hannah, wife of Francis Bowring, *d* May 9. 1870. *a* 60.
Francis Bowring, her husband, *d* June 12, 1877, *a* 78.
　[Formerly a boot and shoemaker in High Street.]

Mary Ann, wife of James Burns, *d* April 12, 1869, *a* 56.

William Joseph Southey, *d* Nov. 23, 1864. *a* 38.
Sarah Southey, his daughter, *d* Jan. 18, 1875, *a* 20.
Alfred, his son, *d* Dec. 10, 1877, *a* 17.
　[Mr. Southey was a chemist at 137, High Street, in the employ of Messrs.
　Crafton and Son.]

Ellen Elizabeth Southey, *d* Feb. 23, 1871, *a* 18.

Jehoiada Stoodley Northcott, *d* March 21, 1881, *a* 61.
　　　　If I still hold closely to Him
　　　　　What hath He at last ?
　　　　Sorrow vanquished, labour ended,
　　　　　Jordan passed.

Sophia, wife of Wm. Bonella, *d* Jan. 9, 1875, *a* 67.
William Bonella, *d* Dec. 21, 1880, *a* 76.

Henry Whittaker, *d* March 5. 1869, *a* 85.

Sophia, wife of W. H. Ray, *d* Sept. 18, 1862. *a* 55.
Thomas Henry, her eldest son, *d* April 27, 1870, *a* 33.
Charles, her second son, *d* Sept. 11, 1872, *a* 30.

John Pettifer, *d* Oct. 28, 1863, *a* 65.
　　　　Let my remembrance often creep,
　　　　Across thy mind, but do not weep,
　　　　But go, so live thy death may be,
　　　　Such as no friend need weep for thee.
Alfred Pettifer, his youngest son, *d* March 26, 1866, *a* 27.
Elizabeth, relict of John Pettifer, *d* Feb. 22, 1869, *a* 67.
Henry Pettifer, *d* Aug. 30, 1873, *a* 39.
　[Mr. John Pettifer was a builder, 65, South End ; he also had a lime kiln on
　the Brighton Road.]

Robt Cleveland, child of Robt. Thomas and Sarah Ann Ready, *d* April 24,
　1865, *a* 7.
Wm. Herbert Ready, *d* April 24, 1865, *a* 1 year and 11 months.

Thomas Neal, *d* May 25, 1863, *a* 47.

Wm. Burrows, after a long and severe illness, *d* March 16, 1868, *a* 43.
Alice Burrows, his daughter, *d* July 12, 1869, *a* 14.
　　　　Just as I am, without one plea,
　　　　But that Thy blood was shed for me.
　　　　And Thou bids't me come to Thee,
　　　　　Oh, Lamb of God, I come.

Lawrence Fielder, *d* Feb. 10, 1866, *a* 68.
　I have trusted in Thy mercy, my heart shall rejoice in Thy salvation, I shall
　be satisfied when I awake with Thy likeness.

Mary Ann Elizabeth, daughter of Henry Bean and Emma Martin, *d* Sept.
　14, 1869, *a* 17 years and 8 months.

Sarah Ann Maria Wicks, *d* March 17, 1865, *a* 30.

Emily, wife of Thomas Cleverly, *d* April 28, 1868, *a* 27.
Also an infant son.

George Bentley, *d* Aug. 26, 1868, *a* 31.

John Betchley, *d* Feb. 11, 1869, *a* 70.
Susan Sarah Hesketh Betchley, *d* May 30, 1870, *a* 59.

> Weep not for us, my children dear,
> We are not dead, but sleeping here,
> Long hath the night of sorrow reigned,
> The dawn shall bring us light,
> God shall appear, and we shall rise,
> With gladness in his sight.

[Mr. John Betchley was a wheelwright in North Place.]

Susan, wife of John Betchley, *d* April 28, 1868, *a* 25.
Sarah Susan Matilda Betchley, *d* Feb. 9, 1873, *a* 1 year and 10 months.

Erected by Edward Hurley in memory of George Lane, who died at his post of duty as gamekeeper, April 22, 1868, *a* 53.

Reuben Dann, *d* May 4, 1868, *a* 65.

Harriott, wife of William Couchman, *d* Oct. 27, 1866, *a* 70.

> Each moment since her dying hour,
> My loss I keenly feel,
> But trust I feel the Saviour's power,
> To sanctify and heal.

Wm. Couchman, her husband, *d* Jan. 10, 1872, *a* 73.

Alfred Broadribb, brother of Mrs. Hookins, of West Street, *d* Nov. 17, 1866, *a* 33.
Frances Broadribb, his sister, *d* July 21, 1876, *a* 50.

Thomas Mallett, Esq., *d* May 29, 1866, *a* 71.

George Joseph Hookins, of West Street, *d* Dec. 27, 1869, *a* 38.

Henry Rix, *d* Dec. 27, 1865, *a* 65.

James Blackman, *d* April 29, 1868, *a* 72.
Elizabeth, wife of Thos. Blackman, *d* April 20, 1864, *a* 82.
Thomas Blackman, a respected resident of this parish, *d* May 15, 1864, *a* 78.

> A sincere Christian, a devoted husband, a faithful friend.

John Edward Bowell, *d* Nov. 28, 1863, *a* 26.

> I wait for the Lord, my soul doth wait, and in His word do I hope.

William Bowell, his father, *d* July 23, 1867, *a* 60.

Thomas Bassett, *d* Jan. 11, 1864, *a* 10.

Alfred Cox, *d* Jan. 30, 1865, *a* 31.
Alfred John Cox, his son, *d* Dec. 31, 1864, *a* 5 months.

> Farewell! farewell! yet not a long adieu,
> For I, if faithful, soon may be with you,
> In blissful regions, where no sin, no pain,
> Nor parting pangs shall sunder us again.

Esther, daughter of Simeon and Ann Shaw, *d* Sept. 18, 1860, *a* 32.
Ann Shaw, her mother, *d* Dec. 23, 1870, *a* 77.

William Agate, *d* Feb. 28, 1864, *a* 86.
Charlotte Agate, his daughter, *d* July 17, 1871, *a* 59.

[Mr. Agate was for many years the proprietor of the well-known nursery in Southbridge Road. He was a worthy, industrious, and successful man; and it is somewhat remarkable that the names of his competitors in business were Diamond, Jewel, Gould, and Batchelar, all of whom have long since joined the majority.]

Estelle, wife of Thomas Charles Bayliss, of Croham Mount, *d* April 25, 1879, *a* 39.

Sarah, wife of Frederick Potter, of Selsdon Road, *d* Dec. 30, 1879, *a* 74.

Charles Coxhead, *d* Dec. 2, 1874, *a* 18.
> Weep not for me, although on earth,
> My time with you is past,
> With Christ above we hope to meet
> Where happiness shall last.

George Coxhead, his father, *d* July 13, 1875, *a* 74.
> Weep not for me, my children dear,
> Though you are left behind,
> Prepare yourselves to follow me
> And bear me in your mind.

Alfred William, son of Alfred Bowell, *d* Dec. 20, 1871, *a* 3 years and 9 months.
Rebecca Bowell, his grandmother, *d* March 8, 1878, *a* 68.

Samuel James Everett, *d* July 10, 1880, *a* 34.

Julia, the beloved and deeply regretted wife of Edgar Francis Carter, and only daughter of Mr. C. Lenney, *d* Oct. 10, 1865, *a* 29.

Samuel Brookes, *d* Aug. 18, 1881, *a* 49.
> " Oh, that thou wouldest hide me in the grave, that thou wouldest keep me secret, until thy wrath be past, that thou wouldest appoint me a set time and remember me."—Job xiv. 13.
> [Mr. Brookes was an architect, living in St. Peter's Road, having offices in George Street.]

Sophia, wife of John Coe, died suddenly Jan. 21, 1872, *a* 58.
John Coe, her husband, *d* Sept. 16, 1880, *a* 71.
> [Mr. Coe was many years manager of the printing department of the Bank of England.]

John Russell, of Dunlewey House, Bedford Park, third son of Thomas Russell, *d* July 9, 1864, *a* 46.
> " In full assurance of the resurrection to eternal life through our Lord Jesus Christ. The Lord gave and the Lord taketh away, blessed be the name of the Lord."
> [This gentleman gave the ground on which the Church stands, and the burial ground surrounding.]

Robt. Horatio Johnson, *d* Feb. 16, 1865, *a* 25.
Sarah Johnson, his mother. *d* Nov. 3, 1881, *a* 76.

Horatio Maynard Chesterman, *d* Jan. 30, 1866, *a* 21.

Mary Day, *d* Dec. 12, 1868, *a* 78.
Joseph Day, her eldest son, *d* July 7, 1865, *a* 42.

William Gaskin, *d* April 25, 1882, *a* 81.
> Because he hath set his love upon Me, therefore will I deliver him; with long life will I satisfy him, and he shall see My salvation.
> [Formerly a builder in Addiscombe Road. He gave the present handsome carved oak pulpit in the parish church.]

William George Stagg, *d* April 14, 1871, *a* 53.
> Erected by a few friends as a mark of respect.

William Edward Johnson, *d* Sept. 20, 1869, *a* 32.

Ann Johnson, died May 16, 1868, *a* 58.
Elizabeth, wife of James Edward Chapman, *d* March 29, 1876, *a* 70.
Henry Chapman, her son, *d* April 3, 1876, *a* 35.
Sarah Ann, wife of John Kilmister, *d* Oct. 4, 1869, *a* 67.
John Kilmister, her husband, *d* Nov. 13, 1876, *a* 78.
> [Old John Kilmister was a well-known character, although in humble life. He was carpenter to the old Workhouse, and eventually died in one of the almshouses.]

William George Butt, *d* June 25, 1875, *a* 52.
> My days are passed, my purposes are broken off, even the thoughts of my
> heart.—Job xvii. 2.

> [Mr. Butt was a blacksmith, and up to the time of his death, verger of St.
> Peter's Church.   His old workshop was situated at the corner of
> Coombe Lane.]

Ann, his wife, *d* June 1, 1882, *a* 66.
> Severe affliction, kindly sent in love,
> Led her to Christ, and trained her for above.
> The end, now seen, how short, how light appear,
> The longest suffering she experienced here !

Thomas Henry Twiddy, *d* June 6, 1871, *a* 29.
> Them also which sleep in Jesus will God bring with Him.

Kate Jane, daughter of Thomas and Mary Jane Young, *d* April 26, 1873,
a 5.

South and West of the Church.

Ann, wife of Joseph Ward, *d* Oct. 24, 1875, *a* 68.
Joseph Ward, her husband, *d* Aug. 20, 1876, *a* 68.

Percy Faulding Dawson, *d* Aug. 12, 1875, *a* 68.

Sarah, wife of Francis Thompson, jun., *d* Oct. 23, 1875, *a* 33.

Rebecca, wife of Wm. Cooper, *d* July 28, 1877, *a* 33.

James Kemp, *d* July 7, 1876, *a* 72.
> [James Kemp kept an oil and colour shop, in High Street.]

Colonel Alfred Bate Richards, for some years, and up to the time of his
death, Editor of the *Morning Advertiser*, *d* Jan. 12, 1876, *a* 56.
Also Marion Richards, *d* Aug. 9, 1877, *a* 38.
> This stone is erected in affectionate remembrance of Colonel Richards by his
> colleagues on the *Morning Advertiser*.

> [Colonel Richards was also author of a play called "Cromwell," enacted
> with considerable success at the Queen's Theatre, London.   At the
> time of his death he resided at 22, Brunswick Square, Bloomsbury. He
> desired to be buried in this churchyard, in order that he might be near
> his old friend, Mr. F. G. Tomkins, whose tomb immediately adjoins.]

Frederick Guest Tomkins, *b* 1804, *d* 1867.
> Whene'er he came
> Into the place, where they who knew him sat,
> Mirth shone beneath the shadow of his eyes,
> In every eye around.

> [On reference to the parish register we find that Mr. Tomkins died on the 27th
> Sept., 1867, aged 63.   His residence is described to be South End, but
> this is evidently an error.   There is an entry further on of the burial of
> Jane Tomkins, his wife, who died at Peckham, on the 15th May, 1871,
> aged 44.   There is no tomb to her memory, nor does her name appear on
> her husband's tomb, although she is buried by his side.]

Agnes May Cooper, fell asleep Aug. 9, 1876, *a* 2 months.

Lieut.-Col. Strachan, 1st W. I. Regt., *d* March 23, 1877, *a* 43.

William Ager, *d* Nov. 14, 1872, *a* 82.
> He opened his mouth with praise, and in his lips was the law of kindness.

Mary Ann Ager, his wife, *d* April 9, 1873, *a* 59.

Ann Paine, of Purley, *d* July 5, 1868, *a* 65.

Elizabeth Corker, *d* Aug. 26, 1863, *a* 80.

Elizabeth Boothman, *d* Aug. 14, 1866, *a* 52.
Edward Boothman, her husband, *d* Sept. 21, 1870, *a* 68.
> [Mr. Boothman came to Croydon to superintend the masonry works during the building of St. Peter's Church. When this work was completed he settled in the town, commenced work on his own account, and met with a fair share of success.]

William Moore, *d* Jan. 13, 1863, *a* 58.
Sarah, his wife, *d* March 4, 1868, *a* 68.
Mary, his daughter, and wife of Charles Peel, *d* Oct. 12, 1876, *a* 36.
> [William Moore kept the Rail View beerhouse in Selsdon Road. He was a man in good circumstances, and had the peculiar hobby of keeping a fast trotting donkey, which he was fond of driving at full pace through the town.]

Elizabeth, wife of Thomas Woodward, *d* June 30, 1868, *a* 70.

Fanny Sarah, wife of Samuel Lovelock, *d* June 18, 1874, *a* 33.

Mary, widow of the late Henry Stone, of Horton, near Epsom, *d* Jan. 23, 1882, *a* 92.

Charlotte Mary, daughter of John and Charlotte Adkins, *d* Jan. 23, 1869, *a* 13.
> He loved her and gave Himself for her. She died trusting in her Saviour Jesus Christ.

Emma, wife of Edward Gibbs, *d* July 4, 1872, *a* 37.

Richard Comber, of Magdala House, *d* Feb. 9, 1870, *a* 69.
Isabella Comber, his wife, *d* Aug. 2, 1877, *a* 80.

Emma, widow of Lieut. Geo. Walter, R.N., *d* Jan. 18, 1870, *a* 60.

Mary Couchman, *d* Aug. 20, 1869, *a* 80.
Benjamin Couchman, her husband, *d* July 10, 1873, *a* 83.
> [A well-known and highly respected carpenter residing in Mint Walk.]

Ernest, son of Walter and Caroline Hall, *d* Nov. 21, 1868, *a* 7.
Jessie Maria, his sister, *d* Jan. 25, 1869, *a* 2.

William Henry Halsey, *d* Nov. 26, 1868, *a* 29.
> Having a desire to depart and be with Christ.

Florence, daughter of Jane and Peter Gunning, *d* Jan. 23, 1869, *a* 13.

Jane, wife of Henry Avis, *d* April 30, 1869, *a* 53.
Henry Avis, her husband, *d* Dec. 12, 1872, *a* 63.

George Twigg, *d* Sept. 10, 1881, *a* 42.

Willie, son of William Thompson and Lilly Brown, *d* Oct. 16, 1874, *a* 6.

James Hardstone, *d* Dec. 29, 1871, *a* 36.
Anne Hardstone, *d* May 2, 1882, *a* 40.

Sarah, wife of Mr. James Hooker, *d* Sept. 27, 1869, *a* 45.

Harper Batty Roberts, Keeley House, North End, *d* July 8, 1874, *a* 51.
> I laid me down and slept.

Frances Jane, his widow, *d* July 13, 1877, *a* 51.

Edward Parris, *d* Nov. 21, 1881, *a* 60.
> " Watch therefore, for ye know not what hour your Lord doth come."

Sarah Jane Knight, *d* Dec. 13, 1871, *a* 3 years and 2 months.

Mary Ann, wife of John Newton, of Park Hill Road, *d* Nov. 1, 1869.

William Barker, *d* Jan. 4, 1875, *a* 67.
Harriet Barker, his wife, *d* Nov. 14, 1879, *a* 63.
> In the sight of the unwise they seemed to die, but they are in peace.

Caroline Grant, *d* Feb. 14, 1870, *a* 49.

Emily Smith Holliday, *d* May 8, 1869, *a* 57.

George Alexander, *d* May 4, 1872, *a* 24.

Henry Close, late of South End, *d* July 28, 1867, *a* 47.
> Yes, he is gone, we are going all,
> Like flowers we wither, and like leaves we fall.

Martha Matilda, wife of William Corden, *d* June 15, 1866, *a* 23.
> Thou art gone to the grave, but I were wrong to deplore thee,
> For God was thy ransom, thy guardian, thy guide;
> He gave thee, He took thee, and He will restore thee,
> And death has no sting since the Saviour has died.

Thomas Telford Campbell, *d* Feb. 28, 1882, *a* 78.

Sarah Ward Presant, wife of Capt. George Presant, of South Town, Great Yarmouth, *d* Aug. 18, 1870, *a* 86.
> We weep with grief that one so dear,
> No more can share our smile and tear,
> But weep with joy that God has given
> The hope to meet again in heaven.

Elizabeth Saker, *d* Feb. 14, 1873, *a* 24.

Mary Rylett, *d* Dec. 29, 1881, *a* 8 months.
> Sweet and lovely little flower,
> Snatched by death so very soon,
> Your parents' hearts are filled with sorrow,
> To lay you in your lonely tomb.

Dear Jessie, child of William and Eliza Horne, whom the Lord called home Dec. 27, 1881, *a* 3 years and 8 months.

Sarah Catchpole, *d* Dec. 13, 1874, *a* 37.

A Memorial of Love.—Dear little Charlie C. T. G., *d* Dec. 6, 1877, *a* 18 months.

Sydney Charles, son of Chas. Wm. and Eliza Ewen, *d* Aug. 20, 1881, *a* 1 month.

Elizabeth, daughter of W. and H. Prevett, *d* April 22, 1872, *a* 12.

William, her brother, *d* April 30, 1872, *a* 11.

John Charles Walker, *d* March 20, 1871, *a* 50.

Sarah Wilson, *d* Jan. 3, 1875, *a* 75.

Emma Mary Allmond, *d* June 7, 1873, *a* 53.

Benjamin Fuller, *d* March 30, 1874, *a* 48.
> Lord Jesus, receive me in glory at last,
> When trial and conflict on earth shall be past,
> To sing with the angels who stand round Thy throne,
> Where sorrow and sin are for ever unknown.

Mrs. Rosamond Say, *d* Jan. 18, 1875, *a* 84.

Mrs. Deborah Crocker, *d* Dec. 3, 1874, aged 80.

Henry Benson Cox, *d* March 18, 1871, *a* 63, buried at Brodas Dorp, Cape of Good Hope.

Fanny, his wife, *d* Jan. 16, 1875, *a* 63.

John Buck, died at Bristol, 1850, *a* 56.

Martha Buck, his widow, *d* March 22, 1875, *a* 77.

Alfred Bowerman, *d* Jan. 6, 1877, *a* 52.

Mary Ann Thompson, *d* Nov. 4, 1880, *a* 67.

William Ansell, *d* June 16, 1880, *a* 25.

Thomas Ridley, after a long and severe affliction, *d* April 3, 1874, *a* 38.

Eleanor Ridley, his most loving and devoted mother, *d* May 21, 1874, *a* 75.

Thomas Ridley, his father, after a prolonged and most industrious life, *d* July 16, 1875, *a* 78.

> They were many years inhabitants of St. Paul's, Covent Garden, beloved and respected by all who knew them.

John Wood, *d* Feb. 7, 1881, *a* 50.

Elizabeth, wife of John Scott, *d* Jan. 15, 1882, *a* 65.

Edith Beatrice Scott Baker, her grandchild, *d* June 24, 1878, *a* 3 years and 11 months.

Anna, widow of Edward Bevan, *d* June 28, 1880, *a* 83.

> My grace is sufficient for thee, for my strength is made perfect in weakness.

Charles Richard Marshall, *d* May 20, 1880, *a* 63.

Sarah Ann Harris, *d* Jan. 10, 1880, *a* 70.

Eliza O'Dwyer, her sister, died at Auckland, New Zealand, Dec. 22, 1880, *a* 67.

Wm. Miller, *d* Feb. 8, 1878, *a* 70.

Wm. Edward Tharp, *d* Feb. 17, 1878, *a* 20.

> Just as I am, thou wilt receive,
> Wilt welcome, pardon, cleanse, receive,
> Because thy promise I believe,
> Oh, lamb of God, I come.

E. Hawick, wife of F. Hawick, *d* April 21, 1881.

> This God is our God for ever and ever, he will be our guide even unto death.

William Notes, *d* Nov. 5, 1877, *a* 62.

George Harland, *d* July 1, 1880, *a* 46.

> A sudden change, I in a moment fell,
> I had not time to bid my friends farewell,
> Think nothing strange, death happens unto all,
> My lot to day; to-morrow you may fall.

Annie Court, *d* Oct. 20, 1878, *a* 23.

Eglantine Grant, daughter of the Rev. James Frances Grant, *d* Dec. 28, 1881, *a* 81.

Elizabeth Malson, *d* Nov. 26, 1881, *a* 65.

Jane Sophia, wife of Eleazar Hayward, *d* April 17, 1881, *a* 73.

William Roff, *d* Feb. 25, 1881, *a* 65.

> This stone is erected as a last token of respect by his affectionate son Henry, of the 22nd Regiment, Allahabad.

Charles Spice, *d* Feb. 3, 1879, *a* 27.

> He sent from above, he took me, he drew me out of many waters.

Arthur Pescud, *d* Feb. 15, 1877, *a* 10.

Charles Baylis, died at Mitcham, Sept. 17, 1876, *a* 31.

> Thou art gone from our midst, but we cannot forget thee,
> Tho' sorrow and darkness encompass the tomb,
> Jesus, the Saviour, has passed it before thee,
> The lamp of his love will guide thee safe home.
> Erected by his widow.

Anna Elizabeth, daughter of Henry C. and Emma Northwood, *d* Nov. 5, 1876, *a* 28.

> I came to Jesus as I was,
> Heavy and worn, and sad,
> I found in him a resting place,
> And He has made me glad.

In memory of our dear mother, Jane Mole, the deeply lamented **wife of** Joseph Mole, *d* Nov. 9, 1876, *a* 57.

Joseph Mole, *d* Dec. 22, 1877, *a* 56.

Richard Henry Easton, *d* Dec. 30, 1876, *a* 3 years and 11 months.

James Philip Walbourn, *d* Jan. 7, 1877, *a* 56.
> Let all thy converse be sincere,
> Thy conscience as the noon-day clear,
> For God's all-seeing eye surveys,
> Thy secret thoughts, thy works, thy ways.

John Richard Candish, *d* Oct. 20, 1876, *a* 30.
John Richard Candish, his father, *d* Dec. 22, 1876, *a* 75.
Mary Candish, his mother, *d* Nov. 8, 1878, *a* 66.

M. A. Catchpoule, *d* Dec. 24, 1875, *a* 53.

Emma Agnes Gates, *d* Aug. 29, 1878, *a* 22.

Ann Apps, wife of George Apps, *d* April 23, 1878, *a* 51.

Mrs. Eliza Dudley, widow of the late T. Dudley, *d* Nov. 18, 1877.

Wm. Henry Maylam, *d* Aug. 20, 1877, *a* 31.
> Farewell ; with a permanent hope of re-union.

William Day, *d* June 18, 1877, *a* 48.
> " Thy will, oh Lord, be done ! "
> Had He asked us, well we know,
> We should cry, " Oh, spare this blow,"
> Yes, with streaming eyes should pray,
> " Lord we love him, let him stay."

Sarah, wife of Benjamin Spice, *d* Nov. 8, 1870, *a* 57.

Robert Strike, chorister, fell asleep, June 2, 1879, *a* 14.
> [Poor boy ! cut off in the prime of youth ; no doubt his friends and **they** whose loving hands decked his grave with flowers, all hope that he has long since joined the heavenly choir, and blended his sweet voice with those of angels.]

Mary, wife of Chas. Stagg, *d* Dec. 31, 1878.
Charles Stagg, *d* Nov. 16, 1881, *a* 49.
> After many years of great suffering, borne with Christian-like fortitude.
> [Mr. Charles Stagg was a builder in Southbridge Road, where his son **now** carries on the business.]

Sarah Jones, wife of Thomas Henry Jones, *d* March 27, 1880, *a* 52.
> I chose the way of truth, and thy judgments I had before me.

Mary Jane, wife of Thos. Young, *d* May 16, 1879, *a* 34.
> Her sun has gone down while it is yet day.

Caroline Gibbons, widow of Geo. David Donkin, Esq., of Wyfold Court, Oxfordshire, and relict of Thomas Gibbon, Esq., *d* June 3, 1877, *a* 59.

Emma, daughter of Mary and Jane Taylor, *d* Oct. 9, 1877, *a* 7.

Arthur Joseph Albury fell asleep Feb. 7, 1879, *a* 12.
> This cross was erected in loving memory by the Sunday School teachers and scholars of St. Peter's.

Arthur Jane, wife of John H. Wren, *d* June 12, 1878, *a* 26.

Christopher Ramsay Fagan, *d* Nov. 9, 1878, *a* 25.
> Lord, all pitying Jesus blest,
> Grant him thine eternal rest.

Bridget, wife of Hugh Venables, *d* Nov. 23, 1878, *a* 63.

John Jerrum, of Violet Lane, *d* Feb. 10, 1879, *a* 68.

Alfred Mason, *d* Dec. 24, 1878, *a* 39.
Caroline and Walter, children, who died in infancy.
> [Mr. Alfred Mason was a builder. He dropped down dead in the street. For some time previously he had suffered from an affection of the heart.]

James Samuel Candish, *d* March 3, 1879, *a* 24.
> He groweth up and is cut down like a flower.

George Pocock, *d* March 23, 1879, *a* 29.

In memory of our little darling, Cecil Alexander Bruce Dagleish, *d* July 29, 1879, *a* 1 year and 11 months.

Fred. Robt. Catchpole, *d* Dec. 19, 1880, *a* 25.

Mary Elizabeth Ward, *d* Oct. 30, 1879, *a* 89.

Richard Burley, *d* March 11, 1879, *a* 49.
Ada Burley, his daughter, *d* Oct. 3, 1875, *a* 6.

Charlotte, wife of Nathaniel Myrtle, *d* Feb. 16, 1879, *a* 59.
Nathaniel Myrtle, *d* Jan. 27, 1881, *a* 68.
> The Lord is gracious and full of compassion, slow to anger,
> and of great mercy.

> [Mr. Myrtle was landlord of the Cricketer's Arms in Southbridge Place, now occupied by his son-in-law, Mr. Alfred Bullock.]

Alfred Leresche, *d* June 11, 1878, *a* 51.

Harriet Smith, sister of Mrs. Loveday, *d* March 20, 1878, *a* 55.
> Oh, call it not death, it is life begun,
> For the waters are passed, the home is won.

James John Cannee, *d* June 25, 1877, *a* 19.

Frances, wife of George Tatum, *d* June 15, 1877, *a* 56.
> No pain, no grief, no anxious fear,
> Invade thy tomb; no mortal woes
> Can reach the peaceful sleeper there,
> While angels watch her sweet repose.

Rebecca, wife of Robert Roffey, *d* June 5, 1880, *a* 70.

John Woodhouse Coulthard, *d* March 16, 1877, *a* 36.

James Jeffery Marshall, *d* Oct. 8, 1877, *a* 17.

Capt. E. M. V. James, late Bombay Staff Corps, *d* April 9, 1878, *a* 42.

Frances Maria, wife of Thomas Cox, *d* June 24, 1878, *a* 61.

Eleanor Maud Goodwin, *d* Feb. 15, 1880, *a* 6.
> We give thee but thine own,
> Whate'er the gift may be,
> All that we have is thine alone,
> A trust, O Lord, from thee.

Rose Minnie, daughter of William and Jane Smith, *d* March 30, 1880, *a* 3.

Hester Saunders, *d* May 8, 1879, *a* 79.

James Williams, D.D., *d* June 9, 1880, *a* 61.

Sophia, wife of David Haines, *d* May 14, 1879, *a* 71.

Muriel Mary, infant daughter of Charles and Mary Edridge, *b* Sept. 10, *d* Sept. 21, 1881.
> Her little harp she tunes so sweet,
> While sitting at the Saviour's feet;
> Angels do stand and listen round,
> I make no doubt, on heavenly ground,
> And then their harps in chorus raise
> To sound the loved Redeemer's praise.

Rev. George Cooke Geldart, B.A., *d* July 15, 1877, *a* 50.

Amelia, wife of Robt. Bailey, *d* April 15, 1879, *a* 26.
Also Robert John, their infant child.

Edward Lote, the much loved husband of Florence Lote, at rest, June 21, 1880.

> I shall be satisfied when I awake with Thy likeness.—Psalm xvii. 15.

> This young man met with his death under peculiarly painful circumstances. On the 16th June, five days before his death, he was married to Miss Ranger, of Warham Road, Croydon. The newly married pair proceeded to spend their honeymoon at Lynton, a pleasant little watering place in Devonshire. On the 21st, he went to bathe with a friend, and in returning they found the tide was setting in, rendering their walk along the sea-shore impossible. The friend climbed some height up the cliffs and determined to wait there until the tide receded. Mr. Lote being anxious to return to his bride, set off alone, by a somewhat difficult route over the cliffs, and was never again seen alive. The friend returned in safety, and was surprised to find Mr. Lote had not arrived. Search was made, but his body was not found until several days afterwards. It was evident that he had met his death by a fall from the cliffs. The corpse was brought to Croydon, and interred in the churchyard, along which he had passed a few days previously a happy bridegroom.

Eliza, the beloved wife of James Spurrier Wright, at rest, June 15, 1880.

> [In loving memory of this estimable and talented lady, a beautiful stained-glass window has been placed in the south aisle of St. Peter's by her husband, Mr. J. S. Wright, which will be found fully described in our account of the church.]

END OF ST. PETER'S CHURCH.

CHRIST CHURCH.

THIS Church is erected near the northern end of the town, at the junction of Handcroft Road and Sumner Road. It was erected by the munificence of Archbishop Sumner, and was consecrated by him on the 27th of July, 1852. Four years later it was enlarged at the cost of the same dignitary, by extending the nave and adding to the chancel. Two hundred more sittings were thus provided. It now contains 1,050 sittings, of which 420 are free. An organ has lately been added. There is a small memorial window in the Church erected to the memory of Chas. Lenox Richardson, who was treacherously killed by the natives in Japan, Sept. 4th, 1862, aged 30. The burial-ground, about two acres in extent, was ordered to be closed when the Cemetery was opened. There are few interesting memorials therein :—

Susanna, wife of John Fowles, *d* Nov. 23, 1852, *a* 43.

> Oh, husband dear, my time is past,
> While life remained my love did last,
> But now for me no sorrow take,
> But love my children for my sake.

Fredk. Fowles, infant son, *d* March 25, 1854.
Thomas Fowles, *d* Sept. 6, 1858, *a* 8.
Susannah Fowles, *d* March 20, 1863, *a* 31.

George Redford, carpenter, second son of Wm. and Mary Batchelar, *d* Oct. 16, 1854, *a* 22.

> How boundless is our Father's grace,
> In height, in depth, in length,
> He made his Son our righteousness
> His spirit is our strength.

Joseph Sharp, *d* May 26, 1858, *a* 72.

Samuel Simons, *d* April 25, 1867, *a* 75.
Ann, his wife, *d* Feb. 27, 1876, *a* 75.

Mary, wife of Thos. Richards, wheelwright, *d* Oct. 31, 1854, *a* 75.
Thomas Richards, her husband, *d* Aug. 25, 1874, *a* 81.

William, son of Jas. and Elizabeth Beadell, *d* Dec. 1, 1854, *a* 23.
James Beadell, his father, *d* June 1, 1859, *a* 71.
Sarah Jane, his sister, *d* May 27, 1864, *a* 25.
Robert, his brother, *d* Jan. 16, 1867, *a* 33.
Elizabeth, his mother, *d* Jan. 12, 1878, *a* 81.

Louisa, wife of John Bennett, *d* Aug. 2, 1855, *a* 32.

Mary Ann, wife of John Carter, *d* June 15, 1873, *a* 57.
Elizabeth, her daughter, *d* Aug., 1861, *a* 18.
Albert Carter, *d* March, 1862, *a* 2.

H

Michael Davies, *d* May 25, 1855, *a* 71.
Amy Davies, his wife, *d* April 8, 1863, *a* 82.

Charlotte Lutter, *d* Aug, 8, 1867, *a* 61.
Sarah, his sister, *d* March 8, 1869, *a* 79.

Sarah Rebekah, daughter of John and Ruth Bradden, *d* Oct. 23, 1865, *a* 3
    years and 10 months.
Sarah Rebekah, daughter of Henry George and Sarah Bradden, *d* March
    4, 1874, *a* 18 months.

George Fox, *d* Sept. 3, 1872, *a* 66.
Ann Fox, *d* March 10, 1861, *a* 83.

Harriet Kempton, *d* Jan. 25, 1866, *a* 64.

George, son of Richd. and Phillis Collis, *d* Oct. 21, 1853, *a* 27.
Richard Collis, *d* Nov. 7, 1854, *a* 71.
Charles Collis, *d* Oct. 12, 1877, *a* 44.
Cecilia Bishop, *d* April 8, 1878, *a* 55.
Phillis Collis, wife of Richard Collis, *d* Jan. 24, 1879, *a* 88.
    [The Collis's were well-known brickmakers. They first had a brick-yard on
       the Selsdon Road, but afterwards removed to Selhurst, where the
       business is carried on now on a considerably enlarged scale.]

Caroline Emily Dixon, *d* March 7, 1856, *a* 2 years and 4 months.
Elizabeth Ann Dixon, *d* March 9, 1856, *a* 8 months.
Jane Dixon, their mother, *d* April 8, 1865, *a* 37.
         A tender mother and a virtuous wife
         Here sleeps in humble hope of better life,
         By side of those she loved and cherished well.
         We leave the judgment-day the rest to tell.

Stephen James Burgess, *d* Jan. 14, 1871, *a* 80.
Ann, his wife, *d* Feb. 5, 1871, *a* 81.
Maria Burgess, *d* Sept. 23, 1872, *a* 84.

Maria, wife of Charles West, *d* Oct. 13, 1860, *a* 31.

Henry Wm. Morrison, *d* Jan. 25, 1865, *a* 46.
George Wm. Morrison, *d* April 26, 1865, *a* 25.

Rev. Charles Davies, late Cathedral Missionary at Calcutta, *d* Oct. 31,
    1858, *a* 33.
    Declare His glory among the heathen, His marvellous works among all
       nations.

Martha, wife of Wm. Dawson, *d* July 20, 1866, *a* 68.
Wm. Dawson, her husband, *d* Sept. 14, 1873, *a* 70.

Amelia Catherine, wife of Edward Stevens, *d* Jan. 20, 1869, *a* 41.

Martha, wife of James T. Brown, *d* Nov. 12, 1863, *a* 23.
       Be thou faithful unto death, and I will give thee a crown of life.

George, son of Catherine and George Cole, *d* Jan. 31, 1856, *a* 82.

Thomas Manser, *d* Sept. 30, 1856, *a* 54.
Robert Manser, *d* Aug. 29, 1868, *a* 41.
Catherine, wife of Thomas Manser, *d* May 27, 1869, *a* 66.

Isaac Sayers, *d* Dec. 22, 1856, *a* 80.
Elizabeth Sayers, his wife, *d* April 9, 1869, *a* 87.

Jane Rose, daughter of Henry and Cary Wright, *d* March 29, 1866, *a* 72.
Wm. Norton Wright, her brother, *d* June 7, 1869, *a* 71.
    [Brother and sister of Mr. J. S. Wright. The former had been in the army,
      and was for some time with his regiment (the 29th Foot) in America,
      and at Gibraltar. He was also in Paris with the Allied Army after
      Waterloo.]

Agnes Lindsay, *d* March 14, 1860, *a* 1 year and 4 months.
Robert Macaulay Lindsay, *d* Jan. 30, 1865, *a* 10.

Frances, widow of John Gray, Esq., *d* Nov. 17, 1856, *a* 78.

George Robert Clemons, *d* March 29, 1869, *a* 14.

Mary Cox, *d* March 17, 1865, *a* 54.

In vain our fancy strives to paint
The moment after death,
The glories that surround the saints
When yielding up their breath.

Sarah Cox, *d* Feb. 28, 1873, *a* 92.

Jane Rebecca, wife of Robt. M. Thompson, *d* Sept. 25, 1863, *a* 59.
Mary, her sister, *d* June 5, 1864, *a* 65.

Martha Towers, a beloved mother, *d* June 4, 1861, *a* 64.

William Neal, *d* Feb. 24, 1866, *a* 41.

The Lord relieveth the fatherless.

Sarah, daughter of Thos. and Sarah Batchelar, *d* Sept. 18, 1864, *a* 45.
Thomas Batchelar, *d* March 2, 1867, *a* 72.

Mrs. Martha Stride, *d* Jan. 20, 1867, *a* 67.

Ann, wife of John Martin, *d* June 4, 1865, *a* 75.
John Martin, her husband, *d* Feb. 25, 1870, *a* 78.
Robt. J. G. Martin, *d* March 3, 1868.

Henry Danton, *d* Dec. 7, 1869, *a* 38.

Susannah Trapnell, *d* June 28, 1865, *a* 84.

Henry Strangemore Couchman, *d* May 30, 1866, *a* 8.
Joseph Strangemore Couchman, his grandfather, *d* June 15, 1868, *a* 74.

Harold John Stanley, of Munich, painter, *d* Nov. 20, 1866, *a* 48.

Scaro duna importuna e grave salma sig noil eterno e dal mondo disuolto qual
fragil legno a te slanco me volto dal orribul pro cella in dolce calma.

John Weller, *d* July 12, 1867, *a* 37.

Edward Randall, *d* Dec. 24, 1861, *a* 38.

Margaret, widow of Thos. Ward, Esq., *d* Sept. 13, 1868, *a* 69.

Helen Evelyn Lloyd Turner, *d* March 26, 1870, *a* 8 months.

Alone unto our Father's will,
One thought hath reconciled,
That He whose love exceeded ours,
Hath taken home his child.
Hold her, oh, Father, in thy arms,
And let her henceforth be,
A messenger of love between,
Our human hearts and Thee.

Helena Sherriff Turner, *d* April 21, 1868, *a* 4.

Richard Jaques Sherriff, *d* Dec. 23, 1859, *a* 47.
Thomas Turner, *d* Dec. 19, 1859, *a* 59.
Mary Jane Turner, his wife, *d* Feb. 14, 1880, *a* 78.

Charlotte, wife of C. H. Tindall, *d* July 10, 1862, *a* 34.

Anna Maria Lodge, *d* Sept. 16, 1858, *a* 28.

"Blessed are the dead which die in the Lord from henceforth." "Yea," saith
the spirit, "that they may rest from their labours and their works do
follow them."

Thomas Lodge, her father, *d* Jan. 20, 1859, *a* 85.

Catherine, relict of Henry Thould, *d* Jan. 28, 1867, *a* 73.

William Gardiner, of H.M's. 19th Foot, died at Shorncliff, May 6, 1859, *a* 17.
Mary Ann, wife of George Hill, his mother, *d* Nov. 8, 1873, *a* 52,

Thomas Escreet, *d* March 7, 1861, *a* 77.
Herbert Thos. Escreet, *d* Oct. 22, 1860, *a* 19 months.

Emma Faulkner, the adopted child of Agur and Martha Faulkner, *d* Feb. 18, 1860, *a* 17.

Ann Godson, *d* May 9, 1865, *a* 59.

George Smith, *d* Oct. 28, 1866, *a* 49.
Sarah Smith, his wife, *d* June 17, 1867, *a* 44.

> Lord, while our dearest earthly ties,
> Are broken one by one,
> Oh, bind us closer to Thyself,
> Thy spirit and Thy Son.

James Smith, his brother, *d* Sept. 12, 1868, *a* 42.

Charles Richard Crouch, *d* May 15, 1871, *a* 45.
Maria Crouch, his mother, *d* Jan. 2, 1874, *a* 98.

> Stop and read before you go,
> For here lies beneath this stone,
> Two sinners saved—and
> By the grace of God alone.

[Mrs. Crouch resided for many years at Bedford Place, Handcroft Road.]

Fanny Adams, *d* Sept. 30, 1865, *a* 22.
Elizabeth Adams, *d* Jan. 1, 1869, *a* 42.
Emma Adams, *d* Sept. 29, 1875, *a* 26.

Alfred Dawson, *d* Sept. 29, 1857, *a* 23.

> Death! where is thy gloomy prison?
> Christ has burst the massy door.
> I shall rise, for He has risen;
> Fear not, He has gone before.

Mrs. Mary May, *d* Dec. 20, 1858, *a* 70.

> Honour widows that are widows indeed.—1 TIM. v. 3.

Susannah, wife of George Matthews, of the Half Moon, Broad Green, *d* May 6, 1859, *a* 45.

Elizabeth Iles, *d* Oct. 26, 1869, *a* 75.

Henry Pocock, *d* July 20, 1864, *a* 40.
Maria Pocock, his daughter, *d* July 17, 1878, *a* 24.

Thomas Lockyer, *d* Dec. 22, 1869, *a* 41.
Kate, his daughter, *d* Dec. 25, 1881, *a* 19.
Alice, his daughter, *d* May 12, 1865, *a* 1.

[Under a spreading willow tree lie the remains of "Tom" Lockyer, one of the best cricketers Surrey ever produced. Tom was born in Mitcham Road, Croydon, and was first initiated into the mysteries of the noble art of cricket on Duppas Hill, like many other Croydon boys. As he grew to manhood, he became more and more proficient in the game, and was the hero of many a local match, and at an early age was admitted into the County Eleven. He afterwards became one of the All England Eleven, and twice represented the Old Country cricketers in their visits to Australia. He was a good all-round player, but as a wicket-keeper he was unrivalled, and it is doubtful whether he had an equal in that particular branch of the game. He died at the Sheldon Arms, in Whitgift Street, at the comparatively early age of 41.]

William James Anderson, *d* Jan. 21, 1862, *a* 62.

George, son of John and Jane N. Need, *d* Oct. 24, 1854, *a* 16.
John Need, his father, *d* Sept. 18, 1868, *a* 67.

Rebecca Morris, *d* Dec. 28, 1859, *a* 61.

Sarah, wife of Stephen Shoesmith, *d* July 7, 1857, *a* 66.
Stephen Shoesmith, *d* May 29, 1873, *a* 85.
Jane Shoesmith, *d* Dec. 4, 1858, *a* 56.

Eliza Cooper, *d* Jan. 2, 1860, *a* 36.
Wm. Henry Cooper, *d* May 9, 1880, *a* 63.

Grace Henley, *d* March 23, 1880, *a* 51.

Kate Constance, infant daughter of the Rev. Octavius Bathurst Byers, M.A., Incumbent of Christ Church, *d* March 20, 1856, *a* 7 months.

Thomas Geo. Lowe West, *d* Oct. 15, 1871, *a* 81.

Elizabeth Winterton Turnour, daughter of the late Hon. and Rev. Edward John Turnour, *d* Jan. 18, 1867.
> [The Hon. and Rev. Edward Turnour was son of the late and brother of the present Earl of Winterton, in the peerage of Ireland.]

Ernest Augustus Harwood, child of John S. Vaughan, *d* Dec. 1, 1869, *a* 3.

Mary Eliza, wife of Josias Serpell, of Croydon Grove, *d* July 7, 1861, *a* 29.
Josias Serpell, *d* April 5, 1869, *a* 77.

Maria, wife of John Merredew, *d* July 28, 1861, *a* 40.
> Mrs. Merredew was formerly mistress of what was called, before her death, "The Mead School," and many of the present good wives of Croydon owe their education to her. The School was built at the lower end of Parson's Mead by the Misses Squire, two maiden ladies of the Society of Friends, who then resided in the London Road, with their brother, in the house now occupied by Mr. Joseph Steele. The school was carried on mainly at the ladies' expense, though a small school fee was charged to the children. On the death of Mrs. Merredew, the school was continued by the Rev. O. B. Byers as a supplementary girls' school for the Christ Church district, the Misses Squire having on the death of their brother, removed to Dorking, where they now reside. The advent of the School Board having rendered this school unnecessary, the premises have been converted into cottages, Nos. 70—73.

Pheby Gill, *d* Nov. 3, 1865, *a* 76.
Jane Gill, *d* Nov. 4, 1870, *a* 73.
John Gill, *d* May 31, 1871, *a* 77.

Mrs. Sarah Stokes, *d* Dec. 9, 1862, *a* 73.

Charlotte, wife of Joseph Nimrod Barrell, *d* Jan. 11, 1861, *a* 33.
Joseph N. Barrell, her husband, *d* June 18, 1869, *a* 41.
Charlotte Barrell, her daughter, *d* Dec. 17, 1878, *a* 23.

Henry George Thornton, *d* March 15, 1868, *a* 68.

Richard Chatfield, *d* Aug. 18, 1877, *a* 46.

Hannah, wife of Wm. Brasier, *d* Nov. 26, 1863, *a* 80.
William Brasier, *d* March 3, 1868, *a* 86.
Louisa Mary Brasier, his daughter, *d* Oct. 19, 1875, *a* 57.

Clara James, *d* July 8, 1868, *a* 20.
Charlotte James, her mother, *d* Dec. 20, 1878, *a* 55.

Richard Parrott, *d* July 15, 1865, *a* 1.
Mary, his sister, *d* Oct. 7, 1877, *a* 22.
Mary Anne Parrott, his mother, *d* May 25, 1878, *a* 54.

Elina Russell, daughter of Miles Braithwaite, Esq., R.N., and Elizabeth Jane his wife, *d* July 26, 1861, *a* 18.

Priscilla Agnes Weaver, *d* Nov. 25, 1866, *a* 64.
John Weaver, her husband, *d* Dec. 30, 1869, *a* 54.

Mary Selmes Dobbs. *d* April 1, 1858, *a* 53.
Harold Oliver Dobbs, *d* Feb. 26, 1863, *a* 14 weeks.

Caroline Georgina, wife of George Henry Pearce, of the Half Moon, Broad
    Green, *d* May 19. 1864, *a* 39.
George Henry Pearce, her husband, *d* March 22, 1871, *a* 46.

Ann, wife of Chas. Hyde, *d* Sept. 23, 1866. *a* 17.

Capt. Edward John Morriss, R.N., *d* Aug. 7, 1870, *a* 77.
Martha, his wife, *d* July 31, 1872. *a* 61.
> What though in lonely grief I sigh,
> For friends beloved, no longer nigh,
> Submissive would I still reply,
>   Thy will be done.

William Charles Hall, *d* July 13, 1857. *a* 18.
Selina Hall, late of Stonehouse, Gloucestershire, his mother, *d* Oct. 25,
    1870, *a* 71.

Louisa Augusta, child of William and Emma Slade, *d* June 30, 1857, *a* 12.
William Slade, her father, *d* Feb. 20, 1867, *a* 67.

Thomas Allen, *d* Nov. 23, 1856, *a* 68.

James Thompson. *d* June 27, 1857, *a* 41.
James Lord, his uncle. *d* Dec. 8, 1859, *a* 67.
Elizabeth Lord, *d* Jan. 6, 1861, *a* 72.

John Ward, *d* July 7, 1858, *a* 61.

Samuel Golding, *d* Nov. 25, 1857, *a* 77.

Samuel Small, *d* May 24. 1857, *a* 34.
Elizabeth Small, his mother, *d* Dec. 18, 1860, *a* 65.
George Jeffery, grandson, *d* Jan. 7, 1871. *a* 5.

Robert Nicholson, *d* Nov. 17, 1860, *a* 49.
Robert, his son, *d* May 26, 1849. *a* 1½.
Phœbe Nicholson, his wife. *d* Feb. 3, 1875, *a* 64.

Caroline Lambert, wife of Richard Knight. *d* June 18, 1860, *a* 58.
Richard Knight, her husband, *d* Feb. 12, 1872, *a* 72.

Joseph Truelove, *d* May 21, 1861, *a* 68.

Harriet Russell, *d* May 1, 1863, *a* 58.

Hannah Lawrence, *d* Jan. 23, 1864, *a* 48.
> When on those dear remains affections shower,
> A voice from Heaven proclaims she is not dead,
> But only sleeps to wait the promised hour,
>   When Jesus will her slumber break,
> And gently lead her to His Father's feet,
>   Where what was sown in weakness
>   Will be raised in power.

Rebecca Crane, *d* June 13, 1864, *a* 69.
Edward Crane, *d* Dec. 16, 1881, *a* 84.

Job Williams, of Mitcham Road, *d* Feb. 17, 1866, *a* 60.
> Whose relative and friendly qualities endeared him to all who
>   were acquainted with him.
[For many years landlord of the Spread Eagle, in the Mitcham Road.]
George Williams, his son, *d* March 23, 1853, *a* 9.
> Beloved, it is well! though deep and sore the smart,
> The hand that wounds knows how to bind and heal a broken heart.

Alfred Arthur, *d* Nov. 20, 1855, *a* 62.
Jane, his wife, *d* June 14, 1870, *a* 70.

Sophia Polton, *d* Oct. 4, 1858. *a* 57.
Charles Polton, *d* March 31, 1877, *a* 75.
  [A wood-broker in Myrtle Street.]

Richard Hermell, *d* Nov. 4, 1864, *a* 64.

Anne Green, *d* Jan. 16, 1854, *a* 76.

Harriot Bower, wife of Thos. James Bower, *d* Feb. 8, 1857, *a* 37.
  " This is a faithful saying and worthy of all acceptation, that Christ Jesus
    came into the world to save sinners, of whom I am the chief." —
    Tim. i. 15 v.

William, only son of Louis Stanislaus and Emma Chartrain, *d* March 16,
  1859, *a* 25.
Emma Chartrain, his mother, *d* March 19, 1867, *a* 56.

Caroline Jeffery, *d* Feb. 11, 1872, *a* 67.
              Oh, Death, where is thy sting,
              Oh, Grave, where is thy victory.

John Jeffery, her grandson, *d* March 6, 1872, *a* 26.

Fredolinda Alexina Ellicia Mentiploy, *d* Jan. 15, 1856, *a* 14 months.
Marrietta, her cousin, *d* July 21, 1853, *a* 6 months.

Catherine Ellis, *d* Jan. 14, 1856, *a* 67.

William, son of Thomas Burstow, of Horsham, *d* July 4, 1853, *a* 22.

Mrs. Eliza Raine, *d* April 27, 1854, *a* 52.
              Father, I bless Thy gentle hand,
                How kind was Thy chastening rod,
              That forced my conscience to a stand,
                And brought my wand'ring soul to God.

William Clarence, *d* Dec. 3, 1855, *a* 77.
Harriet Eleanor Clarence, *d* June 25, 1862, *a* 82.
Jane Louisa Clarence, *d* March 15, 1874, *a* 88.

Elizabeth Hodges, *d* Sept. 17, 1858, *a* 43.
Maria Hodges, *d* April 3, 1869, *a* 47.

Matilda Ann, wife of David Tilling, *d* July 20, 1872, *a* 58.
David Tilling, *d* April 21, 1882, *a* 68.
  Who when living was a man ; now of his kindred dust.
  [The last man buried in this churchyard. He was for many years a plumber
    residing in the Handcroft Road. He was taken ill while attending the
    funeral of his old friend Attwood Bignell, and died a few days
    afterwards.]

William Albert Tilling, *d* Dec. 16, 1856, *a* 2.
Minnigrey Eleanor Tilling, *d* Aug. 23, 1859, *a* 4 months.

Edmund Smith, *d* Feb. 17, 1858, *a* 74.
Mary Ann Smith, his wife, *d* Feb. 23, 1863, *a* 73.

END OF CHRIST CHURCH.

THE FRIENDS' BURIAL GROUND.

THE FRIENDS' MEETING HOUSE is situated in Park Lane. The first meeting of the Friends in Croydon was held about the year 1657. About the year 1696, regular meetings were held in a small building, but where situate we are unable to state, which was rented of Thomas Beck for 40s. per annum. In 1707 the present burial ground was purchased for £25 5s. On the ground thus acquired, a meeting-house was built in 1720; this building now forms a portion of the present premises. The meeting-house now used was built in 1816, but has been altered and enlarged since that date. The oldest stone in the burying ground is dated 1811. Formerly the Friends objected to the use of headstones. Many families at the present time never use them, therefore the stones form a very incomplete record of the dead. As is customary in the Friends' burial grounds, the headstones are made all of one size, and contain nothing more than the simple announcement of the name, age, and date of death.

Richard Crafton, *d* 17th 12th month, 1813, *a* 60.
Elizabeth Crafton, *d* 7th 9th month, 1831, *a* 58.
Ralph Caldwell Crafton, *d* 28th 5th month, 1875, *a* 79.
> [Mr. Crafton was the head of the present firm of Crafton and Son, 137, High Street.]

William Foster Reynolds, *d* 19th 11th month, 1838, *a* 70.
Esther Reynolds, *d* 28th 10th month, 1857, *a* 84.

Augusta Miller, *d* June 28th, 1869, *a* 53.
Mary Miller, *d* July 19th, 1873, *a* 95.

Philip Cyrus Clark, *d* 13th 7th month, 1868, *a* 8.
Sarah Anna Clark, *d* 26th 3rd month, 1869, *a* 40.

John Peacock, late of Sunderland. *d* 10th 12th month, 1868, *a* 78.
Ann Peacock, *d* 7th 7th month, 1876, *a* 68.

Thomas Woodrouffe Smith, *d* 3rd 5th month, 1811.

Ann Woodrouffe Barton, *d* 24th 10th month, 1822, *a* 31.

Ann Woodrouffe Smith, *d* 17th 4th month, 1839, *a* 72.

John Morland, *d* 21st 10th month, 1867, *a* 73.
> [He was a member of the Local Board of Health from 1853 to 1862. His son, Mr. C. C. Morland, has sat on the same Board from 1868 to the present time.]

Sarah Sophia Morland, *d* 21st 8th month, 1852, *a* 32.

Frederick Morland, *d* 20th 5th month, 1856, *a* 14.

Edward Coventry, *d* 14th 9th month, 1867, *a* 95.

Elizabeth Bush Hughes, *d* 4th 12th month, 1867, *a* 71.

Emma Binns, *d* 15th 2nd month, 1868, *a* 50.

Henry Binns, *d* 17th 1st month, 1880, *a* 69.
  [Mr. Binns was for some years one of the most valued speakers at the meetings.]

Rachel Coleman, *d* 17th 3rd month, 1868, *a* 68.

John Coleman, *d* 10th 9th month, 1830, *a* 67.
Deborah Coleman, *d* 2nd 2nd month, 1853, *a* 84.

Mary Reed, *d* 10th 5th month, 1868, *a* 56.

Sarah Moon Cash, widow of Samuel Cash, *d* 1866, *a* 83.

Emma Wood, *d* 25th 3rd month, 1866, *a* 13.

Charlotte Emily Reckitt, *d* 9th 12th month, 1865.
Arthur Edward Reckitt, *d* 19th 12th month, 1870.
    Children of George and Elizabeth Reckitt.

Peter Bedford, *d* 1st 12th month, 1864, *a* 84.

Cyrus Candler, late of Leicester, *d* 17th 11th month, 1863, *a* 77.

James Rokes, *d* 7th 3rd month, 1868, *a* 34.

Phœbe Jane Radley, wife of Joseph Radley, *d* 19th 9th month, 1868, *a* 32.
  [Mrs. Radley was the wife of Mr. Joseph Radley, who was for many years second master of The Friends' School, Park Lane, but afterwards removed to the Ulster Schools, Lisburn, Ireland.]

Lucy Fryer, *d* 23rd 9th month, 1858, *a* 14.

Mary Barrett, *d* 11th 10th month, 1858, *a* 60.

Mary, daughter of P. J. and M. Butler, *d* 20th 6th month, 1869, *a* 13.

Elizabeth North Levitt, *d* 3rd 7th month, 1869, *a* 44.

Joseph Marsh, *d* 3rd 3rd month, 1870, *a* 80.

Anna Coleman, *d* 8th 7th month, 1877.
Robert Coleman, her husband, *d* 5th 5th month, 1871, *a* 77.

Benjamin Abbott, *d* 5th 12th month, 1870, *a* 77.

William Squire Pryor, of Clapham, *d* 5th 3rd month, 1871, *a* 75.

John Squire, *d* 29th 10th month, 1872, *a* 79.

Anna Sophia Dearman, *d* 27th 1st month, 1820.

Ann Brewster, *d* 21st 4th month, 1835, *a* 73.

Richard Brewster, *d* 13th 2nd month, 1832, *a* 46.

Thomas Brewster, *d* 3rd month, 1869, *a* 85.

Eleanor Pim, *d* 21st 10th month, 1832, *a* 37.

John Hewell, *d* 16th 11th month, 1830, *a* 70.

Joseph William Taylor, son of Joseph and Elizabeth Taylor, *d* 2nd 11th month, 1869, *a* 11.

John Dearman, *d* 2nd 3rd month, 1842, *a* 73.

Thomas Hutchinson, *d* 23rd 3rd month, 1839, *a* 20.

John Pine, *d* 6th 2nd month, 1829, *a* 77.

Elizabeth Pim, *d* 11th 12th month, 1860, *a* 68.

Sarah Everitt, *d* 8th 8th month, 1839, *a* 85.
Anne Everitt, *d* 6th 12th month, 1868, *a* 79.

Edward Foster Brady, *d* 11th 4th month, 1838, *a* 35.

Hannah Lucas, *d* 13th 2nd month, 1836. *a* 51.

Sarah Hayhurst Lucas, *d* 14th 6th month, 1873, *a* 86.

Arthur Lucas, *d* 24th 9th month, 1849, *a* 19.

Sarah Ann Lucas, *d* 7th 8th month, 1869, *a* 53.

Sarah, wife of Fredk. Smith, *d* 22nd 4th month, 1825, *a* 69.

Esther Coleman, *d* 2nd 3rd month, 1872, *a* 68.

Jonathan Wilkinson Angus, *d* 16th 11th month, 1879, *a* 90.

Frederick Smith, *d* 22nd 2nd month, 1823, *a* 65.

Florence Mary Barrett, *d* 23rd 3rd month, 1862, *a* 1 year and 4 months.

Deborah Coleman, *d* 8th 1st month, 1876, *a* 84.

Mary Shewell, *d* 10th month, 1842, *a* 85.

Philip Frith, *d* 7th 3rd month, 1844, *a* 77.

Thomas Eaton, *d* 12th 10th month, 1843, *a* 27.

Mary Eaton, *d* 12th 1st month, 1856, *a* 60.

John Ashby, *d* 1st 8th month, 1864. *a* 57.

　　[Mr. Ashby was the founder of the present firm of Ashby, Son, & Allen, steam millers, St. James' Road. He took a prominent part in Croydon towards the repeal of the Corn Laws.]

Elizabeth Candler, *d* 10th 2nd month, 1875.

Charles Ledbetter. *d* 9th 2nd month, 1850. *a* 1 year and 10 months.

Rebecca Prier, *d* 12th 11th month, 1853, *a* 73.

William Prier, her husband. *d* 9th 12th month, 1857, *a* 85.

Edward, their son, *d* 24th 8th month, 1870, *a* 54.

Amy Edgar, *d* 25th 5th month, 1852, *a* 48.

John Edgar, *d* 17th 11th month, 1874, *a* 71.

James Horne, *d* 26th 10th month, 1857. *a* 68.

Mary Ann Horne, *d* 13th 9th month, 1870, *a* 79.

Joseph Neatby, *d* 6th 7th month, 1857, *a* 83.

Alfred Tobias Sturge, *d* 12th 4th month, 1856, *a* 19.

Hannah Horniman, *d* 1st 6th month, 1854, *a* 13.

Catherine Sophia, wife of Alfred Crowley, *d* 13th 1st month, 1854, *a* 27.

Ann Sterry. *d* 28th 1st month, 1864, *a* 76.

Richard Sterry, *d* 23rd 2nd month, 1865, *a* 80.

　　[Mr. Richard Sterry lived for many years in the original Oakfield Park, in the grounds of which stood his residence now converted into the Croydon General Hospital. In 1858 the estate, which was formerly a deer park, was sold and cut up and formed into roads now known as Oakfield, Kidderminster, Lennard, and Farquharson. Mr. Sterry was a member of the Croydon Local Board from its commencement in 1849, till 1855.]

Mary Sterry, *d* 28th 2nd month, 1853. *a* 70.

Sarah Sterry, *d* 25th 2nd month, 1863, *a* 73.

Elizabeth, daughter of Joseph Steele, *d* 21st 3rd month, 1863, *a* 40.

John Sharp, *d* 6th 1st month, 1853, *a* 41.

Hannah Sharp, *d* 24th 12th month, 1864, *a* 60.

Mary Mason, of Waterford, *d* 3rd 1st month, 1853, *a* 45.

Sarah Barrett, *d* 1st 6th month, 1846, *a* 64.

Richard Barrett, *d* 4th 4th month, 1855, *a* 70.

END OF THE FRIENDS' BURIAL GROUND.

PUMP PAIL CHAPEL.

THIS Chapel was erected in 1729, and until the opening of the new cemetery, the small square in front of the chapel was the only place of sepulture for Nonconformists in the whole town, except the ground belonging to the Friends. The Chapel originally belonged to the General Baptists, but they removed to a larger chapel in Tamworth Road in 1866, and it was then purchased for the Congregationalists, who have considerably improved it. Formerly the burial ground was full of memorial stones, but they have been almost all removed, and used for other purposes. We append a copy of the inscriptions still remaining :—

George Sawyers, d Oct. 26, 1852, a 82.
Ann Sawyers, his wife, d Sept. 19, 1852, a 77.

Sarah Tidman, d Aug. 2, 1832, a 82.
Catherine White, her sister, d Nov. 12, 1837, a 62.
Susannah, wife of Joseph Potter, d Sept. 9, 1827, a 62.
Joseph Potter, d July 27, 1845, a 80.

Sarah Credland, d Oct. 6, 1828, a 40.

> My flesh will slumber in the ground,
> Till the last trumpet's joyful sound,
> Then burst the chains with sweet surprise,
> And in my Saviour's image rise.

Amey, wife of Samuel Standen, d Sept. 21, 1801, a 54.
Sarah Ann Davis, her daughter, d June 11, 1813, a 23.
Mary Standen, d Dec. 1, 1830, a 47.
Samuel Standen, d Aug. 29, 1835, a 82.

William Phillips, formerly an auctioneer at Mitcham, d Sept. 29, 1818, a 82.

Frances, wife of Thomas Bassett, d March 29, 1828, a 29.

> Nevertheless, not my will, but Thine be done.

Mary Ward, d March 2, 1824, a 32.

> Let worms devour my wasting flesh,
> And crumble all my bones to dust,
> My God shall raise my frame anew,
> At the revival of the just.

William Townsend, d Oct. 1, 1838, a 88.

Maria, widow of the late Stephen Hersee, d Sept. 29, a 70.

Susannah Collis, d April 18, 1840, a 71.

> A guilty, weak, and helpless worm,
> On Thy kind arms I fall,
> Be Thou my strength and righteousness,
> My Jesus and my all.

Sarah, wife of Eliza Allen, and daughter of Samuel and Sarah Candish,
   d July 17, 1824, a 26.

Samuel Candish, d Jan. 10, 1814, a 37.

Hannah Chandos, d Oct. 30, 1831, a 80.
Elizabeth Chandos, d May 13, 1813, a 71.
Sarah Chandos, her sister, d Oct. 39, 1819, a 71.

John Outram, d April 6, 1850, a 63.

William Hider, d May 28, 1852, a 25.
Mary Hider, his sister, a Jan. 26, 1853, a 31.

END OF PUMP PAIL CHAPEL.

BEDDINGTON CHURCH.

THIS Church is situated about a mile-and-a-half from Croydon in the valley of the River Wandle. There was a Church here when the Domesday Book was compiled, but no part of the present structure can be referred to that era. It would seem, from the style of architecture, to have been erected during the reign of Richard II, and we find that Nicholas de Carew, the first Lord of Beddington of that name, in 1390, bequeathed £20 to the building of the Church. The edifice is dedicated to St. Mary, and consists of a nave and aisles, a chancel, and a tower at the west end, and a monumental chapel for the Carew family, attached to the south side of the chancel, and opening into it. During the present century very extensive repairs have been made to the Church, which had become in a very dilapidated condition. Canon Bridges, the present rector, has thoroughly restored the Church both inside and out. The interior decorations are most elaborate. An addition to the churchyard was made in 1875, and the new ground was consecrated by the Bishop of Winchester " on the feast of St. Matthias " in that year. Very handsome lych gates have been erected to both the new and the old grounds. We commence our record by describing the tombs in the Carew chapel :

Virtutis splendore, et equestri clarus honore, Franciscus Carew conditur hoc tumulo, principibus fidus, percharus amicus amicis, pauperibus largus, munificusque bonis, Hospitio excepit Reges, proceresque frequenter, hospitibus cunctus semper aperta domus. Innocui mores niveo, candore politi, Lingua dolo caruit, meus sine fraude fuit. Laudatum vitam laudandâ morte peregit, solus in extremis anchoræ Christus erat.
Avunculo optimè merito Nepos mœstissimus hoc monumentum honoris et memoriæ ergo posuit.

On the opposite panel is the following inscription :

" Here lieth Sir Francis Carew, Knt., sonne and heire of Sir Nicholas Carew, Knight of the Honorable Order of the Garter, maister of the horse, and privye councellour to King Henry the VIII ; the said Sir Francis living unmarried, adopted Sir Nicholas Throckmorton, sonne of Annie Throckmorton, his sister, to be heire of his estate, and to beare his surname, and having lived 81 yeares, he, in assured hope to rise in Christ, ended this transitory life the 16th day of Maye, 1611."

The figure of Sir Francis is life size, sculptured in alabaster. He is represented in complete armour, wearing a scull-cap; his hands are folded as if in prayer. In front of the tomb, on a low plinth, and kneeling upon cushions, are small figures of a knight in armour, and his lady in a ruff and long cloak, together with five sons and two daughters ; the the latter wearing ruffs and farthingales. Underneath is the following inscription :—

Sir Nicholas Carew, knight, youngest sonne of Sir Nicholas Throckmorton, adopted into the surname and armes of Carew, maried Marie, eldest daughter of Sir George Moore, of Loosely. knight, of whom he had issue Francis, Nicholas, George, Edmund, Oliphie, Elizabeth, and Marie, and to the memory of his deare and well deserving unckle erected this monument.

Sir Francis Carew was son of Sir Nicholas Carew, who, it will be noticed, held several important offices under King Henry VIII, and was at one time in high favour with that monarch, but taking part in some of the Roman Catholic plots, instigated by Reginald Pole, afterwards Cardinal Pole, who aspired to the throne, he was tried, found guilty, and beheaded on Tower Hill on the 3rd March, 1539, at the age of forty-three. He was buried in the Church of St. Botolph, Aldersgate, where there is a small monument inscribed with his name. His estate was sequestrated. By favour of Queen Mary, his son, Sir Francis, obtained the restitution of the estates, and built a beautiful mansion adjoining the church, where he had honour of being twice visited by Queen Elizabeth, as stated in the laudatory verses on his tomb, in the years 1599 and 1600. He died unmarried at the age of 81. He had two sisters, one of whom married Sir Nicholas Throckmorton, as the monument testifies, and whose youngest son inherited the Carew name and property. The second sister married the celebrated Sir Walter Raleigh, founder of the colony of Virginia, who first introduced the use of tobacco into England. He was beheaded in the reign of James 1st, and left one son, Carew Raleigh. The lower monument is to the memory of Sir Francis Throckmorton Carew. He married twice. A son of the " laste " Lady Carew has erected a tablet to her memory near her husband's monument. It reads thus :—

To the memory of my dear mother, the Lady Carew, laste wife of Sir Nicholas Carew, of Bedington.

> Whose virtuous life doth memory deserve,
> Who taught her children Heaven's great God to serve.

She departed this life Dec. 11, in the year 1633.

She was Susanna, second wife of Sir Nicholas Carew, and a daughter of Thomas Bright, draper, of Bury St. Edmunds, and third wife and widow of Francis Barker, citizen and vintner of London.

There is another monument of a more ancient date adjoining the above, to the memory of Sir Richard Carew, Knight Banneret, Governor of Calais, and his wife Malyn or Magdalen, daughter of Sir John Oxenbridge, Knight. On the tomb are two small brasses, lately restored, of a knight in armour and his lady, and along the verge in black letters, this inscription :—

Pray for the soules of Sir Richard Carew and Dame Malyn. his wife, which Sir Richard deceased the xxiii. day of May, anno d'ni mdxxi.. the same Dame Malyn dyed the —— day of ————, mdxxi, on whose souls, Jesus have mercy.

There are several brasses on the floor, some undecipherable, and others covered up. One in the centre is to the memory of Sir Nicholas Carew and his wife, who died in 1432. This knight was sheriff of the county of Surrey in the 15th year of Richard II., and again in the second year of Henry IV.; he also represented the county in several parliaments. In the year 1422. he made a settlement of his estates, from which it appears that he had manors and possessions in at least eighteen different parishes in Surrey.

Sir Nicholas Hackett Carew, Bart., *d* Aug. 10. 1762. *a* 42.
Caroline Lady Carew, his wife, *d* March 18, 1762, *a* 41.
Caroline Carew. their daughter, *d* March 3. 1769, *a* 27.

The above Sir Nicholas Carew was descended in lineal succession from Sir Nicholas Throckmorton Carew. Having no male issue, and his daughter dying unmarried, he left the estate to the eldest son of Richard Gee, Esq., of Orpington, descended from Philippa Carew, his aunt. who in 1780 obtained an Act of Parliament, authorising him to take the name and arms of Carew. There are several monuments to the Gee family in this chapel.

William Gee. of Beddington, Esq.. *d* Aug. 3. 1815. *a* 69.
Ann Paston Gee. his widow. *d* March 28, 1828, *a* 71.
Richard Carew. formerly Richard Gee, of Orpington. Kent, *d* Dec. 18, 1816, *a* 71.

This gentleman dying unmarried, devised all his property to Ann Paston Gee, the widow of his brother, mentioned above. and she having no issue. bequeathed the estates to her first cousin, Admiral Sir Benjamin Hallowell, G.C.B., who pursuant to her will, assumed the name and arms of Carew, by royal license, on the 18th June in the same year. There is a tablet to his memory. It is decorated with a flag (the staff broken), a naval sword, a branch of laurel, and the word *Nile*, in which battle he fought under Nelson. The bravery and talents of Sir Benjamin were noticed in the despatches.

Admiral Sir Benjamin Hallowell Carew, G.C.B., *b* Jan. 1, 1751, *d* Sept. 2, 1834.

The Carew estates afterwards descended to his sons, by whom they were irretrievably lost. The mansion is now occupied by the Female Orphan Asylum, which removed here from the Westminster Bridge Road in 1866. The tombs of the two sons of Admiral Sir Benjamin Hallowell Carew will be found mentioned in our list of tombs in the churchyard.

The following is the last inscription in the Carew Chapel :—

In the vault beneath lie the mortal remains of Patrick Maxwell Shaw
Stewart, R.N., son of Captain Houston Stewart, R.N., G.C.B., born
Aug. 9, 1833, and killed June 25, 1846, by the accidental discharge
of a fowling piece at Beddington Hall.

Innocent, amiable, and warm hearted, he was loved and lamented by all who
knew him.　In life, he never caused his fond parents to shed one tear
of sorrow, and they have now the blessed conviction he is safe in death.

The following inscriptions are copied from tablets in various
parts of the church :—

This brass is placed to the memory of Andrew Collyer Bristowe, Esq., of
Beddington, by his sorrowing widow, *b* Dec 24, 1794, *d* Dec. 2, 1856.

In memory of Mary Whitehall, many years a resident in and a benefactor
by her will to the poor of the parish of Beddington, *d* March 27,
1859, *a* 83.

John Tritton, Esq., *d* Jan. 19, 1832, *a* 44.
Elizabeth Mary, his wife, *d* Jan. 24, 1834, *a* 39.

Mary, wife of John Henton Tritton, Esq., eldest daughter of the late John
Barclay, Esq., *d* Feb. 25, 1827, *a* 71.

John Henton Tritton, Esq., banker, of Lombard Street, *d* March 20, 1833,
a 79.

Mary Tritton, their only daughter, *d* Sept. 5, 1852, *a* 56.

William Bridges, Esq., late of Wallington House, *d* Nov. 21, 1805, *a* 87.

This monument was erected in token of grateful attachment to the memory
of one whose benevolence extended itself to every branch of his family.

The above inscription is taken from a very handsome
monument of white marble on dove-coloured ground, the
work of the younger Bacon. It is ornamented by an
enriched urn, having the arms of the deceased sculptured
on its pedestal.

John Walton, Esq., *d* April 19, 1802, *a* 63.
Mrs. Alice Walton, *d* Aug. 15, 1810, *a* 60.
Annie Walton, spinster, the last of her father's family, *d* July 11, 1826,
a 72.

Elizabetha felice Caroli Proby, Chathame Navalium Curatores uxoris Pauli
Tchitchagoff, Rerum Navalum Muscovitarum Præfecti quæ obiit
Anno Salutis, 1811, Ætatis 36.

[This memorial is the work of Henry Westmacott.　Paul Tchitchagoff was
superintendent of naval affairs in Russia.]

We conclude our copies of the inscriptions in the Interior of
the Church with the following extremely amusing memorial,
in which it will be seen the author puns on his own name.
On the upper portion are the following brief Latin
phrases :—

Mors super. Virides montes. Sicut hora sic Vita.
Tho. Grenhill, borne and bredd in ye famous University of Oxon, Batche-
lour of Artes, and sometyme Student in Magd. Coll., Steward to ye
Noble Kt. Sir Nicholas Carew, of Beddington, who deceased Sept.
17 day, Ano 1634, aged 33 years.
Will. Grenhill, Mr. of Artes, his brother, and Mary, his sister, to his
memory erected this.

　　　　Under thy feete, interr'd is here,
　　　　A native borne in Oxford-sheere,

First life and learning Oxford gave,
Surry to him his death, his grave.
Hee once a Hill was fresh and Greene,
Now wither'd is, not to be scene,
Earth in earth, shoueld up is shut
A Hill into a Hole is put ;
But darksome earth by poure Divine
Bright at last as ye sun may shine.

THE CHURCHYARD.

We now turn to the tombs and stones in the churchyard. The first is a remarkable one to an old servant of the Carew family :—

Here lieth the body of George Hickson, huntsman to the Carews of Beddington, died Sept. 20, 1848, in the 102nd year of his age, in the service of the family he had entered as a boy.

The deceased, shortly before he died, said if he lived until Martinmas, he should have been 90 years in the service of the Carews, an instance of lengthened service almost unparalleled. He was familiarly known as the man who eat his horse, and this arose from the following circumstance : It would seem the hounds had been out for several days without killing, and the old man vowed one morning if they were not more successful that day, he would eat his horse. During the course of the day, the horse he was riding, a young and valuable animal, fell and broke his leg, and it was found necessary to shoot it. Some of the men who had heard the old huntsman's rash vow, cut a slice out of the rump of the animal and sent it to the huntsman's cottage. His housekeeper thinking it was a beef steak, cooked it for his dinner. On his return home, the old man sat down and eat it, and vowed he had never tasted a better steak in his life. He was terribly annoyed the next morning when he was informed from whence his tender steak had been cut. The joke was remembered against him until the day of his death ; but he learned to laugh at it heartily, and the gentlemen of the hunt very frequently asked him when he came with his hounds to the place of meet whether he had made another vow.

Mary, daughter of John Whitehall, *d* Jan. 24, 1824, *a* 14.

Jerusalem, my happy home,
    When shall I come to thee,
My dear Redeemer is above,
    Him will I go to see.
And all my friends in Christ below
    Shall soon come after me.

Charles Hallowell Hallowell Carew, born March 1, 1829, *d* Sept. 17, 1872.
Benjamin Francis Hallowell Carew, born Oct. 3, 1830, *d* April 23, 1879.

William Marsh, D.D., rector of Beddington, *d* Aug. 24, 1864, *a* 89.

On the day before his death he closed the 66th year of his faithful and fruitful ministry with these words, " Tell the clergy to preach Christ, to live Christ, to serve Christ, and they shall have praise in eternity."

I

Johannes Cox, rector hvivs ecclesiæ decessit Octobris xxvii, A.D., 1609, ætatis svæ 49.

Alice, wife of Francis Henry Layban, of Bandon Hill, *d* Dec. 22, 1872, *a* 26.

Charles Berryman, *alias* Brandon, rector of Beddington, *d* Dec. 19, 1671, *a* 49.

Thomas, his son, *d* Feb. 5, 1672, *a* 12.

William Bromfield Ferrers, clerk, *d* June 6, 1841, *a* 83, having been rector of this parish for 59 years.

Sir Charles Henry Rich, of Wallington, *d* Oct. 22, 1857, *a* 73.

Frances Maria, his wife, *d* Feb. 20, 1852, *a* 67,

Frances Maria Dorothea Rich, *d* July 20, 1878.

William Wilkinson, gent., *d* Dec. 6, 1812, *a* 57.

Mary, his widow, *d* June 9, 1821, *a* 70.

> Alas, the sudden hand of death,
> With sudden stroke deprived of breath
> The ashes that lay here.
> My fellow mortal, pray beware,
> And for that fatal hour prepare,
> Unknown to all now here.

Thomas Lawrence lost his life by a fall from a horse, May 12, 1799, *a* 18.

> O Death, that to me no warning gave,
> No time with my dear friends to take my leave,
> But in a moment pierced my tender heart,
> And caused me from my dearest friend to part.
> I hope with them to meet again,
> In heaven for ever to remain.

On a rail is the following :—

> Hail glorious gospel, Heavenly light whereby,
> We live with comfort, and with comfort die,
> And view beyond this gloomy scene, the tomb,
> A life of endless happiness to come.

Frances, eldest daughter of the late Admiral James Pigott, of Beddington Lodge, wife of Morgan Culhaue. M.D., *d* June 17, 1869, *a* 68.

Morgan Culhaue, M.D., Victoria Row, Kensington, *d* Sept. 22, 1876, *a* 84.

Sarah, wife of Wm. Shaw, Wallington, *d* Jan. 8, 1862, *a* 36.

> I was so long with pain oppress'd,
> Which wore my strength away,
> It made me long for endless rest,
> Which never can decay.

Thomas Pratt, *d* May 16, 1819, *a* 67.

Amey Pratt, his wife, *d* July 20, 1815, *a* 65.

> 'Tis religion that must give
> Sweetest pleasure while we live ;
> 'Tis religion must supply
> Solid comfort while we die.
> After death its joy shall be
> Lasting as Eternity.

Benjamin Parker, of Wallington, who exercised a principal trust in the Bank of England for 37 years with earnest trustfulness, to the satisfaction of the Governor and Company, as well as to those who had business with him, *d* Dec. 3, 1739, *a* 60.

Jaspar Swindall, *d* June, 18, 1828, *a* 44.

> Memory be still, and let me tell the praise
> Of him who now beneath this stone do lie ;
> With care he sought each virtuous path to tread,
> He prayed for faith, and died without a sigh.

George Ormerod, *d* Feb. 21, 1811, *a* 60.

> Dear wife, as I in my cold grave do lay,
> You may by chance pass by this way,
> And on my grave may shed a tear,
> For one that once loved you so dear.

[Son of George and Mary Ormerod, of Beddington; he was for upwards of 30 years officer to the Sheriff of Kent, and resided at a house called " Limekilns," in Greenwich.]

John Williams Bristow, Esq., *d* Jan. 17, 1831, *a* 72.
Elizabeth Bristow, *d* Feb. 1, 1837, *a* 75.
John Priest Bristow, his son, *d* Feb. 6, 1837.
Mrs. Ann Bristow, widow of John Williams Bristow, *d* Sept. 4, 1846, *a* 84.
William Bristow, Esq., *d* Oct. 25, 1858, *a* 97.
Andrew Collyer-Bristow, Esq., *d* Dec. 2, 1861, *a* 66.
Mary, his wife, *d* Jan. 14, 1867, *a* 66.

John Pimm, of Croydon, *d* Oct. 10, 1848, *a* 38.

Bristow Collyer, *d* July 12, 1870, *a* 42.

John Cayley, Esq., of Wallington, many years resident of St. Petersburg, *d* March 30, 1831, *a* 72.

> This monument was erected by his afflicted widow to perpetuate as long as so frail a record may endure, the memory of one deeply regretted by all who were acquainted with his virtues.

Harriet, his wife, *d* Feb. 23, 1870, *a* 91.
Edward Cayley, his son, died in Russia, buried in Riga, Feb. 18, 1871, *a* 66.

Honest Robin Betterton, obiit 9th Sept. 1724, æra 57.

> [We have copied the inscription as it appears on the tomb. The word *æra* is evidently intended for *ætat*, a mistake probably caused during the restoration of the tomb. The deceased was formerly a fishmonger, residing in the parish of St. Botolph, Billingsgate, and afterwards of Croydon. In his will, among other small bequests he leaves the sum of £5 to Mrs. Prudence Snow, "wherewith she is to make one treat for the Wednesday club at her house." This club, in all probability consisted of a number of old cronies with whom he was in the habit of associating during his life time.]

Drinkwater, Ann Margaret, May 22, 1873—Faith.
    ,,   Elizabeth Maria, July 5, 1881—Charity.

John Bridges, Esq., of Wallington House, *d* June 29, 1865, *a* 78.
Elizabeth Bridges, his wife, *d* April 5, 1848.
Brook Bridges, *d* July 8, 1807, *a* 21.
Brook Allen Bridges, *d* Nov. 12, 1815.
Sarah, his wife, *d* Dec. 17, 1816.

Thomas Hillar, *d* Oct. 19, 1719, *a* 38.
Sarah, his wife, *d* August, 1752, *a* 69.

William Thos. Goad, Esq., of Hackbridge House, Wallington, *d* Dec. 17, 1863, *a* 87.
George Anthony Goad, Esq., *d* June 15, 1850, *a* 57.

Elizabeth Farquhar, wife of Andrew Alfred Collyer-Bristow, *d* Jan. 12, 1872, *a* 34.

Mary, daughter of Geo. Ball, Esq., of Mitcham, *d* Aug. 10, 1820, *a* 68.

> If souls could always dwell above,
> Thou ne'er hadst left Thy sphere,
> O, could we keep the soul above,
> We ne'er had lost thee here.

The following are some of the Inscriptions in the new ground :—

Henry Tritton, Esq., *d* Jan. 2, 1877.

Edward Richardson, *d* Nov. 13, 1878, *a* 59.

Under a beautiful statue of a young female leaning on a
rustic cross :—

Juliet Borneque, *d* Sept. 1, 1879, *a* 17.

Caroline, 46 years the beloved wife of J. F. Wathen, *d* Aug. 3, 1877, *a* 71.
Josiah Iles Wathen, *d* April 6, 1881, *a* 76.

William Ray Smee, F.S.A., *d* Oct. 27, 1877, *a* 56.

Alfred Smee, F.R.S., *d* Jan. 11, 1877, *a* 59.
Elizabeth, his wife, *d* March 6, 1879, *a* 61.

[Mr. Alfred Smee was the author of " My Garden," a most profusely illus-
trated work describing the innumerable floral and horticultural beauties
of the garden lying at the south western end of Beddington Park.]

Frederick Smee, *d* Aug. 26, 1879, *a* 55.

Eleanor Maria, wife of Jas. Robt. Bouquet, *d* Dec. 23, 1877, *a* 61.

The saints of God their virgil keep,
While yet their mortal bodies sleep,
Till from the dust, they too shall rise,
And soar triumphant to the skies,
Oh, happy saints rejoice and sing,
He quickly comes, your Lord and King.

Eleanor Margaret, wife of Hy. J. Mitchell, *d* Jan. 3, 1880, *a* 44.

Susanna, wife of Joseph Morris, *d* Sept. 20, 1876, *a* 41.

END OF BEDDINGTON CHURCH.

ADDINGTON CHURCH.

THE old Church at Addington was originally built of flint, with window-cases of friable stone; but about the year 1773, the exterior wall of the building were rebuilt with brick by Alderman Trecothick. There is a low square tower at the west end, containing four bells. Originally there was only a small aisle on the south side, but a larger one has lately been added on the north side, considerably extending the accommodation in the building. The present Church dates from the reign of Edward III. In the year 1843 the whole of the Church was renovated, internally and externally, at the expense of Dr. Howley, the Archbishop of Canterbury. The old pews were replaced by backed seats, affording accommodation for about 250 persons. Formerly there were numerous old monuments in this Church, but many are entirely lost.

Abutting on the north wall of the chancel is a costly monument of alabaster and black marble. It was erected by Sir Oliph Leigh, in memory of his father and mother. In the upper part are two niches, under one of which are two figures kneeling, with this inscription :—

John Leigh, of Addington, Esq., sonne of Nicholas Leigh, of Addington, married Joanne, daughter and heire of Sir John Oliph, Knight, by whom he had issue, Sir Oliph Leigh, Knight, John, Charles, Anne, Joanne, Elizabeth, and Katharine : he ended this life 31 March, 1576.

Under the other arch are two more figures also kneeling, with this inscription :—

Nicholas Leigh, of Addington, married Anne, sister to Sir Nicholas Carew, by whom he had issue John Leigh, Malin, Elizabeth, Mary, Anne.

These figures are habited in the dress of the period, and have evidently been coloured. Underneath is a full size recumbent figure of a knight, fully armed, resting on his right elbow. In the lower compartment is the figure of a lady, dressed in the costume of the fifteenth century, leaning on her right hand, and holding a book in her left. There are also two figures of children kneeling, detached from the monument, and probably belonging to some other tomb. Underneath the lady we read :—

Here resteth in peace, Sir Oliph Leigh, knight, who married Jane, daughter of Sir Thomas Brown, by whom he had Francis, his only son and heire, who died 14 March, 1562.

On a slab on the chancel floor is a brass figure of a man in armour, and underneath an inscription in black letter, to Thomas Hatteclyffe, Esq., " sn'tyme one of ye foure masters of the housholde to our sov'aigne Lord King Henry ye VIII."

Near this brass is a tomb, surmounted by a large memorial urn, standing in a recess, which has evidently, at one time been a small window, on the south-east side of the chancel, on which we read this inscription :—

Died May 28, 1775, *a* 56.

In memory of Barlow Trecothick, Esq., Merchant, Alderman, and Lord Mayor of the City of London, much esteemed by the merchants for his integrity and knowledge of commerce, truly beloved by his fellow citizens, who chose him as their representative in Parliament; and sincerely lamented by his friends and relatives, who looked up to and admired his virtues. This last tribute is humbly offered by his affectionate wife, Ann Trecothick, 1776.

Near this is another large memorial tablet to the memory of the above gentleman's first wife :—

In memory of Mrs. Grizzel Trecothick, who to an elegant form and mind united a virtuous and religious disposition; her affectionate husband, Barlow Trecothick, hath placed this monument. She died at Addington, 31st July, 1769, aged 41 years.

The above-named Barlow Trecothick purchased the Addington estate from the representatives of the Leigh family for £38,500. In the particulars of the sale the lands were computed at 5,000 acres ; of which 500 were wood, and 1,000 waste. On the enclosure of Croydon Common in 1797, a large part of the Common, between Addiscombe and Addington, was claimed by Mr. James Trecothick, in right of his proprietorship of the manor of Addington ; and on a trial, the claim was admitted to be just. Mr. Barlow Trecothick is the gentleman who almost re-built Addington Church. He was Lord Mayor of London in 1770, and during his mayoralty (having lost his first wife, Grizzel, in 1769), he was married a second time to Ann Meredith, of Henbury, in Cheshire, who survived him, and who erected the monument to his memory. The Alderman left no issue, and devised his estate at Addington to his nephew, James Ivers, who took the name and arms of Trecothick. In 1803, this gentleman sold the estates in lots, and a Mr. Coles purchased the house and park, and he, in 1807, transferred the same by sale to the Trustees of the Archbishop of Canterbury, and Addington Park thus became the property of the Primate for the time being, instead of the Old Palace at Croydon, which was sold under the authority of an Act of Parliament. There are several other memorials of the Trecothick family, who were buried in the family vault under the chancel of the Church, though after the sale of the property they went to reside at Broadstairs. We append the inscriptions :—

In the family vault in the chancel are deposited the remains of James Trecothick, Esq., youngest son of the late Jas. Trecothick, Esq., who died Sept. 29, 1849, *a* 51; also Susanna Trecothick, his eldest sister, who died at Broadstairs. Dec. 11, 1857, *a* 79; also Charlotte, another sister, who died at Broadstairs. Oct. 7, 1858, *a* 75.

In memory of Louisa Trecothick, died March 22, 1863, *a* 81; also Ann Trecothick, her twin sister, who died Nov. 20, 1865, *a* 84.

James Trecothick, Esq., formerly of Addington, late of Broadstairs, in the Isle of Thanet, died Sept. 11, 1846, *a* 90. For many years he ably discharged the duties of magistrate for Surrey and Kent, and also for the Cinque Ports. He was an affectionate husband and father, a kind landlord, sincerely beloved by his family, much respected by his friends and those among whom he resided. His six surviving children, as a tribute of respect and affection have erected this tablet to his memory.

Since the purchase of Addington House, this little church and churchyard has been selected by the Archbishops as their burial place. Two are buried in vaults under the church, and two in the churchyard. We first append a copy of the tablets in the church, and other inscriptions will be found on the tombs in the churchyard.

Haud Procul hinc situs est. Carolus Manners Sutton. S.T.D. Cantuariensis Archiepiscopus, natus Dei. Feb. 14, 1755. decessit July 21, 1828.

To the memory of John B. Sumner, D.D., Archbishop of Canterbury. He was consecrated Bishop of Chester in 1828, and was translated to the see of Canterbury in 1848, died Sept. 6, 1862, aged 83, and was interred in the vault belonging to the family in the adjoining churchyard.

There is in the north-east corner of the chancel, adjoining the communion table, an altar tomb, which, we understand, once contained a recumbent figure of Archbishop Howley. At some time this figure was removed to Canterbury Cathedral, and the place is now filled up with a cushion, on which rests a large cross, the lower part reaching to the end of the tomb where the feet of the figure would have rested. Underneath is this inscription :—

To the memory of the Most Reverend William Howley. D.D., Archbishop of Canterbury: he was born Feb. 12th, 1766, married, in 1805, Mary Frances, daughter of John Belli, Esq. He died Feb. 11th, 1848.

There is also a tablet to the memory of a son of Archbishop Manners Sutton, who, it will be seen, for eighteen years presided over the House of Commons, and was afterwards elevated to the peerage :—

Chas. Manners Sutton, P.C., G.C.B., Speaker to the House of Commons from 1817 to 1835, in which year he was created Viscount Canterbury and Baron Bottesford, born 29th January, 1780, died 21st July, 1845. His remains are interred in the family vault inside the Church.

The deceased nobleman was remarkable for his dignified appearance and the suavity of his manners. He presided over the House of Commons during the troubled and excited period which preceded and followed the passing of the first Reform Bill. So popular was he among all classes, though known to be a Conservative, he was re-elected to the Speakership by the Liberals when they took office in the first reformed Parliament.

There is one other tablet, to the memory of a son of Archbishop Tait, buried in the churchyard. It runs as follows :—

To the glory of God and in loving memory of the Rev. Craufurd Tait, only son of the Archbishop of Canterbury, called from God's work on earth to do his Father's will in heaven, May 29, 1878. The offering of parishioners of Addington and neighbouring friends.

THE CHURCHYARD.

Fanny, wife of George Heath, *d* Nov. 7, 1869.

Merion Vansittart, daughter of Charles and Charlotte Vansittart Frere, *d* April 26, 1807, *a* 6.

Augusta Fredk. Wm. Hoffman, *a* 82.

Ann Langford, wife of Geo. Langford, *d* April 13, 1875, *a* 75.
George Langford, her husband, *d* Sept. 28, 1879, *a* 79.

Edward Loyd, of Green Hill, Manchester, *d* at Coombe House Jan. 30, 1863, *a* 83.
Sarah, his wife, *d* Jan. 19, 1873, *a* 78.

Catharine and Craufurd Tait, mother and son, *d* Dec. 1 and May 29, 1878.
We took sweet counsel together, and walked in the House of God as friends.
Lovely and pleasant in their lives, in their deaths they were not divided.
When I awake up after Thy likeness I shall be satisfied with it.

The Rev. Craufurd Tate was the only surviving son of the Archbishop of Canterbury. He was born in 1849, at the Deanery, Carlisle, and was therefore only 29 years old when he died, on the 29th of May, 1878. He was a young man universally beloved. When about seven years of age his father was appointed Bishop of London. In process of time the lad was sent to Eton, and thence to Christ Church, Oxford, where he graduated first class in law and history, in 1872. In 1873 he was ordained curate to the Rev. W. D. Maclagan, the Bishop-Elect of Lichfield. The Archbishop, wishing his son to become acquainted with the practical work of the ministry, arranged for him to spend two or three years working in the poorest parts of London. He then became his father's domestic chaplain, and held this post till a year before his death, when he was appointed to the vicarage of St. John's, Notting Hill ; but the seeds of a fatal disorder had already been contracted, and he died at Stone House, St. Peter's, near Margate, whither he had gone for change of air, only a few days after his arrival.

Mrs. Tait, the wife of the Archbishop, died on the 1st December, 1878, while with the Archbishop on a visit to Mr. Pitman, of 11, Great Stuart Street, Edinburgh. Thus, twice within the same year was Addington Palace thrown into grief too great for words to express. Mrs. Tait was the youngest daughter of the Venerable W. Spooner, Archdeacon of Coventry, and was married to the Archbishop, then the Rev. Archibald Campbell Tait, in 1843.

Catherine, the dearly-loved child of Charles and Helen Goschen, of the Ballards, Addington, *d* May 18, 1875, *a* 5.

Benjamin Forrester Scott, *d* at Croydon 14th Oct., 1870, *a* 62.

Charles Thomas Longley, Archbishop of Canterbury, born July 28, 1794, *d* Oct. 27, 1868.

[Archbishop Longley succeeded Archbishop Sumner, and was followed by Dr. Tait.]

Caroline Georgina Levett, *b* July 18. 1842, *d* Oct. 30, 1867.
Blessed are the dead which die in the Lord.

Rosamond Diana Longley, *b* 6th Jan. 1875, *d* 8th Dec. 1876.
And in their mouth was found no guile, for they are without fault before the Throne of God.

Henry Selfe Selfe, *d* Sept. 6, 1870, *a* 60.
Thou wilt keep him in perfect peace, whose mind is stayed on Thee, because he trusteth in Thee.

Edward Henry Selfe, *d* Oct. 17, 1880, *a* 37.
Until the day break and the shadows flee away.

Frances Maud, *a* 11, and Fredk. Maxwell Spooner, *d* July 11, 1871.

Charlotte Maria, wife of Capt. J. D. Clarke, *d* June 29, 1867, *a* 25.
'Yond the shade of death's dark valley,
Now ye lean upon his breast,
Where the wicked cease from troubling,
And the weary are at rest.

George Richardson, of Croydon, *d* March 24, 1879, *a* 62.

Marmaduke Walker, of Addington Lodge, *d* April 16, 1880, *a* 74.

Mr. Marmaduke Walker may claim to have accomplished in agriculture as great a conquest as any which have been achieved on a field of battle. He took a sterile tract of land on the hills, and in a few years converted it into an exceedingly fertile farm; and by the aid of a colony of Irish labourers has shown what perseverance and skill can do. He sat for many years on the Croydon Board of Guardians, and was much respected. He won many prizes with his farm produce.

Emily, wife of Robt. Walker, of Addington Park Farm, *d* Dec. 27, 1855, *a* 43.

Robt. Walker, *d* Nov. 29, 1878, *a* 74.

Christopher Rawlins, priest, 40 years vicar of Thornton-cum-Allerthorpe, Yorkshire, *d* April 1, 1876, *a* 68.

Hariot Walters, *d* Nov. 22, 1855, *a* 62.
Thomas Walters, Esq., of Heathfield, her husband, *d* Aug. 4, 1868, *a* 89.

Mary Ann, wife of Mr. Joshua Lott, of Croydon, *d* June 6, 1857, *a* 43.
Joshua Lott, *d* Nov. 24, 1863, *a* 47.

Emma, wife of Wm. Harry Strudwicke, *d* Oct. 23, 1876, *a* 38.

Francis Emma, wife of the Rev. M. T. Farrer, vicar of this parish, *d* Sept. 3, 1844.

Wm. Middleton, late of Croydon, d Nov. 30, 1847, a 61.
Mary Middleton, his wife, d July 16, 1856, a 63.

Until the day dawn, here resteth all that could die of Louisa Marian
 Benham, the beloved wife of the Vicar of this Parish. She was
 born Aug. 12, 1832, and died in the faith and love of Jesus Christ
 our Lord, Aug. 22, 1870.
 The wisdom that is from above is first pure, then peaceable, gentle, and easy
 to be intreated, full of mercy and good fruits, without partiality and
 without hypocrisy.—JAMES iii, 4.

Alexander Bissett, M.A., of Croydon, d Nov. 4, 1821, a 69.
Sarah, his wife, d Aug. 1, 1818, a 53.
Sarah Ann Eyman, d Dec. 4, 1812, a 22.
Harriet Maria Bissett, a July 27, 1812, a 28.
Elizabeth Eleanor, daughter of Charles Emanuel and Elizabeth Sarah
 Bissett, d Jan. 20, 1833, a 9.
Henry Cowper, her brother, d March 13, 1833, a 16 months.
Elizabeth Sarah Bissett, their mother, d Nov. 26, 1843, a 43.

Edward, son of Richard Furbisher, d Aug. 15, 1850, a 2.
> His tender parents left to mourn,
> Enough to break a heart of stone,
> God grant his blessing to be given
> For them to meet again in Heaven.

> Short was thy life, fair flower, how soon removed,
> Sudden thy summons to the realms above,
> Sleep on, sweet child, and take thy rest,
> For God takes them that He loves best.

Eliza Trecothick, d Feb. 5, 1860, a 79.
B. T., d July 30, 1862.   L. T., d March 22, 1863, a 81.
[Members of the Trecothick family, see tablets in the interior of the Church.]

Jeannie Gillies, d Sep. 3, 1870, a 37.

John Bird Sumner, D.D., Archbishop of Canterbury, and his daughter,
 Marie Thomas.
 Archbishop Sumner succeeded Dr. Howley in the See of
 Canterbury. He built Christ Church, Croydon, in 1852,
 and gave the incumbency to the Rev. O. B. Byers, who
 had married the Archbishop's niece. The Archbishop died
 Sept. 6, 1862.

Mary, only daughter of Wilson Dodie Wilson, Esq., and granddaughter of
 John Bird Sumner, Archbishop of Canterbury, d April 26, 1851, a 14.
 The flower fadeth, but the word of God standeth for ever.
 Blessed are the pure in heart, for they shall see God.

Georgina Wilson, born Feb. 28, 1812, d June 22, 1881.
 I thank my God upon all my remembrance of you.—PHILIPPIANS i, 2.
Also two children.

Robt. Jarvis Fuller, at rest, Maunday Thursday, 1876, a 24.
 Mr. Robt. Jarvis Fuller was the eldest son of Mr. Robt. W.
 Fuller, auctioneer, High Street, Croydon. He was a
 young man of singular promise. Affable in his manner,
 and sincere in his friendship he had won the esteem of all
 with whom he had business or social relations. He was
 taken in the pride of manhood, to the great grief of his
 relatives and friends.

William and George, the beloved infants of Francis and Elizabeth Covell, of Croydon.

Also Elizabeth, wife of Francis Covell, their mother, *d* June 18, 1870, *a* 70.

Francis, her eldest son, *d* Sept. 9, 1879, *a* 47.

Also Francis Covell, for 38 years minister of Providence Baptist Chapel, Croydon, *d* Nov. 26, 1879, *a* 71.

None but Jesus
Can do helpless sinners good.

Mr. Francis Covell was no ordinary man. He was born Dec. 8th, 1808, in High Street, Croydon, where his father carried on the business of a tinman and brazier, and to which trade he was brought up and worked at until June, 1851. In early life he was a regular attendant at the Old Parish Church, but as he grew older, his convictions led him to join the Calvinistic Baptists. He commenced his ministry at his own house on July 14th, 1844, where a few friends gathered to meet him. His hearers increased, and in 1846 they agreed to take a small meeting-house in the Old Town, called Ebenezer Chapel. This chapel soon became too small, and it was determined to build a larger chapel in West Street, which was opened on March 12th, 1848, and here he continued to minister the remainder of his life. It would be out of place in a work of this description to give any opinion of his ministry or the doctrines he held; it will suffice to say that his meeting-house, called Providence Chapel, was invariably filled whenever he occupied the pulpit. He had a great aversion to the prefix " Reverend," and was never addressed by this ministerial designation. It is rather singular that this determined opponent to Arminianism and Sacerdotalism should find a resting place in the churchyard where so many Archbishops are buried. It will be seen, however, that he belonged to a very ancient family, none of whom had a better claim than himself to lie in such a distinguished company of illustrious dead.

Gul. Covell, *d* May 11, 1636.
John Covell, *d* April 14, 1650.
Dorothy Covell, *d* Sept. 13, 1724.
Mary Covell, *d* April 13, 1729.
Francis Covell, *d* Sept. 23, 1729.
Mr. Covell, *d* June, 1751.
John Covell, *d* Nov. 2, 1740.
Prudence Covell, *a* April 27, 1746.
Francis Covell, *d* Dec. 6, 1753.
John Covell, *d* April 7, 1756.
Also Mr. Francis Covell, of Croydon, *d* Feb. 2, 1830, *a* 61.
Jane, his daughter, *d* Oct. 29, 1830, *a* 24.
Mary, his wife, *d* Dec. 18, 1832, *a* 57.

Wm. Howard, *d* Jan. 17, 1795, *a* 78.

With patience to the last he did submit,
And murmured not at what the Lord thought fit ;
All through lingering illness, grief and pain,
Although doctor's skill and physic proved in vain,
He with a Christian courage did resign
His soul to God at His appointed time.

Elizabeth Keely. *d* Dec. 24, 1787, *a* 76.
John Keely, of North End, Croydon, *d* April 17, 1829, *a* 74.
Mary Keely, his relict, *d* May 3, 1839, *a* 72.

Charles Blundell, *d* April 24, 1846, *a* 18.
James Blundell, *d* Sept. 15, 1853, *a* 28.
Ann Blundell, their mother, *d* Nov. 5, 1866, *a* 66.
Joseph Blundell, their father, *d* Dec. 18, 1879, *a* 83.

Rebecca, wife of John Alexander, of South End, Croydon, *d* Feb. 18, 1841,
    a 63.
John Alexander, Esq., her husband, *d* May 20, 1861, *a* 83.

Nannette, daughter of Marmaduke and Nanny Rothwell Walker, of
    Addington Lodge, *d* Nov. 13, 1849, *a* 13.

Hester Palmerine. *d* Nov. 26, 1880, *a* 24.

S. M. C. Boatwright, *d* July 4, 1872, *a* 45.

Sarah Boatwright, *d* May 21, 1832, *a* 52.
James Boatwright, her husband, *d* Feb. 1, 1874, *a* 88.

Edward Fuller, *d* Feb. 18, 1849, *a* 80.
Wm. Fuller, *d* Jan. 25, 1852, *a* 82.

James Filor, house steward to the Archbishop of Canterbury, who has
    caused this stone to be erected in testimony of his worth and
    integrity, his zeal in the service of his master, and his exemplary
    attention to all his duties towards God and man, *d* Dec. 26, 1829,
    a 56.
Sophia, his widow, *d* June 2, 1858, *a* 70.

Mary Ann, daughter of Thomas and Mary Mann, of Croydon, *d* April 18,
    1798, *a* 46.

> Sweet is the sleep which now I take,
> Till Jesus Christ doth me wake,
> And may my soul in Heaven rejoice,
> To hear our blessed Saviour's voice.

END OF ADDINGTON CHURCHYARD.

SHIRLEY CHURCH.

THIS Church is very pleasantly situated near to the boundary of Croydon parish, on the road to Addington. The original chapel was built in the year 1835, pulled down in 1856, when the present edifice was erected. There is a burial ground attached, about two acres in extent, which is still used as a place of interment. The first burial therein took place on the 8th August, 1831. There is one peculiarity about this ground. It would seem the original chapel was not placed due east and west, and the burials followed the direction of the church. When the new church was built, this fault was corrected, and the newer burials are of course laid at the same angle as the church; thus some of the graves lie almost at right angles to the others. An attempt has been made to obviate this peculiarity to some degree, still the difference is plainly perceptible.

Here rests from day's well sustained burden, John James Ruskin, born in Edinburgh, Aug. 10th, 1785. He died in his home in London, March 3rd, 1864. He was an entirely honest merchant, and his memory is to all who keep it, dear and helpfull. His son, whom he loved to the uttermost, and taught to speak truth, says this of him.

The deceased was father of Mr. John Ruskin, the celebrated art critic, and this epitaph is from his son's pen. In the same grave was also buried, in December, 1871, Mrs. Ruskin, wife of the elder Mr. Ruskin, aged 90. There is no monument nor inscription to her memory.

James Hobbs, d April 11, 1880, a 65.
There shall be no more death.

Sacred to the beloved memory of Sir John W. H. Anson, Bart., whom God took to his rest, Aug. 2. 1873, a 56.
Blessed are those servants whom the Lord, when He cometh, shall find watching.

The deceased baronet was killed by an accident on the London and North Western Railway, near Carlisle, on the above date.

Henry Oliver, fourth son of the Rev. Matthew Thos. Farrer, and Maria Louisa, his wife, d Sept. 17, 1854, a 1 year and 4 months.
Blessed are the death which die in the Lord.

[Mr. Farrer was the first curate in charge of Shirley Church.]

Alexander Bankier Freeland, d Feb. 13, 1881, a 54.

Lilian, youngest child of Matthew and Adelaide M. Hodgson, of Shirley Cottage, d Feb. 22, 1881, a 1.

Ralph Chassereau Burgess, a 4½ years.
Jesus, the Shepherd, our little ones keep.

George Pothecary, C.E., who fell asleep, being wearied with his journey, May 17, 1876, *a* 34. His mortal remains were removed from Paris and re-interred here Oct. 8, 1881.

John Pennefather, *d* April 23, 1881.

Laura Russell Tillyer, *d* June 20, 1881, *a* 7.

Ann, wife of J. S. Ancona, went home to her rest Aug. 16, 1881.

In the next grave, though no stone has yet been erected to her memory, lies the body of the Right Honourable Lady Bulwer Lytton, widow of the celebrated novelist and statesman, and mother of the present Lord Lytton, late Governor General of India, who died March 15, 1882, *a* 87.

Charles Lauree, of Addiscombe, *d* March 26, 1882, *a* 58.

David Morice, *d* Sept. 25, 1837, *a* 70.
Elizabeth, his wife, *d* Nov. 25, 1857, *a* 68.

David Simpson, *d* April 21, 1881, *a* 63, and several children.

Catharine Barbara Oldham, *d* Aug. 9, 1850, *a* 69.

George Stack, late of High Street, Croydon, *d* Jan. 4, 1838, *a* 80.

Wm. Dangar Grant, *b* Oct. 19, 1879, *d* Jan. 12, 1880.
Thos. Michell Grant, *b* Oct. 3, 1876, *d* Jan. 30, 1880.
    Children of Henry and Helen Grant, of Sydney Hirst, Croydon.

Henry Cornfield, *d* April 19, 1879, *a* 62.

Lucy Fanny Gurney, of Addiscombe, *d* Aug. 29, 1878, *a* 29.

Wm. Alexander Leslie, late H.M. Madras Medical Service, *d* May 5, 1878, *a* 58.
Elizabeth, his wife, daughter of David Morice, *d* July 6, 1878, *a* 50.

Emily Priscilla, widow of Pressey Granger, *d* Dec. 25, 1875, *a* 43.

Elizabeth (Bessie) wife of Wm. C. Earton, *d* June 27, 1876, *a* 36.

Theodore Lloyd, *d* Jan. 19, 1880, *a* 73.
Anna, his wife, *d* March 23, 1882, *a* 77.
            And at evening time, it shall be light.

Robert Newman Lloyd, *d* April 19, 1873, *a* 37.
    Thou hast made him most blessed for ever, Thou hast made him exceeding glad with Thy countenance.

Eliza Gill, wife of Henry Gill, of Park Hill Rise, Addiscombe, *d* June 15, 1872, *a* 65.

Edward Foss, *d* July 27, 1870, *a* 83.

Henry Young, late of the Bombay Civil Service, *d* Jan. 9, 1869, *a* 60.

William Seymour Quentery, *d* May 14, 1875, *a* 61.

Lavinia Mary, widow of Mark Robert Cockburn Wightman, whom God called Aug. 16, 1875, *a* 60.
Lavinia Mary, daughter of the above, wife of Charles F. Cooke, died at sea, April 3, 1880, *a* 31.

Joanna, wife of W. S. Walkey, of Addiscombe, *d* March 16, 1876, *a* 50.

Julia Sarah, daughter of Wm. B. and Jane Davis, of Croydon, *d* April 8, 1876, *a* 21.

Christiana Charlotte, wife of Thos. Fagg, of Addiscombe, *d* Oct. 27, 1876, *a* 62.
Thos. Fagg, her husband, *d* June 8, 1877, *a* 55.

Margaret Hill, *d* July 30, 1877, *a* 70.

Charles Coppin, *d* March 2, 1877, *a* 58

There is a small triangular shaped stone erected near this
grave. On the one side are engraved these words :—
" This stone marks the centre of Shirley Chapel, built 1835, pulled down
1856."
On the other side :—

" Yet not a hillock mouldered near that spot,
By one dishonour'd or by all forgot,
To some warm heart the present dust was dear,
From some kind age, the meanest claimed a tear,
And oft the living by affection led,
Were wont to walk in spirit with their dead.
    *   *   *   *   *

'Twas not a scene for grief to nourish care,
It breathed of hope, and moved the heart to prayer."

George Brown, of Brickwood House, Croydon, *d* Feb. 15, 1878, *a* 79.

Frederick Frith, *d* Aug. 11, 1878, *a* 77.

Bessie, wife of Richard Maidstone, of Addiscombe, *d* April 26, 1881, *a* 23.

Louisa Harriet Hammond, devoted nurse to the family of Mr. and Mrs.
Lamotte, of Shirley, *d* July 19, 1881, *a* 39.

Isabella Anderson, *d* Jan. 18, 1872, *a* 23.
Margaret Anderson, *d* Feb. 20, 1877, *a* 30.

Elizabeth, wife of Chas. Hingston, Esq., *d* July 19, 1881, *a* 43.

" Rest spirit, free.
In the green pastures of the heavenly shore,
Where sin and sorrow can approach no more,
With all the flock by the Good Shepherd fed,
Beside the stream of life Eternal led,
For ever with thy God and Saviour blest,
Rest, sweetly rest."

Amelia Cooper Austen, *d* Aug. 11, 1872, *a* 47.
William Austen, her husband, *d* Jan. 20, 1874, *a* 52.

The parent's lips when God is nigh,
As life draws near its end,
Trustful may say, " Behold, I die,
But God will be your friend."

William Greenish, *d* Sept. 25, 1872, *a* 85.
Bessie, his daughter, *d* Feb. 25, 1875, *a* 42.

Alexander Gibson, *d* Jan. 19, 1874, *a* 62.
Mary, his wife, *d* March 23, 1881, *a* 61.

Thos. Alexander Loftus, *d* March 27, 1875, *a* 65.

James Biggs, *d* June 24, 1874, *a* 38.
Henry H. Biggs, *d* July 14, 1882, *a* 67.

William Foster, *d* April 19, 1874, *a* 43.

Elizabeth, wife of James Hart, *d* Jan. 26, 1874, *a* 35.
A gentle faithful companion, her life was blameless and her end was peace.

Wm. Henry, son of W. H. and Emma Cooper, *d* Nov. 3, 1873, *a* 23.
William Henry Cooper, his father, *d* July 15, 1876, *a* 49.

William Pare, *d* June 18, 1873, *a* 68.
Write me as one who loved his fellow men.

Percy Watson Tickle and Norman Lester Tickle, children of William
Wilson and Annie E. Tickle, 1, Outram Villa, Addiscombe, *d* Aug.
28, 1871.

Robert Chuter, *d* Feb. 10, 1872, *a* 79.

James Miller, banker, London, *d* at Addiscombe, Jan. 24, 1871, *a* 56.

Samuel Tarrant. *d* Jan. 12, 1865, *a* 87.

Eliza, wife of John Skinner, *d* Dec. 19, 1875, *a* 61.

Robert Nash, accidentally killed at West Croydon Station Yard, Jan. 15, 1876, *a* 55.

William Baker, surgeon R.N., *d* July 1, 1867, *a* 79.

Henry Gill, *d* Oct. 27, 1867, *a* 64.

Many Ann Houghton, *d* Nov. 25, 1867, *a* 59.
John Houghton, her husband, *d* June 16, 1868, *a* 63.

Florence, daughter of Thomas and Christian Fagg, *d* Aug. 22, 1868, *a* 15.
Elizabeth Sarah. her sister, *d* May 5, 1870, *a* 18.

Elizabeth Simpson. eldest daughter of Patrick and Elizabeth J. Punnett, *d* Dec. 17, 1868, *a* 20.

> There is a spot where spirits blend.
> And friend holds fellowship with friend,
> Though sundered far, by faith they meet,
> Around one common mercy seat.

Rebecca. wife of Thos. Grantham Atkinson, of Clyde House, Addiscombe, *d* April 24, 1881.

James Pusey, *d* Jan. 16, 1865, *a* 88.

Thomas Prescott, *d* March 21, 1867, *a* 46.

Mary, wife of Geo. Bradford, farmer, Woodside, *d* Jane 23. 1865, *a* 70.
George Bradford, her husband, *d* Feb. 8, 1867, *a* 68.

Sarah, wife of Jas. Ellis, *d* Feb. 3, 1862, *a* 62.

Joseph Jell, *d* May 26, 1863, *a* 72.
Elizabeth, his widow, *d* April 18, 1880, *a* 90.

Robert Parfitt, *d* June 3. 1856, *a* 49.

William Gorton, of Addiscombe, *d* Dec. 19, 1858, *a* 54.

Ann Innell, died suddenly, March 27, 1866, *a* 71.

Robert Tolhurst, *d* Sept. 24, 1862, *a* 55.

Dear Little Willie Hunt, who was accidentally drowned in Shirley Park, Feb. 28, 1874, *a* 4¾.

Eveline Lizzy, daughter of Alfred G. Patch, *d* April 25, 1870, *a* 7¾.

> By Guardian Angels led,
> Safe from temptation, safe from sin's pollution,
> She lives, whom we call dead.

Mrs. Amelia Hubbard, *d* Feb. 17, 1869, *a* 69.

Florence Maria. daughter of Henry William Colleson, *d* Oct. 27, 1869, *a* 21.

Major Charles J. Strange, youngest son of Sir T. Strange, *d* Jan. 26, 1863, *a* 38.

Harriet Mure, *d* June 13, 1873, *a* 73.

Elizabeth, wife of Jas. Peck, *d* Aug. 3, 1836, *a* 61.

Roger Plumb, *d* July 28, 1840, *a* 64.

Rachel, wife of Thos. Blake, *d* Feb. 13, 1837, *a* 76.
Thomas Blake, *d* Feb. 4, 1855, *a* 81.

Ann Piper, *d* Sept. 2. 1840, *a* 74.
Rebecca, her sister. *d* Aug. 25, 1841, *a* 81.
Joseph Piper, *d* Dec. 26, 1842, *a* 80.

Marianne, wife of Thomas Phillips, of the Hermitage, Woodside, Nov. 18, 1862, *a* 62.

Major Rohde, Esq. *d* July 22, 1846, *a* 68.
Ann Rohde, *d* June 8, 1847, *a* 63.
Eleanor Rohde, *d* Nov. 9, 1859, *a* 76.
> When thou passest through the waters I will be with thee, and through the rivers and they shall not overflow thee, when thou walkest through the fire thou shalt not be burned, neither shall the flame kindle upon thee, for I am the Lord thy God, the Holy One of Israel, thy Saviour.

John Gray, of Addiscombe, *d* May 6, 1875, *a* 54.
Elizabeth, his wife, *d* April 26, 1878, *a* 68.

Harry, son of W. H. Woods, of Addiscombe, *d* July 12, 1877, *a* 13.

Mary Ann, widow of the Rev. C. P. Jones, *d* March 9, 1879, *a* 76.

James Russell, *d* Jan. 1877, *a* 80.

Lydia, wife of Henry Branscombe, of Kondrovo, Park Hill Road, *d* Feb. 12, 1879, *a* 23.
Carmelina Geraldine, fifth and youngest child of the above, *d* Jan 30, 1880, *a* 2.

Fredk. Bethell Lloyd, only child of Fredk. and Ann Lloyd, whom God called to Himself June 5, 1880, *a* 5.

James Allen, of Croydon, *d* Aug. 30, 1881, *a* 81.

Robert Amadeus, Baron Heath, *d* June 5, 1882, *a* 63.
> The deceased Baron was Consul-General for the Kingdom of Italy. His father was created a baron in the Italian peerage by King Victor Emanuel. He lived for many years in Coombe Lane, Croydon, but shortly before his death removed to Coombe House. He died while on a visit to Paris, and was brought home to be buried here. He was a great friend to all the charitable and educational institutions in the town, and most liberally supported every movement of a benevolent character.

Helen Hamilton, widow of Henry Hamilton, *d* Jan. 3, 1882.

Georgiana Isabella Sutherland, *d* June 5, 1881.

John Wm. Sutherland, of Coombe, *d* Aug. 14, 1871, *a* 70.

Hawkins Francis James, *d* March 3, 1860, *a* 53.

Eliza Martha, wife of Henry Fawcett, *d* Nov. 10, 1860, *a* 61.
Henry Fawcett, her husband, *d* Dec. 3, 1881, *a* 73.

Thomas Andrew Gilson, Commander R.N., *d* Oct. 20, 1873, *a* 77.
Ann, his wife, Jan. 13, 1881, *a* 79.

John Bisdee Fawcett, of North Park, *d* May 11, 1877, *a* 40.
Ellen Fawcett, his wife, *d* March 10, 1877, *a* 38.
Eliza Martha, her daughter, *d* March 23, 1877, *a* 17 days.
> In Thy presence is fulness of joy ; at Thy right hand there are pleasures for evermore.

Albrecht Maurice Schenk, *d* March 12, 1879, *a* 17 months.

Wm. Gedge Clarke, *d* Nov. 15, 1878, *a* 5.
Marion Emma Clarke, *d* Nov. 20, 1878, *a* 1 year and 2 months.

Charlotte Augusta, wife of Hy. John Kirby, Esq., *d* Sept. 28, 1870, *a* 62.
Edward Fredk. Kirby, her eldest son, *d* at Otago, New Zealand, July 17, 1862, *a* 28.

K

James Frewer, *d* Feb. 14, 1854, *a* 59.
Elizabeth, his widow, *d* April 2, 1878, *a* 86.

John Grantham, *d* July 10, 1874, *a* 61.

Thomas James, second son of the Rev. Charles Goodwin, rector of
Hildersham, Cambridgeshire, *d* April 25, 1872.

Isabella Stainforth, *d* Nov. 2, 1876, *a* 45.
Sarah Stainforth, her sister, *d* March 7, 1882, *a* 58.

John Martin, *d* June 25, 1881, *a* 51.

Jane, wife of Wm. Price, *d* Oct. 26, 1879, *a* 44.

Reuben Browning, *d* Sept. 6, 1879, *a* 77.
Margaret Browning, his wife, *d* Aug. 19, 1881, *a* 61.

> Together down they sink in social sleep,
> Together free'd their gentle spirits fly,
> To scenes where love and bliss immortal reign.

John Bennington, formerly of St. James, Westminster, *d* Oct. 14, 1877, *a* 72.

Until the day dawn and the shadows flee away, rest the dear children of
Richard and Isabella Borrow : Robert James, *d* June 12, 1874, *a* 5,
and Minnie, *d* March 5, 1875, *a* 7.

Helena Pilcher, "dear little Nellie," born All Saints' Day, 1869, fell asleep
Nov. 3, 1877.

James Fredk. Pilcher, *d* Jan. 2, 1881, *a* 42.

Benjamin Rawlings, of Bensham Manor House, Croydon, *d* Dec. 4, 1878,
a 59.

Frankie, child of Francis and Margaret Napier, *b* July 2, 1869, *d* Feb. 22,
1874.

> God calleth those whom He loveth best.

Agnes Louisa Thomson, *d* Oct. 13, 1879, *a* 27.

Francis Waters, *d* June 6, 1880, *a* 70.
Eliza Waters, his wife, *d* Nov. 4, 1880, *a* 45.

John Wickham Flower, of Park Hill, Croydon, *d* April 11, 1873, *a* 65.

> Nec quæso lacrimis tuis viator, æternam invideas mihi quietam, vixi ut nil
> obiise pienitendum i viator et humanis rebus tantillam fide.

> [There are several memorial windows to the memory of this gentleman in the
> Parish Church, Croydon, see page 2. He sat on the Croydon Local
> Board during the first two years of its existence.]

Charlotte Beaumont, wife of General Spink. K.H., *d* Aug. 24, 1876, *d* 74.
General John Spink, *d* March 14, 1877, *a* 93.

George Hudson, *d* Sept. 4, 1881, *a* 54.

END OF SHIRLEY CHURCHYARD.

CROYDON CEMETERY.

CROYDON CEMETERY is pleasantly situated in the Queen's Road—between Pawson's Road and Princess Road. It comprises about 24 acres of land of good dry gravel soil, and is enclosed with dwarf stone walls and ornamental iron railings.

In the year 1859 the Churchyard of St. John the Baptist (Parish Church) was directed to be closed by Order in Council. The date of closing was ultimately extended to the 31st of August, 1861. The Croydon Local Board of Health was appointed the Burial Board by an Order in Council dated the 3rd of March, 1859. The Board immediately proceeded to acquire the necessary land, and to make arrangements for the formation of a Cemetery. Twenty-four acres of land were purchased at £200 an acre, and £8 per acre for the purchase of a portion of the tithes. The consent of the Secretary of State to the various plans was obtained, and also that of the Lords of the Treasury to the raising of the loans on security of the Poor Rate. Two Mortuary Chapels and a Lodge were erected. The Chapels are built near the centre of the ground, each of them consisting of a simple nave with open timbered roof, the episcopal chapel having the addition of a semi-octagonal apse at the east end. Both Chapels are paved with ornamental tiles. There are three recessed entrances to the grounds, with carved and moulded Bath stone piers between the carriage and foot gates. Down the centre is a straight roadway 20 feet wide, crossed at right angles near the centre by another road running from the side gates in Pawson's Road and Princess Road. The entrance lodge adjoins the Queen's Road. The total cost of the land, erection of Chapels and buildings, including the wall and railings, and the laying out of the grounds, has been £16,000. The amount is charged upon the Poor Rate, a 30th portion of the principal being repaid yearly with 5 per cent. interest on the balance remaining unpaid. Portions of the ground have been set apart for the use of members of the Church of England, Nonconformists, Roman Catholics, and the Society of Friends.

The first portion of the Church of England ground was consecrated by the late Archbishop Sumner on Thursday the 18th of July, 1861, and the remaining portion by the Suffragan Bishop of Dover (acting for the present Archbishop Tait) on the 4th of July, 1871.

The first interment took place in the Nonconformist Ground on the 24th July, 1861, being that of Mr. Garniss, a member of the Board of Guardians, and formerly of Fairfield House School.

Since the opening of the Cemetery the following interments have taken place :—

Year.	Consecrated.	Uncon-secrated.	Year.	Consecrated.	Uncon-secrated.
1861	... 63	... 20	1873	... 524	... 210
1862	... 183	... 59	1874	... 662	... 209
1863	... 228	... 66	1875	... 798	... 261
1864	... 272	... 78	1876	... 713	... 227
1865	... 348	... 93	1877	... 679	... 183
1866	... 356	... 95	1878	... 727	... 241
1867	... 339	... 110	1879	... 727	... 252
1868	... 538	... 111	1880	... 674	... 285
1869	... 503	... 168	1881	... 678	... 273
1870	... 590	... 162	1882(Dec. 1) 733	... 321	
1871	... 604	... 186			
1872	... 536	... 194		11475	3804

The Cemetery grounds are very tastefully laid out, the late Chairman of the Local and Burial Boards, Mr. C. W. Johnson (a practical and skilful horticulturist) rendering very valuable assistance. The grounds are open to visitors daily, subject to certain rules and regulations notified on a board at the entrance.

The Scale of Fees to be charged by the Board were submitted to and adopted at a vestry meeting of the inhabitants, and on the 2th of July, 1861, they were approved by the Secretary of State for the Home Department.

The members of the Burial Board are the same as the Local Board. The Clerk and Registrar is Mr. R. J. Cheeswright, and the Superintendent is Mr. T. Alden.

CHURCH OF ENGLAND GROUND.

We commence with the tombs nearest the Lodge, on the right hand side, and work downwards to the end of the ground.

George, son of Joseph and Louisa Stainburn, *d* May 9, 1870, *a* 29.

Mrs. Rachel Saward, *d* Dec. 21, 1867, *a* 76.
Edward George and Eleanor, children of Edward Puxon.

Eliza, wife of Henry Rhodes, of Sutton, *d* May 15, 1867, *a* 56.
Henry, her husband, *d* June 6, 1878, *a* 69.

Belinda Cornish, *d* Nov. 8, 1877.

Fanny Hemmings, *d* Aug. 25, 1869, *a* 22.
> Hold Thou Thy Cross before my closing eyes,
> Shine through the gloom, and point me to the skies,
> Heaven's morning breaks, and Earth's vain shadows flee,
> In Life, in Death, oh Lord, abide with me.

William Hemmings, *d* Feb. 24, 1854.
Louise Kent, his niece, *d* March 8, 1870, *a* 2.

Elizabeth, widow of Thomas Routledge, late of Denmark Hill, *d* June 23, 1867, *a* 84.

Frank Herbert Davy, *d* March 19, 1879, *a* 15.
> Nothing in my hand I bring,
> Simply to thy cross I cling.

Maria, wife of Richard Morrant, *d* Jan. 3, 1868, *a* 28.
Harry, her infant son, *d* Aug. 3, 1868.

Archibald James, son of James and Agnes Russell, *d* April 8, 1875, *a* 3 months.
> " He is not dead but sleepeth."

Agnes, wife of James Russell, *d* Jan. 6, 1880, *a* 39.
> Asleep in Jesus.

John Henry Klitz, of Dagnall Park, *d* Dec. 6, 1880, *a* 64.
Sarah, his wife, *d* Nov. 6, 1868, *a* 58.

Saxe Bannister, M.A., *d* Sept. 16, 1877, *a* 85.
> " Shew some token upon me for good, that they who hate me may see it and be ashamed; because thou hast holpen me, and comforted me."—Psalm lxxxvi. 17.

Matilda Rayment, *d* April 27, 1878, *a* 61.
Sarah Rayment, her sister, *d* Feb. 2, 1880, *a* 60.
> Trusting in the finished work of Jesus.

Louisa, wife of Henry A. Cleaver, surgeon, *d* Oct. 1, 1877, *a* 63.

Maria Moyse, *d* April 19, 1868, *a* 82.
> " My soul fainteth for Thy salvation, but I hope in Thy word."

Frances Anne Chapple, wife of George Chapple, *d* Oct. 6, 1877, *a* 53.
> " Thy will be done."

Mary Eleanor Duncan, wife of John Foster, *d* Sept. 10, 1877, *a* 29.

In memory of Hannah and her little George.

John Tummons, *d* Dec. 30, 1873, *a* 53.
> Requiescat in pace.

Olive Ann Ireland, youngest daughter of the late C. G. Ireland, Esq., of London, *d* Feb. 26, 1870, *a* 36.
Betsy Frances Ireland, her sister, *d* Oct. 7, 1856, *a* 23.
Mary Ireland, her mother, *d* April 15, 1872, *a* 82.

Ellen, wife of W. B. Hammond, *d* July 31, 1877, and two infant sons.

Annie Jane, daughter of Thomas Joy, *d* July 1, 1869, *a* 4.

James Hubbard, *d* June 6, 1870, *a* 60.
Rose Hubbard, *d* March 5, 1878, *a* 45.

Rev. Lewis Gregory, vicar of Oadly, Leicestershire, *d* May 10, 1869, *a* 61.

John Wilson Bertram, died of apoplexy on board the steamer Nubia, Aug. 14, 1866, *a* 35.
Frederick Bertram, his son, *d* Feb. 13, 1869, *a* 8.
> " Be ye therefore ready also, for the Son of man cometh in an hour when ye think not."

Elizabeth Jackson, *d* Sept. 9, 1876, *a* 47.

John Alexander Hunt, *d* Sept. 25, 1874, *a* 77.
Mary Anne Hunt, *d* Dec. 15, 1879, *a* 82.

John Bechely, *d* Oct. 28, 1877, *a* 62.

Joseph Partridge, *d* May 8, 1867, *a* 76.
Elizabeth, his widow, *d* Sept. 7, 1872, *a* 79.

Edmund T. Brown, *d* Feb. 29, 1876, *a* 27.

Gerald August, second son of Squire John and Jessy Pitt, *d* Oct. 14, 1874, *a* 2.

Ann Sarah, widow of Joshua Blow, *d* Nov. 18, 1871, *a* 79.

Edward Warner, of Mitcham Road, *d* Oct. 30, 1867, *a* 29.
Walter Henry, his nephew, *d* Sept. 30, 1875, *a* 19.
> It is good for me that I have been afflicted,
> Thou, Oh Christ, are all I want !

George Carter, *d* Jan. 9, 1872, *a* 56.
> Weep not dear friends, but be content,
> For I to you was only lent,
> The Lord has only had his due,
> And very soon may call for you.

Mrs. Sarah Carter, widow, *d* July 13, 1878, *a* 61.
> They have gone, we are going all,
> Like leaves we wither, and like leaves they fall.

Wm. Henry Campart, *d* March 19, 1870, *a* 74.
> Deeply respected by all his friends.   An honest man is the noblest work of **God**.

Mr. Campart was a hatter in the High Street, for very many years. He was one of the good old-fashioned tradesmen who disliked innovations of any kind. He had a great antipathy to gas, and would never have it laid on even to his shop, though "Campart's hats" were as noted as "Budgen's clocks."

George Everall, *d* Nov. 27, 1867, *a* 50.
> All gracious God ! Thy will be done,
> It was Thou that did'st the blessing lend,
> And though withdrawn, I'm not alone,
> Thou are the widow's faithful friend.
> Rest in the Lord.

Frances, his wife, died suddenly, June 24, 1871, *a* 69.
> " Be ye also ready."

Ellen Hewitt, *d* Dec. 11, 1867, *a* 36.
> Jesus said, " Him that cometh to me, I will in no wise cast out."
> Asleep in Jesus ! oh, how blessed !
> How sweet her slumberings are !
> From sufferings and from sin released,
> And freed from every snare.

Charlotte Chart, *d* Feb. 6, 1873, *a* 66.

Arthur G. Tate, *d* May 16, 1866, *a* 16 months.

Mary Alice, wife of Wm. Page, *d* Oct. 7, 1869.

Joseph Bond, *d* Sept. 14, 1875, *a* 70.
Elizabeth, his wife, *d* May 5, 1863, *a* 65.
Elizabeth, their daughter, *d* Sept. 20, 1870, *a* 40.

Thomas Alexander Bustard, *d* April 10, 1866, *a* 27.
> Beloved and lamented by all who knew him.

Thomas Bustard, *d* April 11, 1878, *a* 69.
> Then, dearest Lord, in Thine embrace
> Let me resign my fleeting breath,
> And with a smile upon my face
> Pass through the lonesome vale of death.

Elizabeth Meager, *d* Oct. 10, 1868, *a* 67.
Amey Meager, her sister, *d* Feb. 18, 1870, *a* 68.
Catharine Meager, her sister, *d* March 17, 1872, *a* 69.

Miss Harriott White, *d* April 6, 1866, *a* 78.

William Kneller, *d* Jan. 13th, 1869, *a* 74.
> E'en as he died a smile was on his face,
> And in that smile affection loved to trace
> A cheerful trust in Jesu's power to save,
> An aged pilgrim's triumph o'er the grave.

Harriet, daughter of Wm. E. Brockway Rogers, of Lansdowne Road,
d Dec. 30, 1866, *a* 10.

> That little star, but for a moment given,
> Just rose on earth, then set to rise in heaven.

Annie Penrose Skinner, *d* June 21, 1867, *a* 3 months.

Minnie Isabel Skinner, *d* March 11, 1871, *a* 4 months.

Bertha Winifred, second daughter of Charles William and Mary Harriet
Bonus, *d* June 29, 1871, *a* 3.

Mary Harriet Bonus, her mother, *d* Jan. 15, 1879, *a* 38.

Edward, infant son, born and died Dec. 6, 1878.

> " And they shall be Mine, saith the Lord of Hosts, when I make up My
> jewels."

Margaret Bonus, *d* Oct. 7, 1878, *a* 89.

Jane Bonus, *d* Aug. 4, 1878, *d* 74.

Georgina Grise, their faithful servant and friend for 44 years, *d* Oct. 28,
1879, *a* 80.

Mary Jane, wife of Richard Restell, High Street, *d* Feb. 21, 1874, *a* 65.

> " My soul fleeth unto the Lord."

William Caswell, *d* Dec. 28, 1881, *a* 82.

Mariannie, wife of the above, whom she survived only three days, *a* 66.

Henry Mark Shattock, at rest Oct, 3, 1872, *a* 70.

Mary, his wife, at rest July 5, 1880, *a* 71.

> Father, in Thy precious keeping,
> Leave we here Thy servants sleeping.

Agnes Clara, daughter of Francis and Mary Rosina Wright, *d* May 16, 1875.

Francis Wright, of Addiscombe, *d* Jan. 2, 1874, *a* 62.

Mary Rosina Wright, *d* Feb. 14, 1876, *a* 62.

> In their death they were not divided.
>
> In peace, let me resign my breath,
> And Thy salvation see.
> My sins deserve eternal death,
> But Jesus died for me.

Eliza, wife of Thomas Angell, of Woodside, *d* Nov. 3, 1874, *a* 63.

George Meakin, *d* Feb. 4, 1869, *a* 73.

Elizabeth Elliott Orkinstall, widow, *d* Jan. 30, 1874, *a* 74.

Adam Uriah Bryant, *d* June 22, 1871, *a* 70.

Charles Lenny, died suddenly March 15, 1877, *a* 64.

> Mr. Lenny was the well-known and successful carriage builder,
> whose factory was at North End. He was in an extensive
> way of business, and made a name by his manufacture of
> the pretty " Croydon Basket Carriage," which was (in the
> decade from 1855—1865) most extensively patronised, not
> only in England but on the Continent.

Adna Fuller, *d* April 3, 1879, *a* 87.

> After many years suffering. This monument is erected by her loving sister,
> Mrs. Maltby.

Charles Henry Maltby, third son of the Right Rev. Edward Maltby, late
Bishop of Durham, *d* Sept. 22, 1878, *a* 77.

Maria, his wife, *d* March 16, 1880, *d* 84.

Emma, relict of Thomas Froggatt, *d* Aug. 5, 1876, *a* 50.

Jesse Vincent Watkins, *d* June 1, 1881, *a* 82.

Elizabeth, wife of John Moore, Oakwood, Park Hill, *d* July 20, *a* 71.

John Drummond, *d* March 19, 1880, *a* 78.

John Drummond was so well known in Croydon that any remarks referring to him may appear almost superfluous to
his friends ; but as every month brings new inhabitants to
the town and neighbourhood, it may be mentioned that he
was the elder brother of the respected chairman of the
Local Board of Health, and the senior partner of the well-
known firm of solicitors at North End.   He filled the office
of Vestry Clerk for many years (succeeding Mr. George
Penfold), and, like his brother William, he always took an
active part in all affairs relating to the parish.   He was a
good speaker, as we have not only heard him address
public meetings, but have also had the pleasure of hearing
his merry laugh, in days gone by, at the Easter dinners
at the Greyhound, where his speeches and his anecdotes
would always excite the risible nerves of the joyous company.   He was a man " full of wise saws and modern
instances," who had the happy knack of making a " July's
day short as December."

Mary Elizabeth, the dearly loved, honoured, and lamented wife of John
Drummond, *d* July 19, 1876, *a* 74.

Rev. Jonathan Cape, M.A., F.R.S., formerly Professor of Classics and
Mathematics, East India College, Addiscombe, *d* Sept. 9, 1868, *a* 75.

Wm. Sutherland, M.D., *b* in Aberdeen, Sept. 20, 1812, *d* in Croydon, Nov.
25, 1874.

Dr. Sutherland was in practice for many years in Croydon,
and was medical officer to Whitgift's Hospital, by the
inmates of which he was loved and valued.   He was also
a valuable member of the Local Board of Health (from
1858 to 1869), and his opinions were invariably listened to
with respect, and his suggestions frequently adopted.   The
doctor was a skilful practitioner, cheery, straightforward,
and upright, a " man of cheerful yesterdays and confident
to-morrows."   One of those honourable men who would
" prefer a good name to great riches."   The writer of this
note, like many others, by his death, not only lost a skilful
medical man, but a valued and esteemed friend.

George Chasemore, *d* Feb. 9, 1874, *a* 74.

Mr. Chasemore was the senior partner in the well-known firm
of bankers—Chasemore, Robinson, and Sons, of the Union
Bank, High Street.   He formerly resided at Beddington
Corner, afterwards at Waddon, and lastly at Park Lane,
where he died.   He was a wealthy, warm-hearted man,
though sometimes a little brusque in his manner.   He was
a lover of truth, and a hater of chicanery, and in all his
dealings with the world he was most honourable and correct.
His word was his bond, and the public had the utmost
confidence in him.   He was a director of the Croydon Gas
Company, and was not only highly valued by his colleagues,
but by the large body of proprietors.

Augusta Mary Chasemore, wife of Henry Chasemore, *d* June 27, 1870, *a* 38.

Mary Ann, wife of Allen John Lambert, *d* Dec. 31, 1866, *a* 45.

This estimable and amiable lady was the affectionate wife of
Mr. A. J. Lambert, of High Street, and the eldest daughter
of Mr. Henry Overton, the successful brewer, of Surrey
Street. In life she was dearly loved by all her family and
friends ; and in death she was not only deeply regretted by
all her relations, but by all who had the pleasure of knowing
her. This slight tribute to her memory is written by one
who knew her, and values her excellent qualities.

Thomas Farley, *d* at Dovercourt, Thornton Heath, July 19, 1881, *a* 73.
So He giveth His beloved sleep.

Thomas Farley was one of the old Croydon worthies, whose
ancestors had also been old inhabitants of the parish. Mr.
Farley was a wealthy gentleman farmer, and resided at
Thornton Heath all his life. He was a shrewd, clear-
headed man of business, and before he had " fallen into
the sere and yellow leaf," he was most active and useful in
all parish affairs, and it is believed that he had filled
every honorary office in the parish, from overseer and
churchwarden to high constable. He was a member of
the Croydon Board of Guardians for 33 years, a member
of the Local Board of Health for the first 20 years of its
existence, and also one of the old " Homage Jury." It
will thus be seen that he was a useful man, and during his
long life, he no doubt " did the state some service."

Mary Frances, wife of John Farley, *d* Aug. 15, 1882, *a* 56.

James Boyton, Esq., late Hon. E. I. Co.'s service, *d* Sept. 21, 1867, *a* 79.
Susan, his wife, *d* Jan. 6, 1880, *a* 76.

Jane, wife of James Pearce Budden, *d* May 1, 1877, *a* 52.
[For several years of the Greyhound Hotel, Croydon.]

Margaret Burdus, daughter of Edward and Margaret Oliver, *b* Dec. 28,
1860, *d* May 16, 1877.

Caroline Metcalfe Browne, *d* Oct. 30, 1868.

George Browne, Esq., her father, late Hon. E. I. Co.'s service, *d* Feb. 1,
1870, *a* 80.

Caroline Browne, his widow, *d* Feb. 16, 1881, *a* 86.

Elizabeth, wife of John Mortleman Eastty, Esq., *d* March 13, 1864, *a* 43.

Rev. Joseph Henry Eastty, B.A., eldest son of the above, assistant curate
of St. Cross, Holywell, Oxford, *d* Dec. 16, 1872, *a* 28.

Joseph Mortleman Eastty, J.P., *b* Sept. 19, 1819, *d* Jan. 5, 1878.

Mr. Eastty, who resided at Wellesley House (now in the occupation of J. Spencer Balfour, Esq., M.P.), was a magistrate for the county. He was rich and kind-hearted,
liberal and humane, and always had a cheery word for
everyone, which made him very popular, and won him
" golden opinions from all sorts of people ! " He was
always nicely dressed, and invariably wore a pretty button-
hole, and was, in fact, the *beau ideal* of a gentleman who
enjoyed society.

Alice Emma, daughter of Arthur Burrows, Esq., *d* Oct. 1, 1866, *a* 19.

James Cullen, *d* Aug. 1, 1865, *a* 82.
Margaret Jeffrey, his wife, *d* Feb. 13, 1872, *a* 86.
Louisa Wilhelmina Anna Cornelia Cullen, at rest April 2, 1881.

Patrick W. Dolan, Esq., *d* Jan. 27, 1878, *a* 67.
Amelia, his wife, *d* Oct. 10, 1867, *a* 47.

Louisa Wyatt, wife of Herbert Bean, *d* Oct. 23, 1874, *a* 30.
Benjamin Bean, *d* April 20, 1867, *a* 56.

> Mr. Bean, after residing at Croydon for some time, became the proprietor of the Greyhound Hotel, which he conducted successfully for a number of years.   He was respected by his fellow townsmen, and filled most of the parochial offices in the parish.   He was also a useful member of the Local Board of Health from 1859 to 1867.

Elizabeth, his wife, *d* June 3, 1867, *a* 51.
Charlotte, wife of William Bean, *d* Feb. 3, 1875, *a* 36.

Thomas Watson Young, *d* March 10, 1875, *a* 72.
Ann, his wife, *d* July 12, 1871, *a* 58.
James Young, his son, *d* Dec. 3, 1879, *a* 33.

Elizabeth Easted, *d* Oct. 21, 1881, *a* 78,

Sarah Ann, wife of William Sharp, *d* Aug. 8, 1839, *a* 41.
> Interred in Hackney New Churchyard.
Mary, her daughter, *d* Feb. 26, 1869, *a* 39.
William Sharp, *d* Oct. 4, 1877, *a* 83.
Ann, his daughter, *d* Dec. 24, 1880, *a* 48.
Eleanor, second wife of William Sharp, *d* April 19, 1880, *a* 78.

John Rickett, F.R.M.S., late of H. E. I. Co.'s Service, and of Hong Kong, *d* May 11, 1878, *a* 76.
> " Rest weary soul, rest, sweetly rest."

> Mr. Rickett resided in the Wellesley Road for some time, but removed into Dingwall Road before his death.   He was an ardent meteorologist, and kept a perfect set of instruments for recording the weather.   For some time he published these in the *Croydon Advertiser*, but growing infirmities prevented his taking a complete register, and when he could no longer furnish a perfect report he discontinued them altogether.   He was a strict Conservative, and had ideas of his own which made him resolve never to wear an overcoat.

Julia Elizabeth Chatfield, *d* March 27, 1875, *a* 41.

Edward Moseley, *d* Aug. 14, 1876, *a* 72.
> Last survivor of 14 sons of the late Litchfield Moseley, of Somersham, Hants.

Emma Bingham Carter, widow of the late Rev. William Drayton Carter, Vicar of Kirby-Moorside, Yorkshire, *d* June 27, 1873, *a* 81.

Thomas Curtis Vipan, *d* Dec. 25, 1870.
George Francis Vipan, *d* June 21, *a* 12.

James Hamsher, *d* Aug. 24, 1865, *a* 68.
> Severe affliction, kindly sent in love,
> Led him to Christ and trained him for above ;
> The end now seen, how short, how light appear,
> The longest sufferings he experienced here.

George Holdsworth, formerly of Shanghai, *d* Nov. 4, 1878, *a* 34.

Albert Neave Davis, *d* Aug. 12, 1880, *a* 2.

Thomas John Brooker, *d* Nov. 7, 1866, *a* 18.

Sophia, wife of Frederick J. Durban, *d* May 3, 1870, *a* 70.
> Deeply lamented and sincerely respected by all who knew her.

Frederick John Durban, *d* April 4, 1873.
> [Mr. Durban was a pensioned letter carrier, and was one of the most exten-sive newsagents in Croydon—first (in 1857) in Chapel Path, then in North End (now the site of Oxford House), then at No. 106, High Street, where he died.]

Alfred William Davis, after many years intense suffering, *d* June 28, 1865, *a* 24.

Fanny Elizabeth Davis, his sister, *d* July 6, 1865, *a* 22.

Frances Elizabeth Davis, their mother, *d* Jan. 28, 1870, *a* 52.

Thomas Hensall Davis, their father, *d* May 7, 1881, *a* 69.

Samuel Francis Baker, *d* Oct. 23, 1866, *a* 58.
> "God will redeem my soul from the power of the grave, for He shall receive me."

Jane, his wife, *d* Aug. 2, 1874, *a* 62.
> "Them also which sleep in Jesus will God bring with Him, therefore comfort one another with these words."

Maria Henley, *d* Aug. 1, 1868, *a* 59.
> Long lingering sickness gave the silent blow,
> The stroke was final though the effect was slow,
> With wasting pain, death found me sore opprest,
> Pitied my grief, and kindly gave me rest.

John Adam Trenter, *d* Sept. 9, 1880, *a* 74.

Hannah, his wife, *d* Sept. 16, 1868, *a* 67.

Jane, wife of Richard Wells, 43, London Road, Thornton Heath, *d* Oct. 28, 1874, *a* 80.

Richard, her husband, *d* May 17, 1875, *a* 77.

Mrs. Sarah Jones, of the Waldrons, *d* May 7, 1869, *a* 98.

Margaret, wife of R. M. Bennett, *d* April 2, 1876, *a* 61.

Sarah, wife of Samuel Matthews, *d* Sept. 5, 1868, *a* 44.

James, son of the above, drowned near Portland, U.S.

In memory of Little Edith, born Feb. 19, 1873, *d* Feb. 23, 1874.

Mary Lascelles, her sister, *d* April 11, 1875, *a* 15.

Alexander John Moseley, *d* July 19, 1865, *a* 28.

Jane, widow of John Spencer Dickin, Esq., of Wem, in Salop, and daughter of the late Rev. Richard Parker, vicar of Leppington, in the same county, *d* Oct. 12, 1867, *a* 63.

Alexander Fraser, quartermaster of the West Cork Artillery Militia, *d* April 4, 1868, *a* 52.

Robert Smith, *d* April 8, 1872, *a* 29.
> "Shall not the Judge of all the earth do right?"

William Thomas Dickenson, of North End, *d* Oct. 5, 1871.
> "In my afflictions I called upon the Lord, and he heard me and delivered me out of my troubles."

John Hawkins, *d* Jan. 12, 1872, *a* 64.

William Briggs Page, *d* Aug. 9, 1865, *a* 65.

Deborah, his wife, *d* Jan. 9, 1876, *a* 75.

Wm. Briggs Page, his son, *d* May 31, 1874, *a* 38.

Mary, wife of Robt. Newbury, *d* Aug. 12, 1865, *a* 65.

Mary Ann Frost Matthews, *d* July 10, 1876, *a* 82.

George Gatland, *d* May 23, 1874, *a* 58.

William Marshall, youngest son of Robt. Marshall, of South End, *d* Oct. 1, 1865, *a* 29.
Frank, third son, died at Brighton April 6, 1871, *a* 38.

Elizabeth Slatter, *d* Nov, 5, 1873.
John Slatter, *d* Dec. 18, 1878,, *a* 53.

Harry Fowles, *d* Dec. 18, 1878, *a* 26.

Emma Adelaide, wife of Benjamin Bradley, *d* Sept. 6, 1872, *a* 42.
> Whilst on the Father's love relying,
> And Jesus all her need supplying,
> In peace she fell asleep.

Mary Ann, his second wife, *d* Aug. 31, 1876, *a* 52.

Mary, wife of Thomas Pascall, of South Norwood, *d* July 25, 1879, *a* 70.
Thomas Pascall, *d* Oct. 26, 1881, *a* 69.
> [The Pascalls for tile making and red pottery have attained a wide fame in the Home Counties.]

Charles Pascall, *d* June 3, 1868, *a* 19.
> So kind, so young, so gentle, so sincere.
> So loved, so early lost, may claim a tear,
> Yet wherefore mourn, the life resumed by Heaven,
> Doubtless fulfilled the end for which it was given.

James Davis, *d* Nov. 8, 1865, *a* 16.
Herbert Davis, his father, *d* July 22, 1869, *a* 59.

Maria Whetstone, *d* March 16, 1866, *a* 66.
> " My beloved spake, and said unto me, Rise up, my love, my fair one, and come away."

Edward Joyce, *d* April 11, 1868, *a* 66.
Sarah E. Joyce, his wife, *d* Nov. 1, 1877, *a* 64.

Agnes Elizabeth, wife of Christopher P. Armstrong, *d* June 13, 1869, *a* 29.
Christopher Perkins Armstrong, *d* March 1, 1875, *a* 33.

Elizabeth Fuller, *d* Aug. 18, 1867, *a* 69.

Emily Sarah West, daughter of Thomas West, *d* Oct. 9, 1867, *a* 4.

Susannah Elizabeth, wife of Charles Hussey, *d* June 8, 1874, *a* 27.

Susannah, wife of H. Hammond, *d* Dec. 8, 1865, *a* 40.
> Her immortal soul has gone to that bright land of everlasting life and never-ending love, where the weary rest in Christ.

G. W. Hammond, her son, *d* Sept. 1, 1879, *a* 25.
> [Founder of the firm of Hammond & Purrott.]

Henry Hammond, *d* Jan. 21, 1872, *a* 53.
Annie, wife of Henry Hammond, *d* March 6, 1869, *a* 29.

Henry James Wells, licensed victualler, *d* Jan. 9, 1866, *a* 40.

Jane, wife of Atwood Bignell, *d* June 28, 1872, *a* 46.

Harry, second son of Thomas and Anne Day, victualler, *d* May 23, 1866, *a* 7 months.
Margaret W. Day, *d* March 8, 1867, *a* 3 months.
Fredk. Jas. Day, *d* Aug. 19, 1868, *a* 10 days.
Thomas H. Day, *d* July 30, 1870, *a* 12.

Mary Gower, *d* March 21, 1865, *a* 69.
Robert Gower, her husband, *d* May 21, 1873, *a* 77.
> For honest worth, let friendship drop a tear.
> Who knew them best, lament them most sincere.

Emma, wife of Joseph Gillingham, *d* Oct. 16, 1880, *a* 62.

Mary Ann, wife of Geo. Treadaway, *d* Nov. 11, 1874, *a* 67.
Good God, have mercy upon my poor soul.
George Treadaway, *d* Aug. 12, 1875, *a* 64.
[Mr. George Treadaway was a jobbing bricklayer, and lived in his own house in the Handcroft Road.]

Joseph Wilson, late of the Derby Arms, *d* July 30, 1875, *a* 46.

Robt. Milton Spearpoint, 22 years station-master at West Croydon, *d* Nov. 7, 1872, *a* 61.
Grieve not, dear wife, but be content,
For unto thee I was but lent,
My time is o'er, my labour done,
Therefore, dear wife, prepare to come.

Thomas West, timber merchant, *d* Dec. 23, 1866, *a* 53.
[Mr. West first commenced the timber yard now occupied by Messrs. Taylor and Brooker, Pitlake.]

Elizabeth Garner, *d* June 16, 1867, *a* 70.

Wm. Frost, Biggin Cottage, Norwood, *d* March 30, 1872, *a* 86.
Martha, his widow, *d* Dec. 29, 1875, *a* 86.
Yes, they are gone, we are going all,
Like flowers we wither, and like leaves we fall.

John Tebbutt, *d* July 22, 1832, *a* 62.
[For many years landlord of the Fox and Hounds, West Croydon.]

Thomas Wyatt, *d* Jan. 20, 1875, *a* 83.
Thou wilt keep him in perfect peace, whose mind is stayed on Thee.

Mary, widow Arthur Septimus Edlin, *d* March 22, 1871, *a* 54.

Emma, wife of Albert Willing, *d* June 11, 1874, *a* 24.

Jane Annie, widow of Capt. Jackson V. Tuthill, late 2nd Dragoon Guards, *d* June 7, 1874, *a* 66.
Martin Vernon Ayre, grandson, drowned at Brighton, Aug. 17, 1875, *a* 15.
Thou art gone to the grave, but we will not deplore thee,
Whose God was thy ransom, thy guardian, thy guide;
He gave thee, He took thee, and He will restore thee,
And death has no sting, since the Saviour has died.

Elizabeth Matthews, widow, *d* April 2, 1867, *a* 83.

Sarah, wife of John Denning, *d* Dec. 18, 1876, *a* 68.
John Denning, *d* March 1, 1880, *a* 71.

Ada Mary Hatch, *d* March 11, 1879, *a* 1 year.
A fondly-loved treasure in heaven.

Annie Keen, wife of John J. Keen, *d* July 16, 1869, *a* 46.

Domenico Antonio Tonelli, born at Couvalle, near Lucca, Italy, *d* May 11, 1871, *a* 66, after 49 years' residence in England.

John Skynner Bailey, *d* Jan. 19, 1877, *a* 80.
Margaret, his wife, died at The Priory, Croydon, Nov. 14, 1863, *a* 68.
Sweet is the memory of departed worth; her faith rested in her Saviour, Jesus Christ.

Anne, wife of James Denis de Vitré, Esq., of Bedford Park, *d* June 20, 1871, *a* 54.
James Denis de Vitré, *d* Jan. 2, 1875, *a* 82.

Caroline Rosaline, wife of G. W. Allen, Esq., of North-West India, *d* Sept. 30, 1866, *a* 24.

Rebecca Purkess, *d* July 18, 1879, *a* 41.
Wm. Ernest Purkess, her son, *d* Oct. 13, 1879, *a* 6.

Sarah Kinsman, *d* Nov. 7, 1881, *a* 69.

Capt. Matthew Jas. Popplewell, R.N., *d* April 30, 1871, *a* 83.

Philippa Margaret Ellen Watkins, wife of C. R. W. Watkins, *d* March 18,
    1881, *a* 61.
      Her children rise and call her blessed   Not lost, but gone before.
                Until the day break.

Caroline Brown Flint, *d* April 26, 1881, *a* 51.

Thos. Hernon Woodfall, *d* April 13, 1874, *a* 73.
Caroline, his wife, *d* Oct. 14, 1855, buried at Brighton.
George Henry, eldest son, died at Nagasaki, in Japan, Nov. 1, 1861, *a* 25.

Adelaide Beatrice Johnson, *d* Sept. 7, 1871, *a* 3.
Lucy Johnson, her mother, *d* June 25, 1873, *a* 33.

Wm. Henry Alexander Russ, *d* Sept. 17, 1872, *a* 68.

Marjory Gerard Cruikshank, widow of Colonel Colin Mackay, *d* Feb. 23,
    1873, *a* 84.

Elizabeth, wife of A. Jackson, *d* Sept. 14, 1875, *a* 54.
Arthur, her husband, *d* Nov. 24, 1875, *a* 84.

Harriet Schroder, *d* Nov. 23, 1881, *a* 65.

Henry Babington Ross, fell asleep, Jan. 22, 1876, until the daybreak.
    He satisfieth the loving one and filleth the hungry soul, the waves thereof
        are still.   Then are they glad because they are at rest.

Ellen Harriet, wife of Lieut. Gompertz, late Madras Army, *a* Aug. 11,
    1880, *a* 65.

Ann Brealey, *d* Christmas Day, 1881, *a* 62.

Henry Carlyon Phear, *d* March 2, 1880, *a* 54.

    [Mr. Phear was a barrister-at-law, and resided for many years in Bedford Park.
      He was a Christian gentleman in every sense of the word ; an earnest
      supporter of every philanthropic work in Croydon, and his death at so
      comparatively early an age was greatly deplored.]

Elizabeth, wife of William Rigby, *d* March 11, 1879, *a* 64.
Anne, her daughter, *d* June 30, 1878, *a* 32.

Jessy Mackenzie, widow of the Rev. T. Pearson Lammin, of Tamworth,
    d April 27, 1880, *a* 79.

To the glory of God and in loving memory of Admiral Sir Stephen
    Lushington, G.C.B., entered into rest May 28, 1877, *a* 73.
                Be ye also patient.
    So He bringeth them into the haven where they would be ; they are then glad
      because they are at rest.

Henrietta, his wife, daughter of Admiral Sir Henry Prescott, G.C.B., *d* Sept.
    22, 1875, *a* 57.
            " Because I live, ye shall live also."

John Anson Whealler, *d* June 6, 1865, *a* 63.
Louisa, his wife, *d* June 8, 1868, *a* 70.
Mary Winnifred, his grandchild, *d* June 8, 1875, *a* 7.

Evan Jones, *d* May 19, 1878, *a* 85.
Sarah, his wife, *d* March 19, 1867, *a* 77.
Spencer Evan Jones, *d* July 30, 1868, *a* 10.

Catherine Belcher, *d* April 26, 1863, *a* 89.

Herbert, fourth son of Robert Cleara Collis, *d* Dec. 31, 1880, *a* 19.

Henry Richards, *d* Feb. 20, 1868, *a* 63.

Mr. Henry Richards was the predecessor of Mr. W. H. Rowland, solicitor, High Street. He held several offices of importance in the town, in all of which he was very generally respected. He was Clerk to the Local Board of Health ; Registrar of the County Court ; and joint Secretary (with Messrs. Drummonds) to the Croydon Gas Company.

Robert Kynaston, *d* Oct. 14, 1874, *a* 47.
Ethel May, his daughter, *d* July 16, 1873, *a* 13.
[For many years Mr. Kynaston resided at Bensham Villa, Broad Green.]

James Mash, c.e., *d* April 21, 1877, *a* 67.
Caroline, his wife, *d* Nov. 4, 1876, *a* 44.

Euphemia, wife of Arthur Simpson, *d* Aug. 12, 1861, *a* 40.

Louisa Lee, wife of Melbourne Clarke, *d* Jan. 21, 1864, *a* 49.
Mary Caroline, her daughter, *d* Sept. 10, 1878, *a* 28.

Herman Cornelius Rymbende, born in Holland, *d* Feb. 19, 1876, *a* 79.

Eliza, wife of William Wenham, *d* July 16, 1863, *a* 58.
William Wenham, *d* April 20, 1866, *a* 60.
> May their souls rest in peace.
[Landlord of the Gun Inn for many years.]

Sarah Fidler, *d* July 28, 1863, *a* 58.

John Hill, *d* Sept. 14, 1863, *a* 58.
Rose, his granddaughter, *d* Feb. 19, 1867, *a* 18 months.

Catherine Townly, wife of Edward Wm. Townly, jun., *d* Oct. 15, 1863, *a* 32.
> Awhile the stormy life she trod,
> Then meekly closed her eyes and saw her God.

Henry Johnson, *d* March 29, 1862, *a* 48.
> Whate'er the cross in mercy given,
> To lead to Christ, and train for Heaven.
> If meekly born with faith and prayer,
> It ends in joys beyond compare.

Margaret, his widow, *d* Dec. 16, 1875, *a* 65.

Mary Rees, wife of Chas. L. Ward, *d* April 19, 1865, *a* 39.

Emily, wife of Chas. Reading, of Caterham, *d* Oct. 19, 1863, *a* 29.
> Mercy, good Lord, mercy I ask,
> This is the total sum,
> For mercy, Lord, is all my suit,
> Lord, let Thy mercy come.

Adrian Vernon, daughter of Henry and Jane E. Hodges, taken home March 20, 1870, *a* 4.
Emma Hodges, his grandmother, *d* April 29, 1878, *a* 79.

Elizabeth, relict of Chas. Bond, *d* April 7, 1879, *a* 72.

Mary Ellen, daughter of Geo. Whiffin, *d* March 2, 1864, *a* 5.
Maud, infant sister, *d* May 21, 1867, *a* 8 months.

Mary Ann Clark, *d* May 11, 1867, *a* 44.
> Dear Jesus to Thy Glory take me in, for there I long to be.

James Clark, her father, *d* Feb. 15, 1878, *a* 78.
Mary, his wife, *d* July 14, 1880, *a* 72.
Reuben Clark, *d* March 5, 1864, *a* 32.
Percy Clark, *d* April 26, 1864, *a* 9 months.
> Too bright for earth, thou precious one,
> Lord, help me say " Thy will be done."

Mrs. Mary Ann Wren, *d* April 5, 1864, *a* 34.

Mrs. Amy Bennett, *d* Nov. 20, 1863, *a* 74.
Richard Bennett, her husband, *d* July 16, 1873, *a* 86.

Esther Toms, *d* Nov. 1, 1869, *a* 67.
Harriet Toms, her sister, *d* Sept. 3, 1878, *a* 77.

Henry Monk, *d* Jan. 19, 1868, *a* 82.
Edward Rugendyke, his nephew, *d* Aug. 3, 1867, *a* 40.

> Gone to the grave in all thy vigorous prime,
> In full activity of zeal and power,
> A Christian cannot die before his time,
> The Lord's appointment is the servant's hour.

Jane Dorothy Spencely, *d* Oct. 18, 1863, *a* 72.
Mary Spencely, her sister, *d* May 4, 1875, *a* 74.

Robert Rickards, Esq., *d* May 24, 1863, *a* 77.

George Willlam Kershaw, *d* Dec. 11, 1875, *a* 29.

Elizabeth Reed, *d* Jan. 6, 1863, *a* 29.
Samuel Reed, her father, *d* May 13, 1864, *a* 63.
Charles Reed, *d* Jan. 9, 1860, *a* 23.

Eliza Bennett, *d* Nov. 10, 1865, *a* 26.
Mrs. Eliza Bennett, her mother, *d* Dec. 14, 1865, *a* 54.

> They were lovely and pleasant in their lives, and in their death they were not divided.

Mr. Richard Bennett, her father, *d* Sept. 4, 1866, *a* 52.

Sarah Skelton, of Factory Lane, *d* Feb. 14, 1876, *a* 76.

Edward Warner Whiffin, *d* March 14, 1862, *a* 18.
Henry Whiffin, *d* Aug. 3, 1869, *a* 78.

Wm. Jones, *d* Nov. 14, 1875, *a* 70.
Richard James Jones, his brother, *d* Sept. 17, 1878, *a* 69.

Mary Jones, *d* Nov. 13, 1862, *a* 96.
Sarah Hatton, her daughter, *d* Oct. 13, 1865, *a* 58.

John Jones, *d* Sept. 22, 1861, *a* 35.
John Jones, his father, *d* Aug. 21, 1874, *a* 70.

Eliza Jane, relict of Richard George, *d* Feb. 10, 1863, *a* 53.
Mrs. Jane Lodge, her mother, *d* June 10, 1869, *a* 83.

Mary Bailey, *d* May 7, 1862, *a* 69.
John Bailey, her husband, *d* June 13, 1870, *a* 73.
Robert John, his grandson, *d* Aug. 6, 1878, *a* 4 months.

Walter Towse, *d* Aug. 4, 1864, *a* 34.

> A lingering sickness did me seize,
> No physicians could me ease ;
> I sought relief, but all in vain,
> Till God did ease me of my pain.

Edmund Walter Menhennitt, *d* Feb. 28, 1879, *a* 1.

> Farewell, loved child, with angels wing thy way ;
> Amid our tears, we dare not bid thee stay.

George Kirk, *d* Feb. 11, 1864, *a* 73.
Ann, his wife, *d* March 24, 1869, *a* 76.

Emily Edith Owen, *d* March 8, 1863, *a* 3.
Samuel Claydon Owen, *d* Dec. 18, 1874, *a* 44.

Mary, wife of Thos. Eggleton, *d* Feb. 21, 1863, *a* 44.
Thomas Eggleton, sen., *d* Jan. 13, 1864, *a* 82.

Mary, wife of Thomas Pascall, *d* March 5, 1862, *a* 77.

> Lord, she was Thine, and not my own,
> Thou hast not done me wrong.
> I thank thee for the precious gift
> Afforded me so long.

Thomas Pascall, *a* Feb. 89, 1873, *a* 85.

> Far from this world of toil and strife,
> They're present with the Lord,
> The labours of their mortal life
> End in a large reward.

Mrs. Ann Swansborough, *d* Jan. 17, 1861, *a* 75.

Eliza, wife of James Bain, *d* July 31, 1867, *a* 36.

> Gone from earth to rest above,
> Rejoicing in a Saviour's love.

John Batchelor, of Waddon, *d* Jan. 13, 1864, *a* 58.

> When sorrowing o'er the stone we bend,
> Which covers our departed father, friend,
> Thou Saviour mark'st the tears we shed,
> For we do weep o'er our father dead.

Mr. Batchelor was the well-known gardener at Waddon, and was contemporary with the Agates, the Diamonds, and the Jewels. In his time there was only a narrow lane leading by his cottage to Beddington, called Batchelor's Lane, traces of which may still be seen along the quickset hedge on the south-east side of Mr. Philip Crowley's beautiful grounds. When, however, the Epsom Railway was formed, it occupied part of the site of the old lane, and the present wide road was made which leads to the Waddon Station. The garden is still in existence, in the occupation of some of his descendants, but as the site is a most desirable one, it is feared that it will soon be cut up for building purposes. Mr. Batchelor was a jovial man, fond of company, and very musical; and half a century ago there was an excellent glee club held at the Gun Tavern, in Church Street, which attracted much attention, and gave great pleasure to the inhabitants. Mr. Batchelor was a member of this club, where he played second violin. *Apropos* of this club, sometimes, on a summer's evening, the road in front of the Gun was almost impassable in consequence of the number of people who stood listening to those fine old glees, "The Chough and Crow," "The Red Cross Knight," "Life's a Bumper," "How Sleep the Brave?" and many other familiar favourites.

> "Alas! for the joyous hearts that then
> Beat warm, but now are cold."

William Harris, his son-in-law, *d* Dec. 30, 1880, *a* 41.

John Pritchard, *d* Jan, 17, 1865, *a* 62.

Louisa Wilder, wife of James Wilder, married June 12, 1861, died Nov. 12, 1861, *a* 20.

> Lent to thee, my husband dear,
> Only for a short time here,
> With my Saviour now at rest,
> Anchored safe among the blest.
> See the haven full in view,
> Love divine shall bear thee through,
> Trust to that propitious gale,
> Weigh the anchor, spread the sail.
> Shudder not to pass the stream,
> Fearless trust the helm to him,
> He will guide thee safely o'er,
> He has passed this way before.
> Now I wait in Heaven, our home,
> Watching o'er you till you come.

Sarah Jane Quittenton, *d* June 16, 1862, *a* 27.

L

Douglas Augustine Belletti, *d* December 29, 1863, *a* 47.

Rebecca Chilman, *d* March 9, 1865, *a* 65.
Wm. John Bennett, her nephew, *d* Feb. 1863, *a* 33.

Thomas, second son of George Horsley, *d* Nov. 18, 1862, *a* 27.
Frank, fifth son, *d* at Maroin, Brazil, March 26, 1869, *a* 29.

George Smith, *d* March 4, 1875, *a* 52.

Sarah Ann, wife of Samuel Smith, *d* Oct. 21, 1863, *a* 62.
Charles Smith, *d* Dec. 21, 1867, *a* 42.
Samuel Smith, *d* April 1, 1875, *a* 72.

> Mr. Samuel Smith was one of the original Croydon carriers, and acquiring a competence, retired from active life. He was much afflicted, having lost the use of his lower limbs. He was not an idle man, however, as those who could see his portly figure through his open door in George-street (now No. 26) could testify. He worked some beautiful pictures in embroidery, at which he was very clever. But it was as the treasurer to a large Court of Foresters that he was best known. He made the keeping of these accounts his hobby, and for many years it was an honorary office.

George Robert, son of George Smith, *d* Sept. 13, 1863, *a* 2 years and 2 months.
George William, son of William James Smith, *d* April 3, 1882, *a* 4½.

John Martin, *d* March 17, 1862, *a* 69.
Elizabeth, his wife, *d* July 25, 1863, *a* 76.

Hannah Young, *d* Dec. 19, 1861, *a* 52.

Edith, daughter of Frederick William Edgar, *d* May 16, 1863, *a* 9 days.
Kate Margaret Edgar, *d* Dec. 27, 1867, *a* 5 years.
Florence R. Edgar, *d* June 13, 1868, *a* 1.

William Ringham, *d* Dec. 6, 1861, *a* 46.
Sarah Ringham, his relict, *d* June 15, 1881, *a* 69.

William Shepherd, of Carshalton, *d* Dec. 6, 1864, *a* 61.

Alfred Taylor, infant son of E. J. Edgar, *d* Jan. 10, 1866.
Edward James Edgar, *d* March 25, 1871, *a* 35.
Sarah Ann, his wife, *d* May 5, 1873, *a* 38.

Sarah Shephard, *d* Nov. 2, 1861, *a* 69.
Isabella Neale, her niece, *d* Oct. 31, 1879, *a* 63.

Janet, wife of Henry Horne, *d* Jan. 3, 1880, *a* 72.
Henry Horne, *d* July 2, 1881, *a* 81.

Jane, wife of James Willis, *d* Jan. 14, 1863, *a* 53.
Mary Ann, daughter of Francis Potter, fellmonger, *d* Aug. 13, 1861, *a* 72.

Caroline, wife of Charles Potter, *d* June 12, 1875, *a* 47.

Sarah Susannah Vincent, *d* Sept. 18, 1871, *a* 88.

Ann, wife of William Radford, *d* Sept. 30, 1862, *a* 43.
Susannah McLean, her sister, *d* Sept. 3, 1865, *a* 49.

Mary Ann Twort, *d* Dec. 15, 1876, *a* 23.

Frances Georgina Shove, *d* Aug. 30, 1880, *a* 57.

William Dyer, *d* Oct. 20, 1861, *a* 35.
Ann, his relict, *d* Feb. 12, 1869, *a* 41.
Also four children died in infancy.

Henry Stagg, *d* Aug. 5, 1878, *a* 82.

> This old, respected, and well-known inhabitant was formerly in
> business as a grocer (in the shop afterwards occupied by
> Mr. Matthew Hoy) at the back of the Town Hall ; and
> when business no longer prospered he became one of the
> collectors of the Croydon Gas Company, an appointment
> which he held for many years with credit to himself and
> satisfaction to his employers.

Jane Stagg, *d* April 4, 1880, *a* 80.

Jonas Sturt, *d* Aug. 16, 1864, *a* 65.

> Mr. Jonas Sturt was a worthy old Croydonian. He was a farrier
> and shoeing smith, and his old-fashioned house and smithy
> were in Sturt's Yard—so named, doubtless, after his father,
> who lived and carried on business there for a generation or
> two anterior to his son.   Mr. Jonas Sturt was a Chairman
> of the Gas Company, and was an old crony of Mr. H.
> Overton's.   He retired from business some years before his
> death, and resided at Thornton Heath.

Ann Sturt, his mother, *d* Oct. 24, 1867, *a* 96.
Maria Sturt, *d* Nov. 4, 1873, *a* 74.

William Morris, died suddenly May 13, 1878, *a* 67.
Eliza, his wife, *d* Jan. 26, 1875, *a* 59.

Ellen Barry, *d* June 2, 1878, *a* 75.

Robt. Pope, *d* Oct. 24, 1864, *a* 35.
Charles Nicoll, *d* March 23, 1865, *a* 55.

> No more weighed down by pain or strife,
> His spirit is refreshed and free,
> After the battle hour of life,
> Saviour, he findeth rest in Thee.

Joseph Allbright, *d* July 16, 1869, *a* 60.
Lucy Allbright, *d* Dec. 10, 1878, *a* 69.

> And God shall wipe away all tears from their eyes, and there shall be no more
> death, neither sorrow, nor crying, neither shall there be any more pain,
> for the former things have passed away.

Rev. Chas. Maddock Arnold, M.A., minor canon of Westminster Abbey,
   d June 21, 1876, *a* 64.

> [For many years Incumbent of St. Mark's, South Norwood.]

Eliza Frances Hatchett, *d* Nov. 15, 1818, *a* 41.

Richard Watson Pritchard, *d* Sept. 16, 1867, *a* 2 months.
Louisa Pritchard, his mother, *d* Feb. 7, 1868, *a* 31.

Maria, wife of Chas. M. Edwards, *d* July 1, 1879, *a* 55.

> Her children arise up and call her blessed, her husband also, and he praiseth
> her.

In sweetest remembrance of a beloved husband and father, Frederick
   Ditmas, Major R.E., called home June 12, 1876, *a* 64.
Also darling first born and sister, Emily Ditmas, called home July 19, 1876,
   a 26.   They sleep.

> Major Ditmas was an earnest Church worker, and took a
> leading part in several home mission efforts in the St.
> James's district.   He resided several years at No. 3,
> Morland Road, Addiscombe.

Fred. James Campbell, *d* June 19, 1867, *a* 43.

> He is gone, and we weep that we see him no more,
> We mourn his departure, but would not repine,
> We know that the grave shall his body restore,
> And Heaven invest it with lustre divine.

Joseph Kirkham, *d* Jan. 5, 1880, *a* 76.

Samuel Freeman, *d* Jan. 25, 1863, *a* 58.

> Yes, he is gone, and we are going all,
> Like flowers we wither, and like leaves we fall.

Ann, widow of the above, *d* Oct. 10, 1864, *a* 81.

Eliza Warren, *d* Sept. 15, 1872, *a* 15.

> Adieu, dear Eliza, till we meet above,
> In those pure peaceful realms of light and love.
> Grain sown on earth is still its owner's care,
> And evening's sun but sets to rise more fair.

Also Eliza, her mother, *d* Feb. 1, 1876, *a* 56.

Hannah, wife of Wm. Purvis, *d* April 4, 1866, *a* 54.

> Fortified by a firm faith in the redeeming love of Christ, she was sustained through many months of daily increasing suffering unto the end, when, with a joyful heart, she yielded up her soul to God.

William Purvis, her husband, *d* May 23, 1873, *a* 52.

> This gentleman was a man of ability, and was very fortunate in life. He was brought up in the office of Messrs. Drummonds, the eminent solicitors, where he remained as confidential clerk for some years. He afterwards became secretary to the Croydon Gas Company, and was highly valued in both appointments. He was also proprietor of the well-known boot and shoe establishment at No. 3, North End, then known as " Drew and Purvis."

Henry Jas. Wild, Commissary-General, *d* April 28, 1873, *a* 80.

Susan, widow of Colonel Evalt, *d* Oct. 3, 1875, *a* 83.

Elizabeth Newton, *a* Feb. 1, 1869, *a* 28.
Jane Newton, *d* Feb. 14, 1873, *a* 73.

Amy Lucy Woodhouse, wife of E. P. Cearns, *d* Dec. 24, 1871, *a* 27; also an infant son.
Edward Paton Cearns, *d* Jan. 7, 1874, *a* 47.

Martha Sarah Blythe, *d* March 14, 1876, *a* 69.

Wm. Nathaniel Sandell, *d* May 24, 1881, *a* 62.
Ann Elizabeth, his wife, *d* April 11, 1862, *a* 52.

Elizabeth Johnson, *d* June 2, 1862, *a* 52.
Wm. Joseph Johnson, *d* May 3, 1880, *a* 40.

Charles Plowman, *d* May 9, 1865, *a* 53.
Mary Ann, his wife, *d* Jan. 9, 1872, *a* 56.
Wm. Chas. Arthur and Elizabeth Amelia, two children, died in their infancy.

> These lovely buds, so young and fair
> Called hence to early doom,
> Just came to show how sweet such flowers
> In Paradise would bloom.

Thomas Strange, *d* Sept. 25, 1863, *a* 78.
Mary Rebecca, grandchild, *d* Nov. 28, 1863, *a* 7.
David Thomas, *d* Dec. 2, 1863, *a* 3.

Frederick Hopkins, *d* Sept. 23, 1862, *a* 43.
Frederick Samuel Hopkins, *d* Oct. 17, 1878, *a* 87.

> Mr. Hopkins was a most retiring and amiable gentleman (for some time a Poor-law Guardian), whose only daughter was married to Mr. S. L. Rymer, the eminent dentist, of George Street. He was a "monarch retired from a London business," and soon after he came to Croydon he built an excellent residence in the London Road, on land which formerly was a portion of Parson's Mead, where he enjoyed his *otium cum dignitate* for some years.

Keturah, infant daughter of Samuel Lee Rymer, *d* Dec. 14, 1868.
Frances Rymer, *d* Feb. 4, 1870, *a* 72.
Mary, widow of Frederick Samuel Hopkins, *d* May 15, 1879, *a* 86.

Anne Christina, infant daughter of R. and C. Roberts.

Lawrence Lancelot Cowling, *d* July 23, 1863, *a* 27.

Sophia, wife of Robt. Shotton, *a* Feb. 2, 1874.
Elizabeth, widow of John Shotton, of Lamb's Conduit Street, *d* Dec. 29, 1863, *a* 79.

John Trapp, Esq., *d* Jan. 14, 1876, *a* 92.

> Mr. Trapp was a gentleman of the old school, and always appeared on his walks in his drab "smalls" and gaiters, and black coat. He was, unfortunately, not quite *compos mentis*, but was most harmless, and amiable and polite to anyone. He resided for many years with Miss Deacon, in the house now occupied by the Misses Coward. His relations were rich people, and, no doubt, allowed a handsome sum for his maintenance to the lady who had charge of him. He appeared to enjoy life, and, notwithstanding his infirmity, he lived to a green old age.

Mrs. Emily Brooker, *d* Aug. 6, 1863, *a* 63.

Mary, wife of Andrew Dyer, *d* Oct. 1, 1864, *a* 30.

Fanny, relict of Thomas Hintson, *d* Aug. 27, 1865, *a* 87.

Thomas C. Geyle, Master of Croydon Workhouse from Jan. 1855 to 1864, *d* Nov. 3, 1864, *a* 61.

> Mr. Geyle was a fine-looking man, hale and hearty, till he met with an accident at the laying of the memorial stone of the Roman Catholic Chapel in Wellesley Road. While the Bishop of Southwark was engaged in the ceremony, part of the scaffolding gave way, and Mr. Geyle, with several others, was precipitated to the ground about 15 feet below. Mr. Geyle was much shaken by the fall, although no bones were broken ; and being a heavy man, and of good age at the time, he never really recovered from the shock.

Elizabeth, relict of John Town, Esq., of Tunbridge, *d* Nov. 11, 1866, *a* 73.

Mary Puplett, *d* July 21, 1864, *a* 85.
John Puplett, *d* May 3, 1865, *a* 82.

Thomas, son of Thomas and Mary Ann Paine, *d* Sept. 30, 1865, *a* 48.
Thomas, his father, *d* March 7, 1867, *a* 88.

Mary Ann, wife of William Baker, *d* April 2, 1864, *a* 59.

Thomas Pilbeam, late beadle, *d* March 28, 1864, *a* 79.

    Thomas Pilbeam (once beadle of our parish) was a good officer, and a terror
to all evil-doers. His face and figure were known to every one—and so
soon as "old Tom," as he was familiarly called, put in an appearance,
the roughs bolted as quickly as though a shell had fallen amongst them.
But it was on Sundays, when "Tom" was in outward show elaborate,
that he "astonished the groundlings." On the Sabbath he always
appeared at the church door, draped in gold laced hat and coat, with
stick in hand, and all the little boys that passed him—almost shaking
in their shoes—must have considered him as grand, if not grander,
than the Lord Mayor! Pilbeam's father was beadle before him, and
the name becoming so familiar, it is thought that the *canaille* considered
it another name for beadle, and that there were "Pilbeams" in every
town. "Tom's" house adjoined the gaol, in which there was a
remarkably strong room, where he received all visitors, without making
too many enquiries about their antecedents.

Elizabeth, his sister, *d* April 29, 1866, *a* 84.
Eleanor, his wife, *d* Sept. 14, 1880, *a* 89.

Jane Elizabeth, wife of John Hempsted, of South Norwood, *d* March 5,
    1868, *a* 66.
Lucy Brown, her sister, *d* Sept. 11, 1869, *a* 75.
John Hempsted, *d* Aug. 26, 1871, *a* 68.
Lucia Dora Closer, his grandchild, *d* Jan. 17, 1879, *a* 1.

Thomas Turner, after a long and painful illness, *d* April 9, 1864, *a* 70.

    Dear Jesus, smooth my rugged way,
    And lead me to the realms of day,
    To milder skies and lighter plains,
    Where everlasting sunshine reigns.

Jane Turner, *d* April 21, 1869, *a* 41.
Thomas Turner, her husband, *d* April 27, 1869, *a* 77.
Emily, their youngest daughter, *d* Dec. 9, 1874, *a* 32.

John Adolphus Stafford, *d* Jan. 14, 1874, *a* 76.

William Miller, after intense suffering, *d* Aug. 21, 1834, *a* 32.
Also darling little Maud Mary, only child of George and Anne Alsop,
    d Aug. 30, 1866, *a* 3½.
George Wm. Alsop, her father, *d* May 1, 1874, *a* 46.

Caroline Ann, wife of James Griffiths, *d* Oct. 25, 1864, *a* 28.

James Paine, Esq., *d* Dec. 19, 1867, *a* 48.
Elizabeth Paine, his sister, *d* Jan. 13, 1875, *a* 63.

Henry Batchelor, *d* March 19, 1877, *a* 62.
Martha, his wife, *d* Dec. 19, 1879, *a* 62.

Harriet, wife of Thos. George Chapman, *d* Aug. 24, 1879, *a* 63.

    Weep not for me, I'm free from pain,
    My earthly sufferings o'er,
    I hope to meet you all again,
    On a peaceful happy shore.

Mary Ann Herring, *d* Dec. 6, 1865, *a* 73.

John David Julian, beadle of this parish, *d* Dec. 22, 1865, *a* 57.
    This stone is erected by a few friends, in commemoration of his faithful **public**
    services for 35 years in various ranks of the Metropolitan Police.

Caroline, wife of Saml. John Mason, of Penge, *d* Sept. 2, 1864, *a* 59.
Samuel John Mason, *d* Nov. 10, 1872, *a* 77.

Charles Page, *d* May 6, 1864, *a* 45.

Eliza Ann, his daughter, *d* Aug. 7, 1864, *a* 10 months.

> This lovely bud, so young and fair,
> Called hence by early doom,
> Just came to show how sweet a flower,
> In Paradise would bloom.

John Boreman, *d* Feb. 9, 1873, *a* 78.

Anna, wife of Dr. J. Bellwood, of Addiscombe, *d* Oct. 14, 1877, *a* 53.

Wm. Henry Varden, *d* Oct. 29. 1871, *a* 69.

Richard Coates, *d* April 21. 1868, *a* 74.

Mary Ann, his wife, *d* April 23, 1865, *a* 66.

William Harris, *d* June 4, 1878, *a* 84.

> Mr. Harris resided near the Old Church, and was deservedly successful in business as a builder. Fortunately for him, he possessed abundance of *nous*, and had a good share of " go " in him : essentials of the highest importance in this high-pressure age. He was somewhat eccentric and humorous, was in a large way of business, and occasionally employed a large staff of men, whom he managed with tact and judgment. It is doubtless within the memory of many of the inhabitants, that he turned the extensive sheet of water, near St. John's Church, known as the old " Mill Head," into a swimming bath, which he made private by throwing up high banks of earth. The speculation, however, was not a profitable one ; and when the Local Board came into existence, so large a head of water was considered injurious to the neighbourhood, the swimming bath was consequently condemned, the banks were levelled, and it is believed that some of the houses on the south side of St. John's Road were built close to the site. It will thus be seen that more *changes* have taken place near the Parish Church, than those which have been *rung* on the beautiful peal of bells, which, sometimes sound " sweet and musical as Apollo's lute."

Mary, his wife, *d* April 1, 1879, *a* 82.

Julia Desborough Vaux, *d* Sept. 1, 1871, *a* 41.

Emily, widow of Calvert Bowyer Vaux, *d* Feb. 9, 1881, *a* 88.

Wm. George Grantham, *d* April 29, 1865, *a* 34.

> He is not dead, but sleepeth,
> A sleep, how calm, how blest,
> When Christ the spirit keepeth,
> The wearied frame hath rest.

Emanuel Grantham, his brother, *d* Nov. 11, 1869, *a* 66.

Henry Payne, of North End, *d* Feb. 10, 1873, *a* 48.

James Newman, *d* June 7, 1865, *a* 40.

Mary Ann Towers, *d* Dec. 6, 1865, *a* 40.

> For 13 years a faithful and trustworthy servant of Mr. G. Stapelton, High Street, Croydon.

David Thomas, *d* July 16, 1873, *a* 41.

John Thomas Raffe, *d* June 6, 1865, *a* 11.

Hannah Amelia Raffe, *d* Sept. 25, 1865, *a* 15.

William Raffe, *d* Jan. 9, 1873, *a* 65.

> Mr. Raffe was an architect, for many years in the service of Mr. John Berney, of North End. His son was a bookseller, first at No. 85, then at 62, North End.

Eleanor, wife of James Tharp, *d* Nov. 21, 1879, *a* 51.

Also two infant children.

Henry Franklin, *d* Jan. 27, 1867, *a* 59.

Mary Ann Ford, *d* May 12, 1877, *a* 53.
> Farewell, dear husband, my time is past,
> My life to you not long did last ;
> And for me no sorrow take,
> Love my children for my sake.

John Bickersteth Wheeler, *d* Feb. 8, 1870, *a* 14.
Constance Wheeler, *d* Dec. 28, 1880, *a* 16.

Mary, wife of Henry Messenger, *d* June 3, 1866, *a* 42.
Louisa Price, her daughter, *d* Feb. 3, 1880, *a* 33.

John Shepherd, *d* Jan. 23, 1866, *a* 38.
Sarah Cherry, *d* May 24, 1875, *a* 87.

Louisa Francis Jane Tate, *d* Aug. 15, 1865, *a* 54.
Andrew Bruce, infant son of Monkhouse R. Tate, *d* Aug. 23, 1865.

Louisa Elizabeth Norman, *d* July 17, 1865, *a* 7.

William John Bennett, *d* Dec. 23, 1866, *a* 63.
Louisa, his wife, *d* Feb. 15, 1880, *a* 73.

Cecilia Pringle, *d* June 21, 1880, *a* 78.
> "She hath done what she could."

Fanny Grace, wife of William James Carey, *d* Oct. 31, 1871, *a* 41.
Vernon Mansell, her son, *d* Sept. 28, 1870, *a* 1.
Ida Grace, *d* Sept. 29, 1871, *a* 13, during her mother's last illness.

Eliza Withers, sister of Hesther Dosell, *d* Dec. 27, 1879, *a* 70.
James Dosel, *d* July 28, 1876, *a* 81.

Emma Watson, *d* June 27, 1876, *a* 81.
James, her husband, *d* March 2, 1828, *a* 72.

Elizabeth, wife of Wm. Stuart, *d* May 23, 1865, *a* 35.
> Led by simplicity divine,
> She pleased, but never tried to shine.

Joseph Glover, *d* July 25, 1866, *a* 53.

George Matthew, *d* March 16, 1865, *a* 71.
Anne Matthew, *d* Dec. 9, 1878, *a* 79.

William Ireland, *d* July 11, 1865, *a* 42.
> Once the beloved partner of my earthly love
> I yield thee to a dearer Friend above ;
> On Him I rest, who all my love can feel,
> And trust the Hand which gave the blow to heal.

John Sadler Hartley, *d* March 16, 1863, *a* 66.
Sophia Stephens Hartley, his wife, *d* Oct. 2, 1866, *a* 69.

Isabella, wife of George Hayward, *d* May 26, 1863, *a* 52.
Leslie George, her youngest son, died at Leghorn, July 20, 1868, *a* 25.

Rev. Richard Mason, *d* Feb. 12, 1869, *a* 70, late Incumbent of Tovill, Maidstone.

Rev. Henry Campbell Watson, M.A., Incumbent of St. James', Croydon, *d* Jan. 9, 1879, *a* 50.
[A handsome stained glass window is erected to his memory in St. James' Church (see page 57).]

Mary, wife of Chas. Wm. Barkley, *d* July 30, 1875.
Mary, her eldest daughter, *d* July 27, in the same year.

Elizabeth Piercy, *d* July 21, 1862, *a* 53.

Sarah Pearce, *d* Feb. 18, 1865.
Elizabeth Pearce, *d* Jan. 19, 1874, *a* 70.

Mary Elizabeth Barrand, *d* Sept. 2, 1864, *a* 39.
Isabella Jane Towers, *d* Aug. 8, 1867, *a* 77.

Mary Ann Eyles, *d* April 29, 1868, *a* 75.
Elizabeth Eyles, *d* May 19, 1870, *a* 73.
Elizabeth Wells Eyles, *d* Feb. 4, 1879, *a* 44.

Donald McDonald, *d* April 23, 1868, *a* 23.
Chas. Jas. Grant McDonald, *d* Nov. 23, 1869, *a* 34.

Sarah Bentley, *d* July 5, 1862, *a* 71.
Isabella, her sister, *d* March 2, 1877, *a* 80.
Samuel Bentley, her brother, *d* April 13, 1868, *a* 83.

John French Burke, *d* June 8, 1882, *a* 80.

Ada Annie Holden, grandchild of Mrs. Jane Wilmshurst, *d* Oct. 10, 1868, *a* 6.

John Henry Living, *d* Oct. 14, 1881, *a* 72.

Jane Madeline, wife of Wm. John Tapson, of Anerley Park, *d* Oct. 23, 1874, *a* 27, and two children.

Harriott Gresham, *d* March 19, 1862, *a* 67.

William Robinson White, one of Her Majesty's Justices of the Peace for the county of Surrey, *d* Dec. 30, 1863, *a* 59.

> And he shall be like a tree planted by the rivers of water that bringeth forth his fruit in his season, his leaf also shall not wither, and whatsoever he doeth shall prosper.

Mary Ann, his widow, *d* March 28, 1869, *a* 75.

Mary Ann Clark, *d* Jan. 16, 1869, *a* 64.

Thomas Well, *d* July 12, 1868, *a* 74.
Ann, his relict, *d* Feb. 20, 1869, *a* 77.

Thomas Henry Thomas, *d* Jan. 31, 1868, *a* 57.
Frances Thomas, *d* March 21, 1881, *a* 58.

James Birch, *d* June 6, 1868, *a* 95.

Thomas Purritt, *d* July 26, 1872, *a* 19.

Charles Major Herbert, *d* Dec. 24, 1861, *a* 38.
Frances Sophia, his youngest child, *a* 3 years and 9 months.
George Herbert, his eldest son, *d* Oct. 15, 1866, *a* 19.
Jacob Herbert, 32 years secretary to the Corporation of Trinity House, London, *d* Jan 9, 1867, *a* 79.
Charles Herbert, C.B., general in Her Majesty's Indian Army, his brother, *d* Jan. 17, 1867, *a* 87.
Ann, wife of Jacob Herbert, *d* March 24, 1874, *a* 79.

Elizabeth Caroline, wife of Charles Hall, *d* Dec. 20, 1861, *a* 42.

Henry Sawyer, *d* Jan. 11, 1867, *a* 64.
Horace, his fifth son, *d* Nov. 27, 1869, *a* 25.
Adela, his third daughter, *d* March 4, 1871, *a* 26.
Eliza, his widow, *d* Feb. 14, 1872, *a* 62.
Isabella, his second daughter, *d* April 11, 1875, *a* 32.

Henry Alfred Lucas, late H.M. Customs, *d* Oct. 1, 1867, *a* 50.
Harvey Bryer, his only son, *d* Nov. 1, 1869, *a* 6.
Eliza, his relict, *d* May 30, 1876, *a* 42.

Charlotte Pearce, *d* April 22, 1877, *a* 57.

Ann Lomas, *d* Jan. 1, 1868, *a* 41.
John Lomas, her husband, *d* April 13, 1881, *a* 64.
Eliza Lomas, her daughter, *d* June 25, 1868, *a* 6 months.

Arthur, son of Fredk. Wiltshire, *d* Jan. 12, 1873, *a* 2.

George Wiltshire, *d* July 20, 1880, *a* 11.

Zillah Maud Wiltshire, *d* Jan. 23, 1881, *a* 6 months.

Ellen, widow of Jonathan Barrett, *d* Nov. 28, 1880, *a* 70.

John Purdie, of Thornton Heath, *d* Jan. 25, 1880, *a* 81.

William Bilbie Parker, *d* April 11, 1866, *a* 64.
[For many years a coal merchant at East Croydon.]
Lydia, his wife, *d* Sept. 24, 1877, *a* 71.

Ann, wife of John Stedman, *d* Sept. 2, 1868, *a* 52.

John, her husband, *d* Feb. 17, 1877, *a* 71.

Eliza, youngest daughter of Thomas and Mary Ward, *d* May 5, 1870, *a* 54.

Mary, her sister, *d* June 22, 1879.

Sarah Elizabeth Brisenden, *d* June 19, 1869, *a* 88.
Erected by a few of her friends.

William Francis Lock, *d* Sept. 24, 1866, *a* 14.

Herbert George Lock, *d* Dec. 12, 1869, *a* 13.

Sarah, wife of B. Pearson Bartleet, *d* Sept. 24, 1870, *a* 71.

Emily, her eldest daughter, *d* Aug. 11, 1874.

Benjamin Pearson Bartleet, *d* Oct. 13, 1877, *a* 78.

John Brown, of Selhurst Road, *d* Oct. 8, 1879, *a* 71.

Capt. Henry Maynard Bingham, R.N., *d* July 28, 1880, *a* 51.
" Thou wilt keep him in perfect peace, whose mind is stayed on Thee."

Rev. W. J. Friel, M.A., first Incumbent of St. Luke's, Woodside, *d* Dec. 19, 1873.
A workman that needeth not be ashamed.

Mr. Friel had, by untiring energy, worked up a congregation at Woodside, and had ministered in a school-room on Woodside Green for five years. The new church was consecrated in April, 1872, and he died, to the great grief of his parishioners, before the close of the next year.

William Smith, *d* Aug. 19, 1866, *a* 61.
With patience to the last he did submit,
And murmured not at what the Lord thought fit,
With Christian spirit did his soul resign,
Returned to God at His appointed time.

Matilda, his widow, *d* June 22, 1881, *a* 72.

Thomas Rowe Edmonds, *d* March 17, 1866, *a* 9.

Caroline, his sister, *d* May 12, 1875, *a* 15.

Dame Eliza Margaret Fitzgerald, *d* Aug. 3, 1877, *a* 61.

Thomas Echalaz Davison, *d* Jan. 16, 1881, *a* 36.

Elizabeth Bonaker Whittington, *d* Jan. 10, 1867, *a* 70.

Benjamin Whittington, born on the Festival of the Conversion of St. Paul, 1799, who fell asleep March 12, 1871.
Lovingly remembered by all their children, who in their mourning sorrow not (all glory be to God!) as those which have no hope.

Christiana Jane Overbury, *d* April 9, 1876, *a* 59.

John Thomas Twigg, *d* March 4, 1881, *a* 71.

Mrs. Isabella Irwin, *d* Nov. 16, 1877, *a* 72.
Erected by the five children whom she so faithfully nursed.

Joseph Clifford, *d* Oct. 8, 1881, *a* 59.
> Twenty-seven years Waterworks Foreman. This stone was erected by members of the Local Board.
>> Mr. Clifford was an honoured member of the Ancient Order of Foresters, and was for upwards of 20 years secretary of one of the largest Courts in the kingdom. He was familiarly known as " Brother Joe," and had won the esteem of all parties. He had received three testimonials from his brethren, and at his funeral he was honoured by the largest concourse of spectators which ever assembled at the Cemetery.

Sarah Frances, daughter of Capt. H. A. Drought, I.N., *d* May 29, 1868, *a* 11 years and 10 months.

Blanche Mary Braikenridge, *d* March 12, 1881, *a* 26.

George Edmonds, *d* Sept. 13, 1869, *a* 64.

Martha Norroway Gregory, *d* March 9, 1872, *a* 39.

Mrs. Catharine Snelling, *d* Aug. 1, 1867, *a* 86.

Mary, widow of Thomas Stunnell, *d* Nov. 23, 1869, *a* 79.

Charles Gregory, *d* Nov. 2, 1865, *a* 75.
Jane, wife of Charles Gregory, *d* June 23, 1872, *a* 73.

Elizabeth Franks, *d* June 8, 1866, *a* 76.
George, her husband, *d* Nov. 22, 1867, *a* 70.

Richard Alexander Pettit, of Thornton Heath, *d* Sept. 19, 1877, *a* 25.

John Cousens, *d* Dec. 26, 1880, *a* 70. [Of South Norwood.]
Elizabeth, his wife, *d* Jan. 31, 1870, *a* 60.

Mary, wife of Thomas Ready, *d* Aug. 11, 1875, *a* 94.
Thomas Ready, *d* March 16, 1877, *a* 90.

James Moore, *d* March, 1866, *a* 81.
Jane, wife of James Moore, *d* March 27, 1866, *a* 33 ; also 4 children.

Maria, wife of George Thomas Moore, *d* Aug. 30, 1872, *a* 56.

William Ernest Gutteridge, of Southbridge House, *d* April 18, 1880, *a* 7.

Thomas Clift, *d* Oct. 6, 1866, *a* 75.
Harriet, his wife, *d* Dec. 18, 1871, *a* 72.

Charlotte, wife of George Dann, *d* Nov. 11, 1876, *a* 64.

Jane Fairman, *d* June 21, 1866, *a* 40.
> Yes, she is gone, we are going all,
> Like flowers we wither, and like leaves we fall.

Caroline Ellen Faulkner, *d* Jan. 20, 1879, *a* 20.
> This stone is erected in affectionate gratitude for her loving care of Walter de M. Malan, by his parents.

Lucy Ashdown, *d* July 7, 1866, *a* 75.

Ann Barker, wife of Wm. Carter, of South Norwood, *d* Nov. 29, 1877, *a* 63.
Jemima Eliza, his second wife, *d* Dec. 20, 1879, *a* 55.

Elizabeth Haines, *d* Feb. 1, 1871, *a* 65.
> For forty-six years devoted servant to Mr. Benington and family.

Charles Joseph Hewitt, *d* March 8, 1874, *a* 56.

Jonathan Brooks, *d* Sept. 26, 1875, *a* 77.

Maria, wife of Mark Fothergill, *d* Feb. 25, 1870, *a* 64.

Annie Ellen, her daughter, and wife of the Rev. Thos. T. Lightfoot, Canon of St. George's, Capetown, South Africa, died at sea, on her passage to England, Trinity Sunday, 1874.

Elizabeth, widow of Chas. Carter, Esq., *d* Sept. 15, 1871, *a* 82.

George Cumick Wilson, *d* Oct. 7, 1871, *a* 32.

Thomas King, of Parson's Mead, *d* Aug. 8, 1871, *a* 90.

   [Father of Mr. William King, now of the Blue Anchor, South End. He was formerly connected with the Greyhound Livery Stables.]

Ellen, widow of James Martin, *d* Dec. 14, 1873, *a* 72.

Thomas Waldron, *d* Jan. 19, 1875, *a* 61.

Mary, his wife, *d* Jan. 3, 1872, *a* 65.

Mary, daughter of Thos. Kitchen, *d* April 24, 1871, *a* 2.

Marie, her sister, an infant.

Augustus Chas. Andrews, *d* June 29, 1875, *a* 47.

William Merredew, *d* April 8, 1871, *a* 67.

Edith Maria Sandy, *d* March 10, 1871.

      Thou star of comfort, for a moment given,
      Just rose on earth, then set to rise in heaven.

Sarah Webb, *d* Dec. 30, 1878, *a* 86.

Martha Bratton, her cousin, *d* May 20, 1881, *a* 81.

Anthony Cooper, *d* Jan. 22, 1872, *a* 61.

Esther, wife of Wm. Stevenson, 123, High Street, *d* Oct. 28, 1877, *a* 58.

George Longueville Bedingfield, *d* Nov. 21, 1871, *a* 38.

Mr. Josiah Witt, of Cross Road, *d* March 29, 1871, *a* 68.

Sarah, his wife, *d* Sept. 24, 1876, *a* 81.

      Rest our kind and gentle parents,
        From this troubled world of pain,
      We trust you've left us for a better,
        Where we hope to meet again.
      For, though lost from sight, remember'd here,
      A faithful Father and a Mother dear.

George Campbell Ruxton, *d* March 25, 1879, *a* 23.

   [Son of Mr. W. Ruxton, of East Croydon Station.]

Elizabeth Anne, daughter of John Dowden, *d* April 5, 1871, *a* 14.

John Frederick, her brother, *d* Feb. 7, 1872, *a* 17.

      Thou hast called us to resign,
      What most we prized, thou Lord divine,
      We only yield Thee what was Thine,
        Thy will be done.

Ann Price, *d* Dec. 23, 1877, *a* 77.

Edward Price, *d* July 28, 1878, *a* 70.

Ada Maria Smith, *d* Dec. 3, 1874, *a* 16.

   Ten thousand words could not proclaim her goodness nor her worth.

Emma Susannah Ford, *d* Oct. 11, 1877, *a* 58.

Anne Colmore Lambley, who resided as a most cherished friend for many years at the Vicarage, Thornton Heath, *d* Aug. 1, 1877, *a* 49.

Elizabeth, wife of James Ellis, *d* Sept. 12, 1874, *a* 75

James Ellis, *d* May 16, 1882, *a* 79.

Louisa, wife of James Cadburn, *d* Dec. 27, 1870 *a* 72.

James Coates, *d* Feb. 12, 1877, *a* 74.

Henry Parry, son of William Randall, *d* Nov. 29, 1880, *a* 3.
John McCutcheon, *d* April 27, 1874, *a* 39.

Ellen, wife of George Nicoll Price, *d* Jan. 12, 1877, *a* 38.

William Cragg, *d* Jan. 10, 1874, *a* 39.

Frederick West, *d* May 3, 1876, *a* 53.

> Mr. Fredk. West, of the Waldrons, Croydon, had risen to be regarded as one of the first lawyers in London. As partner in the firm of West & King, he was solicitor to the Croydon Local Board of Health, a position now held by his son. He was a liberal supporter of all the institutions in the town of a philanthropic, social, or scientific character. Among the *élite* of society in Croydon he was much esteemed. He died in the prime of life, to the intense grief of his family and friends.

Robert, infant son of Robert and Annie Davidson, *d* March 12, 1875.
Annie Ruby, his sister, *d* Nov. 2, 1877, *a* 2.

Anwyn Mary, widow of Nicol Stenhouse, *d* May 12, 1871, *a* 54.

Fanny Neale, *d* Nov. 3, 1875, *a* 43.

Herbert Hazelgrove, *d* March 15, 1867, *a* 16.

Thomas Brooker, *d* March 5, 1867, *a* 73.
Elizabeth, his wife, *d* April 25, 1871, *a* 69.

Mary Russell, *d* Jan. 20, 1878, *a* 36.

> Lord, she was Thine, and not mine own,
> Thou has not done me wrong,
> I thank Thee for the precious gift,
> Afforded me, but not for long.

John Morley, *d* Feb. 13, 1867, *a* 66.

Mary Ann Russell, *d* March 14, 1867, *a* 48.
Fredk., her husband, *d* Jan. 10, 1869, *a* 53.

> Honoured and loved, and full of days,
> We laid thee in the silent earth,
> And here this humble stone we raise,
> A tribute to a parent's worth.

John Bradbury, *d* March 8, 1865, *a* 40.
Ann Teale, *d* Feb. 13, 1872, *a* 82.

Alice Elizabeth, wife of Thos. Sanders, *d* Aug. 21, 1879, *a* 28.

Thomas Beale, *d* Nov. 28, 1870, *a* 70.

John Smith Waller, *d* July 23, 1873, *a* 31.
Ann Waller, her mother, *d* April 16, 1875, *a* 56.
Joseph Waller, fourth son of David Waller, *d* May 23, 1875, *a* 20.

Louisa, wife of George Bailey, *d* July 21, 1873, *a* 25.

Antonia Caroline, wife of John Harris Danvers, *d* Feb. 4, 1864, *a* 47.

Jane, widow of William Beckley, *d* March 21, 1880.

Thomas Biddulph, *d* Dec. 18, 1877, *a* 41.

Henry Oswald Baber, son of Henry John Strong, M.D., *d* July 11, 1865, *a* 3 years and 10 months.
Maria May, wife of Henry John Strong, M.D., *d* April 22, 1871, *a* 45.
Elizabeth Matilda Grist, *d* Feb. 9, 1878, *a* 51.

Maria Dyke, *d* Dec. 28, 1878, *a* 44.

Leonard Bristow, son of John and Mary Halliwell, *d* July 27, 1866, *a* 9
months.

Charles Herbert, her brother, *d* Sept. 18, 1879, *a* 21.

James Davis, *d* Aug. 27, 1876, *a* 31.

Owen H. Turner, *d* April 8, 1874, *a* 42.
> Though lost to sight, to memory dear ;
> A beloved husband and father lies sleeping here.

George Dean Corbett, *d* Oct. 1, 1874, *a* 59.

Matilda Artindale, *d* July 19, 1875, *a* 85.
John Artindale, *d* Oct. 10, 1858, *a* 62.

George Summersby, *d* March 6, 1871, *a* 48.
> [He kept the level crossing gate where the trains from Norwood to West and
> New Croydon are turned on to their respective lines. He was knocked
> down and killed by a passing train which he had not observed.]

George Hayes, *d* June 8, 1874, *a* 59.

Samuel Townshend Davey, *d* March 18, 1871, *a* 34.

George John Cuckow, *d* Sept. 19, 1880, *a* 85.
Amelia Ann Sedgwick, *d* March 20, 1871, *a* 50.
> Lone are the paths and sad the home,
> Whence thy kind smile is gone ;
> But, oh ! a brighter home than ours,
> In heaven, is now thine own.

Susannah Janet, widow of the Rev. A. J. Bennoch, Vicar of St. Luke's,
Woodside, *d* Dec. 16, 1879, *a* 35.
Jane, widow of Archibald Bennoch, *d* Dec. 12, 1880, *a* 79.
Archibald Bennoch, died at Pine Hill, South Australia, Feb. 20, 1860,
a 58.
Archibald Francis Bennoch, *d* Jan. 3, 1882, *a* 3.

William Grace, *d* Jan. 20, 1859, *a* 53.
Jane Grace, his wife, *d* Nov. 16, 1879, *a* 69.
Jane Johnson, his daughter, *d* Feb. 20, 1880, *a* 47.

Elizabeth, wife of Chas. Cross, of Norwood, *d* Dec. 22, 1874, *a* 67.
Eliza Ellen Tolly, *d* Feb. 6, 1876, *a* 45.

Thos. James, son of Henry Marrion, *d* July 18, 1869, *a* 1 year and 4 months.
Albert Sidney, brother, *d* Dec. 10, 1880, *a* 7 months.
Helen, sister, *d* Dec. 3, 1871, *a* 1 year and 5 months.
Flora, sister, *d* Feb. 8, 1880, *a* 7.

Alice Spencer, child of Edwin Spencer, *d* June 10, 1872.
Albert Spencer, *d* April 13, 1879, *a* 3 years and 8 months.
> These lovely buds, so young and fair,
> Called hence by early doom ;
> Just came to show how sweet such flowers
> In paradise could bloom.

Michael King, *d* Nov. 12, 1871, *a* 70.
Elizabeth, his wife, *d* Jan. 29, 1882, *a* 81.

William James, second son of William James Paxton, *d* March 2, 1874,
a 4 years and 1 month.
Jane Ellen, infant sister.

Elizabeth Blackburne, *d* Jan. 23, 1874, *a* 39.

Annie Adelaide Shardlow, *d* July 25, 1872, *a* 10.

Mary Jane, wife of William Reeves, *d* July 14, 1877, *a* 29.

Emanuel Butt, *d* June 7, 1876, *a* 45.

Sarah Sares, *d* April 27, 1875, *a* 50.

George Cooper, surgeon, *d* Oct. 31, 1880, *a* 70.
[An old resident of Croydon, having lived many years in George Street. He was police surgeon, and of quiet and retired habits.]

Alfred Cooper, his son, *d* Nov. 25, 1875, *a* 23.

Mary Jane, wife of George French, *d* March 10, 1877, *a* 74.

> When last we looked on her we loved,
> Whom in life we held most dear,
> We then turned submissive to our God,
> But could not suppress the tear.

Elizabeth Jane Collier, *d* Oct. 25, 1876, *a* 59.

Thomas Arthur, son of J. F. A. Norton Beecher, *d* July 9, 1876, *a* 7.

> He is not dead, the child of our affection,
> But gone unto that school,
> Where he no longer needs our poor protection,
> And Christ himself doth rule.

Also Mabel, his infant sister.

Maria Maidment, *d* May 29, 1877, *a* 66.

William Henry Puttick, *d* Sept. 16, 1876, *a* 4.
Mary Puttick, *d* Oct. 7, 1877, *a* 7½.
Maria Masters, *d* Sept. 4, 1877, *a* 44.

Joseph Webb, *d* Sept. 5, 1876, *a* 64.
William Hudson Beckwith, *d* Aug. 23, 1876, *a* 14.

Edmund John Henry, son of H. G. Harris, surgeon, *d* June 6, 1874, *a* 10.

Emma, wife of Henry Thomas Dellar, *d* Dec. 13, 1873, *a* 63.

Francis Ann, wife of Francis M. Mercer, *d* Aug. 6, 1873, *a* 43.

Thomas Williams, *d* Sept. 1, 1873, *a* 74.
Rebecca, his widow, *d* Nov. 19, 1881, *a* 81.
Elizabeth Roberts, widow, *d* Nov. 19, 1873, *a* 93.
Thomas Williams, *d* Sept. 22, 1877, *a* 49.

Isabella, wife of D. G. McReddie, *d* March 24, 1874, *a* 32.

Charles Gage, *d* Aug. 29, 1873, *a* 55.

Hannah Sarah Elizabeth, wife of Edward James Ulph, *d* Oct. 21, 1872, *a* 49.

> Thou art gone to the grave, but we will not deplore thee,
> Though sorrows and darkness encompass the tomb.
> The Saviour has passed through its portals before thee,
> And the lamp of His love is thy guide through the gloom.

Edward James Ulph, *d* Jan. 14, 1879, *a* 54.

George Marston, *d* April 9, 1878, *a* 24.

Jessie Susannah, child of John and Jessie Humphreys, *d* Feb. 15, 1876, *a* 8.

> Here our darling Jessie sleeps
> But her soul our Shepherd keeps
> With his host of lambs above,
> See his everlasting love.

Rev. Wm. Deacon Isaac, *d* June 21, 1875, *a* 60.

Chas. Wm. Gibson, *d* March 17, 1879, *a* 48.
Jessie, his daughter, *d* July 3, 1873, *a* 15.

Mary Goadby, *d* Feb. 23, 1873, *a* 68.
She was 44 years in the service of one family, by whom she was much regretted.

Robert Rosier Ray, *d* Feb. 25, 1875, *a* 76.

Matilda Thyer, *d* Jan. 25, 1873, *a* 26.
> Oh, weep not for her, 'tis unkindness to weep,
> The weary weak frame is but fallen to sleep,
> No more of fatigue and endurance she knows,
> Oh, weep not, oh, break not the gentle repose.

Annie, wife of Henry Smith, Whitehorse Road, *d* April 22, 1873.
Henry Smith, *d* March 11, 1881, *a* 53.

Susan, wife of W. A. Isaac, *d* July 13, 1873, *a* 53.
Percival Hadden, her grandson, *d* Jan. 6, 1876, *a* 4½.

Richard Rowley Collier, *d* July 18, 1873, *a* 65.

Lieut.-Col. Edward Thomas Tierney, late 28th B. N. Infantry, *d* Dec. 25, 1872, *a* 64.
> Erected by three loving friends.

Frank Henry, son of Henry and Elizabeth Salt, of Thornton Heath, *d* July 9, 1874, *a* 4.

Albert Layton, *d* Oct. 31, 1872, *a* 39.
Alice, his sister, *d* July 8, 1878, *a* 61.

Joseph Booker, *d* March 17, 1873, *a* 44.

Julia Legg, *d* Nov. 18, 1872, *a* 56.

Sarah Wallis, *d* Dec. 21, 1873, *a* 47.

Mary, wife of John Wood, *d* Oct. 15, 1872, *a* 24.

Keturah, wife of Alfred P. Hughes, *d* Dec. 29, 1875, *a* 40.

Caroline Matilda, wife of C. W. Johnson, *d* March 17, 1874.
Eva Caroline, her daughter, *a* 12.

Ann Langridge, *d* Oct. 29, 1873, *a* 76.
Thomas, her husband, *d* Feb. 14, 1881, *a* 84.
> Released from sorrow, sin, and pain,
> And free from every care,
> By angel hands to Heaven conveyed,
> To rest for ever there.

Josiah Ludlow, *d* July 8, 1872, *a* 37.
> My God hast called me to resign,
> What most I prized, it ne'er was mine,
> I only yielded what was thine,
> Thy will be done.
> Grieve not for me, but be content
> For unto you I was but lent,
> In love we lived, in peace I died,
> You asked my life, but 'twas denied.

Jane Freeman, *d* Feb. 5, 1874, *a* 52.

James Charles Brady, *d* Sept. 29, 1874, *a* 55.

Eliza Shepherd Bowman, widow of Deputy-Commissioner General Bowman, *d* June 2, 1872, *a* 72.

Edward Leese, *d* Jan. 22, 1875, *a* 62.

Jane Caroline Drury, second daughter of the late Rev. C. Taylor, of Barnby, Nottinghamshire, *d* May 14, 1872, *a* 42.

Wm. Henry Eustace Hide, died Vigil of St. Mark, 1872, *a* 27.
Lily Verena, his daughter, *d* Aug. 4, 1872.

Mary Ann, wife of Stephen Ferrett, *d* May 12, 1872, *a* 38.

Albert George, son of Thomas Mills, *d* July 24, 1878, *a* 7½.

Charles William Dawson, *d* Sept. 27, 1878, *a* 37.

George Martin, *d* March 10, 1869, *a* 53.
Mary, his mother, *d* June 28, 1874, *a* 84.

John Foster F. Fresson, youngest son of the late Capt. Fresson, *d* Jan. 17, 1865, *a* 18.
Eliza Fresson, *d* July 6, 1869, *a* 41.

Joseph Jas. Welch, of Beaulieu, South Norwood, *d* June 12, 1872, *a* 67.
Joseph Archibald Welch, his grandson, *d* June 18, 1873, *a* 2.

Frederick Rumble, *d* Oct. 16, 1866, *a* 33.

Ann, wife of Richard H. Trott, *d* June 19, 1867, *a* 67.
Richard Howard Trott, *d* Jan. 28, 1868, *a* 67.

Maria, wife of William Edward Parker, *d* Feb. 23, 1872, *a* 23.

Captain James Holland, late 69th Regt., 20 years Paymaster and Quarter-master Highland Borderers, Light Infantry Militia, *d* Jan. 31, 1879, *a* 81.
> Erected by the officers who served with him in the last named regiment.

George McMillen, Esq., *d* Sept. 1872, *a* 27.
> He now sleeps in Jesus and is blest,
> How soft his slumbers are,
> From suffering, and from sin released,
> And freed from every care.

Frederick Moore Lloyd, *d* Sept. 15, 1879, *a* 31.

Edith Lucy Steed, *d* Dec. 8, 1875, *a* 1 year and 5 months.
Jane Elizabeth Steed, her mother, *d* Oct. 25, 1876, *a* 34.

George Peskett, *d* Dec. 15, 1875, *a* 36.
> Weep not for me, my children dear,
> Although you're left behind,
> Prepare yourselves to follow me,
> And bear me in your mind.

Arthur George Inglis, *d* Dec. 27, 1875, *a* 4½.

Henry Randall, *d* April 1, 1876, *a* 28.
Charles Randall, *d* Nov. 28, 1881, *a* 24.
> Not gone from memory, not gone from love,
> But gone to his Father's home above.

Jane Rebecca McKay, *d* March 9, 1876, *a* 51.
George Daniel McKay, *d* Jan. 2, 1880, *a* 62.

Sarah Kathrine, wife of Robert Gear, *d* Feb. 11, 1876, *a* 30.
> Consumption sapped her youthful life,
> My children lost a mother, and I a wife;
> As human skill could not death arrest,
> May she live in Heaven among the blest.

Jane Hale, *d* April 15, 1876, *a* 57.
Nathaniel Hale, her brother, *d* Jan. 4, 1867, *a* 41.

Catherine Mary, wife of Alfred Bywater, *d* April 30, 1876, *a* 24.

Margaret Mary Clutton, *d* Feb. 30, 1875, *a* 53.
> The winter of trouble is past,
> The storm of affliction is o'er,
> Her trials are ended at last,
> And sorrow can reach her no more.

Clara, her daughter, *d* July 22, 1882, *a* 36.
> Most dearly loved, most deeply mourned, by all who knew her.

Thomas Wells, lost his life at Selhurst Station, Dec. 16, 1874, *a* 37.

Sophia Priscilla Sirr, *d* Jan. 7, 1875.

M

Emma Arthur, *d* Feb. 3, 1875, *a* 86.

Richard Beaver, *d* Sept. 20, 1874, *a* 71.
Jane, his wife, *d* Dec. 31, 1878, *a* 72.

Maria Walker, for many years serving woman in the Parish Church of Croydon, *d* March 30, 1875.
> This stone was erected by members of the congregation.

Eliza, wife of D. W. Lanham, *d* April 4, 1875, *a* 41.

John Holland, *d* April 2, 1875, *a* 79.
> "Yea, though I walk through the valley of the shadow of death, I will fear no evil, for Thou art with me, Thy rod and Thy staff comfort me."

Eliza, wife of J. J. Murray, *d* April 10, 1875, *a* 53.
> Asleep in Jesus! oh, for me,
> May such a blissful refuge be!
> Securely shall my ashes lie,
> Waiting the summons from on high.

Eleanor Phœbe, wife of James Read, *d* April 7, 1875, *a* 27.

Martha Meads, *d* May 19, 1875, 62.

Alice, daughter of Walter Albert and Hettie Andress, *d* Dec. 27, 1875, *a* 1 year and 9 months
Albert, infant son, *d* June 25, 1875.

Sarah, wife of John Middleton, Esq., *d* April 1, 1876, *a* 73.

Ann Julia Young, *d* July 28, 1876.

Cassandra, wife of Jas. H. Sanderson, *d* June 10, 1879, *a* 38.
Basil Walker, her son, *d* Dec. 23, 1876, *a* 2.

John Hatter, *d* Sept. 4, 1876, *a* 54.
> The winter of trouble is past,
> The storm of affliction is o'er,
> His trials are ended at last,
> And sorrow can reach him no more.

George Dodd, *d* May 15, 1875, *a* 59.
> Dear Saviour, though unworthy,
> Yet this my only plea,
> Thy all atoning merit,
> For Thou hast died for me.

John Birch, *d* June 3, 1875, *a* 75,
> His languishing head is at rest,
> Its thinking and aching is o'er,
> His quiet immovable breast,
> Is heaved by affliction no more.

Our darling baby, Eve Francis Ann Saunders, *d* June 11, 1877.

Adelina Margaret Oldfield, *d* May 3, 1879, *a* 12.

Mary Ann Hersee, *d* May 12, 1879, *a* 80.

Elizabeth Sarah, wife of Wm. Harris, *d* Jan. 31, 1879, *a* 50.
Sidney Wm. Harris, *d* March 17, 1870, *a* 6 months.

Rachel Martha, wife of Henry Clarke, *d* Jan. 27, 1870, *a* 68.
> Stranger, pause! think what a woman should be, for such was she.

Wm. Hy. Scudamore Ward, *d* March 12, 1879, *a* 50.
> They that sow in tears shall reap in joy.

John Ellis, of Neville-road, *d* Dec. 5, 1877, *a* 74.
Maria Ellis, his wife, *d* July 15, 1878, *a* 78.

Sarah D. Allanson, *d* Jan. 10, 1879, *a* 65.

Benjamin Tett Palmer, *d* Dec. 17, 1877, *a* 49.

George Patterson, Staff Commander, R.N., *d* April 28, 1877, *a* 42.

Ann King, of South Norwood, *d* Sept. 13, 1877, *a* 79.

Frances, wife of J. E. D. Rodgers, surgeon, *d* Jan. 3, 1879, *a* 58.

Hannah, wife of Richd. Balcomb, *d* Dec. 7, 1877, *a* 60.

Mary Ann Geal, *d* Sept. 7, 1877, *a* 66.
Wm. Henry Geal, her brother, *d* May 5, 1882, *a* 44.

Mary Ann, wife of P. R. T. Martin, *d* April 6, 1878, *a* 52.
Mary Ann, her daughter, *d* Sept. 1, 1877, *a* 27.

Charles James Gates, *d* Dec. 23, 1877, *a* 77.

Wm. Arlett, *d* March 25, 1874, *a* 86.
Jane, his daughter, *d* Oct. 10, 1877, *a* 49.

Kate Ellen Mayhew, *d* Sept. 23, 1879, *a* 49.

Thomas Solkeld Martin, *d* April 11, 1877, *a* 54.
> For many years a resident in South Africa.

Alice Hamp, *d* Dec. 9, 1877, *a* 1,

Wm. Gambrill, *d* May 9, 1877, *a* 68.
> Lord, all pitying Jesu bless,
> Grant him thine eternal rest.

Fanny, wife of George Ladd, *d* May 2, 1877, *a* 72.

Ellen Wall, *d* April 24, 1877, *a* 54.

Jonathan Richardson, *d* March 2, 1877, *a* 68.
Fanny, his wife, *d* April 25, 1881, *a* 44.

Jessie Ann, wife of Richd. Harding, *d* Dec. 17, 1876, *a* 42.

Thomas Hole, *d* Jan. 17, 1877, *a* 8.
> Joyful, joyful, will the meeting be,
> When from sin our hearts are pure and free,
> And we shall gather, Saviour, with thee,
> In our eternal home.

James George Allan, *d* Nov. 27, 1876, *a* 67.

Walford Izod, *d* April 8, 1880, *a* 24.

Marcella Sarah Heading, *d* Oct. 19, 1875, *a* 31.
Robert Heading, her father, *d* Feb. 9, 1880, *a* 66.
Mary, wife of Thomas White, *d* Sept. 5, 1875, *a* 53.

Albert Edward Holman, *d* Aug. 8, 1875, *a* 5.
> Without a fault before the throne of God.
Nellie Holman, *d* Jan. 1, 1880, *a* 4 years and 8 months.
> The cup was bitter, the loss severe,
> To part with her we loved so dear.

Catherine Ada, *d* July 6, 1875, *a* 32.

Emily Mary Atkinson, *d* Nov. 8, 1876, *a* 39.

Joseph Young, *d* July 7, 1875, *a* 42.

Amelia Bull, *d* Jan. 8, 1880, *a* 77.

Chas. Edward Pocock, *d* Jan. 8, 1875, *a* 22.
Elizabeth, his sister, *d* Jan. 13, 1875, *a* 26.
> When blooming youth is snatched away,
> By death's resistless hand,
> Our hearts the mournful tribute pay,
> Which pity must demand.

Mary Ellen, daughter of Capt. J. H. Anderson, *d* Jan. 12, 1875, *a* 24.

Edward Maxwell, *d* Feb. 20, 1875, *a* 46.

Eliza, wife of Thomas Gregory, *d* Nov. 21, 1875, *a* 66.
> We cannot tell who next may fall,
>   Beneath the chastening rod,
> One must be first, then let us all,
>   Prepare to meet our God.

Augusta Hill James, *d* Jan. 23, 1878, *a* 62.

Charles Anderson Read, F.R.H.S., *d* Jan. 23, 1878, *a* 36.
This memorial is erected by his friends.

John Chappell, *d* Jan. 28, 1878, *a* 64.
> He is not lost, he is within the door,
>   That shuts out loss, and every hurtful thing,
> With angels bright, and loved ones gone before,
>   In his Redeemer's presence evermore,
> And God himself, His Lord, and Judge, and King.

Mary Jane Chappell, *d* Jan. 22, 1880, *a* 71.

Emma Constable, *d* Feb. 15, 1877, *a* 53.
John Constable, her husband, *d* May 2, 1878, *a* 55.

Charles Hart, *d* March 20, 1877, *a* 37.
> Weep not for me, my wife and children dear,
> I am not lost, but sleeping here,
> Though like the blossom plucked from the tree,
> So death has parted you and me.

Georgina Elizabeth Tarver, *d* Feb. 15, 1878, *a* 60.

Wm. Henry Webb, *d* Feb. 28, 1878, *a* 30.

Harold I'Anson, *d* Jan. 6, 1878, *a* 2.

William Miriam, *d* Sept. 6, 1878, *a* 51.

Susan Brown Salmon, 70, Albert Road, *d* Sept. 3, 1878, *a* 84.

J. W. Martin, *d* Sept. 6, 1878, *a* 51.

Sarah Foster, *d* June 24, 1878, *a* 85.
> I came to Jesus as I was,
>   Weary and worn and sad,
> I found in Him a resting place,
>   And He has made me glad.

Florence Beatrice Mayhew, *d* July 23, 1878, *a* 9 months.

Susannah, wife of Wm. Parker, *d* Aug. 9, 1879, *a* 70.
Ernest Pottinger, her grandson, *d* July 28, 1878, *a* 7 months.

Mary Ann Glisbey, *d* Aug. 13, 1878, *a* 49.

Wm. Brooker, lost his life while on duty at Norwood Junction, April 1, 1876, *a* 58.
> Sleep, dear husband, sleep,
>   Time will soon pass away,
> When I shall cease to weep,
>   And calmly with thee lay.

Rose Harriet Ann, his granddaughter, *d* Jan. 30, 1878, *a* 2½.

Amy, wife of Isaiah Wilkins, *d* Dec. 20, 1875, *a* 66.

Thomas Hedgis, *d* Nov. 24, 1875, *a* 66.
[For very many years a wheelwright at "Hedgis' Yard," North End.]

Henry Greenhead, *d* Aug. 22, 1875, *a* 63.
Rebecca, his wife, after a long and painful illness, *d* July 17, 1880, *a* 59.

Sarah Jane Vinall, *d* Jan. 1, 1876, *a* 18.
>Beneath this turf of ashes rest,
>Whose memory lingers dear,
>She sleeps unconscious of the tear,
>That tells my tale of sorrow here.

Richd. Simmons, *d* Aug. 22, 1878, *a* 40.

Susanna Ingram, *d* Oct. 8, 1878, *a* 48.
John Ingram, her husband, *d* May, 1866, *a* 42.
Beatrice Ethel Bush, *d* Jan. 14, 1882, *a* 2.

Allen John Fredk. Kotze, *d* June 27, 1878, *a* 4.
>Ere sin could harm or sorrow fade,
>Death came with friendly care,
>The opening bud to Heaven conveyed,
>And bade it blossom there.

Harriet Thorn, *d* April 24, 1881, *a* 62.
Moses, her husband, *d* March 2, 1882, *a* 60.
>[For many years a hairdresser in Handcroft Road.]

Mary Leaver, *d* Dec. 29, 1881, *a* 47.
>A loving wife, a sister dear,
>A fond and faithful friend when here;
>She lived in love, she died in peace,
>We trust her joys will never cease.

Catherine, wife of Lieut.-Colonel H. W. L. Paddon, late of the Royal
Fusiliers, *d* Aug. 12, 1881, *a* 36.
>A wife after God's own heart, chosen and precious.
>Thou art all fair, my love,
>There is no spot in thee!—*Song.*
>Severed only till He come.

Edward Ewer, *d* Nov. 14, 1881, *a* 53.
>Day by day a voice saith, " Come,
>Enter thine eternal home,"
>Asking not if we can spare
>This dear soul it summons there;
>Had He asked us, well we know
>We should cry, " Oh, spare this blow!"
>Yes, with streaming eyes should pray,
>" Lord, we love him, let him stay!"

Harriet Elizabeth, wife of Nathaniel Jacob, *d* Aug. 7, 1881, *a* 26.
>The smile of life has taken flight
>To a world unknown to mortal life;
>Her time was short with husband dear;
>How sweet indeed while life was here!
>The infant was her joy of thought,
>Which none but mother's love has brought;
>Still left by God's kind will behind
>To calm the mourner's troubled mind.

Also Lily Maud, infant daughter, *d* April 1, 1882, *a* 8 months.
>Lay her playthings all away,
>She will never need them more;
>Gone, the sunlight of our day,
>Gone to yonder happy shore;
>Little baby's gone to sleep,
>While we gently round her weep;
>Angels bade our darling come
>To her Father's happy home;
>Sweet the mother's meeting now will be
>In heaven through all eternity.

Mary Ann, widow of Christopher Hildyard, of Brigg, Lincolnshire, *d* Nov. 8, 1878, *a* 78.

Rebecca Ridpath, *d* Aug. 29, 1880, *a* 61.

> Farewell, farewell, I go to join the number,
> Who wait through watches long,
> I rest in peace, for that which breaks the slumber
> Shall be the angel's song.

Jessie Kettles, *d* July 11, 1879, *a* 2.

George Smith Orton, *d* July 25, 1880, *a* 30.
Ellen Alice, his wife, *d* July 26, 1879, *a* 28.
Ellen Alice, his daughter, *d* Sept. 6, 1878, *a* 4.
Jessie, second daughter, *d* Aug. 15, 1879, *a* 10.

James W. Newbery, *d* Aug. 20, 1879, *a* 35.

> His sun went down while it was yet day.

George Kelly King, late W.M. of Lodge 1,797 ; P.M. of No. 4, and No. 1,541 ; S.W. of No. 1,141 ; P.G.S. The stone was erected by members of the above Lodges, in testimony of the untiring zeal and energy of his devotion to the Brotherhood, *d* Aug. 24, 1879, *a* 63.
Eliza King, who survived him only four months, *d* Dec. 29, 1879, *a* 68.

Cyril Alfred Scrivener, *d* May 5, 1880, *a* 7.

Harriett Dow, *d* July 1, 1879, *a* 68.

Thomas Stone, *d* July 17, 1879, *a* 63.

> Strange are His judgments, and His ways past finding out.

John Walton, of St. James's Road, *d* May 19, 1879, *a* 39.

Wm. Fudge, *d* May 18, 1879, *a* 54.

C. Michaelwaite, *d* Aug. 1879, *a* 20.

Annie Carthew Trewheela, *d* May 21, 1879, *a* 41,

> To one who loved her her place is empty always.

Edward Burchatt, *d* June 11, 1879, *a* 36.

Fredk. Berwick Montague, *d* June 1874, *a* 41.

Francis Tarrant, of Whitgift College, *d* June 29, 1879, *a* 88.

Wm. H. G. Mason, *d* May 14, 1879, *a* 68.

John Moorley, *d* April 18, 1879, *a* 68.
Phœbe Norkett, mother of Mary Moorley, *d* Nov. 5, 1879, *a* 65.

Hannah, wife of Thos. Tubb, *d* March 23, 1879, *a* 38.

Charles Langley, *d* Feb. 28, 1879, *a* 41.

> Weep not for me, my wife and children dear,
> I am not dead, but sleeping here,
> Stay a little while in peace and love,
> And trust in God to meet above.

Richd. Beams Paull, of Lansdowne Road, *d* suddenly at Purley, Feb. 7, 1879, *a* 52.

> Mr. Paull was for several years principal of the Grammar School in the Lansdowne Road. In this capacity he had the training and education of many of the children of the leading gentry in the town, of whom he had won universal respect. He was a favourite reader at popular entertainments, and it was while reading at a school room at Purley that he suddenly expired, to the inexpressible grief of his family and friends.

Henry Walker, *d* Feb. 20, 1879, *a* 57.

Simon Barton, *d* Aug. 29, 1876, *a* 59.

William Linn, *d* April 20, 1879, *a* 59.

> My God, my Father, while I stray,
> Far from my home, on life's rough way,
> Oh, teach me from my heart to say,
> Thy will be done.

Elizabeth Jane Linn, his daughter, *d* Jan. 23, 1856, *a* 15.

Mary Rudge, *d* Nov. 26, 1878, *a* 16.

James Dryden, *d* Nov. 11, 1878, *a* 55.

Philadelphia Sarah, daughter of Joseph Dean, *d* Nov. 4, 1878, *a* 32.

Charlotte, widow of Joseph Carham, *d* Dec. 24, 1879, *a* 89.

James Quelch, *d* Jan. 4, 1879, *a* 72.

Fanny Wood, *d* Sept. 17, 1876, *a* 27.

> This cross is erected by Maud, Amy, Charles, and Robt. Buxton, as a token of affection for their nurse, who devoted nine years of her life to their care.

Katie, wife of James L. Browning, *d* March 6, 1880, *a* 27.

Mary Hunt, *d* May 10, 1880.

> Struck by death's unerring dart,
> All physicians still proved vain.
> She endured the bitter smart,
> Till eased by God from pain.

Wm. George Harden, *d* Oct. 31, 1879, *a* 68.

> Weeping may endure for a night,
> But joy cometh in the morning.

Mary Ann Lawrence, *d* June 15, 1880, *a* 76.

Hermon Capern, *d* Nov. 23, 1879, *a* 65.

Thomas Punnett, *d* March 30, 1880, *a* 64.

> May his memory be long blessed, and his soul be happy for ever.

Katherine Greaves, *d* Jan. 21. 1880, *a* 84.

Ellen Margaret, wife of Thomas Stuchberry, *d* May 10, 1880, *a* 34.

John Pitts, *d* Jan. 22, 1880, *a* 19.

> Fixed in his eternal state,
> He is gone from all below ;
> We a little longer wait,
> But how little none can know.

John Sharp, *d* March 26, 1880, *a* 48.

> Many years resident in Port Elizabeth, South Africa.

Charles Edward Rivers, *d* March 7, 1880, *a* 4.

John Little, *d* April 22, 1881, *a* 74.
Patience, his wife, *d* Dec. 23, 1878, *a* 69.

George Osborn, " Black Horse Inn," Woodside, *d* July 3, 1877, *a* 46.

John Robt. Hotson, *d* June 15, 1877, *a* 39.

Sarah Constable, *d* April 21, 1877, *a* 74.

Robt. Eade, *d* Aug. 8, 1877, *a* 62.

Annie Catherine, widow of John Scotland, Esq., W.S., *d* Feb. 1, 1880, *a* 64.

James Bray Cutting, *d* June 5, 1880, *a* 73.

Robert Spencer, *d* March 17, 1878, *a* 64.

Wm. Robert, his youngest son, *d* Oct. 19, 1875, *a* 10.

Hugh Maitland, son of Maitland Gardner, *d* Feb. 3, 1880, *a* 8.

Eliza Mead, *d* March 9, 1880, *a* 64.

Sarah Ellen, daughter of John Watson Greenwood, *d* Jan. 13, 1880, *a* 29.

Eliza, wife of J. R. Worcester, *d* May 11, 1880.

Eli Beagley, *d* Dec. 24, 1878, *a* 69.

Fredk. Lucas, *d* May 29, 1879, *a* 44.

George Wm. F. Berresford, *d* Dec. 4, 1878, *a* 7 months.
> Not in cruelty, not in wrath,
> The reaper came that day ;
> 'Twas an angel visited the green earth,
> And took our darling child away.

Matilda Harland, *d* Sept. 20, 1877, *a* 66.
> My wearied limbs will toil no more,
> Suffering and pain with me are o'er.
> Forbear, dear friends, to mourn and weep,
> Whilst sweetly in the dust I sleep ;
> This toilsome world I've left behind,
> A glorious crown I hope to find.

John Cole White, *d* May 20, 1879, *a* 52.

Richard Hazelgrove, *d* Feb. 16, 1881, *a* 85.

Fredk. Geo. Shattock, *d* Feb. 26, 1879, *a* 71.

Edward Sturgeon, *d* Nov. 4, 1881, *a* 26.
> Released from sorrow, sickness, and pain,
> And free from every care ;
> By angels' hands to Heaven conveyed,
> To rest for ever there.

Percy Francis, *d* Nov. 9, 1880, *a* 3.
Herbert Owen, *d* Nov. 11, 1880, *a* 4.
> Children of George Fredk. and Frances Claredge.

Wm. Jacob, son of John Henry Freestone, *d* Jan. 3, 1881, *a* 22.

Jane, wife of George Smith, *d* Nov. 24, 1881, *a* 66.
> We bring our years to an end as a tale that is told.

Harriet Symonds, *d* May 16, 1880, *a* 71.

Matilda Hungerford Lattrell, *d* Sept. 7, 1869, *a* 56.

Hannah Death, *d* May 3, 1880, *a* 81.

Richd. Henley, *d* June 25, 1880, *a* 40.

George Morton, *d* Jan. 23, 1881, *a* 61.
> What I do thou knowest not now, but thou shalt know hereafter.

Dear little Annie, child of George and Anne Smith, *d* July 1, 1881, *a* 4.

Thomas Ingleton, *d* Oct. 5, 1881, *a* 66.

Anne, wife of Henry Arnold Cowley, *d* Nov. 8, 1860.

Isabel, daughter of Jas. and C. Scott, *d* Aug. 17, 1880, *a* 20.

Ernest William, son of Wm. and Helen Broad, *d* Dec. 17, 1880, *a* 15.
Herbert Edward, his brother, *d* Feb. 14, 1882, *a* 2.

Our dear little Bertie, dear child of Richd. and Sarah Crookes, *d* March 20, 1882, *a* 6½.

Harriot Eliza Cole, *d* Feb. 15, 1882, *a* 85.

Caroline Louisa, wife of Wm. Dyer, *d* Oct. 27, 1881, *a* 57.

Wm. Paston Robinson, *d* Dec. 5, 1880, *a* 47.
Our little darling Harvey Paston, only son of the above, *d* Dec. 2, 1880, *a* 4.
  [Mr. Robinson was for twenty years a journalist in Croydon.]

William Weller, *d* Jan. 2, 1882, *a* 75.

Gertrude Horsley, *d* Nov. 28, 1880, *a* 2½.

William Henry Hulbert, *d* June 13, 1882, *a* 74.

Louisa, wife of John Wm. Vint, *d* March 1, 1881, *a* **25**.

William Dearling, *d* Feb. 12, 1881, *a* 68.

Dear little Tim—Thomas Herbert Tapson, *d* June 4, 1882, *a* 1 year 10 months.

Walter John Fulker, *d* April 8, 1882, *a* 26.

Emily, wife of William Clarke, *d* Jan. 4, 1873, *a* 34.
Elizabeth, second wife, *d* March 8, 1881, *a* 36.
Herbert William, infant son, *d* April 17, 1881.

Matilda, wife of John Turtill Ward, *d* May 26, 1875, *a* 45.
William Collier Ward, his son, *d* June 11, 1877, *a* 18.

George Baber, *d* March 12, 1874, *a* 73.
  [For many years a confidential clerk to Mr. Henry Richards, solicitor.]

Henry James Long, *d* March 19, 1874, *a* 22.
Sarah, his mother, *d* April 18, 1874, *a* 47.

John Dyer, *d* Nov. 21, 1873, *a* 74.

Mabel Caroline, daughter of W. H. Snelling, *d* Feb. 10, 1876, *a* 4.

Hamel Smith, *d* Jan. 18, 1873, *a* 12.
Philip Smith, *d* Oct. 5, 1875, *a* 12.
               Children of Hamel Lewis Smith.

Ellen, wife of George Brooke, *d* July 15, 1871, *a* 31.
        We weep for our loss, we rejoice at her gain,
        Like her, we would pass from sin, sorrow, and pain ;
        We long for the time when, with angels above,
        We join them in praising the Saviour they love.

Mary Ann Bavridge, *d* Nov. 8, 1872, *a* 22.

Caroline, wife of Fredk. Nash, *d* Dec. 27, 1880, *a* 24.

Catherine, widow of the late Capt. Peter B. Man, Madras Army, *d* May 29, 1873, *a* 82.
Lieut.-Colonel H. Garnet Man, *d* Nov. 4, 1873, *a* 69.

George Poole, of Beulah Grove, *d* Aug. 1, 1873, *a* 55.

Jane, wife of William Haden, *d* June 14, 1874, *a* 57.
        How loved, how valued once, avails thee not,
        To whom related, or by whom forgot ;
        A heap of dust alone remains of thee,
        'Tis all thou art, and all the proud shall be.
Also Wm. Haden, *d* Feb. 13, 1877, *a* 60.
  " And there shall be no night there, and they need no candle, neither light of
    the sun, for the Lord God giveth them light, and they reign for ever
    and ever."
            Oh, glorious hour ! oh, blest abode !
            I shall be near and like my God,
            And flesh and sense no more control
            The endless pleasures of the soul.

Richard Wood, *d* May 3, 1875, *a* 65.
John Wood, his brother, *d* Oct. 28, 1880, *a* 82.
We all do fade as a leaf.

William Line, *d* May 29, 1879, *a* 60.
Caroline, his wife, *d* Dec. 11, 1874, *a* 57.

Rebecca, widow of Henry Gillingham, thirty-five years a householder of Norwood, *d* Jan. 8, 1875, *a* 75.
Captain Henry Constable, her grandson, *d* March 1, 1875, *a* 13.

Lydia Payne, wife of Henry Payne, jun., *d* Jan. 27, 1871, *a* 22.
Charles Portsmouth, *d* Feb. 22, 1871, *a* 29.

George Holmden, *d* March 27, 1876, *a* 31.
> See from the earth the fading lily rise,
> It springs, it grows, it flourishes, and dies,
> So these fair flowers scarce blossomed for a day,
> Short was the blossom, and early the decay.

Lucy Maria, relict of the late Rev. John W. Hughes, rector of St. Clement's, Oxford, *d* June 11, 1866, *a* 67.

Wm. Bryant, *d* Jan. 27, 1866, *a* 46.

Mary Bryant, *d* May 27, 1871, *a* 74.
James Bryant, her husband, *d* Jan. 5, 1881, *a* 85.

The remaining inscriptions on the tombs of the Church or consecrated portion of the Cemetery will be found on two sections in the upper part of the Cemetery, on the *left-hand* side of the main path.

Charles Godwin, *d* Dec. 27, 1870, *a* 65.
Emma Elizabeth Madock, *d* March 21, 1875, *a* 77.

B. C. Staples, of Sydenham Road, *d* April 26, 1872, *a* 45.
Percival Herbert, infant son, *d* Feb. 11, 1872.

Mary Chalklin, *d* Feb. 4, 1871, *a* 64.

Fredk. Turner, *d* Jan. 9, 1871, *a* 57.
> We trust her soul has found a home
> Among the faithful blest,
> Where the wicked cease from troubling,
> And the weary are at rest.

Sarah Ann, wife of Charles Day, of Addiscombe, *d* April 27, 1881, *a* 58.
> In life a pure and holy bride,
> With look angelic as she died,
> And passed away in peace.

Catherine, wife of Edwd. R. Gibbon, *d* Oct. 30, 1874, *a* 21.
> She is not dead, the loved of our affection,
> But gone into that school
> Where she no longer needs our poor protection,
> And Christ Himself doth rule;
> Day after day we think what she is doing
> In that bright realm of air,
> Year after year her tender steps pursuing,
> Behold her crown more fair
> In that great cloister's stillness and seclusion,
> By guardian angels led;
> Safe from temptation, safe from sin's pollution,
> She lives whom we call dead.

James King, builder, of Portland Road, South Norwood, *d* Oct. 27, 1873,
 a 64.

Ellen, daughter of G. W. Smith, of Wellesley Terrace, *d* May 15, 1871,
 a 17.

John Howell, *d* June 1, 1874, *a* 52.
John Girault Bailey, his nephew, *d* Aug. 30, 1875, *a* 21.
   Safe sheltered from the storms of life.

Sophia Bartlett, *d* July 30, 1870.

Henry Simpson, *d* Sept. 27, 1871, *a* 53.
 The dust shall return to the earth as it was, and the spirit shall return to the
  God who gave it.

Wm. Jermyn Burch, *d* Sept. 28, 1871, *a* 91,
Charlotte, his wife, *d* Feb. 28, 1874, *a* 80,
Emma, his eldest daughter, *d* May 15, 1881.
Sarah Holmwood, her sister, *d* Oct. 16, 1878.

Robert Martin, *d* Nov. 17, 1871, *a* 49.

Sarah Elizabeth, daughter of John George Marks, *d* April 22, 1873, *a* 2
 years and 4 months.
Sarah Marks, her mother, *d* April 3, 1880, *a* 39.
 Her pure bright spirit, beautiful unselfish nature, loving heart, wise and
  earnest-minded views, made her the guide and blessing of her husband
  and her boys, and endeared her to all who knew her.

Edward Elliff, *d* Dec. 26, 1869, *a* 60.

George Waters, of George Street, *d* April 10, 1872, *a* 76.
 Mr. Waters was the originator of the famous Croydon Basket
 Carriages, and founder of the present firm in George
 Street. He was of a quiet unobtrusive nature, and died
 with the respect of all who knew him.

Eliza Jane Waters, his grand-daughter, *d* Jan. 14, 1876, *a* 12.

Wm. Evans Briden, M.D., *d* April 15, 1873, *a* 79.

Wm. Gardner, *d* Aug. 2, 1873, *a* 55.

Elizabeth Smith Oliphant, *d* May 26, 1872, *a* 54.

John Callow, *d* October 10, 1874, *a* 47.
Ann, widow of John Callow, *d* Oct. 10, 1877, *a* 54.

Mary Ann Wilcox, *d* March 12, 1875, *a* 70.

Ann Martin, *d* Feb. 11, 1870, *a* 70.

George Butcher, *d* Dec. 6, 1869, *a* 38.
   A dutiful son, and a loving husband.

Josiah James Rickett, *d* Feb. 13, 1875, *a* 61.

Charles Bennett, *d* Sept. 2, 1870, *a* 62.

Elizabeth, wife of Amos Weaver, *d* Dec. 18, 1872, *a* 72.
   There is a cross in every lot,
    And an earnest need of prayer,
   But a lowly heart that leans on God,
    Is happy everywhere.
Also Amos Weaver, *d* Feb. 25, 1878, *a* 82.

Thomas Baker, Bensham Lane, *d* March 26, 1871, *a* 75.
   In life, oh, how beloved, his death,
    How dear, we can but mourn.
 A husband, father, loving friend, beneath this stone is buried.
Sarah, his wife, *d* Dec. 8, 1874, *a* 71.

Mary Ann Eastey, *d* April 16, 1871, *a* 78.
Catharine Georgiana Eastey, *d* Feb. 7, 1879, *a* 74.

Sophie Amelie Williams, wife of C. G. Williams, *d* Oct. 14, 1872, *a* 62.
Charles Gummow Williams, her husband, *d* June 18, 1877, *a* 74.

Susannah Mary Wilkinson, *d* July 18, 1871, *a* 81.
Little Willie, her grandchild, *d* Feb. 8, 1871, *a* 10 months.

Thomas Oakley, *d* Sept. 10, 1875, *a* 76.
Jane, his wife, *d* July 18, 1874, *a* 65.

Thos. Fielder, Leslie Park, *d* Dec. 28, 1871, *a* 55.
Hetty, his wife, *d* June 29, 1878, *a* 63.

Maria, widow of Geo. Moorcroft, *d* Nov. 30, 1871, *a* 87.
> And there with all the blood-bought throng,
> From sin and sorrow free,
> I'll sing the new eternal song,
> Of Jesu's love for me.

Emma, wife of Samuel Barnes, *d* June 20, 1873, *a* 23.

Henrietta Yeoell, *d* Nov. 3, 1874, *a* 30.

Daniel Belton, *d* May 25, 1873, *a* 70.
Jane, his wife, *d* Dec. 23, 1875, *a* 68.

Samuel Banister, *d* Jan. 11, 1870, *a* 79.

Matilda Pollard, *d* Sept. 20, 1869, *a* 5.
> Gone early to rest.

William Attridge, *d* Aug. 26, 1869, *a* 63.

Emily Louisa Tyler, *d* Jan. 54, 1875, *a* 15.
> Be my last thought, how sweet to rest,
> For ever on my Saviour's breast.

Richard Alder, *d* Oct. 18, 1873, *a* 66.

James Gilbert, *d* Dec. 15, 1872, *a* 39.
Julia Ann Gilbert, his wife, *d* Aug. 18, 1870, *a* 30.
Sidney Gilbert, his son, *d* April 19, 1870, *a* 11 months.

Jane Elizabeth, daughter of Joseph Willis, South Norwood, *d* March 22, 1874, *a* 19.

Frances Elizabeth, widow of John Ely Fisher, *d* April 11, 1874, *a* 86.

Hannah Elizabeth Wright, *d* Jan. 27, 1870, *a* 91.

Susanna, wife of John Simmons, *d* April 26, 1870, *a* 54.

Catherine Willcox King, *d* Aug. 1870, *a* 61.
John Geo. King, her husband, *d* April 13, 1875, *a* 61.

Francis Tummons, *d* Nov. 9, 1878, *a* 60.
> We cannot tell who next may fall,
> Beneath the chastening rod,
> One must be first, but let us all,
> Prepare to meet our God.

John Ridge, *d* March 27, 1879, *a* 64.

Catherine Christiana, wife of Job H. West, of Thornton Heath, *d* Aug. 7, 1876, *a* 75.
Job Henry West, *d* July 23, 1880, *a* 78.
> A father kind, and most dear,
> And to the end he was sincere,
> Though great the loss we all sustain,
> We hope in Heaven to meet again.

John Allsop, *d* Aug. 27, 1872, *a* 52.
    [Well known as a public man in Croydon, having served on the Local Board
        and Board of Guardians.]

John Marston Allsop, *d* June 13, 1877, *a* 34.

George Day, *d* Dec. 13, 1877, *a* 51.
    [Many years landlord of the Railway Bell, North End.]

John Greenhill, jun., *d* June 29, 1879, *a* 34.
              God moves in a mysterious way,
                His wonders to perform.

Thomas Goodwin, *d* March 7, 1873. *a* 53.
    [A foremost man in the County elections, and one of the principal originators
        of the Croydon races.]

Thomas Wigley, *d* Jan. 20, 1882, *a* 72.

Arthur Robt. Potter, *d* Oct. 31, 1879. *a* 40.

Laura Louisa, his sister, wife of William Griffin Davis, *d* March 6, 1881,
    a 35.

Emma, wife of J. T. Murray, of Coodnor, East Indies, *d* Dec. 11, 1830,
    a 35.

Mary, wife of Richd. Harman, Dunheved House, West Croydon, *d* Sept.
    15. 1880, *a* 48.

Charles Stanley Masterman, *d* Jan. 6, 1870, *a* 88.
    " He died and was gathered unto his people, being old and full of days, and
        his sons buried him."
    [A solicitor residing in the Wellesley Road.]

Ann Cadogan, *d* Dec. 25, 1879, *a* 67.

Eliza Pulford, *d* July 12, 1869. *a* 46.

Mary Ann Ringham, *d* May 21, 1880, *a* 43.

James Thomson, 150, Leadenhall Street, *d* Sept. 16, 1870, *a* 49.

Rev. Charles H. A. Ormerod, M.A., *d* Feb. 5. 1874, *a* 44.
    For we know that if our earthly house of this tabernacle were dissolved. we
        have a building of God, an house not made with hands, eternal in the
        heavens."

Laura Gertrude Ormerod, *d* Sept. 5, 1878, *a* 15.

Archie, at rest on the morning of April 22, 1879.
                Love follows him.

Marianne Marsh, *d* Nov. 7, 1876, *a* 77.

Mary Elizabeth Harcourt, *d* June 6, 1866, *a* 49.

Edward Allen Berney, *d* Oct. 17, 1870, *a* 18.

William Tice, *d* March 29, 1879, *a* 73.
Louisa Perryman, *d* July 26, 1873, *a* 84.
Martha, wife of Wm. Tice, died of consumption, July 19, 1866, *a* 26.
    She bowed with meekness to the stroke. and fell asleep in Christ.
             Calm on the bosom of thy God,
                Fair spirit, rest thee now,
             E'en while with mine thy footsteps trod
                His seal was on thy brow.
             Dust to its narrow house beneath,
                Soul to its place on high ;
             They that have seen thy look in death
                No more may fear to die.

James Norrington, *d* July 28, 1872. *a* 75.
Sarah, his wife, *d* Oct. 23, 1872, *a* 68.

Jane, daughter of Wm. and Martha Tice, *d* of bronchitis, March 23, 1868,
  a 9 and 4 months.
> Thou art gone to the grave, but 'twere wrong to deplore thee,
>   When God was thy Ransom, thy Guardian, thy Guide ;
> He gave thee, He took thee, and soon will restore thee
>   Where death hath no sting, since the Saviour hath died.

Also George, her brother, *d* July 11, 1875, *a* 19.
> Not gone from memory or love,
> But to our Father's home above.

Also William Tice, the father, *d* March 29, 1881, *a* 51.

William Barham, *d* Sept. 17, 1877, *a* 72.
> All gracious God, Thy will be done,
>   'Twas Thou that didst the blessing lend,
> And though withdrawn, I'm not alone,
>   Thou art the widow's faithful Friend.

Elizabeth, his wife, *d* Aug. 23, 1879, *a* 67.
> A tender mother and a virtuous wife
> Here sleeps in humble hope of better life,
> By side of him she loved and cherished well ;
> We leave the Judgment Day the rest to tell.

Henry Prior Farr, *d* Sept. 4, 1866, *a* 86.
Elizabeth Chilton Farr, *d* Dec. 20, 1876, *a* 84.

Ann Pratt, *d* June 23, 1875, *a* 47.
> While on the Father's love relying,
> And Jesus all her need supplying,
>   In peace she slept.

George Ansell Crippen, *d* Sept. 7, 1867, *a* 69.
Susannah Layton, his wife, *d* June 18, 1870, *a* 69.

Frederick Herbert, son of Stephen and Mary Eglantine Quelch, *d* Jan. 15
  1877, *a* 12.
> It is well with the child ; it is well.

Walter Tracy Walker, *d* Sept. 16, 1872, *a* 27.

Wm. Taylor Bruce, *d* Oct. 8, 1867, *a* 54.
Hannah T. Bruce, his wife, *d* Aug. 24, 1871, *a* 57.

Marianne, child of A. E. and E. C. Ginner, *a* 9 years and 10 months.
> These is a rest for little children,
>   Above the bright blue sky,
> Who love the blessed Saviour,
>   And to his Father cry,
> A rest from every trouble,
>   From sin and danger free,
> There every little pilgrim,
>   Shall rest eternally.

Mary, wife of James Pilbeam, *d* Aug. 10, 1875, *a* 64.
William, her son, *d* March 21, 1879, *a* 34.

Ann Kerrell, *d* Jan. 14, 1870, *a* 71.
Wm. Kerrell, her husband, *d* Feb, 10, 1878, *a* 80.
> For ever with the Lord,
>   Amen, so let it be,
> Life from the dead is in that word,
>   And immortality.

Carry, *d* April 20, 1868, *a* 8 ; Charles, *d* Jan. 8, 1869, *a* 3 ; Lizzie, *d* Feb. 9,
  1869, *a* 18 months ; children of Thomas and Caroline Hipwell.

Ann Warburton, *d* Oct. 6, 1878, *a* 80.

Sarah Maria Windle, *d* Feb. 5, 1877, *a* 85.
> Patent in suffering; cheerful under the affliction; full of love for others; sweet is the remembrance of thee, dear mother.

Rachel, wife of W. Blitz, *d* June 3, 1878, *a* 40.

Henry Farrant, *d* Oct. 7, 1870, *a* 68.
Ann, his wife, *d* Dec. 17, 1858, *a* 53.

Susanna Milward, *d* July 19, 1818, *a* 9.
> The hoary head is a crown of glory if it is found in the way of righteousness.

Samuel Simpson Toulmin, barrister-at-law, *d* March 7, 1871, *a* 68.
Susanna, his wife, *d* Sept. 11, 1881, *a* 67.

Eliza, widow of Capt. O'Shea, *d* June 13, 1874.

Henry Owens, M.D., *d* Sept. 9, 1878, *a* 40.

Lionel Foster, *d* Oct. 26, 1878, *a* 23.

Eleonora Sophia, relict of Lieut. James Love, R.H.A., *d* June 4, 1880, *a* 77.

Richard Batchelar, *d* Aug. 11, 1868, *a* 54.
> All gracious God, Thy will be done,
> 'Twas Thou that didst the blessing lend,
> And though withdrawn, I'm not alone;
> Thou art the widow's faithful friend.

Charles Mortimer, *d* May 7, 1868, *a* 2 years and 10 months; Frederick Harry, *d* May 13. 1868. *a* 1 year and 3 months; children of Harry Toulmin and Louisa Flower, of Enmore Park, South Norwood.

Edmund Lorant, *d* March 14, 1879, *a* 40.

William Holman, 8, High Street, *d* March 17, 1870, *a* 2.

Alfred Walter, son of Robt. Mills, *d* May 7, 1868, *a* 3 years and 7 months.

Margaret, wife of Robt. Lumley, *d* June 16, 1878, *a* 49.

Jean, wife of James Norris, *d* Jan. 1, 1870, *a* 77.

Cornelius Pugh, *d* Aug. 4, 1869, *a* 38.

Eliza, wife of Samuel Redman, *d* Dec. 29, 1873, *a* 53.

Robt. Wm. Farrant, *d* Dec. 3, 1872, *a* 31.
> [Mr. Farrant's bright hopeful nature brought a gleam of sunshine wherever he went.]

Little Annie, *d* June 12, 1867, *a* 4 months.

Thomas Robinson Read. *a* March 8, 1874, *a* 17.
Henry Robt. Read, *d* March 30, 1874, *a* 6.
Philip Chas. Read, *d* Nov. 1, 1877, *a* 18.

Henry Richard Martin, *d* March 26, 1880, *a* 46.
> His work concluded, ere the day was done,
> Sudden the Saviour stooped, and caught him to His throne.

Henry Sharp, *d* April 8, 1870. *a* 47.
> We wait Thy time, our Father,
> Then in the home above
> We shall be re-united
> By Christ's redeeming love.

John Rowlett, *d* July 17, 1875, *a* 86.

Wm. John Sharp, *d* Oct. 6, 1876, *a* 80.

Fanny Grant, *d* Feb. 18, 1875, *a* 51.
> I came to Jesus as I was,
> Weary and worn and sad,
> I found in Him a resting place,
> And He has made me glad.

Nellie Amelia Richards, *d* May 19, 1867, *a* 13.
Charles Thomas Richards, her father, *d* May 9, 1872, *a* 49.

Cecile Heloise Eliza Cooke, *d* Dec. 4, 1868, *a* 16.
  The sweet tender rosebud hath withered and passed away, but the thorn, alas,
    remaineth behind.

Ann Maria Chatfield, *d* Sept. 16, 1879, *a* 44.
          Though lost to sight, to memory dear,
          A loved wife lies sleeping here.

William Crickmere, for 47 years a faithful servant of the London Society
  for Promoting Christianity among the Jews, *d* June 30, 1870, *a* 78.

Susannah Clements, wife of Richd. Clements, *d* Nov. 20, 1870, *a* 51.

Wm. Henry Gardner, *d* June 15, 1869, *a* 29.
          Dearest, thou art gone before me,
          And thy soul, we trust, is flown
          Where tears are wiped from every eye,
          And sorrow is unknown.
          Where thou art sure to meet the good,
          Whom on earth thou lovedst best,
          Where the wicked cease from troubling,
          And the weary are at rest.
  Erected by his affectionate lover, E. Halls.

Mary, wife of Thomas Southgate, *d* Aug. 21, 1875, *a* 64.
          While on her Father's love relying,
          And Jesus all her need supplying,
            In peace she slept.

Also Thomas Southgate, *d* Oct. 13, 1876, *a* 69.

Selina Hillman, *d* Oct. 6, 1872.
Elizabeth Hillman, *d* Dec. 4, 1878, *a* 85.

Henry Gale, *d* Sept. 23, 1872, *a* 24.

William Blackburn, *d* March 30, 1875, *a* 70.

Susannah Mary, daughter of Robt. Dods, *d* Oct. 21, 1868, *a* 20.

George Kember, *d* Oct. 8th, 1868, *a* 35.
Henrietta May, his daughter, *d* March 22, 1868, *a* 7.

Major Richard William Meheux, *d* at Sydenham, Nov, 20, 1868, *a* 59.

Mary Maltby, widow, *d* May 17, 1874, *a* 75.

James Steer, *d* April 2, 1874, *a* 51.
Mary, his wife, *d* March 11, 1874, *a* 47.
  In life they were together, and in death were not divided.

Charles Goodwin, *d* March 5, 1875, *a* 46.
          Since Thou hast called me to resign
          What most I prized, it ne'er was mine,
          I only yielded what was Thine.
            Thy will be done.

Caroline Gillespie, wife of Commander R. Patton Jenkins, R.N., *d* Feb. 15,
    1881, *a* 39.
Caroline Mary Beatrice, *d* Dec. 12, 1877, *a* 10.
Alice Eleanor Maud, *d* April 20, 1873, *a* 6 months.

Sarah Moxam, spinster, *d* March 14, 1869, *a* 81.

Joseph Hollidge, *d* Oct. 4, 1873, *a* 51.

Ann James, *d* Aug. 29, 1873, *a* 65,
          This humble stone records no titled fame,
          But better far, a Christian servant's name.

F. Bowden, High Street, *d* Feb. 26, 1878, *a* 46.
Also two children.

> He was a good husband, a kind father, and a sincere friend.

> [Mr. Bowden was one of the most respected of the Croydon tradesmen, and his early loss was universally deplored. He had formerly been in the service of Messrs. Hammond & Purrott ; and was subsequently partner in the firm of Redgrove & Bowden, ironmongers, High Street.]

Charles Chambers, *d* July 16, 1881, *a* 59.
Mary Chambers, *d* June 26, 1881, *a* 67.

> Lovely and pleasant were their lives, and in death they were not divided.

James Elliott, *d* March 15, 1869.
Jane, his widow, *d* Oct. 1, 1880.

Sophia, wife of Edward Samuel Edwards, *d* Nov. 3, 1880, *a* 63.

George Link, *d* July 25, 1881, *a* 80.

Mary, wife of Philip Secretan, Esq., of Harestone, Caterham, *d* March 11, 1869, *a* 54.
Philip Secretan, *d* April 4, 1877, *a* 58.

John Steer, *d* June 21, 1869, *a* 74.
Ann, his wife, *d* June 17, 1879, *a* 87.

Eliza Ann, daughter of John Thomas Burgess, *d* Jan. 18, 1869, *a* 3½.

Mary Punnett, *d* Feb. 1, 1873, *a* 51.
Rebecca, her sister, relict of Alfred Veriom, Esq., of Chumbra, Weynaad, Malabar, *d* Nov. 15, 1872, *a* 41.

William Henry Hughes, *d* Oct. 24, 1878, *a* 42.

Eliza Hawes, wife of Wm. Fox Hawes, of North Park, *d* April 7, 1878, *a* 39.

James Tart, *d* Feb. 18, 1874 *a* 59.
Frank Leonard, infant grandson, *d* Feb. 21, 1874.

Mary Ann, wife of Wm. Godson, *d* Nov. 27, 1868, *a* 47.
Wm. Godson, *d* Dec. 5. 1872, *a* 72.

> [For a number of years chief clerk at the Union Bank, Croydon.]

Arthur Butchers, *d* July 11, 1877, *a* 64.

John Paull Lang, *d* Nov. 29, 1873, *a* 39.

Elizabeth Carrick, *d* Nov. 8, 1868, *a* 64.

Emily Godfrey, *d* May 10, 1872, *a* 66.

Mary, wife of Wm. Godfrey, *d* Sept. 14, 1868, *a* 69.

> Long time I've been a sufferer,
> But the Lord has set me free,
> And called me to his own elect,
> So do not weep for me.

Mary Needland, wife of Benjamin Gibbins, *d* April 9, 1879.

Anne, wife of John Quittenton, *d* May 8, 1873, *a* 60.

> The winter of trouble is past,
> The storms of affliction are o'er,
> Her struggle is ended at last,
> And sorrow and death are no more.

John Quittenton, *d* Dec. 17, 1875, *a* 59.

John Chauncey Jones, *d* Dec. 23, 1879, *a* 61.
Clarissa, his wife, *d* Nov. 11, 1872, *a* 51.

Charlotte, wife of Wm. Todman, *d* July 23, 1881, *a* 72.

N

Samuel Stovell, *d* Aug, 2, 1877, *a* 59.

Mr. Stovell was the principal poulterer in the town, and carried on an extensive business in the High-street. After he had secured the assistance of his sons, like others who have plodded along the dusty road of life, he required a little leisure and relaxation, and in order to secure these advantages, he built a pretty cottage in Warrington-road, Duppas Hill; but notwithstanding his walks to and from his shop, the salubrity of the atmosphere, and the pleasures he derived from his suburban residence, his health failed, and to the great grief of his family and friends, he passed away at a comparatively early age.

Isabella Stovell, *d* Aug. 13, 1882, *a* 1 year and 10 months.

Thomas Trilleo, *d* May 18, 1882, *a* 69.
   [A former landlord of the "Fox and Hounds," West Croydon.]
Mary Ann, his wife, *d* Nov. 17, 1881, *a* 62.

Thomas Boileau Trilleo, *d* July 8, 1874, *a* 31.
   This stone was erected by his sister.
   "And God shall wipe away all tears from their eyes, and there shall be no more death, neither sorrow, nor crying, neither shall there be any more pain, for the former things have passed away."

John George Drinkwater, *d* April 26, 1877.

Robert Streeter, *d* April 23, 1873, *a* 79.

Mr. Streeter was formerly a butcher in Surrey-street (then called Butchers' Row), and carried on business in the shop now occupied by Mr. Dunham. His father also carried on an extensive business as a butcher for many years, and the family were well known and respected.

Louisa, his daughter, and wife of Thos. Henry Ebbutt, *d* Nov. 29, 1874, *a* 41.

Joseph Steer, *d* Jan. 29, 1872, *a* 73.
Elizabeth Mary Steer, *d* March 11, 1879, *a* 80.

Susannah Harding, *d* June 3, 1870, *a* 9.

In memory of our only one, Ernest Page, *d* Aug. 24, 1870, *a* 6 months.
   Our little boy gone.

Emeline Mary Moore, daughter of John Rhodes, *d* April 1, 1870, *a* 1 year.
Mary Agnes Moore, *d* Jan. 14, 1876, *a* 16 months.

William, son of Rose and Wm. Prodham, *d* April 19, 1870, *a* 5½.
Valentine (dear little Julie), *d* Aug. 3, 1877, *a* 1 years and 8 months.

Henry Selby Hayr, of Linden lodge, Thornton Heath, *d* June 28, 1881, *a* 43.
   [A partner with Mr. Stephen West, wholesale butcher, Church Street.]

Emma Jane, wife of Wm. M. Perkins, *d* June. 24, 1879, *a* 47.
   I heard the voice of Jesus say,
   "Come unto me and rest."

Eleanor, wife of Edward Garaty, *d* Dec. 4, 1880, *a* 50.

Thomas Whiffin, who was killed at Cannon Street Railway Station, Nov. 17, 1879, *a* 82.

Elizabeth, wife of George Harmer, *d* July 30, 1881, *a* 50.

Samuel Webb, of 36. Surrey Street, *d* Jan. 7, 1881, *a* 50.

> He is not dead, but lieth sleeping,
> In the sweet refuge of his Master's breast,
> And far away from sorrow, toil, and weeping ;
> He is not dead, but only taking rest.

Samuel William Webb, his only son, *d* Jan. 11, 1882, *a* 17.

> With love I gazed on thee, dear boy,
> And watched the opening bloom ;
> But all the hopes I had in thee
> Are withered in the tomb.

George Holliday Holledge, late of Sunnydene, London Road, *d* June 30th, 1882, *a* 66.

> [Mr. Holledge, with Mr. Freeman, secured the land for the Croydon Ceme-
> tery, and were voted £100 each by the Burial Board for their success.]

Eliza, his wife, *d* Sept. 23, 1882, *a* 65.

> It is the voice of Jesus that I hear
> His are the hands stretched out to draw me near,
> And His the blood that can for all atone,
> And set me faultless there before the Throne.

Henry James Grantham, *d* Oct. 1, 1882, *a* 25.

Alfred Draper, *b* Aug. 6, 1838, *d* Oct. 2, 1882.

William Henry Hulbert, *d* June 13, 1882, *a* 74.

> " Sorrow may endure for a night, but joy cometh in the morning."

Mary Elizabeth, wife of H. J. Close, at rest April 21, 1882, *a* 85.

Henry Thomas Smith, *d* July 4, 1882. *a* 60.
Eleanor Mary, his wife, *d* May 12, 1882, *a* 61.

> After many years' suffering, borne with Christian fortitude.

Mary Stone, at rest, Aug. 27, 1881.

> Thine eyes shall see the King in His glory.

James Gordon, *d* June 27, 1882, *a* 69.

End of Church of England Ground.

NONCONFORMIST SIDE,

Commencing at the end nearest Queen's Road.

Robert Orr. of Orland Villa. Bedford Park, *d* Jan. 5, 1874, *a* 80.

> [Mr. Orr had amassed an ample fortune during his younger years abroad, and
> spent the evening of his life in quiet retirement in Croydon. where his
> tall, commanding figure was as well known as his sedate yet courteous
> manner was esteemed.]

George Spooner, of Church Road, Upper Norwood, *d* March 12, 1874. *a* 49
Charles Spooner, his son, drowned at Trinidad, West Indies, March 2 1870, *a* 18.

Thomas Oxford, *d* April 8, 1874, *a* 41.

> Jesus loves me, he who died,
> Heaven's gate to open wide,
> He has washed away my sin,
> Let his loved one enter in.

Sarah, wife of Thos. Jas. Marrion, of South Norwood, *d* Aug. 18, 1882. *a* 74.

> I am so tired, let me rest.
> " Come unto me all ye that are weary and heavy laden, and I will give you
> rest."

Louisa Ann, wife of Mr. John Gray, Dingwall Road, *d* March 4, 1866, *a* 60.

John Gray, Buckland Lodge, born (to die) June 2, 1807, died (to live again) May 20, 1877.

> Mr. Gray was the successful and highly-respected printer and bookseller of High-street (afterwards Gray and Warren, and now Roffey and Clark). He was also a printer and bookseller's valuer, in which profession he ranked very high. He was *facile princeps* as an arithmetician, and he has been heard to observe that he delighted in disentangling accounts that were intricate and complicated. We believe that after he had left business as a bookseller, and had retired to Buckland Lodge, he still retained the trade of a valuer, in which he was most successful. He was also a valuable Director of the Gas Company, and was missed and regretted by his colleagues; and taking him for " all in all," it is hardly an exaggeration to state that " none but himself could be his parallel."

Elizabeth Harrison, widow, *d* March 30, 1874, *a* 74.

Penelope, wife of John Wilson. Lansdowne Road, *d* Dec. 13, 1866, *a* 41.

> After very long and intense suffering endured with wonderful patience and Christian resignation.

Sarah Maria Aris, *d* May 20, 1880, *a* 50.

Elizabeth, wife of Wm. J. Lewis, *d* March 18, 1865, *a* 60.

Edwin Coleman, *d* March 27, 1867, *a* 26.

Charles, his brother, *d* May 1, 1868, *a* 22.

Mary Bullock, of Lansdowne Road, who suddenly but very peacefully passed away June 30. 1874, *a* 68.

> Nothing in my hand I bring,
> Simply to Thy cross I cling.

George Axford, *d* July 28, 1874, *a* 27.

> I came to Jesus as I was,
> Weary and worn and sad,
> I found in Him a resting-place,
> And He has made me glad.

Also Mary Jane Axford, his niece, *d* Sept. 20, 1878, *a* 3 years and 9 months.

Christian Jane Carpenter, *d* Dec. 29, 1868, *a* 73.

> One gentle sigh her fetters broke,
> We scarce could say, she's gone,
> Before her willing spirit took
> Its mansion near the throne.

William Carpenter, her husband, *d* June 10, 1874, *a* 73.

> His dying testimony—
> A guilty weak and worthless worm,
> On Thy kind arm I fall ;
> Be Thou my strength and righteousness,
> My Jesus and my All.

Ruth Smith, *d* July 2, 1871, *a* 76.

> A loving and beloved mother.
> Father, I bless thy gentle hand,
> How kind was the chastening rod,
> That forced my conscience to a stand,
> And brought my wand'ring soul to God.

William Thrift, *d* Dec. 30, 1879, *a* 84.
> So he giveth his beloved sleep.

Eliza Dickson, *d* March 12, 1871, *a* 69.

Deborah Anscombe, *d* Jan. 1, 1869, *a* 20.

Eliza Jane Axford, *d* July 31, 1881, *a* 29.

Alfred Richardson, *d* Oct. 1, 1863, *a* 18.
George William Richardson, *d* Jan. 2, 1880, *a* 37.
Annie Richardson, *d* Feb. 7, 1871, *a* 22.

Ann Walden, *d* Sept. 20, 1876, *a* 77.

Ellen, wife of Joseph Staples, *d* Nov. 9, 1875, *a* 27.

George Easton, *d* Oct. 18, 1871, *a* 21.

Richard Mott, *d* Feb. 17, 1866, *a* 63.
> On Christ the solid rock I stand,
> All other props are sinking sand.

Elizabeth, wife of G. Shirley, *d* Feb. 7, 1870, *a* 58.
> For 38 years a faithful member of the Wesleyan Society.
> When this poor lisping stammering tongue
> Lies silent in the grave,
> Then in a nobler sweeter song
> I'll sing His power to save.

Louisa Clarissa Gray, *d* Jan. 38, 1865, *a* 78.

William Goff, *d* June 4, 1874, *a* 85.

Rev. John Nelson, who during 54 years of his life, at home and abroad, was a faithful minister of Christ, *b* 1798, *d* 1873.
> The religious shall be in everlasting remembrance.

When the congregation of Baptists removed from Pump Pail to the new chapel in the Tamworth Road, Mr. Nelson, who was then living in a well-earned retirement in Croydon, took the old Salem Chapel, and gratuitously conducted the services for some time as well as his failing health would allow him. His ministrations to the poor were much appreciated and blessed, his memory being held in just affection.

Susannah, wife of Thomas Crutchett, *d* Sept. 12, 1875, *a* 38.

Rev. Joseph Whiting, minister of South Croydon Congregational Church, *d* Oct. 14, 1875, *a* 58.
> Blessed are the dead which die in the Lord, from henceforth; yea, saith the Spirit, that they may rest from their labours, and their works do follow them.
> I gave unto them eternal life, and they shall never perish, neither shall any pluck them out of my hand.

Mr. Whiting was for many years a Congregational minister at Bideford, and had chosen Croydon to spend the evening of his life. His love for the cause of religion, however, induced him to take charge of the South Croydon congregation, then worshipping in an iron chapel at the corner of Parker Road. This soon proving too small, he mainly by his own untiring efforts, built the present handsome Church in the Aberdeen Road. He was a Christian gentleman in every sense of the word, a classical scholar, and a cheerful companion. He lived at Sedgfield Villa, St. Peter's Road.

Henrietta Wratten, *d* June 23, 1870, *a* 14.

Eliza Willis, *d* Sept. 21, 1870, *a* 27.

Edward Parsons, *d* March 17, 1876, *a* 10 months.

Keziah, wife of John Wratten, *d* April 7, 1879, *a* 68. †

Mary, wife of John Roberts, *d* April 28, 1879, *a* 68.

Wm. Henry Rivers, *d* Jan. 21, 1866, *a* 63.

Grace, relict of the Rev. C. N. Davies, late tutor of Brecon College, South Wales, *d* Feb. 26, 1874, *a* 76.

Sarah Elizabeth Mary Ann, wife of Wm. Toy, *d* May 29, 1865, *a* 24.

Rev. Wm. Matthew Robertson, *d* June 30, 1866, *a* 36.

Lydianna, his wife, *d* Jan. 2, 1865, *a* 31.

Richard Cort, Esq., *d* March 4, 1866, *a* 82.
> The last surviving son of the late Henry Cort, the father of the British Iron Trade, and the Tubal Cain of our country.—*Times*, July 29, 1856.

Thomas Chard, *d* Oct. 22, 1867, *a* 41.

Thomassinia Chard, *d* Feb. 16, 1876, *a* 76.

James Axford, *d* April 21, 1874, *a* 67.
> Why should our tears in sorrow flow,
> When God recalls his own,
> And bids them leave a world of woe,
> For an immortal crown.

John Kent, *d* Feb. 20, 1866, *a* 59.
> Being taken from you for a short time in presence, not in heart.

Lucy Plowman, *d* July 8, 1865, *a* 28.
> Waiting here the morning of the first resurrection.

Mary, wife of Wm. Batchelar, *d* March 4, 1866, *a* 58.

Wm. Batchelar, *d* Jan. 20, 1881, *a* 72.

Julian Brack, wife of Andrew Kerr, *d* July 24, 1864.
> Thus we part, but not for ever,
> Joyful hopes our bosoms swell,
> They who love the Saviour never,
> Know a long, a last farewell,
> Blissful unions
> Lie beyond this parting vale.

Helen Murray Liddell, her granddaughter, *d* Nov. 11, 1874, *a* 22.

Caroline Stollens, *d* Jan. 19, 1873, *a* 25.

Ebenezer Palmer, formerly of Paternoster Row, *d* March 22, 1866, *a* 82.

George Savage, *d* June 15, 1866, *a* 31.

Bertha, *b* July 29, 1862, *d* Dec. 4, 1865.
> Gone from this room into the next.

George Shurlock, suddenly snatched away June 26, 1866, *a* 47.
> Reader, art thou ready to meet thy God ?
> [Formerly an undertaker in Tamworth Road.]

Walter, son of J. and C. Burton, *d* July 10, 1865, *a* 2.

Alfred Burton, *d* July 4, 1881, *a* 20.

Joseph Brown, *d* April 21, 1876, *a* 66.
> The Lord is good, a stronghold in the day of trouble ; and He knoweth them that trust in Him.

Mary Ellen, wife of Alfred S. Groom, of Thornton Heath, *d* April 29, 1873, *a* 28.

Lily, infant daughter, *d* April 28, 1873.
> So he bringeth them unto their desired haven.

Richard Goddard, *d* Aug. 2, 1866, *a* 45.
    " The voice said, Cry! And he said, What shall I cry? All flesh is grass, and all the goodliness thereof is as the flower of the field."

Mary Newman, *d* May 11, 1870, *a* 82.

Ellen Johnson, *d* Feb. 28, 1874, *a* 44.
Ann Johnson, her mother, *d* June 2, 1874, *a* 74.
              If thou should'st call me to resign,
              What most I prize, it ne'er was mine,
              I only yield thee what was thine,
                    Thy will be done.

Hettey, wife of Henry Appleby, *d* Oct. 31, 1863, *a* 36.

Margaret, wife of William Lowe, *d* July 12, 1872, *a* 47.
William Lowe, *d* Dec. 27, 1881, *a* 56.

George Norton, of Westerham, Kent, *d* July 25, 1874, *a* 78.
              My hope is fixed on nothing less,
              Than Jesu's blood and righteousness.

Mary Ann Tancock, *d* Feb. 20, 1875.

Emily Louisa, daughter of George Thomas King, of Holloway, *d* Nov. 12, 1870, *a* 5 years and 8 months.

Hannah, wife of Jabez Smith, *d* Oct. 27, 1875, *a* 43.
              What cheering words are these,
              Their sweetness who can tell;
              In time and to eternal days
              'Tis with the righteous well.

Joseph Tennison, *d* July 14, 1875, *a* 65.

Alfred Runacres, *d* Dec. 17, 1873, *a* 42.

Eliza Mary, wife of George Auber, *d* April 4, 1878, *a* 45.
Walter, her son, *d* Sept. 4, 1871, *a* 7.

John Edward Arnold, *d* Aug. 8, 1878, *a* 39.
    [Of the firm of Arnold and Coldwells. His comparatively early death from consumption was much deplored by his family and friends.]
James, his son, *d* Jan. 2, 1873, *a* 7.

Frank Marmion, son of Frank M. and Maria Coldwells, *d* Sept. 11, 1871, *a* 17.
    [A most promising lad when he was untimely snatched away by fever.]
Margaret Alice Coldwells, *d* Sept. 9, 1872, *a* 8 months.
                  The flower fadeth.

Caroline, wife of Henry Theobald, *d* March 4, 1871, *a* 30.
Henry Theobald, *d* Nov. 24, 1871, *a* 31.

Harry, son of James R. and Mary Payne, *d* July 29, 1869, *a* 11.
Mrs. Mary Kirkham, his grandmother, *d* Oct. 9, 1866, *a* 90.

Sarah, wife of Geo. Perkins, *d* Nov. 9, 1871, *a* 53.
              Be still, and know that I am God.

Ann Merrick, *d* March 9, 1867, *a* 75.
           If I am found in Jesu's hands, my soul cannot be lost.

Wm. Bishop, died suddenly March 14, 1869, *a* 73.
Emma Bishop, his wife, *d* Oct. 23, 1878, *a* 79.
Also infant grandson.

Elizabeth Ann, wife of Thos. Candy, *d* Sept. 21, 1872, *a* 43.
    Her kindness of heart and self-sacrificing disposition endeared her to all who knew her. Safe with Jesus, not a wave of trouble rolls across her peaceful breast.

Amos, youngest son of John and Mary Fuller, *d* April 6, 1872, *a* 27.

Jane, wife of Charles Sheppard, *d* Sept. 25, 1866, *a* 57.
> Reader! art thou prepared to die?   Now is the accepted time ; now is the day of salvation.

Mary, wife of George Sherrin, *d* Jan. 11, 1868, *a* 74.

Johanna Mary, wife of James Browning, *d* Nov. 28, 1878, *a* 56.

Elizabeth Roberts, wife of P. R. H. Henson, *d* May 10, 1869, *a* 49.

James Wm., son of Joseph and Jane Campbell, *d* April 8, 1866, *a* 3.
Joseph, his elder brother, *d* Jan 14, 1882, *a* 28.

Lydia Sarah, daughter of J. and S. Thomson, *d* April 15, 1865, *a* 1½.
> Here our little Lydia lies,
> But her soul our Shepherd keeps,
> With the host of lambs above,
> In His everlasting love.

J. R. Thomson, *d* Sept. 3, 1880, *a* 19.
J. S. Thomson, *d* Jan. 29, 1868, *a* 9 months.

Emily, daughter of Joseph Hallett, *d* July 11, 1863, *a* 3.

Ann, wife of George Sparkes, *d* Jan. 24, 1880, *a* 59.

Thomas May Simson, *d* Nov. 21, 1873, *a* 76.
Rosa, his widow, *d* Dec. 14, 1876, *a* 54.

Ruth, daughter of Samuel Page, *d* April 5, 1875, *a* 5.

George Alfred Hinton, *d* Sept. 2, 1874, *a* 23.

Alice, widow of Robt. Smith Stubbs, *d* Jan. 21, 1871, *a* 69.

Elizabeth, wife of Chas. J. Moss, *d* July 9, 1870, *a* 34.
Wilfred Moss, their son, *d* Jan. 19, 1877, *a* 8.

Dr. David Munro, *d* April 23, 1869, *a* 29.
> More than conquerors through Him that loved us.

Agnes Jervis, *d* Aug. 20, 1867, *a* 62.

Mary Ann, daughter of James H. and S. Sanders, *d* Dec. 11, 1864, *a* 41.

Philippa, wife of Samuel Miles Benson, *d* May 31, 1873, *a* 49.
> Hear what God, the Lord, hath spoken,
> Oh, my people, faint and few,
> Comfortless, afflicted, broken,
> Fair abodes I build for you.
>
> Thorns of heartfelt tribulation,
> Shall no more perplex your ways,
> You shall name your walls salvation,
> And your gates shall all be praise.

Joseph Charles Philpot, M.A., late of Stamford, *d* Dec. 9, 1869, *a* 67.
> He was widely known and greatly beloved by the living family of God, for whom he laboured abundantly by tongue and pen.   He being dead yet speaketh.
> This monument is erected by his bereaved widow and children.

Adelaide Ann Mary, daughter of Reuben Vincent and Mary Ann Barrow, *d* July 26, 1875, *a* 13.

Nathaniel Bogle French, *d* Sept. 11, 1876, *a* 48.
> With Christ which is far better.
> For our light affliction, which is but for a moment, worketh for us a far more exceeding and eternal weight of glory.

Rev. Samuel Barrows, of Shanklin, Isle of Wight, *d* Feb. 4, 1881 ; and Mary Ann, his widow, *d* Jan. 26, 1879, *a* 71.

John Atkin, of Thorn Bank, Chepstow Road, *d* July 3, 1876, *a* 47.

Lydie A. King, *d* Oct. 20, 1876. *a* 42.
Howard Shepherd King, *a* 3 months.

Mary, wife of Wm. Clarkson, 1882.

Herbert Stradling Skeates, *d* Oct. 12, 1881, *a* 53.
[A son-in-law of the late Edward Miall, editor of *The Nonconformist*.]
Herbert Allan, his son, *d* March 20, 1878, *a* 26.

Elizabeth Virgin, widow of James Billings, who after a self sacrificing and Christian life, sweetly entered into rest July 8, 1879, *a* 82.
My days of praise shall ne'er be past,
While life. and thought. and being last.
Or immortality endure.

To the sweet memory of Alice Cecil, fifth daughter of John Reid and Susan Jackson, *d* Oct. 17, 1877. *a* 34.
Purified and made white. among the lilies, by the grace of God. She has been a succourer of many and of myself also.

Eliza, wife of R. W. Russell, *d* March 26, 1879, *a* 67.

Mary Ann, wife of Wm. Wheeler. *d* March 21, 1879, *a* 69.
A sinner saved by grace.

William Wheeler, *d* May 30, 1881, *a* 70.

David, son of Wm. Ashby, *d* April 30. 1872, *a* 10.

Mr. James Warren, *d* Dec. 21, 1867. *a* 57.
Deeply lamented by his sorrowing wife, for he was an affectionate husband, and a sincere friend.
Weep not, dear friends, although on earth
My time with you is past,
With Christ alone we hope to meet,
Where happiness will last.

Sarah, wife of Thomas Shadbolt. *d* Feb. 21, 1878, *a* 51.
Josephine Elizabeth, his daughter, *d* Nov. 7, 1861, *a* 9.

George Matthew, *d* Sept. 16. 1879, *a* 62.

John Bishop, *d* Dec. 20, 1867.

Althea Sophia, wife of John C. Kersey, *d* June 3, 1879.

Susan Dennis, spinster, *d* April 3. 1882.
Thirty years faithful servant in the family of the late Thomas Diller, of Thornton Heath.

Thomas H. Graley, of Thornton Heath, *d* July 14, 1876, *a* 74.
Louisa Graley, his sister, *d* Aug. 26, 1875, *a* 60.
Fondly loved and deeply regretted by all who knew her.

John Greenwood Graley, *d* Sept. 22, 1881, *a* 79.

Elizabeth, wife of G. R. Bell, *d* Feb. 4, 1875, *a* 52.
George Alexander Bell, *d* June 26, 1877, *a* 60.
"And they shall be mine, saith the Lord of Hosts, in the day when I make up my jewels."

Ann, wife of Thomas Brooker, *d* Nov. 18, 1875, *a* 54.

Thomas Garniss, *d* July 19, 1861, *a* 64.
[Mr. Garniss was formerly principal of the late Fairfield House School, in which he was succeeded by Mr. A. Twentyman. He was the first man buried in this Cemetery.]
Anne, his widow, *d* March 16, 1877, *a* 80.
William Ridley Garniss, *d* Feb. 20, 1864, *a* 3.
Frederick William, his brother, *d* July 21, 1868, *a* 7 months.

William Lewis, *d* Aug. 16, 1861, *a* 67.

> Dear friends, farewell, at God's command,
> I summoned was before His bar to stand ;
> This sudden stroke of death calls loud on thee
> For to prepare yourselves to follow me.

James Lewis, his son, *d* Sept. 27, 1861, *a* 37.

Richard Brain, *d* Dec. 18, 1864, *a* 81.

> Oh, glorious hour ; oh, blessed abode,
> I shall be near and like my God,
> And flesh and sense no more control
> The sacred pleasures of my soul.

Mary Brain, his wife, *d* June 2, 1866, *a* 77.

Phœbe Mary, daughter of Robt. and Phœbe Brain, *d* May 8, 1872.

> Great the joy, the union sweet,
> When the saints in glory meet,
> Where the theme is still the same,
> Where they praise Jehovah's name.

John Sugden, *d* April 28, 68, *a* 61.

> His soul the second death defies,
> And reigns eternal in the skies.

Sarah, wife of Robt. Mortimer, *d* Nov. 30, 1861, *a* 45.

> With patience to the last, she did submit,
> And murmured not at what the Lord thought fit,
> With Christian spirit did her soul resign,
> Returned to God at His appointed time.

Mrs. Jane Mortimer, *d* May 17, 1871, *a* 86.

W. M. Chambers, *d* May 23, 1866, *a* 66.
Mary, his wife, *d* Oct. 20, 1872.

Esther Ann, wife of James Dryland, of 42, Thornton Heath, *d* Dec. 13, 1874, *a* 76.

Mary Kentish, *d* March 31, 1862, *a* 82.

Thomas Diller, of Thornton Heath, *d* Dec. 10, 1871, *a* 85.

Mary Ann, widow of Thomas Penson, *d* July 18, 1863, *a* 64.

Rachael Mary, wife of Chas. Penson, *d* Feb. 7, 1874, *a* 28.

Thomas Holliday, builder, *d* suddenly Jan. 26th, 1875, *a* 55.

> A kind, intelligent, and affectionate husband and father, greatly beloved and regretted by all who knew him.

William West, *d* Jan. 26, 1876, *a* 73.
Fredk. Evans, his grandson, *d* Feb. 12, 1876, *a* 6.

Elizabeth Hannah Rogers, *d* Dec. 17, 1862, *a* 2 years and 8 months.
Fredk. Rogers, *d* Dec. 16, 1867, *a* 7 months.
Florence Emily Rogers, *d* Sept. 13, 1878, *a* 17.

> Children of Edward and Elizabeth Rogers, and grandchildren of Wm. West, sen.

William West, of North End, *d* Oct. 13, 1878, *a* 40.

> For me to live is Christ, and to die is gain.
> Then farewell to evil, a final farewell,
> Shut in for ever with Jesus to dwell.

Elizabeth Pennick Hickmott, *d* Aug. 9, 1878, *a* 79.

Kate West, *d* Jan. 9, 1871, *a* 4 months.
Alfred West, *d* Dec. 14, 1873, *a* 7 months.

> Children of Wm. and Eleanor Elliott West, of North End.

Rachael Mannerson, *d* Sept. 23, 1872, *a* 58.

Henry Glover, *d* Nov. 3, 1876, *a* 69.

Robert Knell, *d* Oct. 21, 1877. *a* 84.

Vincent Wm. Ballard, *d* Feb. 5, 1877, *a* 33.
> Who lived in that faith and died in the hope of an eternal inheritance. which Christ the Redeemer of all the elect family of God wrought out by His glorious resurrection from the dead.

To the pure soul of Matilda, wife of James Francis Morgan, *d* Feb. 7. 1880. *a* 62.

Sarah Ann, wife of Arthur Richard May, *d* Sept. 12, 1863, *a* 23.

Ann Martin, for many years the faithful and affectionate housekeeper to the family of James Taylor, Esq., Ravenswood, *d* Jan. 14, 1865, *a* 79.

Mary, wife of Geo. W. H. Tharp, *d* Feb. 17, 1864, *a* 39.

Oliver Samuel (Olly). youngest son of Jesse W. and Maria Ward, who passed away 23rd Nov., 1877, *a* 3½.
> " For of such is the kingdom of heaven."

Emily, wife of Richard Landon, *d* July 25, 1881, *a* 41.

Emily Charlotte, daughter of A. C. Jones, *d* Nov. 27, 1863, *a* 6 months.

Edward Brown, *d* Feb. 29, 1864. *a* 74.

Mrs. Ann Dalton, his sister, *d* May 6, 1867, *a* 81.

Mary Ann Thomas Candish, *d* Aug. 6, 1864, *a* 68.

Sarah Collins, *d* Aug. 3, 1876, *a* 82.

Martha, wife of Chas. John Lee, *d* March 6, 1873, *a* 49.

John Thorn, son of Wm. and Elizabeth Thorn, *d* Feb. 13, 1873, *a* 9½.

Mary, wife of Richd. Gaston, *d* Feb. 1, 1864, *a* 75.
> Now the grave's a downy bed,
> Embroidered round with blood,
> Say not the believer's dead,
> She only rests in God.

Mary Ann, wife of Joseph Brown, *d* Oct. 15, 1868, *a* 36.
> Every moment since her dying hour,
> My loss I keenly feel,
> But trust I feel the Saviour's power,
> To sanctify and heal.

Eliza, wife of Edward Dixon. *d* March 25, 1877, *a* 46.

Wm. Edward, her son, *d* March 21, 1864, *a* 6 years and 10 months.

Philip Denny, *d* July 31, 1877, *a* 37.

Alfred Woodhams, *d* April 9, 1865, *a* 49.
> Having a desire to depart and be with Christ.

James Shankland, 11, Katharine Street, died suddenly April 14, 1872, *a* 42.
> Let manhood think that death may come,
> When least it seemeth nigh,
> And though content with this bright home,
> Yet be prepared to die.

Richd. Dallow, *d* March 21, 1874, *a* 21.

Jane Jenkins, *d* Sept. 8, 1874, *a* 23.
> She's safe in her Father's home above,
> In the place prepared by her Saviour's love.

Mrs. Emma White, *d* Jan. 25, 1872, *a* 66.

Elizabeth, wife of John Evans, of Waddon New Road, *d* Sept. 29, 1872, *a* 50.

Arabella Palmer, *d* May 17, 1871, *a* 33.
> I will see you again.—JOHN xvi, 32.

Wm. Hall, *d* Feb. 5, 1878, *a* 66.

Emily, wife of Edgar Newby, of Walpole Cottage, Whitehorse Road,
     d June 10, 1878, *a* 66.

William Childs, of Selhurst, *d* March 10, 1874, *a* 44.

Samuel Rogers, *d* March 28, 1875, *a* 41.
Anna Agnes Kate Rogers, *d* Feb. 7, 1882, *a* 18.

Parnel, wife of Thos. Forman, of South Norwood, *d* Nov. 29, 1870, *a* 42.

Jane Mary, wife of A. W. P. Keep, *d* Jan. 29, 1877, *a* 49.

John Skere, *d* Jan. 7, 1870, *a* 68.
Frances, his wife, *d* Oct. 31, 1871, *a* 78.

George Richard, infant son of Geo. John and Ann Jones, High Street, *d*
     Oct. 13, 1874, *a* 4 months.
Wm. Henry, his brother, *d* March 12, 1876, *a* 4 months.
Elizabeth Ann, his sister, *d* April 4, 1879, *a* 3.

Emma, wife of Jas. Hanscomb, *d* May 18, 1880, *a* 65.
> Rest from thy labour, rest
> Soul of the just, set free;
> Blest be thy memory, and blest
> Thy bright example be.

James Hanscomb, *d* May 18, 1882, *a* 80.

Emma, wife of Alfred Brooks, *d* May 2, 1882, *a* 62.
> No one knows how much we miss her,
> None but aching hearts can tell;
> Earth has lost her, Heaven has won her,
> Jesus doeth all things well!

John Thomas Walford, *d* Feb. 21, 1876, *a* 86.
> Absent from the body, but present with the Lord.

Dear little Florry, third child of Charles and Louisa Hunt, *d* July 1, 1875,
     a 2.
> To us for two short years,
> Her infant smiles were given,
> And then she bade farewell to earth,
> And went to dwell in heaven.

David Lauchlan, *d* Oct. 30, 1869, *a* 64.
Wm. Thomas, his youngest son, *d* March 30, 1877, *a* 13.

Emily Ann Broughton, *d* June 8, 1875, *a* 30.
> Safe in the arms of Jesus,
> Safe on His gentle breast,
> There by His love o'ershaded,
> Sweetly my soul doth rest.

John Albert Broughton, her youngest son, *d* Sept. 9, 1881, *a* 8.

Jonathan Johnson Martin, *d* Sept. 10, 1875, *a* 36.
> Waiting until the day break.

James Gray, *d* May 1, 1869, *a* 74.
> For some years deacon of the Congregational Church, George Street.

Eliza, wife of George H. Couch, *d* Nov. 14, 1878, *a* 36.
> We shall not all sleep, but we shall all be changed.

Percy Charles, infant son of J. Compton Rickett, *d* Aug. 19, 1877.

Chas. Wm. W. Frisch, *d* Oct. 30, 1875, *a* 26.

Jane, wife of John Couch, *d* July 8, 1869, *a* 63.

George Couch Gunn, his grandson, *d* Dec. 21, 1868, *a* 13.

Esther Mary, wife of Robt. Edward Hart, 57, High Street, *d* July 7, 1872, *a* 27.

> Knowing as I am known,
> How shall I love that word,
> And oft repeat before the throne,
> " For ever with the Lord."

Richd. Trotman, *d* Feb. 13, 1872, *a* 68.

Elizabeth, his wife, *d* April 12, 1874, *a* 63.

Emily, eldest daughter of Wm. and Mary Lock, *d* Aug. 26, 1881, *a* 30.

Annie, the dearly loved wife of Lindon Parkyn, of Christ Church, Addiscombe, *d* May 21, 1881, *a* 30.

Florence Elizabeth, daughter of J. W. Buckley and Louisa, his wife, *d* May 11, 1862, *a* 4.

Joseph Wilson Buckley, *d* Jan. 30, 1874, *a* 57.

> [Mr. Buckley was a deacon at George Street Chapel, Croydon, but removed to Dorking a few years before his death.]

Richard Pengilly, for nearly 40 years pastor of the Baptist Church, Newcastle-on-Tyne, *d* March 22, 1865, *a* 83.

Eliza, his wife, *d* Jan. 7, 1869, *a* 82.

Edgar Rowland Witherby, *a* 6 years and 10 months.

> A moment o'er the stone, dear children stay,
> " Do you love God ? " was Edgar wont to say,
> In rosy health, and now his early grave
> Shall ask, " Is Jesus, who our souls to save
> Was nailed upon the cross, your Saviour dear ? "
> If yes ! then children you have nought to fear.
> E'en from the silence of our darling's tomb,
> The name of Jesus penetrates the gloom
> Of death ! Come quickly Saviour, bid us rise
> With all thy lambs to meet Thee in the skies.

Until the morning of the first resurrection, here sleeps the body of our dearly beloved boy, Henry Dawson Witherby, whose spirit was called away October 4, 1868, *a* 3 years and 8 months.

> Jesus said, " Suffer little children to come unto me ; rejoice with me for I have found my sheep which was lost."
> Among the countless ransomed children there,
> Our darling we shall know,
> Again shall find him, and while passing fair
> The same we loved below.

Annie Witherby passed away June 2, 1879, *a* 17.

> Not long before she fell asleep she said, " We shall have plenty of happy days in Heaven." And again, " After all, this is only just the beginning of life—only like a few days."
> " Eye hath not seen, nor ear heard, neither have entered into the heart of man, the things which God hath prepared for them that love Him ; but God hath revealed them unto us by His spirit."

Mary Ann, wife of Chas. Coles, *d* Jan. 20, 1880, *a* 36.

> Not gone from memory, not gone from love,
> But gone to her Father's home above.

Chas. Joseph McIvor, only son of A. and G. M. Acheson, *d* July 8, 1868, *a* 20.

> And his body rests here until the resurrection from among the dead.

Georgina Margaret Acheson, *d* July 8, 1868, *a* 20.

> To depart, and be with Christ, which is far better.

Ann Heatley, *d* Feb. 12, 1867, *a* 72.
> Reader,—I ask have you found that peace
> That only Christ can give ;
> Have you by power divine been changed,
> For Christ and heaven to live ?

Mrs. Charlotte Herbert, *d* Nov. 21, 1870, *a* 91.

Thomas Surman, *d* May 31, 1875, *a* 75.

Harriette Amelia, wife of Charles Hingston, *d* Sept. 3, 1878, *a* 37.
> There is no death.   What seems so is transition.
> This life of mortal breath
> Is but a suburb of the life Elysian,
> Whose portal we call death.

Agnes Gray, wife of William Gardiner, *d* March 28, 1872, *a* 23.

Helen Eliza, her daughter, *d* June 24, 1872, *a* 3¼.

Emma, 42 years the affectionate and helpful wife of Thomas C. Carter, *d* March 28, 1875, *a* 64.
> By the grace of God I am what I am.

Hannah Vincent, for 16 years a faithful servant in the family of Mr. E. Moore, No. 2, Stanley Villas, St. James's Road, *d* April 2, 1875.

Artie, child of John and Jessy Walker, *d* Jan. 11, 1875, *a* 11.

Robert Cathcart Matheson, *d* Dec. 8, 1871, *a* 33.

Eliza Margaret, daughter of Benjamin and Margaret J. Lees, *d* April 15, 1872, *a* 26.

Benjamin, her father, *d* Aug. 13, 1872, *a* 52.

Alfred Goldsmith, *d* March 5, 1871, *a* 48.
> Humbly we hope that death to him was gain,
> To whom God's mercy through his blessed Son,
> Gave gracious strength through long continued pain,
> Meekly to trust, and say " Thy will be done."

Zachariah Westbrook, *d* April 2, 1875, *a* 81.

Sarah, his wife, died on the 8th of the same month, *a* 75.
> Both safe in the arms of Jesus.

Henry Kirkby, *d* Feb. 2, 1867, *a* 50.

Mary Annie, his daughter, *d* July 5, 1875, *a* 23.

Amy Florence Lewis, of Thornton Heath, *d* Jan. 9, 1866, *a* 4 months.
> A lovely babe lies sleeping here
> Short was on earth her stay,
> For at the age of four months old,
> Alas, 'twas took away.

Thomas Wm. Lewis, *d* Oct. 17, 1868, *a* 5.
> He was not loved by one, but all,
> He left this world when God did call,
> Knock'd at the door, death did so soon,
> His morning sun went down at noon.
> Grieve not for me my parents dear,
> I do lie here till Christ appear.

Grace Eleanor Lewis, *d* Dec. 13, 1878, *a* 7.
> She is not among the dying now,
> For she has life for ever,
> Yet links remain to hearts below,
> No stroke of death can sever.
> We mourn the wreck which death hath made,
> But shed not hopeless tears,
> Her body 'neath this sod is laid,
> Her soul in Heaven appears.

Harriet Waghorne, *d* March 3, 1881, *a* 63.
Maria Bambridge, her sister, *d* Feb. 21, 1862, *a* 33.

Stephen Scott, of Woodside, *d* April 19, 1864, *a* 58.

Elizabeth Ann Trindal Reep, widow of the late Capt. Reep, R.N., *d* Oct. 29, 1864, *a* 80.

Mary, wife of Jacob Venning, *d* Dec. 11, 1865, *a* 26.

> What is there here to court my stay,
>   Or hold me back from home,
> While angels beckon me away,
>   And Jesus bids me come
> Away to yonder realms of light,
>   There multitudes redeemed with blood,
> Enjoy the beatific sight,
>   And dwell for ever with their God.

James Martin, *d* Nov. 5, 1868, *a* 73.

Susannah Layton, wife of Bryan Bishop, *d* April 12, 1878, *a* 74.

Richard Wallis, *d* Aug. 11, 1878, *a* 82.
Maria, his wife, *d* May 5, 1862, *a* 67.

Charlotte Dobin, *d* Nov. 18, 1878, *a* 54.

Kate Adeney (Kitty), *d* July 28, 1879, *a* 2.
Francis G. Farrow, *d* July 13, 1878, *a* 2 months.

Mary Smith, *d* July 12, 1878, *a* 53.

Mary Ann Palmer, *d* Sept. 27, 1878, *a* 44.

Hannah Kimber, *d* Jan. 15, 1829, *a* 30.

Major-General James Campbell, R.A., *d* March 4, 1878.

Alfred Frederick Bell, *d* April 20, 1878, *a* 33.

James Peerless, *d* Sept. 14, 1877, *a* 74.

Robt. W. W. Vickery, *d* Sept. 11, 1876, *a* 65.

Selina, wife of James Woodman, *d* March 28, 1877, *a* 38.

> Released from sorrow, sin, and pain,
>   And free from every care,
> By angels' hands to Heaven conveyed,
>   To rest for ever there.

Mary Ann Jefferies, who lived for 46 years with the late Mr. Garniss, of No. 8, Park Lane, *d* Jan. 8, 1878, *a* 76.

Sarah Ann Peskett, of South End, *d* April 11, 1877, *a* 52.

> Blessed are they and only they
>   Who in the Lord their Saviour die ;
> Their bodies wait redemption day,
>   They sleep in peace where'er they lie.

Mary Smith, *d* May 5, 1877, *a* 77.

Fanny, infant daughter of Alexander Shapcott, *a* 5 months.

Mary, wife of William Robinson, died suddenly at New Thornton Heath, Feb. 3, 1877, *a* 40.
William Robinson, her husband, *d* April 10, 1877, *a* 42.

Laurie, son of Charles B. Ingham, *d* Nov. 26, 1876, *a* 3½.

Fred George Whitfield, son of Walter Holt, *d* Aug. 12, 1877, *a* 1.
Wm. Henry Peckham, *d* March 14, 1876, *a* 35.

Hannah, wife of Stephen Willcock, *d* Jan. 7, 1876, *a* 81.
Jemima Duthort, her sister, *d* Oct. 9, 1881, *a* 70.

In remembrance of Little Charlie, son of Edwin Alden, *d* Jan. 6, 1878, *a* 6
   months.

> That beautiful flower was lent awhile,
>   To cheer us on our way,
> But Jesus took it to a fairer clime,
>   To bloom in endless day.

John Ling, *d* May 31, 1879, *a* 75.

Ann, wife of Henry Johnson, *d* Jan. 10, 1880, *a* 63.

> Her toils are past, her work is done,
>   And she is fully blest,
> She fought the fight, the vict'ry won,
>   And entered into rest.

Emily, wife of Richd. John Coventry, *d* May 9, 1877, *a* 30.

William Martin, *d* Dec. 2, 1879, *a* 53.

Mary Grace, wife of Ebenezer S. Pears, of Broad Green, *d* April 7, 1878,
   a 29.

> Shall not the Judge of all do right ?

George H. Owen, 2, Grosvenor Road, South Norwood, *d* Dec. 10, 1878,
   a 20.

Frank, infant son of Ebenezer Wilson, *d* Dec. 6, 1878.

> He metes thy days, my little one, who gave thee life.

Charles Westrope, *b* Aug. 31, *d* Sept. 18, 1877.
Pattie Westrope, *b* Aug. 31, *d* Oct. 31, 1877.

> Twin infants of Charles and Martha Bowman, of London Road.

Isabella, wife of John Tanner, *d* April 23, 1880, *a* 62.

Henry Iles, *d* July 18, 1880, *a* 65.

Margaret Jane Smith, *d* April 2, 1881, *a* 76.

Charles Watts, of Canterbury Road, *d* Jan. 18, 1880, *a* 65.

Ann, wife of Wm. Newling, *d* Dec. 11, 1880.

> Her hope was built on nothing less
> Than Jesu's blood and righteousness.

Rebecca, wife of Benjamin Haines, *d* Oct. 8, 1881, *a* 26.

Mary, wife of Edward Granville, *d* Sept. 30, 1881, *a* 78.

Elizabeth, wife of Alfred Claudius Collins, *d* March 27, 1881, *a* 88.

Clarence Henry, infant son of Hy. Peters, of Croydon Grove, *d* Aug. 15,
   1879, *a* 6 months.

> From adverse blasts and low'ring storms,
>   His favoured soul He bore,
> And with yon bright angelic forms,
>   He lives to die no more.

Little Walter, only child of Chas. and Sarah Heathfield, *d* May 19, 1879, *a*
   5 months.

Alice, daughter of Jane C. and Mary King, *d* Aug. 26, 1879, *a* 12.

> Pain and sickness ne'er shall enter,
>   Grief nor woe her lot shall share ;
> But in that celestial centre,
>   She a crown of life shall wear.

Robert Mapletoft, *d* Sept. 5, 1881, *a* 50.

> Just as I am, without one plea,
>   But that Thy blood was shed for me,
> And that Thou bidst me come to Thee,
>   Oh, Lamb of God, I come.

Samuel Robinson, *d* May 26, 1880, *a* 58.
John Robinson, his brother, *d* March 13, 1882, *a* 68.

Edward Odd, *d* Dec. 27, 1880, *a* 42.

Louisa Block, *d* Sept. 24, 1880, *a* 41.
> She was endowed with a mind so clear,
> That all who knew her, loved her far and near,
> But God, her Father, loved her best,
> And took her to her Heavenly rest.

Charles Smith, *d* May 1, 1880, *a* 43.
Hannah, his wife, *d* Nov. 22, 1881, *a* 45.

Alice Evelyn Freebody, *d* June 17, 1881, *a* 4½.
> " And Jesus called a little child unto Him."

Emma, widow of Wm. Slade, *d* March 12, 1882, *a* 75.
Thomas Douglas, her son, *d* April 11, 1880, *a* 37.

James Pilbeam, of South End, *d* Jan. 30, 1882, *a* 84.

Sarah Davis, *d* Sept. 13, 1881, *a* 98.
> She was a member of the Wesleyan Church 74 years.

Richard Hanks, of Church Street, *d* Oct. 21, 1880, *a* 55.

Mary Ann, wife of George Horn, *d* Jan. 2, 1879, *a* 49.

Jane Row, *d* May 21, 1879, *a* 70.

Thomas Dartnell, *d* Nov. 15, 1879, *a* 75.

Ophelia Jane, wife of John Hunt, of South Norwood, *d* July 1, 1879, *a* 38.
> Jesus protects ; my fears be gone,
> What can the Rock of Ages move ?
> Safe in Thy arms, I lay me down,
> Thy everlasting arms of love.

Arnold C. Westlake, her nephew, *d* Jan. 4, 1882, *a* 1.

Samuel Overton, *d* May 28, 1879, *a* 60.
> Until the day break, and the shadows flee away.

George Henry Checker, *d* Feb. 1, 1877, *a* 48.
George Checker, his son, *d* March 1, 1877, *a* 18.

Elizabeth, wife of Thos. Jeffery Duke, *d* July 9, 1877, *a* 50.
> [Late Matron of the Croydon Workhouse.]

John Kew, *d* March 19, 1879. *a* 68.
> Oh, Death, where is thy victory,
> Oh, Grave, where is thy sting ?

Thomas Ray, of North End, *d* March 23, 1871, *a* 76.
Harriot, his wife, *d* Dec. 11, 1877, *a* 73.
> Let them be at rest that die in the Lord.

Sarah, widow of the late Rev. R. Inchbald, D.C.L., late of Aldwick Hall.
Doncaster, *d* July 15, 1872, *a* 75.

Margaret Hodgson, *d* March 28, 1882, *a* 62.
> " Be ye therefore followers of God, as dear children."

Richard Astington, died suddenly, Jan. 26, 1882, *a* 74.
> [For many years a tailor in Church Street, much respected.]

Caroline, his widow, *d* May 15, 1882, *a* 68.

William Potter, *d* Oct. 17, 1882, *a* 63.
> Blessed are they whose fault is gone,
> Whose sins are washed away with blood,
> Whose hope is fixed on Christ alone,
> Whom Christ has reconciled to God.

Rev. Henry Mitchell, M.A., *d* May 9, 1867, *a* 62.

William Lowndes, *d* July 3, 1882.

Thomas Edwards, late of Llanfyllion, Montgomeryshire, *d* Oct. 22, 1881, *a* 78.

Janet, wife of Leigh Paul Tebbutt, *d* Feb. 12, 1882, *a* 35.

Percy Tebbutt, *d* Feb. 17, 1882, *a* 13 days.
   [Mother and babe fell victims to that terrible disease, small-pox.]

SOCIETY OF FRIENDS.

A small portion of the Unconsecrated Ground is devoted to the burial of Members of the Society of Friends. The following is a copy of the gravestones therein :—

Alfred Crowley, *d* 16th 1st month, 1876, *a* 51.
   Alfred Crowley was a principal member of the ancient firm of brewers at Croydon and Alton. He took an active interest in public affairs, and sat on the Local Board of Health from 1858 until his death. Gifted with much general knowledge, his experience in commercial matters was very wide, and his common sense opinions were invariably expressed tersely and fearlessly.

Guy Robt., son of Alfred and Mary Crowley, *d* 20th 8th month, 1873, *a* 7 months.

Helen, daughter of John and Alice Ward, *d* 2nd 12th month, 1878, *a* 1 year and 8 months.

Louisa Cruickshank, *d* 6th 4th month, 1875, *a* 22.

Mary Harrisson, *d* 15th 10th month, 1874, *a* 72.

Charles Dearman, *d* 2nd 9th month, 1872, *a* 73.

John Harry McGill, *d* 31st 5th month, 1875, *a* 13.

Sarah Sidney Beach, *d* 5th 10th month, 1871, *a* 38.

Thomas Beach, *d* 9th 4th month, 1875, *a* 76.

Arthur Godfrey, *d* 25th 5th month, 1875, *a* 15.

Robert Harvey, *d* 15th 3rd month, 1867, *a* 61.

Matilda Harvey, *d* 5th 7th month, 1875, *a* 74.

ROMAN CATHOLICS.

The Roman Catholics have two pieces of ground near the Nonconformist Chapel.

To my child, *d* 10th May, 1875.

James Lynch, *d* Nov. 19, 1879, *a* 26.

Benjamin Hoar, R.N., *d* May 17, 1878.
   We have loved him in life, let us not forget him in death.

Catherine Caplis, *d* April 3, 1869, *a* 38.

Eloy Eugenio da Silva, 1877.

Susannah Rousch, *d* Jan. 18, 1876, *a* 50.

Jacob Henry Cattaneo, who met with a fatal accident Nov. 22, 1881, *a* 28.
   On whose soul, sweet Jesus have mercy.

Hugh Hastings, *d* Dec. 21, 1867, *a* 57.

Edward James Lane, *d* April 3, 1865, *a* 55.
> Pray for the repose of his soul.

Orate pro animabus Joannes Pace et Anna Mariæ, ejus uxoris, qui obierunt illa 16 Mai, 1864, æt. 48 ; ille 15th Jan. 1876, æt. 67.
> Morte disjuncti nunc morti juncti.
> Requiescant in pace.

Edward Gustavus Norton, *d* April 13, 1871, *a* 44.

Ernest Thomas Hammond, *d* May 12. 1863, *a* 31.

Charles A. Cattaneo, *d* Aug. 25, 1870. *a* 19.
Marcelina Jane Cattaneo, *d* Dec. 2, 1876, *a* 35.
Winifred Catherine Hanlon, *d* Aug. 21, 1862, *a* 4.
Mary Hanlon, her mother, *d* Aug. 16, 1871, *a* 37.
Edward Hanlon, *d* March 9, 1875, *a* 43.
> [Mr. Hanlon formerly was a leather cutter at 31, High Street.]

Calieto Hanrie, *d* July 25, 1863, *a* 56.

Anna Maria Vernon, of Penge, *d* June 27, 1863, *a* 38.

Eda J. M. Alexander, of Thornton Heath, *d* Aug. 27, 1870, *a* 16.

Ellen Mary Cattaneo, *d* May 30, 1864, *a* 4.
Catharine Mary, wife of Pasquale Cattaneo, *d* Feb. 24, 1866, *a* 46.
Peter Thomas Cattaneo, *d* March 4. 1866, *a* 3.
George Francis Cattaneo, *d* Dec. 7, 1869, *a* 15.
Julia Mary Kate Cattaneo, *d* May 2, 1870, *a* 12.

Mary Blanche, daughter of M. G. Lavers, Esq., *d* July 5, 1869, *a* 14.

John Walton Teevan, M.A., *d* Dec. 27. 1871, *a* 32.
Henry James, his second son, *d* Nov. 26. 1868, *a* 7.
Arthur Walton, third son, *d* Nov. 26, 1868, *a* 5.
William Walton, fourth son, *d* Nov. 27, 1868, *a* 3.
Edward Walton, sixth son, *d* Dec. 10, 1870, *a* 1.

Thomas J. Woods, *d* Feb. 8, 1870, *a* 59.

Etienne Toussant Désiré Benôit, of the Royal Military Academy, Woolwich, *d* Feb. 14, 1868, *a* 53.

Jane Harvey, *d* March 4, 1880, *a* 84.

Alfred Patrick Ryan, *d* July 27, 1872, *a* 35.
> [Mr. Ryan was a mahogany and timber merchant at the steam saw mills in Morland Road.]

John Carley, Esq., *d* March 7, 1870, *a* 68.

Wm. Phelen, *d* March 29, 1868, *a* 45.

Bryan Wynn, Esq., *d* Jan. 31, 1869, *a* 73.
> [Formerly an accountant at 56, High Street, living in Parson's Mead.]

Lieut. Geo. Alfred Devereux, R.N., *d* July 7, 1867, *a* 80.
Ann Mary Devereux, *d* Feb. 9, 1872, *a* 81.

Eliza, wife of M. O'Riordan, *d* July 7, 1867, *a* 43.
> Have mercy on me, have pity on me, at least you, my friends.

On your charity, pray for the repose of the soul of Susan Mary Agatha Pearson, of Penge, *d* Aug. 23, 1869, fortified with the rites of Holy Church.
> On whose soul, sweet Jesus, have mercy.
> We loved her during life, let us not forsake after death.—*St. Ambrose.*
> May her soul rest in peace.—Amen.

Georgina Devereux, *d* April 30, 1880.

Charles Evan McDougall, *d* April 10, 1872.

Mrs. Margaret Turner, *d* Nov. 27, 1868, *a* 48.

John Edmund Hastings, *d* Oct. 22, 1872, *a* 54.

Ethel Mary Sidgreaves, *d* Oct. 11, 1881, *a* 5.

Marie Anna, daughter of Napoleon Alexander and Mathilde Coste, *d* Feb. 8, 1882, *a* 26.

John Lawless, Esq., *d* June 9, 1869.

Daniel O'Driscoll, *d* July 28, 1877, *a* 24.
Catherine, his mother, *d* Nov. 22, 1881, *a* 58.

Simon Kelly, of South Norwood, *d* Nov. 6, 1873, *a* 65.

Wm. Thomas Doyle, *d* Sept. 12, 1874, *a* 22.
Mary Ann Doyle, his mother, *d* Aug. 18, 1878, *a* 67.
George Doyle, *d* Sept. 25, 1879, *a* 69.

Francisco Augusto J. N. Gomez, born in Hong Kong, May 16, 1864, died in Croydon, May 19, 1882.

    [He was a very promising student in St. George's Roman Catholic College, in the Wellesley Road.]

John Nathaniel Clarke, *d* April 16, 1873, *a* 32.

John Murray, *d* June 15, 1868, *a* 96.

ImTheStory.com

Lightning Source UK Ltd.
Milton Keynes UK
UKOW02f1126231214

243593UK00021B/1318/P